Mastering Predictive Analytics with R

Master the craft of predictive modeling by developing
strategy, intuition, and a solid foundation in
essential concepts

Rui Miguel Forte

BIRMINGHAM - MUMBAI

Mastering Predictive Analytics with R

First published: June 2015

Production reference: 1100615

Published by Packt Publishing Ltd.
Livery Place
35 Livery Street
Birmingham B3 2PB, UK.

ISBN 978-1-78398-280-6

www.packtpub.com

Credits

Author

Rui Miguel Forte

Reviewers

Ajay Dhamija

Prasad Kothari

Dawit Gezahegn Tadesse

Commissioning Editor

Kartikey Pandey

Acquisition Editor

Subho Gupta

Content Development Editor

Govindan Kurumangattu

Technical Editor

Edwin Moses

Copy Editors

Stuti Srivastava

Aditya Nair

Vedangi Narvekar

Project Coordinator

Shipra Chawhan

Proofreaders

Stephen Copestake

Safis Editing

Indexer

Priya Sane

Graphics

Sheetal Aute

Disha Haria

Jason Monteiro

Abhinash Sahu

Production Coordinator

Shantanu Zagade

Cover Work

Shantanu Zagade

About the Author

Rui Miguel Forte is currently the chief data scientist at Workable. He was born and raised in Greece and studied in the UK. He is an experienced data scientist who has over 10 years of work experience in a diverse array of industries spanning mobile marketing, health informatics, education technology, and human resources technology. His projects include the predictive modeling of user behavior in mobile marketing promotions, speaker intent identification in an intelligent tutor, information extraction techniques for job applicant resumes, and fraud detection for job scams. Currently, he teaches R, MongoDB, and other data science technologies to graduate students in the business analytics MSc program at the Athens University of Economics and Business. In addition, he has lectured at a number of seminars, specialization programs, and R schools for working data science professionals in Athens. His core programming knowledge is in R and Java, and he has extensive experience working with a variety of database technologies, such as Oracle, PostgreSQL, MongoDB, and HBase. He holds a master's degree in electrical and electronic engineering from Imperial College London and is currently researching machine learning applications in information extraction and natural language processing.

Acknowledgments

Behind every great adventure is a good story, and writing a book is no exception. Many people contributed to making this book a reality. I would like to thank the many students I have taught at AUEB, whose dedication and support has been nothing short of overwhelming. They should be rest assured that I have learned just as much from them as they have learned from me, if not more. I also want to thank Damianos Chatziantoniou for conceiving a pioneering graduate data science program in Greece. Workable has been a crucible for working alongside incredibly talented and passionate engineers on exciting data science projects that help businesses around the globe. For this, I would like to thank my colleagues and in particular, the founders, Nick and Spyros, who created a diamond in the rough. I would like to thank Subho, Govindan, Edwin, and all the folks at Packt for their professionalism and patience. To the many friends who offered encouragement and motivation I would like to express my eternal gratitude. My family and extended family have been an incredible source of support on this project. In particular, I would like to thank my father, Libanio, for inspiring me to pursue a career in the sciences and my mother, Marianthi, for always believing in me far more than anyone else ever could. My wife, Despoina, patiently and fiercely stood by my side even as this book kept me away from her during her first pregnancy. Last but not least, my baby daughter slept quietly and kept a cherubic vigil over her father during the book's final stages of preparation. She helped in ways words cannot describe.

About the Reviewers

Ajay Dhamija is a senior scientist working in Defense R&D Organization, Delhi. He has more than 24 years' experience as a researcher and instructor. He holds an MTech (computer science and engineering) degree from IIT, Delhi, and an MBA (finance and strategy) degree from FMS, Delhi. He has more than 14 research works of international repute in varied fields to his credit, including data mining, reverse engineering, analytics, neural network simulation, TRIZ, and so on. He was instrumental in developing a state-of-the-art Computer-Aided Pilot Selection System (CPSS) containing various cognitive and psychomotor tests to comprehensively assess the flying aptitude of the aspiring pilots of the Indian Air Force. He has been honored with the Agni Award for excellence in self reliance, 2005, by the Government of India. He specializes in predictive analytics, information security, big data analytics, machine learning, Bayesian social networks, financial modeling, Neuro-Fuzzy simulation and data analysis, and data mining using R. He is presently involved with his doctoral work on *Financial Modeling of Carbon Finance data* from IIT, Delhi. He has written an international best seller, *Forecasting Exchange Rate: Use of Neural Networks in Quantitative Finance* (`http://www.amazon.com/Forecasting-Exchange-rate-Networks-Quantitative/dp/3639161807`), and is currently authoring another book on R named *Multivariate Analysis using R*.

Apart from analytics, Ajay is actively involved in information security research. He has associated himself with various international and national researchers in government as well as the corporate sector to pursue his research on ways to amalgamate two important and contemporary fields of data handling, that is, predictive analytics and information security.

You can connect with Ajay at the following:

LinkedIn:	`ajaykumardhamija`
ResearchGate:	`Ajay_Dhamija2`
Academia:	`ajaydhamija`
Facebook:	`akdhamija`
Twitter:	`akdhamija`
Quora:	`Ajay-Dhamija`

While associating with researchers from Predictive Analytics and Information Security Institute of India (PRAISIA @ www.praisia.com) in his research endeavors, he has worked on refining methods of big data analytics for security data analysis (log assessment, incident analysis, threat prediction, and so on) and vulnerability management automation.

I would like to thank my fellow scientists from Defense R&D Organization and researchers from corporate sectors such as Predictive Analytics & Information Security Institute of India (PRAISIA), which is a unique institute of repute and of its own kind due to its pioneering work in marrying the two giant and contemporary fields of data handling in modern times, that is, predictive analytics and information security, by adopting custom-made and refined methods of big data analytics. They all contributed in presenting a fruitful review for this book. I'm also thankful to my wife, Seema Dhamija, the managing director of PRAISIA, who has been kind enough to share her research team's time with me in order to have technical discussions. I'm also thankful to my son, Hemant Dhamija, who gave his invaluable inputs many a times, which I inadvertently neglected during the course of this review. I'm also thankful to a budding security researcher, Shubham Mittal from MakeMyTrip, for his constant and constructive critiques of my work.

Prasad Kothari is an analytics thought leader. He has worked extensively with organizations such as Merck, Sanofi Aventis, Freddie Mac, Fractal Analytics, and the National Institute of Health on various analytics and big data projects. He has published various research papers in the American Journal of Drug and Alcohol Abuse and American public health. His leadership and analytics skills have been pivotal in setting up analytics practices for various organizations and helping grow them across the globe.

Dawit Gezahegn Tadesse is currently a visiting assistant professor in the Department of Mathematical Sciences at the University of Cincinnati, Cincinnati, Ohio, USA. He obtained his MS in mathematics and PhD in statistics from Auburn University, Auburn, AL, USA in 2010 and 2014, respectively. His research interests include high-dimensional classification, text mining, nonparametric statistics, and multivariate data analysis.

www.PacktPub.com

Support files, eBooks, discount offers, and more

For support files and downloads related to your book, please visit
www.PacktPub.com.

Did you know that Packt offers eBook versions of every book published, with PDF
and ePub files available? You can upgrade to the eBook version at www.PacktPub.
com and as a print book customer, you are entitled to a discount on the eBook copy.
Get in touch with us at service@packtpub.com for more details.

At www.PacktPub.com, you can also read a collection of free technical articles,
sign up for a range of free newsletters and receive exclusive discounts and offers
on Packt books and eBooks.

https://www2.packtpub.com/books/subscription/packtlib

Do you need instant solutions to your IT questions? PacktLib is Packt's online digital
book library. Here, you can search, access, and read Packt's entire library of books.

Why subscribe?

- Fully searchable across every book published by Packt
- Copy and paste, print, and bookmark content
- On demand and accessible via a web browser

Free access for Packt account holders

If you have an account with Packt at www.PacktPub.com, you can use this to access
PacktLib today and view 9 entirely free books. Simply use your login credentials for
immediate access.

This book is dedicated to my loving wife Despoina, who makes all good things better and every adventure worthwhile. You are the light of my life and the flame of my soul.

Table of Contents

Preface

Predictive analytics, and data science more generally, currently enjoy a huge surge in interest, as predictive technologies such as spam filtering, word completion and recommendation engines have pervaded everyday life. We are now not only increasingly familiar with these technologies, but these technologies have also earned our confidence. Advances in computing technology in terms of processing power and in terms of software such as R and its plethora of specialized packages have resulted in a situation where users can be trained to work with these tools without needing advanced degrees in statistics or access to hardware that is reserved for corporations or university laboratories. This confluence of the maturity of techniques and the availability of supporting software and hardware has many practitioners of the field excited that they can design something that will make an appreciable impact on their own domains and businesses, and rightly so.

At the same time, many newcomers to the field quickly discover that there are many pitfalls that need to be overcome. Virtually no academic degree adequately prepares a student or professional to become a successful predictive modeler. The field draws upon many disciplines, such as computer science, mathematics, and statistics. Nowadays, not only do people approach the field with a strong background in only one of these areas, they also tend to be specialized within that area. Having taught several classes on the material in this book to graduate students and practicing professionals alike, I discovered that the two biggest fears that students repeatedly express are the fear of programming and the fear of mathematics. It is interesting that these are almost always mutually exclusive. Predictive analytics is very much a practical subject but one with a very rich theoretical basis, knowledge of which is essential to the practitioner. Consequently, achieving mastery in predictive analytics requires a range of different skills, from writing good software to implement a new technique or to preprocess data, to understanding the assumptions of a model, how it can be trained efficiently, how to diagnose problems, and how to tune its parameters to get better results.

It feels natural at this point to want to take a step back and think about what predictive analytics actually covers as a field. The truth is that the boundaries between this field and other related fields, such as *machine learning, data mining, business analytics, data science* and so on, are somewhat blurred. The definition we will use in this book is very broad. For our purposes, predictive analytics is a field that uses data to build models that predict a future outcome of interest. There is certainly a big overlap with the field of machine learning, which studies programs and algorithms that learn from data more generally. This is also true for data mining, whose goal is to extract knowledge and patterns from data. Data science is rapidly becoming an umbrella term that covers all of these fields, as well as topics such as information visualization to present the findings of data analysis, business concepts surrounding the deployment of models in the real world, and data management. This book may draw heavily from machine learning, but we will not cover the theoretical pursuit of the feasibility of learning, nor will we study unsupervised learning that sets out to look for patterns and clusters in data without a particular predictive target in mind. At the same time, we will also explore topics such as time series, which are not commonly discussed in a machine learning text.

R is an excellent platform to learn about predictive analytics and also to work on real-world problems. It is an open source project with an ever-burgeoning community of users. Together with Python, they are the two most commonly used languages by data scientists around the world at the time of this writing. It has a wealth of different packages that specialize in different modeling techniques and application domains, many of which are directly accessible from within R itself via a connection to the *Comprehensive R Archive Network (CRAN)*. There are also ample online resources for the language, from tutorials to online courses. In particular, we'd like to mention the excellent *Cross Validated* forum (http://stats.stackexchange.com/) as well as the website *R-bloggers* (http://www.r-bloggers.com/), which hosts a fantastic collection of articles on using R from different blogs. For readers who are a little rusty, we provide a free online tutorial chapter that evolved from a set of lecture notes given to students at the Athens University of Economics and Business.

The primary mission of this book is to bridge the gap between low-level introductory books and tutorials that emphasize intuition and practice over theory, and high-level academic texts that focus on mathematics, detail, and rigor. Another equally important goal is to instill some good practices in you, such as learning how to properly test and evaluate a model. We also emphasize important concepts, such as the bias-variance trade-off and overfitting, which are pervasive in predictive modeling and come up time and again in various guises and across different models.

From a programming standpoint, even though we assume that you are familiar with the R programming language, every code sample has been carefully explained and discussed to allow readers to develop their confidence and follow along. That being said, it is not possible to overstress the importance of actually running the code alongside the book or at least before moving on to a new chapter. To make the process as smooth as possible, we have provided code files for every chapter in the book containing all the code samples in the text. In addition, in a number of places, we have written our own, albeit very simple implementations of certain techniques. Two examples that come to mind are the pocket perceptron algorithm in *Chapter 4, Neural Networks* and AdaBoost in *Chapter 7, Ensemble Methods*. In part, this is done in an effort to encourage users to learn how to write their own functions instead of always relying on existing implementations, as these may not always be available.

Reproducibility is a critical skill in the analysis of data and is not limited to educational settings. For this reason, we have exclusively used freely available data sets and have endeavored to apply specific seeds wherever random number generation has been needed. Finally, we have tried wherever possible to use data sets of a relatively small size in order to ensure that you can run the code while reading the book without having to wait too long, or force you to have access to better hardware than might be available to you. We will remind you that in the real world, patience is an incredibly useful virtue, as most data sets of interest will be larger than the ones we will study.

While each chapter ends in two or more practical modeling examples, every chapter begins with some theory and background necessary to understand a new model or technique. While we have not shied away from using mathematics to explain important details, we have been very mindful to introduce just enough to ensure that you understand the fundamental ideas involved. This is in line with the book's philosophy of bridging the gap to academic textbooks that go into more detail. Readers with a high-school background in mathematics should trust that they will be able to follow all of the material in this book with the aid of the explanations given. The key skills needed are basic calculus, such as simple differentiation, and key ideas in probability, such as mean, variance, correlation, as well as important distributions such as the binomial and normal distribution. While we don't provide any tutorials on these, in the early chapters we do try to take things particularly slowly. To address the needs of readers who are more comfortable with mathematics, we often provide additional technical details in the form of tips and give references that act as natural follow-ups to the discussion.

Sometimes, we have had to give an intuitive explanation of a concept in order to conserve space and avoid creating a chapter with an undue emphasis on pure theory. Wherever this is done, such as with the backpropagation algorithm in *Chapter 4, Neural Networks*, we have ensured that we explained enough to allow the reader to have a firm-enough hold on the basics to tackle a more detailed piece. At the same time, we have given carefully selected references, many of which are articles, papers, or online texts that are both readable and freely available. Of course, we refer to seminal textbooks wherever necessary.

The book has no exercises, but we hope that you will engage your curiosity to its maximum potential. Curiosity is a huge boon to the predictive modeler. Many of the websites from which we obtain data that we analyze have a number of other data sets that we do not investigate. We also occasionally show how we can generate artificial data to demonstrate the proof of concept behind a particular technique. Many of the R functions to build and train models have other parameters for tuning that we don't have time to investigate. Packages that we employ may often contain other related functions to those that we study, just as there are usually alternatives available to the proposed packages themselves. All of these are excellent avenues for further investigation and experimentation. Mastering predictive analytics comes just as much from careful study as from personal inquiry and practice.

A common ask from students of the field is for additional worked examples to simulate the actual process an experienced modeler follows on a data set. In reality, a faithful simulation would take as many hours as the analysis took in the first place. This is because most of the time spent in predictive modeling is in studying the data, trying new features and preprocessing steps, and experimenting with different models on the result. In short, as we will see in *Chapter 1, Gearing Up for Predictive Modeling*, exploration and trial and error are key components of an effective analysis. It would have been entirely impractical to compose a book that shows every wrong turn or unsuccessful alternative that is attempted on every data set. Instead of this, we fervently recommend that readers treat every data analysis in this book as a starting point to improve upon, and continue this process on their own. A good idea is to try to apply techniques from other chapters to a particular data set in order to see what else might work. This could be anything, from simply applying a different transformation to an input feature to using a completely different model from another chapter.

As a final note, we should mention that creating polished and presentable graphics in order to showcase the findings of a data analysis is a very important skill, especially in the workplace. While R's base plotting capabilities cover the basics, they often lack a polished feel. For this reason, we have used the ggplot2 package, except where a specific plot is generated by a function that is part of our analysis. Although we do not provide a tutorial for this, all the code to generate the plots included in this book is provided in the supporting code files, and we hope that the user will benefit from this as well. A useful online reference for the ggplot2 package is the section on graphs in the *Cookbook for R* website (http://www.cookbook-r.com/Graphs).

What this book covers

Chapter 1, Gearing Up for Predictive Modeling, begins our journey by establishing a common language for statistical models and a number of important distinctions we make when categorizing them. The highlight of the chapter is an exploration of the predictive modeling process and through this, we showcase our first model, the k Nearest Neighbor (kNN) model.

Chapter 2, Linear Regression, introduces the simplest and most well-known approach to predicting a numerical quantity. The chapter focuses on understanding the assumptions of linear regression and a range of diagnostic tools that are available to assess the quality of a trained model. In addition, the chapter touches upon the important concept of regularization, which addresses overfitting, a common ailment of predictive models.

Chapter 3, Logistic Regression, extends the idea of a linear model from the previous chapter by introducing the concept of a generalized linear model. While there are many examples of such models, this chapter focuses on logistic regression as a very popular method for classification problems. We also explore extensions of this model for the multiclass setting and discover that this method works best for binary classification.

Chapter 4, Neural Networks, presents a biologically inspired model that is capable of handling both regression and classification tasks. There are many different kinds of neural networks, so this chapter devotes itself to the multilayer perceptron network. Neural networks are complex models, and this chapter focuses substantially on understanding the range of different configuration and optimization parameters that play a part in the training process.

Chapter 5, Support Vector Machines, builds on the theme of nonlinear models by studying support vector machines. Here, we discover a different way of thinking about classification problems by trying to fit our training data geometrically using maximum margin separation. The chapter also introduces cross-validation as an essential technique to evaluate and tune models.

Chapter 6, Tree-based Methods, covers decision trees, yet another family of models that have been successfully applied to regression and classification problems alike. There are several flavors of decision trees, and this chapter presents a number of different training algorithms, such as CART and C5.0. We also learn that tree-based methods offer unique benefits, such as built-in feature selection, support for missing data and categorical variables, as well as a highly interpretable output.

Chapter 7, Ensemble Methods, takes a detour from the usual motif of showcasing a new type of model, and instead tries to answer the question of how to effectively combine different models together. We present the two widely known techniques of bagging and boosting and introduce the random forest as a special case of bagging with trees.

Chapter 8, Probabilistic Graphical Models, tackles an active area of machine learning research, that of probabilistic graphical models. These models encode conditional independence relations between variables via a graph structure, and have been successfully applied to problems in a diverse range of fields, from computer vision to medical diagnosis. The chapter studies two main representatives, the Naïve Bayes model and the hidden Markov model. This last model, in particular, has been successfully used in sequence prediction problems, such as predicting gene sequences and labeling sentences with part of speech tags.

Chapter 9, Time Series Analysis, studies the problem of modeling a particular process over time. A typical application is forecasting the future price of crude oil given historical data on the price of crude oil over a period of time. While there are many different ways to model time series, this chapter focuses on ARIMA models while discussing a few alternatives.

Chapter 10, Topic Modeling, is unique in this book in that it presents topic modeling, an approach that has its roots in clustering and unsupervised learning. Nonetheless, we study how this important method can be used in a predictive modeling scenario. The chapter emphasizes the most commonly known approach to topic modeling, Latent Dirichlet Allocation (LDA).

Chapter 11, Recommendation Systems, wraps up the book by discussing recommendation systems that analyze the preferences of a set of users interacting with a set of items, in order to make recommendations. A famous example of this is Netflix, which uses a database of ratings made by its users on movie rentals to make movie recommendations. The chapter casts a spotlight on collaborative filtering, a purely data-driven approach to making recommendations.

Introduction to R, gives an introduction and overview of the R language. It is provided as a way for readers to get up to speed in order to follow the code samples in this book. This is available as an online chapter at `https://www.packtpub.com/sites/default/files/downloads/Mastering_Predictive_Analytics_with_R_Chapter`.

What you need for this book

The only strong requirement for running the code in this book is an installation of R. This is freely available from `http://www.r-project.org/` and runs on all the major operating systems. The code in this book has been tested with R version 3.1.3.

All the chapters introduce at least one new R package that does not come with the base installation of R. We do not explicitly show the installation of R packages in the text, but if a package is not currently installed on your system or if it requires updating, you can install it with the `install.packages()` function. For example, the following command installs the `tm` package:

```
> install.packages("tm")
```

All the packages we use are available on CRAN. An Internet connection is needed to download and install them as well as to obtain the open source data sets that we use in our real-world examples. Finally, even though not absolutely mandatory, we recommend that you get into the habit of using an Integrated Development Environment (IDE) to work with R. An excellent offering is *RStudio* (`http://www.rstudio.com/`), which is open source.

Who this book is for

This book is intended for budding and seasoned practitioners of predictive modeling alike. Most of the material of this book has been used in lectures for graduates and working professionals as well as for R schools, so it has also been designed with the student in mind. Readers should be familiar with R, but even those who have never worked with this language should be able to pick up the necessary background by reading the online tutorial chapter. Readers unfamiliar with R should have had at least some exposure to programming languages such as Python. Those with a background in MATLAB will find the transition particularly easy. As mentioned earlier, the mathematical requirements for the book are very modest, assuming only certain elements from high school mathematics, such as the concepts of mean and variance and basic differentiation.

Conventions

In this book, you will find a number of text styles that distinguish between different kinds of information. Here are some examples of these styles and an explanation of their meaning.

Code words in text, database table names, folder names, filenames, file extensions, pathnames, dummy URLs, user input, and Twitter handles are shown as follows: "Finally, we'll use the sort() function of R with the index.return parameter set to TRUE."

A block of code is set as follows:

```
> iris_cor <- cor(iris_numeric)
> findCorrelation(iris_cor)
[1] 3
> findCorrelation(iris_cor, cutoff = 0.99)
integer(0)
> findCorrelation(iris_cor, cutoff = 0.80)
[1] 3 4
```

New terms and important words are shown in **bold**.

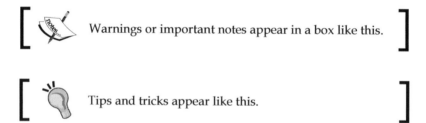

> Warnings or important notes appear in a box like this.

> Tips and tricks appear like this.

Reader feedback

Feedback from our readers is always welcome. Let us know what you think about this book—what you liked or disliked. Reader feedback is important for us as it helps us develop titles that you will really get the most out of.

To send us general feedback, simply e-mail feedback@packtpub.com, and mention the book's title in the subject of your message.

If there is a topic that you have expertise in and you are interested in either writing or contributing to a book, see our author guide at www.packtpub.com/authors.

Customer support

Now that you are the proud owner of a Packt book, we have a number of things to help you to get the most from your purchase.

Downloading the example code

You can download the example code files from your account at http://www. packtpub.com for all the Packt Publishing books you have purchased. If you purchased this book elsewhere, you can visit http://www.packtpub.com/support and register to have the files e-mailed directly to you.

Errata

Although we have taken every care to ensure the accuracy of our content, mistakes do happen. If you find a mistake in one of our books — maybe a mistake in the text or the code — we would be grateful if you could report this to us. By doing so, you can save other readers from frustration and help us improve subsequent versions of this book. If you find any errata, please report them by visiting http://www.packtpub.com/submit-errata, selecting your book, clicking on the **Errata Submission Form** link, and entering the details of your errata. Once your errata are verified, your submission will be accepted and the errata will be uploaded to our website or added to any list of existing errata under the Errata section of that title.

To view the previously submitted errata, go to https://www.packtpub.com/books/content/support and enter the name of the book in the search field. The required information will appear under the Errata section.

Piracy

Piracy of copyrighted material on the Internet is an ongoing problem across all media. At Packt, we take the protection of our copyright and licenses very seriously. If you come across any illegal copies of our works in any form on the Internet, please provide us with the location address or website name immediately so that we can pursue a remedy.

Please contact us at copyright@packtpub.com with a link to the suspected pirated material.

We appreciate your help in protecting our authors and our ability to bring you valuable content.

Questions

If you have a problem with any aspect of this book, you can contact us at questions@packtpub.com, and we will do our best to address the problem.

1
Gearing Up for Predictive Modeling

In this first chapter, we'll start by establishing a common language for models and taking a deep view of the predictive modeling process. Much of predictive modeling involves the key concepts of statistics and machine learning, and this chapter will provide a brief tour of the core distinctions of these fields that are essential knowledge for a predictive modeler. In particular, we'll emphasize the importance of knowing how to evaluate a model that is appropriate to the type of problem we are trying to solve. Finally, we will showcase our first model, the k-nearest neighbors model, as well as `caret`, a very useful R package for predictive modelers.

Models

Models are at the heart of predictive analytics and for this reason, we'll begin our journey by talking about models and what they look like. In simple terms, a model is a representation of a state, process, or system that we want to understand and reason about. We make models so that we can draw inferences from them and, more importantly for us in this book, make predictions about the world. Models come in a multitude of different formats and flavors, and we will explore some of this diversity in this book. Models can be equations linking quantities that we can observe or measure; they can also be a set of rules. A simple model with which most of us are familiar from school is Newton's Second Law of Motion. This states that the net sum of force acting on an object causes the object to accelerate in the direction of the force applied and at a rate proportional to the resulting magnitude of the force and inversely proportional to the object's mass.

We often summarize this information via an equation using the letters *F*, *m*, and *a* for the quantities involved. We also use the capital Greek letter sigma (Σ) to indicate that we are summing over the force and arrows above the letters that are vector quantities (that is, quantities that have both magnitude and direction):

$$\sum \vec{F} = m\vec{a}$$

This simple but powerful model allows us to make some predictions about the world. For example, if we apply a known force to an object with a known mass, we can use the model to predict how much it will accelerate. Like most models, this model makes some assumptions and generalizations. For example, it assumes that the color of the object, the temperature of the environment it is in, and its precise coordinates in space are all irrelevant to how the three quantities specified by the model interact with each other. Thus, models abstract away the myriad of details of a specific instance of a process or system in question, in this case the particular object in whose motion we are interested, and limit our focus only to properties that matter.

Newton's Second Law is not the only possible model to describe the motion of objects. Students of physics soon discover other more complex models, such as those taking into account relativistic mass. In general, models are considered more complex if they take a larger number of quantities into account or if their structure is more complex. Nonlinear models are generally more complex than linear models for example. Determining which model to use in practice isn't as simple as picking a more complex model over a simpler model. In fact, this is a central theme that we will revisit time and again as we progress through the many different models in this book. To build our intuition as to why this is so, consider the case where our instruments that measure the mass of the object and the applied force are very noisy. Under these circumstances, it might not make sense to invest in using a more complicated model, as we know that the additional accuracy in the prediction won't make a difference because of the noise in the inputs. Another situation where we may want to use the simpler model is if in our application we simply don't need the extra accuracy. A third situation arises where a more complex model involves a quantity that we have no way of measuring. Finally, we might not want to use a more complex model if it turns out that it takes too long to train or make a prediction because of its complexity.

Learning from data

In this book, the models we will study have two important and defining characteristics. The first of these is that we will not use mathematical reasoning or logical induction to produce a model from known facts, nor will we build models from technical specifications or business rules; instead, the field of predictive analytics builds models from data. More specifically, we will assume that for any given predictive task that we want to accomplish, we will start with some data that is in some way related to or derived from the task at hand. For example, if we want to build a model to predict annual rainfall in various parts of a country, we might have collected (or have the means to collect) data on rainfall at different locations, while measuring potential quantities of interest, such as the height above sea level, latitude, and longitude. The power of building a model to perform our predictive task stems from the fact that we will use examples of rainfall measurements at a finite list of locations to predict the rainfall in places where we did not collect any data.

The second important characteristic of the problems for which we will build models is that during the process of building a model from some data to describe a particular phenomenon, we are bound to encounter some source of randomness. We will refer to this as the **stochastic** or **nondeterministic component** of the model. It may be the case that the system itself that we are trying to model doesn't have any inherent randomness in it, but it is the data that contains a random component. A good example of a source of randomness in data is the measurement of the errors from the readings taken for quantities such as temperature. A model that contains no inherent stochastic component is known as a **deterministic model**, Newton's Second Law being a good example of this. A stochastic model is one that assumes that there is an intrinsic source of randomness to the process being modeled. Sometimes, the source of this randomness arises from the fact that it is impossible to measure all the variables that are most likely impacting a system, and we simply choose to model this using probability. A well-known example of a purely stochastic model is rolling an unbiased six-sided die. Recall that in probability, we use the term **random variable** to describe the value of a particular outcome of an experiment or of a random process. In our die example, we can define the random variable, Y, as the number of dots on the side that lands face up after a single roll of the die, resulting in the following model:

$$P(Y = y) = \frac{1}{6}, y \in \{1, 2, 3, 4, 5, 6\}$$

This model tells us that the probability of rolling a particular digit, say, three, is one in six. Notice that we are not making a definite prediction on the outcome of a particular roll of the die; instead, we are saying that each outcome is equally likely.

Probability is a term that is commonly used in everyday speech, but at the same time, sometimes results in confusion with regard to its actual interpretation. It turns out that there are a number of different ways of interpreting probability. Two commonly cited interpretations are the **Frequentist probability** and the **Bayesian probability**. Frequentist probability is associated with repeatable experiments, such as rolling a one-sided die. In this case, the probability of seeing the digit three, is just the relative proportion of the digit three coming up if this experiment were to be repeated an infinite number of times. Bayesian probability is associated with a subjective degree of belief or surprise in seeing a particular outcome and can, therefore, be used to give meaning to one-off events, such as the probability of a presidential candidate winning an election. In our die rolling experiment, we are equally surprised to see the number three come up as with any other number. Note that in both cases, we are still talking about the same probability numerically (1/6), only the interpretation differs.

In the case of the die model, there aren't any variables that we have to measure. In most cases, however, we'll be looking at predictive models that involve a number of independent variables that are measured, and these will be used to predict a dependent variable. Predictive modeling draws on many diverse fields and as a result, depending on the particular literature you consult, you will often find different names for these. Let's load a data set into R before we expand on this point. R comes with a number of commonly cited data sets already loaded, and we'll pick what is probably the most famous of all, the *iris data set*:

To see what other data sets come bundled with R, we can use the data() command to obtain a list of data sets along with a short description of each. If we modify the data from a data set, we can reload it by providing the name of the data set in question as an input parameter to the data() command, for example, data(iris) reloads the iris data set.

```
> head(iris, n = 3)
  Sepal.Length Sepal.Width Petal.Length Petal.Width Species
1          5.1         3.5          1.4         0.2  setosa
2          4.9         3.0          1.4         0.2  setosa
3          4.7         3.2          1.3         0.2  setosa
```

The iris data set consists of measurements made on a total of 150 flower samples of three different species of iris. In the preceding code, we can see that there are four measurements made on each sample, namely the lengths and widths of the flower petals and sepals. The iris data set is often used as a typical benchmark for different models that can predict the species of an iris flower sample, given the four previously mentioned measurements. Collectively, the sepal length, sepal width, petal length, and petal width are referred to as **features**, **attributes**, **predictors**, **dimensions**, or **independent variables** in literature. In this book, we prefer to use the word feature, but other terms are equally valid. Similarly, the species column in the data frame is what we are trying to predict with our model, and so it is referred to as the **dependent variable**, **output**, or **target**. Again, in this book, we will prefer one form for consistency, and will use output. Each row in the data frame corresponding to a single data point is referred to as an **observation**, though it typically involves observing the values of a number of features.

As we will be using data sets, such as the iris data described earlier, to build our predictive models, it also helps to establish some symbol conventions. Here, the conventions are quite common in most of the literature. We'll use the capital letter, Y, to refer to the output variable, and subscripted capital letter, X_i, to denote the ith feature. For example, in our iris data set, we have four features that we could refer to as X_1 through X_4. We will use lower case letters for individual observations, so that x_1 corresponds to the first observation. Note that x_1 itself is a vector of feature components, x_{ij}, so that x_{12} refers to the value of the second feature in the first observation. We'll try to use double suffixes sparingly and we won't use arrows or any other form of vector notation for simplicity. Most often, we will be discussing either observations or features and so the case of the variable will make it clear to the reader which of these two is being referenced.

When thinking about a predictive model using a data set, we are generally making the assumption that for a model with n features, there is a true or ideal function, f, that maps the features to the output:

$$Y = f\left(X_1, X_2, \ldots, X_n\right)$$

We'll refer to this function as our **target function**. In practice, as we train our model using the data available to us, we will produce our own function that we hope is a good estimate for the target function. We can represent this by using a caret on top of the symbol *f* to denote our predicted function, and also for the output, *Y*, since the output of our predicted function is the predicted output. Our predicted output will, unfortunately, not always agree with the actual output for all observations (in our data or in general):

$$\hat{Y} = \hat{f}\left(X_1, X_2, \ldots, X_n\right)$$

Given this, we can essentially summarize the process of predictive modeling as a process that produces a function to predict a quantity, while minimizing the error it makes compared to the target function. A good question we can ask at this point is, where does the error come from? Put differently, why are we generally not able to exactly reproduce the underlying target function by analyzing a data set?

The answer to this question is that in reality there are several potential sources of error that we must deal with. Remember that each observation in our data set contains values for *n* features, and so we can think about our observations geometrically as points in an *n*-dimensional feature space. In this space, our underlying target function should pass through these points by the very definition of the target function. If we now think about this general problem of fitting a function to a finite set of points, we will quickly realize that there are actually infinite functions that could pass through the same set of points. The process of predictive modeling involves making a choice in the type of model that we will use for the data thereby constraining the range of possible target functions to which we can fit our data. At the same time, the data's inherent randomness cannot be removed no matter what model we select. These ideas lead us to an important distinction in the types of error that we encounter during modeling, namely the **reducible error** and the **irreducible error** respectively.

The reducible error essentially refers to the error that we as predictive modelers can minimize by selecting a model structure that makes valid assumptions about the process being modeled and whose predicted function takes the same form as the underlying target function. For example, as we shall see in the next chapter, a linear model imposes a linear relationship between the features in order to compose the output. This restrictive assumption means that no matter what training method we use, how much data we have, and how much computational power we throw in, if the features aren't linearly related in the real world, then our model will necessarily produce an error for at least some possible observations. By contrast, an example of an irreducible error arises when trying to build a model with an insufficient feature set. This is typically the norm and not the exception. Often, discovering what features to use is one of the most time consuming activities of building an accurate model.

Sometimes, we may not be able to directly measure a feature that we know is important. At other times, collecting the data for too many features may simply be impractical or too costly. Furthermore, the solution to this problem is not simply an issue of adding as many features as possible. Adding more features to a model makes it more complex and we run the risk of adding a feature that is unrelated to the output thus introducing noise in our model. This also means that our model function will have more inputs and will, therefore, be a function in a higher dimensional space. Some of the potential practical consequences of adding more features to a model include increasing the time it will take to train the model, making convergence on a final solution harder, and actually reducing model accuracy under certain circumstances, such as with highly correlated features. Finally, another source of an irreducible error that we must live with is the error in measuring our features so that the data itself may be noisy.

Reducible errors can be minimized not only through selecting the right model but also by ensuring that the model is trained correctly. Thus, reducible errors can also come from not finding the right specific function to use, given the model assumptions. For example, even when we have correctly chosen to train a linear model, there are infinitely many linear combinations of the features that we could use. Choosing the model parameters correctly, which in this case would be the coefficients of the linear model, is also an aspect of minimizing the reducible error. Of course, a large part of training a model correctly involves using a good optimization procedure to fit the model. In this book, we will at least give a high level intuition of how each model that we study is trained. We generally avoid delving deep into the mathematics of how optimization procedures work but we do give pointers to the relevant literature for the interested reader to find out more.

The core components of a model

So far we've established some central notions behind models and a common language to talk about data. In this section, we'll look at what the core components of a statistical model are. The primary components are typically:

- A set of equations with parameters that need to be tuned
- Some data that are representative of a system or process that we are trying to model
- A concept that describes the model's goodness of fit
- A method to update the parameters to improve the model's goodness of fit

As we'll see in this book, most models, such as neural networks, linear regression, and support vector machines have certain parameterized equations that describe them. Let's look at a linear model attempting to predict the output, Y, from three input features, which we will call X_1, X_2, and X_3:

$$Y = \beta_0 + \beta_1 X_1 + \beta_2 X_2 + \beta_3 X_3$$

This model has exactly one equation describing it and this equation provides the linear structure of the model. The equation is parameterized by four parameters, known as coefficients in this case, and they are the four β parameters. In the next chapter, we will see exactly what roles these play, but for this discussion, it is important to note that a linear model is an example of a parameterized model. The set of parameters is typically much smaller than the amount of data available.

Given a set of equations and some data, we then talk about training the model. This involves assigning values to the model's parameters so that the model describes the data more accurately. We typically employ certain standard measures that describe a model's goodness of fit to the data, which is how well the model describes the training data. The training process is usually an iterative procedure that involves performing computations on the data so that new values for the parameters can be computed in order to increase the model's goodness of fit. For example, a model can have an objective or error function. By differentiating this and setting it to zero, we can find the combination of parameters that give us the minimum error. Once we finish this process, we refer to the model as a trained model and say that the model has learned from the data. These terms are derived from the machine learning literature, although there is often a parallel made with statistics, a field that has its own nomenclature for this process. We will mostly use the terms from machine learning in this book.

Our first model: k-nearest neighbors

In order to put some of the ideas in this chapter into perspective, we will present our first model for this book, **k-nearest neighbors**, which is commonly abbreviated as **kNN**. In a nutshell, this simple approach actually avoids building an explicit model to describe how the features in our data combine to produce a target function. Instead, it relies on the notion that if we are trying to make a prediction on a data point that we have never seen before, we will look inside our original training data and find the k observations that are most similar to our new data point. We can then use some kind of averaging technique on the known value of the target function for these **k neighbors** to compute a prediction. Let's use our iris data set to understand this by way of an example. Suppose that we collect a new unidentified sample of an iris flower with the following measurements:

```
> new_sample
 Sepal.Length  Sepal.Width  Petal.Length   Petal.Width
 4.8           2.9          3.7            1.7
```

We would like to use the kNN algorithm in order to predict which species of flower we should use to identify our new sample. The first step in using the kNN algorithm is to determine the k-nearest neighbors of our new sample. In order to do this, we will have to give a more precise definition of what it means for two observations to be similar to each other. A common approach is to compute a numerical distance between two observations in the feature space. The intuition is that two observations that are similar will be close to each other in the feature space and therefore, the distance between them will be small. To compute the distance between two observations in the feature space, we often use the **Euclidean distance**, which is the length of a straight line between two points. The Euclidean distance between two observations, x_1 and x_2, is computed as follows:

$$d\left(x_1, x_2\right) = \sqrt{\sum_j \left(x_{1j}, x_{2j}\right)^2}$$

Recall that the second suffix, j, in the preceding formula corresponds to the jth feature. So, what this formula is essentially telling us is that for every feature, take the square of the difference in values of the two observations, sum up all these squared differences, and then take the square root of the result. There are many other possible definitions of distance, but this is one of the most frequently encountered in the kNN setting. We'll see more distance metrics in *Chapter 11, Recommendation Systems*.

In order to find the nearest neighbors of our new sample iris flower, we'll have to compute the distance to every point in the iris data set and then sort the results. First, we'll begin by subsetting the iris data frame to include only our features, thus excluding the species column, which is what we are trying to predict. We'll then define our own function to compute the Euclidean distance. Next, we'll use this to compute the distance to every iris observation in our data frame using the `apply()` function. Finally, we'll use the `sort()` function of R with the `index.return` parameter set to `TRUE`, so that we also get back the indexes of the row numbers in our iris data frame corresponding to each distance computed:

```
> iris_features <- iris[1:4]
> dist_eucl <- function(x1, x2) sqrt(sum((x1 - x2) ^ 2))
> distances <- apply(iris_features, 1,
                     function(x) dist_eucl(x, new_sample))
> distances_sorted <- sort(distances, index.return = T)
```

```
> str(distances_sorted)
List of 2
 $ x : num [1:150] 0.574 0.9 0.9 0.949 0.954 ...
 $ ix: int [1:150] 60 65 107 90 58 89 85 94 95 99 ...
```

The $x attribute contains the actual values of the distances computed between our sample iris flower and the observations in the iris data frame. The $ix attribute contains the row numbers of the corresponding observations. If we want to find the five nearest neighbors, we can subset our original iris data frame using the first five entries from the $ix attribute as the row numbers:

```
> nn_5 <- iris[distances_sorted$ix[1:5],]
> nn_5
     Sepal.Length Sepal.Width Petal.Length Petal.Width    Species
60            5.2         2.7          3.9         1.4 versicolor
65            5.6         2.9          3.6         1.3 versicolor
107           4.9         2.5          4.5         1.7  virginica
90            5.5         2.5          4.0         1.3 versicolor
58            4.9         2.4          3.3         1.0 versicolor
```

As we can see, four of the five nearest neighbors to our sample are the *versicolor* species, while the remaining one is the *virginica* species. For this type of problem where we are picking a class label, we can use a majority vote as our averaging technique to make our final prediction. Consequently, we would label our new sample as belonging to the versicolor species. Notice that setting the value of *k* to an odd number is a good idea, because it makes it less likely that we will have to contend with tie votes (and completely eliminates ties when the number of output labels is two). In the case of a tie, the convention is usually to just resolve it by randomly picking among the tied labels. Notice that nowhere in this process have we made any attempt to describe how our four features are related to our output. As a result, we often refer to the kNN model as a **lazy learner** because essentially, all it has done is memorize the training data and use it directly during a prediction. We'll have more to say about our kNN model, but first we'll return to our general discussion on models and discuss different ways to classify them.

Types of models

With a broad idea of the basic components of a model, we are ready to explore some of the common distinctions that modelers use to categorize different models.

Supervised, unsupervised, semi-supervised, and reinforcement learning models

We've already looked at the iris data set, which consisted of four features and one output variable, namely the species variable. Having the output variable available for all the observations in the training data is the defining characteristic of the **supervised learning** setting, which represents the most frequent scenario encountered. In a nutshell, the advantage of training a model under the supervised learning setting is that we have the correct answer that we should be predicting for the data points in our training data. As we saw in the previous section, kNN is a model that uses supervised learning, because the model makes its prediction for an input point by combining the values of the output variable for a small number of neighbors to that point. In this book, we will primarily focus on supervised learning.

Using the availability of the value of the output variable as a way to discriminate between different models, we can also envisage a second scenario in which the output variable is not specified. This is known as the **unsupervised learning** setting. An unsupervised version of the iris data set would consist of only the four features. If we don't have the species output variable available to us, then we clearly have no idea as to which species each observation refers. Indeed, we won't know how many species of flower are represented in the data set, or how many observations belong to each species. At first glance, it would seem that without this information, no useful predictive task could be carried out. In fact, what we can do is examine the data and create groups of observations based on how similar they are to each other, using the four features available to us. This process is known as **clustering**. One benefit of clustering is that we can discover natural groups of data points in our data; for example, we might be able to discover that the flower samples in an unsupervised version of our iris set form three distinct groups which correspond to three different species.

Between unsupervised and supervised methods, which are two absolutes in terms of the availability of the output variable, reside the **semi-supervised** and **reinforcement learning** settings. Semi-supervised models are built using data for which a (typically quite small) fraction contains the values for the output variable, while the rest of the data is completely unlabeled. Many such models first use the labeled portion of the data set in order to train the model coarsely, then incorporate the unlabeled data by projecting labels predicted by the model trained up this point.

In a reinforcement learning setting the output variable is not available, but other information that is directly linked with the output variable is provided. One example is predicting the next best move to win a chess game, based on data from complete chess games. Individual chess moves do not have output values in the training data, but for every game, the collective sequence of moves for each player resulted in either a win or a loss. Due to space constraints, semi-supervised and reinforcement settings aren't covered in this book.

Parametric and nonparametric models

In a previous section, we noted how most of the models we will encounter are **parametric models**, and we saw an example of a simple linear model. Parametric models have the characteristic that they tend to define a **functional form**. This means that they reduce the problem of selecting between all possible functions for the target function to a particular family of functions that form a parameter set. Selecting the specific function that will define the model essentially involves selecting precise values for the parameters. So, returning to our example of a three feature linear model, we can see that we have the two following possible choices of parameters (the choices are infinite, of course; here we just demonstrate two specific ones):

$$Y_1 = 0.68 + 2.54X_1 + 9.12X_2 - 0.13X_3$$
$$Y_2 = 4.56 + 3.08X_1 - 2.29X_2 + 1.11X_3$$

Here, we have used a subscript on the output Y variable to denote the two different possible models. Which of these might be a better choice? The answer is that it depends on the data. If we apply each of our models on the observations in our data set, we will get the predicted output for every observation. With supervised learning, every observation in our training data is labeled with the correct value of the output variable. To assess our model's goodness of fit, we can define an error function that measures the degree to which our predicted outputs differ from the correct outputs. We then use this to pick between our two candidate models in this case, but more generally to iteratively improve a model by moving through a sequence of progressively better candidate models.

Some parametric models are more flexible than linear models, meaning that they can be used to capture a greater variety of possible functions. Linear models, which require that the output be a linearly weighted combination of the input features, are considered strict. We can intuitively see that a more flexible model is more likely to allow us to approximate our input data with greater accuracy; however, when we look at overfitting, we'll see that this is not always a good thing. Models that are more flexible also tend to be more complex and, thus, training them often proves to be harder than training less flexible models.

Models are not necessarily parameterized, in fact, the class of models that have no parameters is known (unsurprisingly) as **nonparametric models**. Nonparametric models generally make no assumptions on the particular form of the output function. There are different ways of constructing a target function without parameters. **Splines** are a common example of a nonparametric model. The key idea behind splines is that we envisage the output function, whose form is unknown to us, as being defined exactly at the points that correspond to all the observations in our training data. Between the points, the function is locally interpolated using smooth polynomial functions. Essentially, the output function is built in a piecewise manner in the space between the points in our training data. Unlike most scenarios, splines will guarantee 100 percent accuracy on the training data, whereas, it is perfectly normal to have some errors in our training data. Another good example of a nonparametric model is the k-nearest neighbor algorithm that we've already seen.

Regression and classification models

The distinction between **regression** and **classification** models has to do with the type of output we are trying to predict, and is generally relevant to supervised learning. Regression models try to predict a numerical or quantitative value, such as the stock market index, the amount of rainfall, or the cost of a project. Classification models try to predict a value from a finite (though still possibly large) set of classes or categories. Examples of this include predicting the topic of a website, the next word that will be typed by a user, a person's gender, or whether a patient has a particular disease given a series of symptoms. The majority of models that we will study in this book fall quite neatly into one of these two categories, although a few, such as neural networks can be adapted to solve both types of problems. It is important to stress here that the distinction made is on the output only, and not on whether the feature values that are used to predict the output are quantitative or qualitative themselves. In general, features can be encoded in a way that allows both qualitative and quantitative features to be used in regression and classification models alike. Earlier, when we built a kNN model to predict the species of iris based on measurements of flower samples, we were solving a classification problem as our species output variable could take only one of three distinct labels. The kNN approach can also be used in a regression setting; in this case, the model combines the numerical values of the output variable for the selected nearest neighbors by taking the mean or median in order to make its final prediction. Thus, kNN is also a model that can be used in both regression and classification settings.

Real-time and batch machine learning models

Predictive models can use **real-time machine learning** or they can involve **batch learning**. The term real-time machine learning can refer to two different scenarios, although it certainly does not refer to the idea that real-time machine learning involves making a prediction in real time, that is, within a predefined time limit which is typically small. For example, once trained, a neural network model can produce its prediction of the output using only a few computations (depending on the number of inputs and network layers). This is not, however, what we mean when we talk about real-time machine learning.

A good example of a model that uses real-time machine learning is a weather predictor that uses a stream of incoming readings from various meteorological instruments. Here, the real time aspect of the model refers to the fact that we are taking only a recent window of readings in order to predict the weather. The further we go back in time, the less relevant the readings will be and we can, thus, choose to use only the latest information in order to make our prediction. Of course, models that are to be used in a real-time setting must also be able to compute their predictions quickly — it is not of much use if it takes hours for a system taking measurements in the morning to compute a prediction for the evening, as by the time the computation ends, the prediction won't be of much value.

When talking about models that take into account information obtained over a recent time frame to make a prediction, we generally refer to models that have been trained on data that is assumed to be representative of all the data for which the model will be asked to make a prediction in the future. A second interpretation of real-time machine learning arises when we describe models that detect that the properties of the process being modeled have shifted in some way. We will focus on examples of the first kind in this book when we look at time series models.

The process of predictive modeling

By looking at some of the different characterizations of models, we've already hinted at various steps of the predictive modeling process. In this section, we will present these steps in a sequence and make sure we understand how each of these contributes to the overall success of the endeavor.

Defining the model's objective

In a nutshell, the first step of every project is to figure out precisely what the desired outcome is, as this will help steer us to make good decisions throughout the course of the project. In a predictive analytics project, this question involves drilling into the type of prediction that we want to make and understanding the task in detail. For example, suppose we are trying to build a model that predicts employee churn for a company. We first need to define this task precisely, while trying to avoid making the problem overly broad or overly specific. We could measure churn as the percentage of new full time hires that defect from the company within their first six months. Notice that once we properly define the problem, we have already made some progress in thinking about what data we will have to work with. For example, we won't have to collect data from part-time contractors or interns. This task also means that we should collect data from our own company only, but at the same time recognize that our model might not necessarily be applicable to make predictions for the workforce of a different company. If we are only interested in churn, it also means that we won't need to make predictions about employee performance or sick days (although it wouldn't hurt to ask the person for whom we are building the model, to avoid surprises in the future).

Once we have a precise enough idea of the model we want to build, the next logical question to ask is what sort of performance we are interested in achieving, and how we will measure this. That is to say, we need to define a performance metric for our model and then a minimum threshold of acceptable performance. We will go into substantial detail on how to assess the performance of models in this book. For now, we want to emphasize that, although it is not unusual to talk about assessing the performance of a model after we have trained it on some data, in practice it is important to remember that defining the expectations and performance target for our model is something that a predictive modeler should discuss with the stakeholders of a project at the very beginning. Models are never perfect and it is easy to spiral into a mode of forever trying to improve performance. Clear performance goals are not only useful in guiding us to decide which methods to use, but also in knowing when our model is good enough.

Finally, we also need to think about the data that will be available to us when the time comes to collect it, and the context in which the model will be used. For example, suppose we know that our employee churn model will be used as one of the factors that determine whether a new applicant in our company will be hired. In this context, we should only collect data from our existing employees that were available before they were hired. We cannot use the result of their first performance review, as these data won't be available for a prospective applicant.

Collecting the data

Training a model to make predictions is often a data-intensive venture, and if there is one thing that you can never have too much of in this business, it is data. Collecting the data can often be the most time and resource consuming part of the entire process, which is why it is so critical that the first step of defining the task and identifying the right data to be collected is done properly. When we learn about how a model, such as logistic regression works we often do this by way of an example data set and this is largely the approach we'll follow in this book. Unfortunately, we don't have a way to simulate the process of collecting the data, and it may seem that most of the effort is spent on training and refining a model. When learning about models using existing data sets, we should bear in mind that a lot of effort has usually gone into collecting, curating, and preprocessing the data. We will look at data preprocessing more closely in a subsequent section.

While we are collecting data, we should always keep in mind whether we are collecting the right kind of data. Many of the sanity checks that we perform on data during preprocessing also apply during collection, in order for us to spot whether we have made a mistake early on in the process. For example, we should always check that we measure features correctly and in the right units. We should also make sure that we collect data from sources that are sufficiently recent, reliable, and relevant to the task at hand. In the employee churn model we described in the previous section, as we collect information about past employees we should ensure that we are consistent in measuring our features. For example, when measuring how many days a person has been working in our company, we should consistently use either calendar days or business days. We must also check that when collecting dates, such as when a person joined or left the company, we invariably either use the US format (month followed by day) or the European format (day followed by month) and do not mix the two, otherwise a date like 03/05/2014 will be ambiguous. We should also try to get information from as broad a sample as possible and not introduce a hidden bias in our data collection. For example, if we wanted a general model for employee churn, we would not want to collect data from only female employees or employees from a single department.

How do we know when we have collected enough data? Early on when we are collecting the data and have not built and tested any model, it is impossible to tell how much data we will eventually need, and there aren't any simple rules of thumb that we can follow. We can, however, anticipate that certain characteristics of our problem will require more data. For example, when building a classifier that will learn to predict from one of three classes, we may want to check whether we have enough observations representative of each class.

The greater the number of output classes we have, the more data we will need to collect. Similarly, for regression models, it is also useful to check that the range of the output variable in the training data corresponds to the range that we would like to predict. If we are building a regression model that covers a large output range, we will also need to collect more data compared to a regression model that covers a smaller output range under the same accuracy requirements.

Another important factor to help us estimate how much data we will need, is the desired model performance. Intuitively, the higher the accuracy that we need for our model, the more data we should collect. We should also be aware that improving model performance is not a linear process. Getting from 90 to 95 percent accuracy can often require more effort and a lot more data, compared to making the leap from 70 to 90 percent. Models that have fewer parameters or are simpler in their design, such as linear regression models, often tend to need less data than more complex models such as neural networks. Finally, the greater the number of features that we want to incorporate into our model, the greater the amount of data we should collect. In addition, we should be aware of the fact that this requirement for additional data is also not going to be linear. That is to say, building a model with twice the number of features often requires much more than twice the amount of original data. This should be readily apparent, if we think of the number of different combinations of inputs our model will be required to handle. Adding twice the number of dimensions results in far more than twice the number of possible input combinations. To understand this, suppose we have a model with three input features, each of which takes ten possible values. We have $10^3 = 1000$ possible input combinations. Adding a single extra feature that also takes ten values raises this to 10,000 possible combinations, which is much more than twice the number of our initial input combinations.

There have been attempts to obtain a more quantifiable view of whether we have enough data for a particular data set but we will not have time to cover them in this book. A good place to start learning more about this area of predictive modeling is to study **learning curves**. In a nutshell, with this approach we build consecutive models on the same data set by starting off with a small portion of the data and successively adding more. The idea is that if throughout this process the predictive accuracy on testing data always improves without tapering off, we probably could benefit from obtaining more data. As a final note for the data collection phase, even if we think we have enough data, we should always consider how much it would cost us (in terms of time and resources) in order to get more data, before making a choice to stop collecting and begin modeling.

Picking a model

Once we are clear on the prediction task, and we have the right kind data, the next step is to pick our first model. To being with, there is no best model overall, not even a best model using a few rules of thumb. In most cases, it makes sense to start off with a simple model, such as a Naïve Bayes model or a logistic regression in the case of a classification task, or a linear model in the case of regression. A simple model will give us a starting baseline performance, which we can then strive to improve. A simple model to start off with might also help in answering useful questions, such as how each feature contributes to the result, that is, how important is each feature and is the relationship with the output positively or negatively correlated. Sometimes, this kind of analysis itself warrants the production of a simple model first, followed by a more complex one, which will be used for the final prediction.

Sometimes a simple model might give us enough accuracy for the task at hand so that we won't need to invest more effort in order to give us a little bit extra. On the other hand, a simple model will often end up being inadequate for the task, requiring us to pick something more complicated. Choosing a more complex model over a simpler one is not always a straightforward decision, even if we can see that the accuracy of the complex model will be much better. Certain constraints, such as the number of features we have or the availability of data, may prevent us from moving to a more complex model. Knowing how to choose a model involves understanding the various strengths and limitations of the models in our toolkit. For every model we encounter in this book, we will pay particular attention to learning these points. In a real-world project, to help guide our decision, we often go back to the task requirements and ask a few questions, such as:

- What type of task do we have? Some models are only suited for particular tasks such as regression, classification, or clustering.

- Does the model need to explain its predictions? Some models, such as decision trees, are better at giving insights that are easily interpretable to explain why they made a particular prediction.

- Do we have any constraints on prediction time?

- Do we need to update the model frequently and is training time, therefore, important?

- Does the model work well if we have highly correlated features?

- Does the model scale well for the number of features and amount of data that we have available? If we have massive amounts of data, we may need a model whose training procedure can be parallelized to take advantage of parallel computer architectures, for example.

In practice, even if our first analysis points toward a particular model, we will most likely want to try out a number of options before making our final decision.

Preprocessing the data

Before we can use our data to train our model, we typically need to preprocess them. In this section, we will discuss a number of common preprocessing steps that we usually perform. Some of these are necessary in order to detect and resolve problems in our data, while others are useful in order to transform our data and make them applicable to the model we have chosen.

Exploratory data analysis

Once we have some data and have decided to start working on a particular model, the very first thing we'll want to do is to look at the data itself. This is not necessarily a very structured part of the process; it mostly involves understanding what each feature measures and getting a sense of the data we have collected. It is really important to understand what each feature represents and the units in which it is measured. It is also a really good idea to check the consistent use of units. We sometimes call this investigative process of exploring and visualizing our data **exploratory data analysis**.

An excellent practice is to use the summary() function of R on our data frame to obtain some basic metrics for each feature, such as the mean and variance, as well as the largest and smallest values. Sometimes, it is easy to spot that a mistake has been made in data collection through inconsistencies in the data. For example, for a regression problem, multiple observations with identical feature values but wildly different outputs may (depending on the application) be a signal that there are erroneous measurements. Similarly, it is a good idea to know whether there are any features that have been measured in the presence of significant noise. This may sometimes lead to a different choice of model or it may mean that the feature should be ignored.

Another useful function used to summarize features in a data frame is the describe() function in the psych package. This returns information about how skewed each feature is, as well as the usual measures of a location (such as the mean and median) and dispersion (such as the standard deviation).

An essential part of exploratory data analysis is to use plots to visualize our data. There is a diverse array of plots that we can use depending on the context. For example, we might want to create box plots of our numerical features to visualize ranges and quartiles. Bar plots and mosaic plots are useful to visualize the proportions of our data under different combinations of values for categorical input features. We won't go into further detail on information visualization, as this is a field in its own right.

R is an excellent platform to create visualizations. The `base` R package provides a number of different functions to plot data. Two excellent packages to create more advanced plots are `lattice` and `ggplot2`. Good references for these two, which also cover principles used to make effective visualizations, are *Lattice: Multivariate Data Visualization with R* and *ggplot2: Elegant Graphics for Data Analysis*, both of which are published by Springer under the Use R! series.

Feature transformations

Often, we'll find that our numerical features are measured on scales that are completely different to each other. For example, we might measure a person's body temperature in degrees Celsius, so the numerical values will typically be in the range of 36-38. At the same time, we might also measure a person's white blood cell count per microliter of blood. This feature generally takes values in the thousands. If we are to use these features as an input to an algorithm, such as kNN, we'd find that the large values of the white blood cell count feature dominate the Euclidean distance calculation. We could have several features in our input that are important and useful for classification, but if they were measured on scales that produce numerical values much smaller than one thousand, we'd essentially be picking our nearest neighbors mostly on the basis of a single feature, namely the white blood cell count. This problem comes up often and applies to many models, not just kNN. We handle this by transforming (also referred to as scaling) our input features before using them in our model.

We'll discuss three popular options for feature scaling. When we know that our input features are close to being normally distributed, one possible transformation to use is **Z-score normalization**, which works by subtracting the mean and dividing it by the standard deviation:

$$x_{z-score} = \frac{x - E(x)}{\sqrt{Var(x)}}$$

$E(x)$ is the expectation or mean of x, and the standard deviation is the square root of the variance of x, written as $Var(x)$. Notice that as a result of this transformation, the new feature will be centered on a mean of zero and will have unit variance. Another possible transformation, which is better when the input is uniformly distributed, is to scale all the features and outputs so that they lie within a single interval, typically the unit interval $[0,1]$:

$$x_{unit-interval} = \frac{x - \min(x)}{\max(x) - \min(x)}$$

A third option is known as the **Box-Cox transformation**. This is often applied when our input features are highly skewed (asymmetric) and our model requires the input features to be normally distributed or symmetrical at the very least:

$$x_{box-cox} = \frac{x^{\lambda} - 1}{\lambda}$$

As λ is in the denominator, it must take a value other than zero. The transformation is actually defined for a zero-valued λ: in this case, it is given by the natural logarithm of the input feature, $ln(x)$. Notice that this is a parameterized transform and so there is a need to specify a concrete value of λ. There are various ways to estimate an appropriate value for λ from the data itself. Indicatively, we'll mention a technique to do this, known as cross-validation, which we will encounter later on in this book in *Chapter 5, Support Vector Machines*.

The original reference for the Box-Cox transformation is a paper published in 1964 by the Journal of the Royal Statistical Society, titled *An analysis of Transformations* and authored by *G. E. P. Box* and *D. R. Cox*.

To get a feel for how these transformations work in practice, we'll try them out on the Sepal.Length feature from our iris data set. Before we do this, however, we'll introduce the first R package that we will be working with, caret.

The caret package is a very useful package that has a number of goals. It provides a number of helpful functions that are commonly used in the process of predictive modeling, from data preprocessing and visualization, to feature selection and resampling techniques. It also features a unified interface for many predictive modeling functions and provides functionalities for parallel processing.

The definitive reference for predictive modeling using the caret package is a book called *Applied Predictive Modeling*, written by *Max Kuhn* and *Kjell Johnson* and published by *Springer*. *Max Kuhn* is the principal author of the caret package itself. The book also comes with a companion website at http://appliedpredictivemodeling.com.

When we transform our input features on the data we use to train our model, we must remember that we will need to apply the same transformation to the features of later inputs that we will use at prediction time. For this reason, transforming data using the caret package is done in two steps. In the first step, we use the prePprocess() function that stores the parameters of the transformations to be applied to the data, and in the second step, we use the predict() function to actually compute the transformation. We tend to use the prePprocess() function only once, and then the predict() function every time we need to apply the same transformation to some data. The prePprocess() function takes a data frame with some numerical values as its first input, and we will also specify a vector containing the names of the transformations to be applied to the method parameter. The predict() function then takes the output of the previous function along with the data we want to transform, which in the case of the training data itself may well be the same data frame. Let's see all this in action:

```
> library("caret")
> iris_numeric <- iris[1:4]
> pp_unit <- preProcess(iris_numeric, method = c("range"))
> iris_numeric_unit <- predict(pp_unit, iris_numeric)
> pp_zscore <- preProcess(iris_numeric, method = c("center",
  "scale"))
> iris_numeric_zscore <- predict(pp_zscore, iris_numeric)
> pp_boxcox <- preProcess(iris_numeric, method = c("BoxCox"))
> iris_numeric_boxcox <- predict(pp_boxcox, iris_numeric)
```

Downloading the example code

You can download the example code files from your account at http://www.packtpub.com for all the Packt Publishing books you have purchased. If you purchased this book elsewhere, you can visit http://www.packtpub.com/support and register to have the files e-mailed directly to you.

We've created three new versions of the numerical features of the iris data, with the difference being that in each case we used a different transformation. We can visualize the effects of our transformations by plotting the density of the Sepal. Length feature for each scaled data frame using the density() function and plotting the results, as shown here:

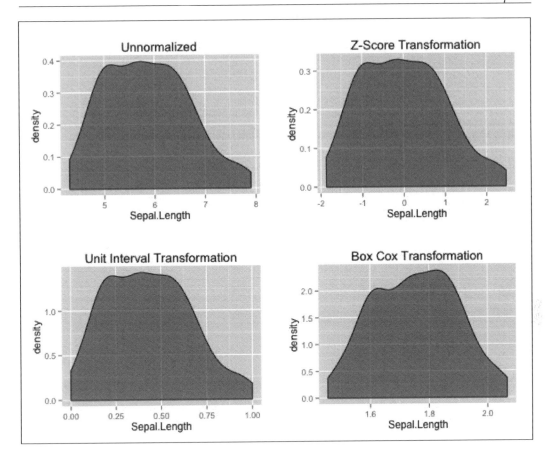

Notice that the Z-score and unit interval transformations preserve the overall shape of the density while shifting and scaling the values, whereas the Box-Cox transformation also changes the overall shape, resulting in a density that is less skewed than the original.

Encoding categorical features

Many models, from linear regression to neural networks, require all the inputs to be numerical, and so we often need a way to encode categorical fields on a numerical scale. For example, if we have a size feature that takes values in the set {*small, medium, large*}, we may want to represent this with the numerical values 1, 2, and 3, respectively. In the case of ordered categories, such as the size feature just described, this mapping probably makes sense.

The number 3 is the largest on this scale and this corresponds to the *large* category, which is further away from the *small* category, represented by the number 1 than it is from the *medium* category, represented by the value 2. Using this scale is only one possible mapping, and in particular, it forces the *medium* category to be equidistant from the *large* and *small* categories, which may or may not be appropriate based on our knowledge about the specific feature. In the case of unordered categories, such as brands or colors, we generally avoid mapping them onto a single numerical scale. For example, if we mapped the set *{blue, green, white, red, orange}* to the numbers one through five, respectively, then this scale is arbitrary and there is no reason why *red* is closer to *white* and far from *blue*. To overcome this, we create a series of indicator features, I_i, which take the following form:

$$I_i = I(x = x_i) = \begin{cases} 1 \ if \ x = x_i \\ 0 \ if \ x \neq x_i \end{cases}$$

We need as many indicator features as we have categories, so for our color example, we would create five indicator features. In this case, I_1, might be:

$$I_1 = I(x = blue) = \begin{cases} 1 \ if \ x = blue \\ 0 \ if \ x \neq blue \end{cases}$$

In this way, our original color feature will be mapped to five indicator features and for every observation, only one of these indicator features takes the value 1 and the rest will be 0 as each observation will involve one color value in our original feature. Indicator features are binary features as they only take on two values: 0 and 1.

 We may often encounter an alternative approach that uses only *n-1* binary features to encode *n* levels of a factor. This is done by choosing one level to be the reference level and is indicated where each one of the *n-1* binary features takes the value 0. This can be more economical on the number of features and avoids introducing a linear dependence between them, but it violates the property that all features are equidistant from each other.

Missing data

Sometimes, data contain missing values, as for certain observations some features were unavailable or could not properly be measured. For example, suppose that in our iris data set, we lost the measurement for a particular observation's petal length. We would then have a missing value for this flower sample in the `Petal.Length` feature. Most models do not have an innate ability to handle missing data. Typically, a missing value appears in our data as a blank entry or the symbol *NA*. We should check whether missing values are actually present in our data but have been erroneously assigned a value, such as *0*, which is often a very legitimate feature value.

Before deciding how to handle missing data, especially when our approach will be to simply throw away observations with missing values, we should recognize that the particular values that are missing might follow a pattern. Concretely, we often distinguish between different so-called mechanisms for missing values. In the ideal **Missing Completely At Random (MCAR)** scenario, missing values occur independently from the true values of the features in which they occur, as well as from all other features. In this scenario, if we are missing a value for the length of a particular iris flower petal, then this occurs independently from how long the flower petal actually was and the value of any other feature, such as whether the observation was from the *versicolor* species or the *setosa* species. The **Missing At Random (MAR)** scenario is a less ideal situation. Here, a missing value is independent of the true value of the feature in question, but may be correlated with another feature. An example of this scenario is when missing petal length values mostly occur in the *setosa* samples in our iris data set, as long as they still occur independently of the true petal length values. In the **Missing Not At Random (MNAR)** scenario, which is the most problematic case, there is some sort of a pattern that explains when values might be missing based on the true values of the feature itself. For example, if we had difficulty in measuring very small petal lengths and ended up with missing values as a result, simply removing the incomplete samples would result in a sample of observations with above average petal lengths, and so our data would be biased.

There are a number of ways to handle missing values but we will not dig deep into this problem in this book. In the rare cases where we have missing values, we will exclude them from our data sets, but be aware that in a real project, we would investigate the source of the missing values in order to be sure that we can do this safely. Another approach is to attempt to guess or impute the missing values. The kNN algorithm itself is one way to do this by finding the nearest neighbors of a sample with a missing value in one feature. This is done by using a distance computation that excludes the dimension which contains the missing value. The missing value is then computed as the mean of the values of the nearest neighbors in this dimension.

The interested reader can find a detailed treatment of how to handle missing values in *Statistical Analysis with Missing Data, Second Edition*, by *Roderick J. A. Little* and *Donald B. Rubin*, published by Wiley.

Outliers

Outliers are also a problem that often needs to be addressed. An outlier is a particular observation that is very far from the rest of the data in one or more of its features. In some cases, this may represent an actual rare circumstance that is a legitimate behavior for the system we are trying to model. In other cases, it may be that there has been an error in measurement. For example, when reporting the ages of people, a value of 110 might be an outlier, which could happen because of a reporting error on an actual value of 11. It could also be the result of a valid, albeit extremely rare measurement. Often, the domain of our problem will give us a good indication of whether outliers are likely to be measurement errors or not, and if so, as part of preprocessing the data, we will often want to exclude outliers from our data completely. In *Chapter 2, Linear Regression*, we will look at outlier exclusion in more detail.

Removing problematic features

Preprocessing a data set can also involve the decision to drop some of the features if we know that they will cause us problems with our model. A common example is when two or more features are highly correlated with each other. In R, we can easily compute pairwise correlations on a data frame using the `cor()` function:

```
> cor(iris_numeric)
             Sepal.Length Sepal.Width Petal.Length Petal.Width
Sepal.Length    1.0000000  -0.1175698    0.8717538   0.8179411
Sepal.Width    -0.1175698   1.0000000   -0.4284401  -0.3661259
Petal.Length    0.8717538  -0.4284401    1.0000000   0.9628654
Petal.Width     0.8179411  -0.3661259    0.9628654   1.0000000
```

Here, we can see that the `Petal.Length` feature is very highly correlated with the `Petal.Width` feature, with the correlation exceeding 0.96. The `caret` package offers the `findCorrelation()` function, which takes a correlation matrix as an input, and the optional `cutoff` parameter, which specifies a threshold for the absolute value of a pairwise correlation. This then returns a (possibly zero length) vector which shows the columns to be removed from our data frame due to correlation. The default setting of `cutoff` is 0.9:

```
> iris_cor <- cor(iris_numeric)
> findCorrelation(iris_cor)
[1] 3
> findCorrelation(iris_cor, cutoff = 0.99)
integer(0)
> findCorrelation(iris_cor, cutoff = 0.80)
[1] 3 4
```

An alternative approach to removing correlation is a complete transformation of the entire feature space as is done in many methods for dimensionality reduction, such as **Principal Component Analysis (PCA)** and **Singular Value Decomposition (SVD)**. We'll see the former shortly, and the latter we'll visit in *Chapter 11, Recommendation Systems*.

In a similar vein, we might want to remove features that are **linear combinations** of each other. By linear combination of features, we mean a sum of features where each feature is multiplied by a scalar constant. To see how caret deals with these, we will create a new iris data frame with two additional columns, which we will call Cmb and Cmb.N, as follows:

```
> new_iris <- iris_numeric
> new_iris$Cmb <- 6.7 * new_iris$Sepal.Length –
                  0.9 * new_iris$Petal.Width
> set.seed(68)
> new_iris$Cmb.N <- new_iris$Cmb +
                    rnorm(nrow(new_iris), sd = 0.1)
> options(digits = 4)
> head(new_iris,n = 3)
  Sepal.Length Sepal.Width Petal.Length Petal.Width   Cmb Cmb.N
1          5.1         3.5          1.4         0.2 33.99 34.13
2          4.9         3.0          1.4         0.2 32.65 32.63
3          4.7         3.2          1.3         0.2 31.31 31.27
```

As we can see, Cmb is a perfect linear combination of the Sepal.Length and Petal.Width features. Cmb.N is a feature that is the same as Cmb but with some added Gaussian noise with a mean of zero and a very small standard deviation (*0.1*), so that the values are very close to those of Cmb. The caret package can detect exact linear combinations of features, though not if the features are noisy, using the findLinearCombos() function:

```
> findLinearCombos(new_iris)
$linearCombos
$linearCombos[[1]]
[1] 5 1 4


$remove
[1] 5
```

As we can see, the function only suggests that we should remove the fifth feature (Cmb) from our data frame, because it is an exact linear combination of the first and fourth features. Exact linear combinations are rare, but can sometimes arise when we have a very large number of features and redundancy occurs between them. Both correlated features as well as linear combinations are an issue with linear regression models, as we shall soon see in *Chapter 2, Linear Regression*. In this chapter, we'll also see a method of detecting features that are very nearly linear combinations of each other.

A final issue that we'll look at for problematic features, is the issue of having features that do not vary at all in our data set, or that have near zero variance. For some models, having these types of features does not cause us problems. For others, it may create problems and we'll demonstrate why this is the case. As in the previous example, we'll create a new iris data frame, as follows:

```
> newer_iris <- iris_numeric
> newer_iris$ZV <- 6.5
> newer_iris$Yellow <- ifelse(rownames(newer_iris) == 1, T, F
> head(newer_iris, n = 3)
  Sepal.Length Sepal.Width Petal.Length Petal.Width  ZV Yellow
1          5.1         3.5          1.4         0.2 6.5   TRUE
2          4.9         3.0          1.4         0.2 6.5  FALSE
3          4.7         3.2          1.3         0.2 6.5  FALSE
```

The ZV column has the constant number of 6.5 for all observations. The Yellow column is a fictional column that records whether an observation had some yellow color on the petal. All the observations, except the first, are made to have this feature set to FALSE and so this is a near zero variance column. The caret package uses a definition of near zero variance that checks whether the number of unique values that a feature takes as compared to the overall number of observations is very small, or whether the ratio of the most common value to the second most common value (referred to as the frequency ratio) is very high. The nearZeroVar() function applied to a data frame returns a vector containing the features which have zero or near zero variance. By setting the saveMetrics parameter to TRUE, we can see more information about the features in our data frame:

```
> nearZeroVar(newer_iris)
[1] 5 6
> nearZeroVar(newer_iris, saveMetrics = T)
             freqRatio percentUnique zeroVar   nzv
Sepal.Length     1.111       23.3333   FALSE FALSE
Sepal.Width      1.857       15.3333   FALSE FALSE
Petal.Length     1.000       28.6667   FALSE FALSE
Petal.Width      2.231       14.6667   FALSE FALSE
ZV               0.000        0.6667    TRUE  TRUE
Yellow         149.000        1.3333   FALSE  TRUE
```

Here, we can see that the `ZV` column has been identified as a zero variance column (which is also by definition a near zero variance column). The `Yellow` column does have a nonzero variance, but its high frequency ratio and low unique value percentage make it a near zero variance column. In practice, we tend to remove zero variance columns, as they don't have any information to give to our model. Removing near zero variance columns, however, is tricky and should be done with care. To understand this, consider the fact that a model for species prediction, using our newer iris data set, might learn that if a sample has yellow in its petals, then regardless of all other predictors, we would predict the *setosa* species, as this is the species that corresponds to the only observation in our entire data set that had the color yellow in its petals. This might indeed be true in reality, in which case, the yellow feature is informative and we should keep it. On the other hand, the presence of the color yellow on iris petals may be completely random and non-indicative of species but also an extremely rare event. This would explain why only one observation in our data set had the yellow color in its petals. In this case, keeping the feature is dangerous because of the aforementioned conclusion. Another potential problem with keeping this feature will become apparent when we look at splitting our data into training and test sets, as well as other cases of data splitting, such as cross-validation, described in *Chapter 5, Support Vector Machines*. Here, the issue is that one split in our data may lead to unique values for a near zero variance column, for example, only `FALSE` values for our `Yellow` iris column.

Feature engineering and dimensionality reduction

The number and type of features that we use with a model is one of the most important decisions that we will make in the predictive modeling process. Having the right features for a model will ensure that we have sufficient evidence on which to base a prediction. On the flip side, the number of features that we work with is precisely the number of dimensions that the model has. A large number of dimensions can be the source of several complications. High dimensional problems often suffer from **data sparsity**, which means that because of the number of dimensions available, the range of possible combinations of values across all the features grows so large that it is unlikely that we will ever collect enough data in order to have enough representative examples for training. In a similar vein, we often talk about the **curse of dimensionality**. This describes the fact that because of the overwhelmingly large space of possible inputs, data points that we have collected are likely to be far away from each other in the feature space. As a result, local methods, such as k-nearest neighbors that make predictions using observations in the training data that are close to the point for which we are trying to make a prediction, will not work as well in high dimensions. A large feature set is also problematic in that it may significantly increase the time needed to train (and predict, in some cases) our model.

Consequently, there are two types of processes that feature engineering involves. The first of these, which grows the feature space, is the design of new features based on features within our data. Sometimes, a new feature that is a product or ratio of two original features might work better. There are many ways to combine existing features into new ones, and often it is expert knowledge from the problem's particular application domain that might help guide us. In general though, this process takes experience and a lot of trial and error. Note that there is no guarantee that adding a new feature will not degrade performance. Sometimes, adding a feature that is very noisy or highly correlated with an existing feature may actually cause us to lose accuracy.

The second process in feature engineering is feature reduction or shrinkage, which reduces the size of the feature space. In the previous section on data preprocessing, we looked at how we can detect individual features that may be problematic for our model in some way. **Feature selection** refers to the process in which the subset of features that are the most informative for our target output are selected from the original pool of features. Some methods, such as tree-based models, have built-in feature selection, as we shall see in *Chapter 6, Tree-based Methods*. In *Chapter 2, Linear Regression*, we'll also explore methods to perform feature selection for linear models. Another way to reduce the overall number of features, a concept known as **dimensionality reduction**, is to transform the entire set of features into a completely new set of features that are fewer in number. A classic example of this is **Principal Component Analysis (PCA)**.

In a nutshell, PCA creates a new set of input features, known as **principal components**, all of which are linear combinations of the original input features. For the first principal component, the linear combination weights are chosen in order to capture the maximum amount of variation in the data. If we could visualize the first principal component as a line in the original feature space, this would be the line in which the data varies the most. It also happens to be the line that is closest to all the data points in the original feature space. Every subsequent principal component attempts to capture a line of maximum variation, but in a way that the new principal component is uncorrelated with the previous ones already computed. Thus, the second principal component selects the linear combination of original input features that have the highest degree of variation in the data, while being uncorrelated with the first principal component.

The principal components are ordered naturally in a descending order according to the amount of variation that they capture. This allows us to perform dimensionality reduction in a simple manner by keeping the first N components, where we choose N so that the components chosen incorporate a minimum amount of the variance from the original data set. We won't go into the details of the underlying linear algebra necessary to compute the principal components.

Instead, we'll direct our attention to the fact that this process is sensitive to the variance and scale of the original features. For this reason, we often scale our features before carrying out this process. To visualize how useful PCA can be, we'll once again turn to our faithful iris data set. We can use the caret package to carry out PCA. To do this, we specify pca in the method parameter of the preProcess() function. We can also use the thresh parameter, which specifies the minimum variance we must retain. We'll explicitly use the value 0.95 so that we retain 95 percent of the variance of the original data, but note that this is also the default value of this parameter:

```
> pp_pca <- preProcess(iris_numeric,  method = c("BoxCox",
  "center", "scale", "pca"), thresh = 0.95)
> iris_numeric_pca <- predict(pp_pca, iris_numeric)
> head(iris_numeric_pca, n = 3)
      PC1      PC2
1 -2.304  -0.4748
2 -2.151   0.6483
3 -2.461   0.3464
```

As a result of this transformation, we are now left with only two features, so we can conclude that the first two principal components of the numerical iris features incorporate over 95 percent of the variation in the data.

If we are interested in learning the weights that were used to compute the principal components, we can inspect the rotation attribute of the pp_pca object:

```
> options(digits = 2)
> pp_pca$rotation
                PC1     PC2
Sepal.Length   0.52  -0.386
Sepal.Width   -0.27  -0.920
Petal.Length   0.58  -0.049
Petal.Width    0.57  -0.037
```

This means that the first principal component, PC1, was computed as follows:

$$0.52 \cdot Sepal.Length - 0.27 \cdot Sepal.Width + 0.58 \cdot Petal.Length + 0.57 \cdot Petal.Width$$

Sometimes, instead of directly specifying a threshold for the total variance captured by the principal components, we might want to examine a plot of each principal component and its variance. This is known as a **scree plot**, and we can build this by first performing PCA and indicating that we want to keep all the components. To do this, instead of specifying a variance threshold, we set the pcaComp parameter, which is the number of principal components we want to keep. We will set this to 4, which includes all of them, remembering that the total number of principal components is the same as the total number of original features or dimensions we started out with. We will then compute the variance and cumulative variance of these components and store it in a data frame. Finally, we will plot this in the figure that follows, noting that the numbers in brackets are cumulative percentages of variance captured:

```
> pp_pca_full <- preProcess(iris_numeric,  method = c("BoxCox",
  "center", "scale", "pca"), pcaComp = 4)
> iris_pca_full <- predict(pp_pca_full, iris_numeric)
> pp_pca_var <- apply(iris_pca_full, 2, var)
> iris_pca_var <- data.frame(Variance =
  round(100 * pp_pca_var / sum(pp_pca_var), 2), CumulativeVariance
  = round(100 * cumsum(pp_pca_var) / sum(pp_pca_var), 2))
> iris_pca_var
    Variance CumulativeVariance
PC1   73.45               73.45
PC2   22.82               96.27
PC3    3.20               99.47
PC4    0.53              100.00
```

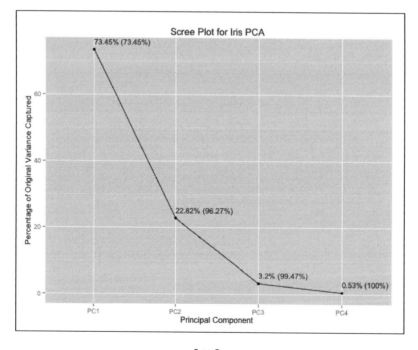

As we can see, the first principal component accounts for 73.45 percent of the total variance in the iris data set, while together with the second component, the total variance captured is 96.27 percent. PCA is an unsupervised method for dimensionality reduction that does not make use of the output variable even when it is available. Instead, it looks at the data geometrically in the feature space. This means that we cannot ensure that PCA will give us a new feature space that will perform well in our prediction problem, beyond the computational advantages of having fewer features. These advantages might make PCA a viable choice even when there is reduction in model accuracy as long as this reduction is small and acceptable for the specific task. As a final note, we should point out that we weights of the principal components, often referred to as **loadings** are unique within a sign flip as long as they have been normalized. In cases where we have perfectly correlated features or perfect linear combinations we will obtain a few principal components that are exactly zero.

Training and assessing the model

In our earlier discussion of parametric models, we saw that they come with a procedure to train the model using a set of training data. Nonparametric models will typically either perform lazy learning, in which case there really isn't an actual training procedure at all beyond memorizing the training data, or as in the case of splines, will perform local computations on the training data.

Either way, if we are to assess the performance of our model, we need to split our data into a **training set** and a **test set**. The key idea is that we want to assess our model based on how we expect it to perform on unseen future data. We do this by using the test set, which is a portion (typically 15-30 percent) of the data we collected and set aside for this purpose and haven't used during training. For example, one possible divide is to have a training set with 80 percent of the observations in our original data, and a test set with the remaining 20 percent. The reason why we need a test set is that we cannot use the training set to fairly assess our model performance, since we fit our model to the training data and it does not represent data that we haven't seen before. From a prediction standpoint, if our goal was to maximize performance on our training data alone, then the best thing to do would be to simply memorize the input data along with the desired output values and our model would thus be a simple look-up table!

A good question to ask would be how we decide between how much data to use for training and testing. There is a trade-off that is involved here that makes the answer to this question nontrivial. On the one hand, we would like to use as much data as possible in our training set, so that the model has more examples from which to learn. On the other, we would like to have a large test set so that we can test our trained model using many examples in order to minimize the variance of our estimate of the model's predictive performance. If we only have a handful of observations in our test set, then we cannot really generalize about how our model performs on unseen data overall.

Another factor that comes into play is how much starting data we have collected. If we have very little data, we may have to use a larger amount in order to train our model, such as an 85-15 split. If we have enough data, then we might consider a 70-30 split so that we can get a more accurate prediction on our test set.

To split a data set using the `caret` package, we can use the `createDataPartition()` function to create a sampling vector containing the indices of the rows we will use in our training set. These are selected by randomly sampling the rows until a specified proportion of the rows have been sampled, using the `p` parameter:

```
> set.seed(2412)
> iris_sampling_vector <- createDataPartition(iris$Species, p =
                        0.8, list = FALSE)
```

 It is good practice when reporting the results of a statistical analysis involving a random number generation, to apply the `set.seed()` function on a randomly chosen but fixed number. This function ensures that the random numbers that are generated from the next function call involving random number generation will be the same every time the code is run. This is done so that others who read the analysis are able to reproduce the results exactly. Note that if we have several functions in our code that perform random number generation, or the same function is called multiple times, we should ideally apply `set.seed()` before each one of them.

Using our sampling vector, which we created for the iris data set, we can construct our training and test sets. We'll do this for a few versions of the iris data set that we built earlier on when we experimented with different feature transformations.

```
> iris_train       <- iris_numeric[iris_sampling_vector,]
> iris_train_z     <- iris_numeric_zscore[iris_sampling_vector,]
> iris_train_pca <- iris_numeric_pca[iris_sampling_vector,]
> iris_train_labels <- iris$Species[iris_sampling_vector]
>
> iris_test         <- iris_numeric[-iris_sampling_vector,]
```

```
> iris_test_z      <- iris_numeric_zscore[-iris_sampling_vector,]
> iris_test_pca    <- iris_numeric_pca[-iris_sampling_vector,]
> iris_test_labels <- iris$Species[-iris_sampling_vector]
```

We are now in a position to build and test three different models for the iris data set. These are the in turn, the unnormalized model, a model where the input features have been centered and scaled with a Z-score transformation, and the PCA model with two principal components. We could use our test set in order to measure the predictive performance of each of these models after we build them; however, this would mean that in our final estimate of unseen accuracy, we will have used the test set in the model selection, thus producing a biased estimate. For this reason, we often maintain a separate split of the data, usually as large as the test set, known as the **validation set**. This is used to tune model parameters, such as *k* in kNN, and among different encodings and transformations of the input features before using the test set to predict unseen performance. In *Chapter 5*, *Support Vector Machines*, we'll discuss an alternative to this approach known as cross-validation.

Once we split our data, train our model by following the relevant training procedure that it requires, and tune our model parameters, we then have to assess its performance on the test set. Typically, we won't find the same performance on our test set as on our training set. Sometimes, we may even find that the performance we see when we deploy our model does not match what we expected to see, based on the performance on our training or test sets. There are a number of possible reasons for this disparity in performance. The first of these is that the data we may have collected may either not be representative of the process that we are modeling, or that there are certain combinations of feature inputs that we simply did not encounter in our training data. This could produce results that are inconsistent with our expectations. This situation can happen both in the real world, but also with our test set if it contains outliers, for example. Another common situation is the problem of model **overfitting**.

Overfitting is a problem in which some models, especially more flexible models, perform well on their training data set but perform significantly worse on an unseen test set. This occurs when a model matches the observations in the training data too closely and fails to generalize on unseen data. Put differently, the model is picking up on spurious details and variations in a training data set, which are not representative of the underlying population as a whole. Overfitting is one of the key reasons why we do not choose our model based on its performance on the training data. Other sources of discrepancy between training and test data performance are model bias and variance. Together, these actually form a well-known trade-off in statistical modeling known as the **bias-variance tradeoff**.

The variance of a statistical model refers to how much the model's predicted function would change, should a differently chosen training set (but generated from the exact same process or system that we are trying to predict as the original) be used to train the model. A low variance is desired because essentially, we don't want to predict a very different function with a different training set that is generated from the same process. Model bias refers to the errors inherently introduced in the predicted function, as a result of the limitation as to what functional forms the specific model can learn. For example, linear models introduce bias when trying to approximate nonlinear functions because they can only learn linear functions. The ideal scenario for a good predictive model is to have both a low variance and a low bias. It is important for a predictive modeler to be aware of the fact that there is a bias-variance trade-off that arises from the choice of models. Models that are typically more complex because of the fact that they make fewer assumptions on the target function are prone to less bias but higher variance than simpler but more restrictive models, such as linear models. This is because more complex models are able to approximate the training data more closely due to their flexibility, but as a result, they are more sensitive to changes in training data. This, of course, is also related to the problem of overfitting that complex models often exhibit.

We can actually see the effects of overfitting by first training some kNN models on our iris data sets. There are a number of packages that offer an implementation of the kNN algorithm, but we will use the knn3() function provided by the caret package with which we are familiar. To train a model using this function, all we have to do is provide it with a data frame that contains the numerical input features, a vector of output labels, and k, the number of nearest neighbors we want to use for the prediction:

```
> knn_model      <- knn3(iris_train, iris_train_labels, k = 5)
> knn_model_z    <- knn3(iris_train_z, iris_train_labels, k = 5)
> knn_model_pca <- knn3(iris_train_pca, iris_train_labels, k = 5)
```

To see the effect of different values of k, we will use the iris PCA model that is conveniently available in two dimensions for us to visualize and repeatedly train:

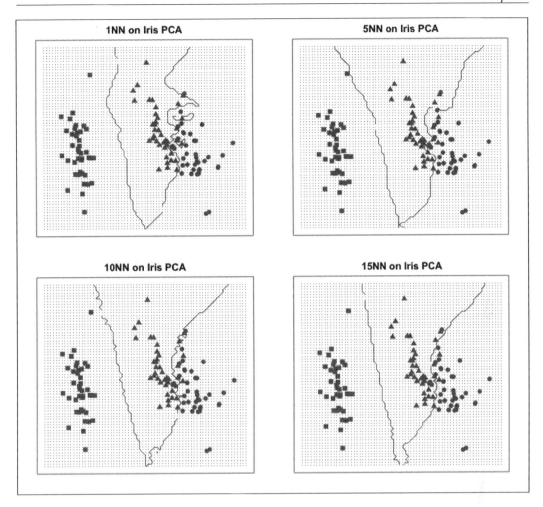

In the preceding plots, we have used different symbols to denote data points corresponding to different species. The lines shown in the plots correspond to the **decision boundaries** between the different species, which are the class labels of our output variable. Notice that using a low value of k, such as 1, captures local variation in the data very closely and as a result, the decision boundaries are very irregular. A higher value of k uses many neighbors to create a prediction, resulting in a smoothing effect and smoother decision boundaries. Tuning k in kNN is an example of tuning a model parameter to balance the effect of overfitting.

We haven't mentioned any specific performance metrics in this section. There are different measures of model quality relevant to regression and classification, and we will address these after we wrap up our discussion on the predictive modeling process.

Repeating with different models and final model selection

During the first iteration of this process (and this is very much an iterative process!), we usually arrive at this stage, having trained and assessed a simple model. Simple models usually allow us to get to a quick and dirty solution with minimum effort, thus giving us an early sense of how far away we are from a model that will make predictions with reasonable accuracy. Simple models are also great at giving us a baseline level of performance against which we can benchmark the performance of future models. As modelers, we often acquire a preference toward one method over others, but it is important to remember that it is generally well worth the effort to try out different approaches to a problem and use the data to help us decide which one we should end up using.

Before picking the final model, it is worth considering whether it might be a good idea to use more than one model to solve our problem. In *Chapter 7, Ensemble Methods*, we spend an entire chapter on studying techniques that involve many models working together to boost the predictive accuracy of the overall system.

Deploying the model

Once we have chosen the final model to use, we want to finalize its implementation so that the end users can use it reliably. Programmers refer to this process as **deploying to production**. This is where sound software engineering principles become extremely important. The following guidelines offer some useful advice:

- The model should be optimized to improve the speed at which it computes predictions. For example, this means ensuring that any features that are computed at runtime are done so efficiently.

- The model should be well documented. The final input features should be clearly defined, and the method and data used for training should be stored so that it can easily be retrained if changes need to be made. The original performance on the training and test set should also be stored as a reference for subsequent improvements.

- The model's performance should be monitored over time. This is important, not only as a means of verifying that the model works as intended, but also in order to catch any potential data shifts. If the process that is being modeled changes over time, it is likely that our model performance will degrade and this will signal the need for a new model to be trained.

- The software used to implement the model should be properly tested using standard unit and integration tests. Often, we will use a lot of existing R packages whose functions have already undergone testing, but the final deployment of a model may require us to write some additional code ourselves, such as for feature computation.

- The deployed model should be able to handle errors in the input. For example, if some of the input features are missing, it should be made very clear to the user why the model is unable to make a prediction through appropriate error messages. Errors and warnings should also be logged, especially if the model is deployed for continuous predictions in real-time settings.

Performance metrics

In the previous section where we talked about the predictive modeling process, we delved into the importance of assessing a trained model's performance using training and test data sets. In this section, we will look at specific measures of performance that we will frequently encounter when describing the predictive accuracy of different models. It turns out that depending on the class of the problem, we will need to use slightly different ways of assessing performance. As we focus on supervised models in this book, we will look at how to assess regression models and classification models. For classification models, we will also discuss some additional metrics used for the binary classification task, which is a very important and frequently encountered type of problem.

Assessing regression models

In a regression scenario, let's recall that through our model we are building a function $\hat{f}$ that is an estimate of a theoretical underlying target function f. The model's inputs are the values of our chosen input features. If we apply this function to every observation, x_i, in our training data, which is labeled with the true value of the function, y_i, we will obtain a set of $(y_i, \hat{y}_i)$ pairs. To make sure we are clear on this last point, the first entry is the actual value of the output variable in our training data for the ith observation, and the second entry is the predicted value for this particular observation produced by using our model on the feature values for this observation.

If our model has fit the data well, both values will be very close to each other in the training set. If this is also true for our test set, then we consider that our model is likely to perform well for future unseen observations. To quantify the notion that the predicted and correct values are close to each other for all the observations in a data set, we define a measure known as the **Mean Square Error (MSE)**, as follows:

$$MSE = \frac{1}{n}\sum_{i=1}^{n}\left(y_i - \hat{y}_i\right)^2, \ \ \hat{y}_i = \hat{f}\left(x_i\right)$$

Here, n is the total number of observations in the data set. Consequently, this equation tells us to first compute the squared difference between an output value and its predicted value for every observation, i, in the test set, and then take the average of all these values by summing them up and dividing by the number of observations. Thus, it should be clear why this measure is called the mean square error. The lower this number, the lower the average error between the actual value of the output variable in our observations and what we predict and therefore, the more accurate our model. We sometimes make reference to the **Root Mean Square Error (RMSE)**, which is just the square root of the MSE and the **Sum of Squared Error (SSE)**, which is similar to the MSE but without the normalization which results from dividing by the number of training examples, n. These quantities, when computed on the training data set, are valuable in the sense that a low number will indicate that we have trained a model sufficiently well. We know that we aren't expecting this to be zero in general, and we also cannot decide between models on the basis of these quantities because of the problem of overfitting. The key place to compute these measures is on the test data. In a majority of cases, a model's training data MSE (or equally, RMSE or SSE) will be lower than the corresponding measure computed on the test data. A model m_1 that overfits the data compared to another model m_2 can often be identified as such when the m_1 model produces a lower training MSE but higher test MSE than model m_2.

Assessing classification models

In regression models, the degree to which our predicted function incorrectly approximates an output, y_i, for a particular observation, x_i, is taken into account by the MSE. Specifically, large errors are squared and so a very large deviation on one data point can have a more significant impact than a few small deviations across more than one data point. It is precisely because we are dealing with a numerical output in regression that we can measure not only for which observations we aren't doing a good job at predicting, but also how far off we are.

For models that perform classification, we can again define an error rate, but here we can only talk about the number of misclassifications that were made by our model. Specifically, we have an error rate given by:

$$ER = \frac{1}{n} \sum_{1}^{n} I\left(y_i \neq \hat{y}_i\right)$$

This measure uses the indicator function to return the value of 1 when the predicted class is not the same as the labeled class. Thus, the error rate is computed by counting the number of times the class of the output variable is incorrectly predicted, and dividing this count by the number of observations in the data set. In this way, we can see that the error rate is actually the percentage of misclassified observations made by our model. It should be noted that this measure treats all types of misclassifications as equal. If the cost of some misclassifications is higher than others, then this measure can be adjusted by adding in weights that multiply each misclassification by an amount proportional to its cost.

If we want to diagnose the greatest source of error in a regression problem, we tend to look at the points for which we have the largest error between our predicted value and the actual value. When doing classifications, it is often very useful to compute what is known as the **confusion matrix**. This is a matrix that shows all pairwise misclassifications that were made on our data. We shall now return to our iris species classification problem. In a previous section, we trained three kNN models. We'll now see how we can assess their performance. Like many classification models, kNN can return predictions either as final class labels or via a set of scores pertaining to each possible output class. Sometimes, as is the case here, these scores are actually probabilities that the model has assigned to every possible output. Regardless of whether the scores are actual probabilities, we can decide on which output label to pick on the basis of these scores, typically by simply choosing the label with the highest score. In R, the most common function to make model predictions is the predict() function, which we will use with our kNN models:

```
> knn_predictions_prob <- predict(knn_model, iris_test,
  type = "prob")
> tail(knn_predictions_prob, n = 3)
      setosa versicolor virginica
[28,]      0        0.0       1.0
[29,]      0        0.4       0.6
[30,]      0        0.0       1.0
```

In the kNN model, we can assign output scores as direct probabilities by computing the ratio of the nearest neighbors that belong to each output label. In the three test examples shown, the *virginica* species has unit probabilities in two of these, but only 60 percent probability for the remaining example. The other 40 percent belong to the *versicolor* species, so it seems that in the latter case, three out of five nearest neighbors were of the *virginica* species ,whereas the other two were of the *versicolor* species. It is clear that we should be more confident about the two former classifications than the latter. We'll now compute class predictions for the three models on the test data:

```
> knn_predictions <- predict(knn_model, iris_test, type = "class")
> knn_predictions_z <- predict(knn_model_z, iris_test_z,
                               type = "class")
> knn_predictions_pca <- predict(knn_model_pca, iris_test_pca,
                                 type = "class")
```

We can use the `postResample()` function from the `caret` package to display test set accuracy metrics for our models:

```
> postResample(knn_predictions, iris_test_labels)
 Accuracy      Kappa
0.9333333 0.9000000
> postResample(knn_predictions_z, iris_test_labels)
 Accuracy      Kappa
0.9666667 0.9500000
> postResample(knn_predictions_pca, iris_test_labels)
Accuracy      Kappa
    0.90      0.85
```

Here, accuracy is one minus the error rate and is thus the percentage of correctly classified observations. We can see that all the models perform very closely in terms of accuracy, with the model that uses a Z-score normalization prevailing. This difference is not significant given the small size of the test set. The **Kappa statistic** is defined as follows:

$$Kappa = \frac{Observed\ Accuracy - Expected\ Accuracy}{1 - Expected\ Accuracy}$$

The Kappa statistic is designed to counterbalance the effect of random chance and takes values in the interval, [-1,1], where 1 indicates perfect accuracy, -1 indicates perfect inaccuracy, and 0 occurs when the accuracy is exactly what would be obtained by a random guesser. Note that a random guesser for a classification model guesses the most frequent class. In the case of our iris classification model, the three species are equally represented in the data, and so the expected accuracy is one third. The reader is encouraged to check that by using this value for the expected accuracy, we can obtain the observed values of Kappa statistic from the accuracy values.

We can also examine the specific misclassifications that our model makes, using a confusion matrix. This can simply be constructed by cross-tabulating the predictions with the correct output labels:

```
> table(knn_predictions, iris_test_labels)
                iris_test_labels
knn_predictions setosa versicolor virginica
      setosa       10         0         0
      versicolor    0         9         1
      virginica     0         1         9
```

 The caret package also has the very useful confusionMatrix() function, which automatically computes this table as well as several other performance metrics, the explanation of which can be found at http://topepo.github.io/caret/other.html.

In the preceding confusion matrix, we can see that the total number of correctly classified observations is 28, which is the sum of the numbers 10, 9, and 9 on the leading diagonal. The table shows us that the *setosa* species seems to be easier to predict with our model, as it is never confused with other species. The *versicolor* and *virginica* species, however, can be confused with each other and the model has misclassified one instance of each. We can therefore surmise that computing the confusion matrix serves as a useful exercise. Spotting class pairs that are frequently confused will guide us to improve our model, for example by looking for features that might help distinguish these classes.

Assessing binary classification models

A special case of classification known as a **binary classification** occurs when we have two classes. Here are some typical binary classification scenarios:

- We want to classify incoming e-mails as spam or not spam using the e-mail's content and header
- We want to classify a patient as having a disease or not using their symptoms and medical history
- We want to classify a document from a large database of documents as being relevant to a search query, based on the words in the query and the words in the document
- We want to classify a product from an assembly line as faulty or not
- We want to predict whether a customer applying for credit at a bank will default on their payments, based on their credit score and financial situation

In a binary classification task, we usually refer to our two classes as the **positive class** and the **negative class**. By convention, the positive class corresponds to a special case that our model is trying to predict, and is often rarer than the negative class. From the preceding examples, we would use the positive class label for our spam e-mails, faulty assembly line products, defaulting customers, and so on. Now consider an example in the medical diagnosis domain, where we are trying to train a model to diagnose a disease that we know is only present in 1 in 10,000 of the population. We would assign the positive class to patients that have this disease. Notice that in such a scenario, the error rate alone is not an adequate measure of a model. For example, we can design the simplest of classifiers that will have an error rate of only 0.01 percent by predicting that every patient will be healthy, but such a classifier would be useless. We can come up with more useful metrics by examining the confusion matrix. Suppose that we had built a model to diagnose our rare disease and on a test sample of 100,000 patients, we obtained the following confusion matrix:

```
> table(actual,predicted)
         predicted
actual      negative positive
   negative    99900       78
   positive        9       13
```

The binary classification problem is so common that the cells of the binary confusion matrix have their own names. On the leading diagonal, which contains the correctly classified entries, we refer to the elements as the **true negatives** and **true positives**. In our case, we had 99900 true negatives and 13 true positives. When we misclassify an observation as belonging to the positive class when it actually belongs to the negative class, then we have a **false positive**, also known as a **Type I error**. A **false negative** or **Type II error** occurs when we misclassify a positive observation as belonging to the negative class. In our case, our model had 78 false positives and 9 false negatives.

We'll now introduce two very important measures in the context of binary classification, which are **precision** and **recall**. Precision is defined as the ratio of number of correctly predicted instances of the positive class to the total number of predicted instances of the positive class. Using the labels from the preceding binary confusion matrix, precision is given by:

$$Precision = \frac{True\ Positives}{True\ Positives + False\ Positives}$$

Precision, thus, essentially measures how accurate we are in making predictions for the positive class. By definition, we can achieve 100 percent precision by never making any predictions for the positive class, as this way we are guaranteed to never make any mistakes. Recall, by contrast, is defined as the number of correct predictions for the positive class over all the members of the positive class in our data set. Once again, using the labels from the binary confusion matrix, we can see the definition of recall as:

$$Recall = \frac{True\,Positives}{True\,Positives + False\,Negatives}$$

Recall measures our ability to identify all the positive class members from our data set. We can easily achieve maximum recall by always predicting the positive class for all our data points. We will make a lot of mistakes, but we will never have any false negatives. Notice that precision and recall form a tradeoff in our model performance. At one end, if we don't predict the positive class for any of our data points, we will have 0 recall but maximum precision. At the other end, if all our data points are predicted as belonging to the positive class (which, remember, is usually a rare class), we will have maximum recall but extremely low precision. Put differently, trying to reduce the Type I error leads to increasing the Type II error and vice-versa. This inverse relationship is often plotted for a particular problem on a **precision-recall curve**. By using an appropriate threshold parameter, we can often tune the performance of our model in such a way that we achieve a specific point on this precision-recall curve that is appropriate for our circumstances. For example, in some problem domains, we tend to be biased toward having a higher recall than a higher precision, because of the high cost of misclassifying an observation from the positive class into the negative class. As we often want to describe the performance of a model using a single number, we define a measure known as the **F1 score**, which combines precision and recall. Specifically, the F1 score is defined as the harmonic mean between precision and recall:

$$F1 = 2 \cdot \frac{Precision \cdot Recall}{Precision + Recall}$$

The reader should verify that in our example confusion matrix, precision is 14.3 percent, recall is 59.1 percent, and the F1 score is 0.23.

Summary

In this chapter, we explored the fundamental ideas surrounding predictive models. We saw that there are many ways to categorize models, learning important distinctions in the process, such as supervised versus unsupervised learning and regression versus classification. Next, we outlined the steps involved in building a predictive model, starting from the process of data collection all the way to model evaluation and deployment. Critically, this process is an iterative one, and most often we arrive at our final model after having tried out and trained a number of different models. In order to compare the performance of the different models that we create, we established some fundamental notions of model performance, such as the mean squared error for regression and the classification error rate for classification.

We also introduced our first model, the k-nearest neighbor model, which is useful in performing classification and regression alike. kNN is a very flexible model that doesn't make any explicit assumptions about the underlying data. Thus, it can fit a very complex decision boundary. It is a lazy learner, in that it doesn't construct a model to describe the relationship between the input features and the output variable. As a result, it doesn't require a long period of training. On the other hand, for data with many dimensions, it may take a long time to produce a prediction, and because the model needs to remember all the training data in order to find the nearest neighbors of a target point, it often also requires a lot of memory. kNN doesn't distinguish the importance of different features, and the fact that it uses a distance metric in its prediction means that, on the one hand, it does not have any built-in way to handle missing data and on the other, it often requires features to be transformed to similar scales. Finally, the model can be tuned by choosing an appropriate value of k, the number of nearest neighbors, so as to balance the degree of overfitting. With a firm grounding in the basics of the predictive modeling process, we will look at linear regression in the next chapter.

2
Linear Regression

We learned from the previous chapter that regression problems involve predicting a numerical output. The simplest but most common type of regression is linear regression. In this chapter, we'll explore why linear regression is so commonly used, its limitations, and extensions.

Introduction to linear regression

In **linear regression**, the output variable is predicted by a linearly weighted combination of input features. Here is an example of a simple linear model:

$$\hat{y} = \beta_1 x + \beta_0$$

The preceding model essentially says that we are estimating one output, denoted by $\hat{y}$, and this is a linear function of a single predictor variable (that is, a feature) denoted by the letter x. The terms involving the Greek letter β are the parameters of the model and are known as **regression coefficients**. Once we train the model and settle on values for these parameters, we can make a prediction on the output variable for any value of x by a simple substitution in our equation. Another example of a linear model, this time with three features and with values assigned to the regression coefficients, is given by the following equation:

$$\hat{y} = 1.91 x_1 + 2.56 x_2 - 7.56 x_3 + 0.49$$

In this equation, just as with the previous one, we can observe that we have one more coefficient than the number of features. This additional coefficient, β_0, is known as the **intercept** and is the expected value of the model when the value of all input features is zero. The other β coefficients can be interpreted as the expected change in the value of the output per unit increase of a feature. For example, in the preceding equation, if the value of the feature x_1 rises by one unit, the expected value of the output will rise by 1.91 units. Similarly, a unit increase in the feature x_3 results in a decrease of the output by 7.56 units. In a simple one-dimensional regression problem, we can plot the output on the y axis of a graph and the input feature on the x axis. In this case, the model predicts a straight-line relationship between these two, where β_0 represents the point at which the straight line crosses or intercepts the y axis and β_1 represents the slope of the line. We often refer to the case of a single feature (hence, two regression coefficients) as **simple linear regression** and the case of two or more features as **multiple linear regression**.

Assumptions of linear regression

Before we delve into the details of how to train a linear regression model and how it performs, we'll look at the model assumptions. The model assumptions essentially describe what the model believes about the output variable y that we are trying to predict. Specifically, linear regression models assume that the output variable is a weighted linear function of a set of feature variables. Additionally, the model assumes that for fixed values of the feature variables, the output is normally distributed with a constant variance. This is the same as saying that the model assumes that the true output variable y can be represented by an equation such as the following one, shown for two input features:

$$y = \beta_2 x_2 + \beta_1 x_1 + \beta_0 + \varepsilon$$

Here, ε represents an error term, which is normally distributed with zero mean and constant variance σ^2:

$$\varepsilon \sim N\left(0, \sigma^2\right)$$

We might hear the term **homoscedasticity** as a more formal way of describing the notion of constant variance. By homoscedasticity or constant variance, we are referring to the fact that the variance in the error component does not vary with the values or levels of the input features. In the following plot, we are visualizing a hypothetical example of a linear relationship with **heteroskedastic** errors, which are errors that do not have a constant variance. The data points lie close to the line at low values of the input feature, because the variance is low in this region of the plot, but lie farther away from the line at higher values of the input feature because of the higher variance.

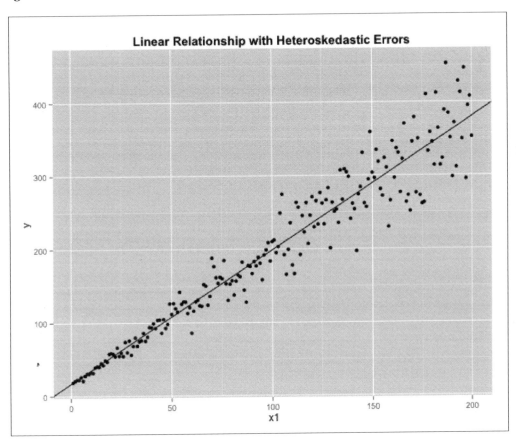

* Heteroskedasticity refers to the circumstance in which the variability of a variable is unequal across the range of values of a second variable that predicts it

The ε term is an irreducible error component of the true function y and can be used to represent random errors, such as measurement errors in the feature values. When training a linear regression model, we always expect to observe some amount of error in our estimate of the output, even if we have all the right features, enough data, and the system being modeled really is linear. Put differently, even with a true function that is linear, we still expect that once we find a line of best fit through our training examples, our line will not go through all, or even any of our data points because of this inherent variance exhibited by the error component. The critical thing to remember, though, is that in this ideal scenario, because our error component has zero mean and constant variance, our training criterion will allow us to come close to the true values of the regression coefficients given a sufficiently large sample, as the errors will cancel out.

Another important assumption relates to the independence of the error terms. This means that we do not expect the **residual** or error term associated with one particular observation to be somehow correlated with that of another observation. This assumption can be violated if observations are functions of each other, which is typically the result of an error in the measurement. If we were to take a portion of our training data, double all the values of the features and outputs, and add these new data points to our training data, we could create the illusion of having a larger data set; however, there will be pairs of observations whose error terms will depend on each other as a result, and hence our model assumption would be violated. Incidentally, artificially growing our data set in such a manner is never acceptable for any model. Similarly, correlated error terms may occur if observations are related in some way by an unmeasured variable. For example, if we are measuring the malfunction rate of parts from an assembly line, then parts from the same factory might have a correlation in the error, for example, due to different standards and protocols used in the assembly process. Therefore, if we don't use the factory as a feature, we may see correlated errors in our sample among observations that correspond to parts from the same factory. The study of **experimental design** is concerned with identifying and reducing correlations in error terms, but this is beyond the scope of this book.

Finally, another important assumption concerns the notion that the features themselves are statistically independent of each other. It is worth clarifying here that in linear models, although the input features must be linearly weighted, they themselves may be the output of another function. To illustrate this, one may be surprised to see that the following is a linear model of three features, $sin(z_1)$, $ln(z_2)$, and $exp(z_3)$:

$$y = 0.8\sin\left(z_1\right) - 0.6\ln\left(z_2\right) + 2.3e^{z_3}$$

We can see that this is a linear model by making a few transformations on the input features and then making the replacements in our model:

$$x_1 = \sin(z_1)$$
$$x_2 = \ln(z_2)$$
$$x_3 = e^{z_3}$$
$$y = 0.8x_1 - 0.6x_2 + 2.3x_3$$

Now, we have an equation that is more recognizable as a linear regression model. If the previous example made us believe that nearly everything could be transformed into a linear model, then the following two examples will emphatically convince us that this is not in fact the case:

$$y_1 = x_1^{\beta_1} + \beta_0$$
$$y_2 = \beta_2 \sin(\beta_1 x_1) + \beta_0$$

Both models are not linear models because of the first regression coefficient (β_1). The first model is not a linear model because β_1 is acting as the exponent of the first input feature. In the second model, β_1 is inside a sine function. The important lesson to take away from these examples is that there are cases where we can apply transformations on our input features in order to fit our data to a linear model; however, we need to be careful that our regression coefficients are always the linear weights of the resulting new features.

Simple linear regression

Before looking at some real-world data sets, it is very helpful to try to train a model on artificially generated data. In an artificial scenario such as this, we know what the true output function is beforehand, something that as a rule is not the case when it comes to real-world data. The advantage of performing this exercise is that it gives us a good idea of how our model works under the ideal scenario when all of our assumptions are fully satisfied, and it helps visualize what happens when we have a good linear fit. We'll begin by simulating a simple linear regression model. The following R snippet is used to create a data frame with 100 simulated observations of the following linear model with a single input feature:

$$y = 1.67x_1 - 2.93 + N(0, 2^2)$$

Here is the code for the simple linear regression model:

```
> set.seed(5427395)
> nObs = 100
> x1minrange = 5
> x1maxrange = 25
> x1 = runif(nObs, x1minrange, x1maxrange)
> e = rnorm(nObs, mean = 0, sd = 2.0)
> y = 1.67 * x1 - 2.93 + e
> df = data.frame(y, x1)
```

For our input feature, we randomly sample points from a uniform distribution. We used a uniform distribution to get a good spread of data points. Note that our final `df` data frame is meant to simulate a data frame that we would obtain in practice, and as a result, we do not include the error terms, as these would be unavailable to us in a real-world setting.

When we train a linear model using some data such as those in our data frame, we are essentially hoping to produce a linear model with the same coefficients as the ones from the underlying model of the data. Put differently, the original coefficients define a **population regression line**. In this case, the population regression line represents the true underlying model of the data. In general, we will find ourselves attempting to model a function that is not necessarily linear. In this case, we can still define the population regression line as the best possible linear regression line, but a linear regression model will obviously not perform equally well.

Estimating the regression coefficients

For our simple linear regression model, the process of training the model amounts to an estimation of our two regression coefficients from our data set. As we can see from our previously constructed data frame, our data is effectively a series of observations, each of which is a pair of values (x_i, y_i) where the first element of the pair is the input feature value and the second element of the pair is its output label. It turns out that for the case of simple linear regression, it is possible to write down two equations that can be used to compute our two regression coefficients. Instead of merely presenting these equations, we'll first take a brief moment to review some very basic statistical quantities that the reader has most likely encountered previously, as they will be featured very shortly.

The **mean** of a set of values is just the average of these values and is often described as a measure of location, giving a sense of where the values are centered on the scale in which they are measured. In statistical literature, the average value of a random variable is often known as the **expectation**, so we often find that the mean of a random variable X is denoted as E(X). Another notation that is commonly used is bar notation, where we can represent the notion of taking the average of a variable by placing a bar over that variable. To illustrate this, the following two equations show the mean of the output variable y and input feature x:

$$\overline{y} = \frac{1}{n}\sum_{i=1}^{n} y_i$$

$$\overline{x} = \frac{1}{n}\sum_{i=1}^{n} x_i$$

A second very common quantity, which should also be familiar, is the **variance** of a variable. The variance measures the average square distance that individual values have from the mean. In this way, it is a measure of dispersion, so that a low variance implies that most of the values are bunched up close to the mean, whereas a higher variance results in values that are spread out. Note that the definition of variance involves the definition of the mean, and for this reason, we'll see the use of the x variable with a bar on it in the following equation that shows the variance of our input feature x:

$$Var(x) = \frac{1}{n}\sum_{i=1}^{n}(x_i - \overline{x})^2$$

Finally, we'll define the **covariance** between two random variables x and y using the following equation:

$$Cov(x, y) = \frac{1}{n}\sum_{i=1}^{n}(x_i - \overline{x})(y_i - \overline{y})$$

From the previous equation, it should be clear that the variance, which we just defined previously, is actually a special case of the covariance where the two variables are the same. The covariance measures how strongly two variables are correlated with each other and can be positive or negative. A positive covariance implies a positive correlation; that is, when one variable increases, the other will increase as well. A negative covariance suggests the opposite; when one variable increases, the other will tend to decrease. When two variables are statistically independent of each other and hence uncorrelated, their covariance will be zero (although it should be noted that a zero covariance does not necessarily imply statistical independence).

Armed with these basic concepts, we can now present equations for the estimates of the two regression coefficients for the case of simple linear regression:

$$\hat{\beta}_1 = \frac{Cov(x,y)}{Var(x)} = \frac{\sum_{i=1}^{n}(x_i - \bar{x})(y_i - \bar{y})}{\sum_{i=1}^{n}(x_i - \bar{x})^2}$$

$$\hat{\beta}_0 = \bar{y} - \hat{\beta}_1 \bar{x}$$

The first regression coefficient can be computed as the ratio of the covariance between the output and the input feature, and the variance of the input feature. Note that if the output feature were to be independent of the input feature, the covariance would be zero and therefore, our linear model would consist of a horizontal line with no slope. In practice, it should be noted that even when two variables are statistically independent, we will still typically see a small degree of covariance due to the random nature of the errors, so if we were to train a linear regression model to describe their relationship, our first regression coefficient would be nonzero in general. Later, we'll see how significance tests can be used to detect features we should not include in our models.

To implement linear regression in R, it is not necessary to perform these calculations as R provides us with the `lm()` function, which builds a linear regression model for us. The following code sample uses the `df` data frame we created previously and calculates the regression coefficients:

```
> myfit <- lm(y~x1, df)
> myfit

Call:
lm(formula = y ~ x1, data = df)

Coefficients:
(Intercept)           x1
     -2.380        1.641
```

N

In the first line, we see that the usage of the `lm()` function involves first specifying a formula and then following up with the `data` parameter, which in our case is our data frame. For the case of simple linear regression, the syntax of the formula that we specify for the `lm()` function is the name of the output variable, followed by a tilde (~) and then by the name of the single input feature. We'll see how to specify more complex formulas when we look at multiple linear regression further along in this chapter. Finally, the output shows us the values for the two regression coefficients. Note that the β_0 coefficient is labeled as the intercept, and the β_1 coefficient is labeled by the name of the corresponding feature (in this case, `x1`) in the equation of the linear model.

The following graph shows the population line and the estimated line on the same plot:

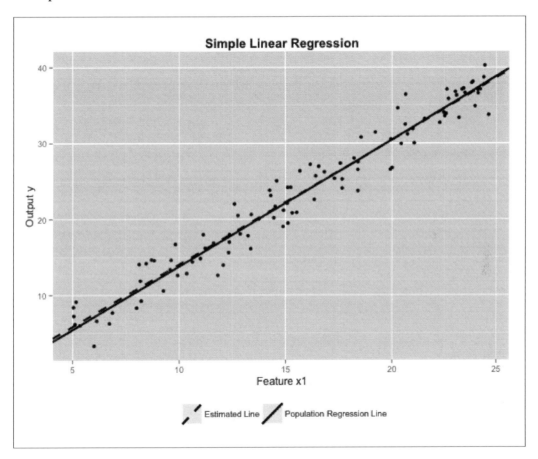

As we can see, the two lines are so close to each other that they are barely distinguishable, showing that the model has estimated the true population line very closely. From *Chapter 1, Gearing Up for Predictive Modeling*, we know that we can formalize how closely our model matches our data set, as well as how closely it would match an analogous test set using the mean square error. We'll examine this as well as several other metrics of model performance and quality in this chapter, but first, we'll generalize our regression model to deal with more than one input feature.

Multiple linear regression

Whenever we have more than one input feature and want to build a linear regression model, we are in the realm of multiple linear regression. The general equation for a multiple linear regression model with k input features is:

$$y = \beta_k x_k + \beta_{k-1} x_{k-1} + \cdots + \beta_1 x_1 + \beta_0 + \varepsilon$$

Our assumptions about the model and about the error component ε remain the same as with simple linear regression, remembering that as we now have more than one input feature, we assume that these are independent of each other. Instead of using simulated data to demonstrate multiple linear regression, we will analyze two real-world data sets.

Predicting CPU performance

Our first real-world data set was presented by the researchers *Dennis F. Kibler*, *David W. Aha*, and *Marc K. Albert* in a 1989 paper titled *Instance-based prediction of real-valued attributes* and published in *Journal of Computational Intelligence*. The data contain the characteristics of different CPU models, such as the cycle time and the amount of cache memory. When deciding between processors, we would like to take all of these things into account, but ideally, we'd like to compare processors on a single numerical scale. For this reason, we often develop programs to benchmark the relative performance of a CPU. Our data set also comes with the published relative performance of our CPUs and our objective will be to use the available CPU characteristics as features to predict this. The data set can be obtained online from the UCI Machine Learning Repository via this link: http://archive.ics.uci.edu/ml/datasets/Computer+Hardware.

> The UCI Machine Learning Repository is a wonderful online resource that hosts a large number of data sets, many of which are often cited by authors of books and tutorials. It is well worth the effort to familiarize yourself with this website and its data sets. A very good way to learn predictive analytics is to practice using the techniques you learn in this book on different data sets, and the UCI repository provides many of these for exactly this purpose.

The `machine.data` file contains all our data in a comma-separated format, with one line per CPU model. We'll import this in R and label all the columns. Note that there are 10 columns in total, but we don't need the first two for our analysis, as these are just the brand and model name of the CPU. Similarly, the final column is a predicted estimate of the relative performance that was produced by the researchers themselves; our actual output variable, PRP, is in column 9. We'll store the data that we need in a data frame called `machine`:

```
> machine <- read.csv("machine.data", header = F)
> names(machine) <- c("VENDOR", "MODEL", "MYCT", "MMIN",
  "MMAX", "CACH", "CHMIN", "CHMAX", "PRP", "ERP")
> machine <- machine[, 3:9]
> head(machine, n = 3)
  MYCT MMIN  MMAX CACH CHMIN CHMAX PRP
1  125  256  6000  256    16   128 198
2   29 8000 32000   32     8    32 269
3   29 8000 32000   32     8    32 220
```

The data set also comes with the definition of the data columns:

Column name	Definition
MYCT	The machine cycle time in nanoseconds
MMIN	The minimum main memory in kilobytes
MMAX	The maximum main memory in kilobytes
CACH	The cache memory in kilobytes
CHMIN	The minimum channels in units
CHMAX	The maximum channels in units
PRP	The published relative performance (our output variable)

The data set contains no missing values, so no observations need to be removed or modified. One thing that we'll notice is that we only have roughly 200 data points, which is generally considered a very small sample. Nonetheless, we will proceed with splitting our data into a training set and a test set, with an 85-15 split, as follows:

```
> library(caret)
> set.seed(4352345)
> machine_sampling_vector <- createDataPartition(machine$PRP,
    p = 0.85, list = FALSE)
> machine_train <- machine[machine_sampling_vector,]
> machine_train_features <- machine[, 1:6]
> machine_train_labels <- machine$PRP[machine_sampling_vector]
> machine_test <- machine[-machine_sampling_vector,]
> machine_test_labels <- machine$PRP[-machine_sampling_vector]
```

Now that we have our data set up and running, we'd usually want to investigate further and check whether some of our assumptions for linear regression are valid. For example, we would like to know whether we have any highly correlated features. To do this, we can construct a correlation matrix with the `cor()` function and use the `findCorrelation()` function from the `caret` package to get suggestions for which features to remove:

```
> machine_correlations <- cor(machine_train_features)
> findCorrelation(machine_correlations)
integer(0)
> findCorrelation(machine_correlations, cutoff = 0.75)
[1] 3
> cor(machine_train$MMIN, machine_train$MMAX)
[1] 0.7679307
```

Using the default cutoff of `0.9` for a high degree of correlation, we found that none of our features should be removed. When we reduce this cutoff to `0.75`, we see that `caret` recommends that we remove the third feature (MMAX). As the final line of preceding code shows, the degree of correlation between this feature and MMIN is `0.768`. While the value is not very high, it is still high enough to cause us a certain degree of concern that this will affect our model. Intuitively, of course, if we look at the definitions of our input features, we will certainly tend to expect that a model with a relatively high value for the minimum main memory will also be likely to have a relatively high value for the maximum main memory. Linear regression can sometimes still give us a good model with correlated variables, but we would expect to get better results if our variables were uncorrelated. For now, we've decided to keep all our features for this data set.

Predicting the price of used cars

Our second data set is in the cars data frame included in the `caret` package and was collected by *Shonda Kuiper* in 2008 from the *Kelly Blue Book* website, www.kbb.com. This is an online resource to obtain reliable prices for used cars. The data set is comprised of 804 GM cars, all with the model year 2005. It includes a number of car attributes, such as the mileage and engine size as well as the suggested selling price. Many features are binary indicator variables, such as the Buick feature, which represents whether a particular car's make was Buick. The cars were all in excellent condition and less than one-year old when priced, so the car condition is not included as a feature. Our objective for this data set is to build a model that will predict the selling price of a car using the values of these attributes. The definitions of the features are as follows:

Column name	Definition
Price	The suggested retail price in USD (our output variable)
Mileage	The number of miles the car has been driven
Cylinder	The number of cylinders in the car's engine
Doors	The number of doors
Cruise	The indicator variable representing whether the car has cruise control
Sound	The indicator variable representing whether the car has upgraded speakers
Leather	The indicator variable representing whether the car has leather seats
Buick	The indicator variable representing whether the make of the car is Buick
Cadillac	The indicator variable representing whether the make of the car is Cadillac
Chevy	The indicator variable representing whether the make of the car is Chevy
Pontiac	The indicator variable representing whether the make of the car is Pontiac
Saab	The indicator variable representing whether the make of the car is Saab
Saturn	The indicator variable representing whether the make of the car is Saturn
convertible	The indicator variable representing whether the type of the car is a convertible
coupe	The indicator variable representing whether the type of the car is a coupe

Column name	Definition
hatchback	The indicator variable representing whether the type of the car is a hatchback
sedan	The indicator variable representing whether the type of the car is a sedan
wagon	The indicator variable representing whether the type of the car is a wagon

As with the machine data set, we should investigate the correlation between input features:

```
> library(caret)
> data(cars)
> cars_cor <- cor(cars_train_features)
> findCorrelation(cars_cor)
integer(0)
> findCorrelation(cars_cor, cutoff = 0.75)
[1] 3
> cor(cars$Doors,cars$coupe)
[1] -0.8254435
> table(cars$coupe,cars$Doors)

      2    4
  0  50  614
  1 140    0
```

Just as with the machine data set, we have a correlation that shows up when we set `cutoff` to `0.75` in the `findCorrelation()` function of `caret`. By directly examining the correlation matrix, we found that there is a relatively high degree of correlation between the `Doors` feature and the `coupe` feature. By cross-tabulating these two, we can see why this is the case. If we know that the type of a car is a coupe, then the number of doors is always two. If the car is not a coupe, then it most likely has four doors.

Another problematic aspect of the cars data is that some features are exact linear combinations of other features. This is discovered using the `findLinearCombos()` function in the caret package:

```
> findLinearCombos(cars)
$linearCombos
$linearCombos[[1]]
[1] 15  4  8  9 10 11 12 13 14

$linearCombos[[2]]
```

```
[1]  18   4   8   9 10 11 12 13 16 17
```

```
$remove
[1]  15 18
```

Here, we are advised to drop the `coupe` and `wagon` columns, which are the 15th and 18th features, respectively, because they are exact linear combinations of other features. We will remove both of these from our data frame, thus also eliminating the correlation problem we saw previously.

Next, we'll split our data into training and test sets:

```
> cars <- cars[,c(-15, -18)]
> set.seed(232455)
> cars_sampling_vector <- createDataPartition(cars$Price, p =
   0.85, list = FALSE)
> cars_train <- cars[cars_sampling_vector,]
> cars_train_features <- cars[,-1]
> cars_train_labels <- cars$Price[cars_sampling_vector]
> cars_test <- cars[-cars_sampling_vector,]
> cars_test_labels <- cars$Price[-cars_sampling_vector]
```

Now that we have our data ready, we'll build some models.

Assessing linear regression models

We'll proceed once again with using the `lm()` function to fit linear regression models to our data. For both of our data sets, we'll want to use all the input features that remain in our respective data frames. R provides us with a shorthand to write formulas that include all the columns of a data frame as features, excluding the one chosen as the output. This is done using a single period, as the following code snippets show:

```
> machine_model1 <- lm(PRP ~ ., data = machine_train)
> cars_model1 <- lm(Price ~ ., data = cars_train)
```

Training a linear regression model may be a one-line affair once we have all our data prepared, but the important work comes straight after, when we study our model in order to determine how well we did. Fortunately, we can instantly obtain some important information about our model using the `summary()` function. The output of this function for our CPU data set is shown here:

```
> summary(machine_model1)

Call:
```

```
lm(formula = PRP ~ ., data = machine_train)

Residuals:
    Min      1Q  Median      3Q     Max
-199.29  -24.15    6.91   26.26  377.47

Coefficients:
              Estimate Std. Error t value Pr(>|t|)
(Intercept) -5.963e+01  8.861e+00  -6.730 2.43e-10 ***
MYCT         5.210e-02  1.885e-02   2.764 0.006335 **
MMIN         1.543e-02  2.025e-03   7.621 1.62e-12 ***
MMAX         5.852e-03  6.867e-04   8.522 7.68e-15 ***
CACH         5.311e-01  1.494e-01   3.555 0.000488 ***
CHMIN        7.761e-02  1.055e+00   0.074 0.941450
CHMAX        1.498e+00  2.304e-01   6.504 8.20e-10 ***
---
Signif. codes:  0 '***' 0.001 '**' 0.01 '*' 0.05 '.' 0.1 ' ' 1

Residual standard error: 61.31 on 172 degrees of freedom
Multiple R-squared:  0.874,   Adjusted R-squared:  0.8696
F-statistic: 198.8 on 6 and 172 DF,  p-value: < 2.2e-16
```

Following a repeat of the call we made to the `lm()` function itself, the information provided by the `summary()` function is organized into three distinct sections. The first section is a summary of the model residuals, which are the errors that our model makes on the observations in the data on which it was trained. The second section is a table containing the predicted values of the model coefficients as well as the results of their significance tests. The final few lines display overall performance metrics for our model. If we repeat the same process on our cars data set, we will notice the following line in our model summary:

```
Coefficients: (1 not defined because of singularities)
```

This occurs because we still have a feature whose effect on the output is indiscernible from other features due to underlying dependencies. This phenomenon is known as **aliasing**. The `alias()` command shows the features we need to remove from the model:

```
> alias(cars_model1)
Model :
Price ~ Mileage + Cylinder + Doors + Cruise + Sound + Leather +
    Buick + Cadillac + Chevy + Pontiac + Saab + Saturn +
    convertible + hatchback + sedan

Complete :
```

```
        (Intercept) Mileage Cylinder Doors Cruise Sound
Saturn  1           0       0        0     0      0
        Leather Buick Cadillac Chevy Pontiac Saab convertible
Saturn  0       -1    -1       -1    -1      -1   0
        hatchback sedan
Saturn  0         0
```

As we can see, the problematic feature is the `Saturn` feature, so we will remove this feature and retrain the model. To exclude a feature from a linear regression model, we include it in the formula after the period and prefix it with a minus sign:

```
> cars_model2 <- lm(Price ~. -Saturn, data = cars_train)
> summary(cars_model2)

Call:
lm(formula = Price ~ . - Saturn, data = cars_train)

Residuals:
    Min      1Q  Median      3Q     Max
-9324.8 -1606.7   150.5  1444.6 13461.0

Coefficients:
              Estimate Std. Error t value Pr(>|t|)
(Intercept)  -954.1919  1071.2553  -0.891  0.37340
Mileage        -0.1877     0.0137 -13.693  < 2e-16 ***
Cylinder     3640.5417   123.5788  29.459  < 2e-16 ***
Doors        1552.4008   284.3939   5.459 6.77e-08 ***
Cruise        330.0989   324.8880   1.016  0.30998
Sound         388.4549   256.3885   1.515  0.13022
Leather       851.3683   274.5213   3.101  0.00201 **
Buick        1104.4670   595.0681   1.856  0.06389 .
Cadillac    13288.4889   673.6959  19.725  < 2e-16 ***
Chevy        -553.1553   468.0745  -1.182  0.23772
Pontiac     -1450.8865   524.9950  -2.764  0.00587 **
Saab        12199.2093   600.4454  20.317  < 2e-16 ***
convertible 11270.4878   597.5162  18.862  < 2e-16 ***
hatchback   -6375.4970   669.6840  -9.520  < 2e-16 ***
sedan       -4441.9152   490.8347  -9.050  < 2e-16 ***
---
Signif. codes:  0 '***' 0.001 '**' 0.01 '*' 0.05 '.' 0.1 ' ' 1

Residual standard error: 2947 on 669 degrees of freedom
Multiple R-squared:  0.912,   Adjusted R-squared:  0.9101
F-statistic: 495.1 on 14 and 669 DF,  p-value: < 2.2e-16
```

Residual analysis

A residual is simply the error our model makes for a particular observation. Put differently, it is the difference between the actual value of the output and our prediction:

$$e_i = y_i - \hat{y}_i$$

Analyzing residuals is very important when building a good regression model, as residuals reveal various aspects of our model, from violated assumptions and the quality of the fit to other problems, such as outliers. To understand the metrics in the residual summary, imagine ordering the residuals from the smallest to the largest. Besides the minimum and maximum values that occur at the extremes of this sequence, the summary shows the first and third quartiles, which are the values one quarter along the way in this sequence and three quarters, respectively. The **median** is the value in the middle of the sequence. The **interquartile range** is the portion of the sequence between the first and third quartiles, and by definition, this contains half of the data. Looking first at the residual summary from our CPU model, it is interesting to note that the first and third quartiles are quite small in value compared to the minimum and maximum value. This is a first indication that there might be a few points that have a large residual error. In an ideal scenario, our residuals will have a median of zero and will have small values for the quartiles. We can reproduce the residuals summary from the summary function by noting that the model produced by the `lm()` function has a `residuals` attribute:

```
> summary(cars_model2$residuals)
    Min. 1st Qu.  Median    Mean 3rd Qu.    Max.
 -9325.0 -1607.0   150.5     0.0  1445.0 13460.0
> mean(cars_train$Price)
[1] 21320.2
```

Note that in the preceding example for our cars model, we need to compare the value of the residuals against the average value of the output variable, in order to get a sense of whether the residuals are large or not. Thus, the previous results show that the average selling price of a car in our training data is around $21k, and 50% of our predictions are roughly within ± $1.6k of the correct value, which seems fairly reasonable. Obviously, the residuals for our CPU model are all much smaller in the absolute value because the values of the output variable for that model, namely the published relative performance, are much smaller than the values for `Price` in the cars model.

In linear regression, we assume that the irreducible errors in our model are randomly distributed with a normal distribution. A diagnostic plot, known as the **Quantile-Quantile plot (Q-Q plot)**, is useful in helping us visually gauge the extent to which this assumption holds. The key idea behind this plot is that we can compare two distributions by comparing the values at their **quantiles**. The quantiles of a distribution are essentially evenly spaced intervals of a random variable, such that each interval has the same probability; for example, quartiles are 4-quantiles because they split up a distribution into four equally probable parts. If the two distributions are the same, then the graph should be a plot of the line $y = x$. To check whether our residuals are normally distributed, we can compare their distribution against a normal distribution and see how close to the $y = x$ line we land.

There are many other ways to check whether the model residuals are normally distributed. A good place to look is the `nortest` R package, which implements a number of well-known tests for normality, including the Anderson-Darling test and the Lilliefors test. In addition, the `stats` package contains the `shapiro.test()` function for performing the Shapiro-Wilk normality test.

The following code generates Q-Q plots for our two data sets:

```
> par(mfrow = c(2, 1))
> machine_residuals <- machine_model1$residuals
> qqnorm(machine_residuals, main = "Normal Q-Q Plot for CPU
  data set")
> qqline(machine_residuals)
> cars_residuals <- cars_model2$residuals
> qqnorm(cars_residuals, main = "Normal Q-Q Plot for Cars
  \data set")
> qqline(cars_residuals)
```

The following diagram displays the Q-Q plots:

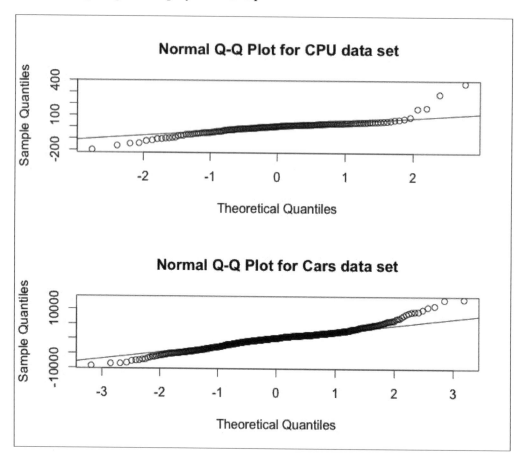

The residuals from both models seem to lie reasonably close to the theoretical quantiles of a normal distribution, although the fit isn't perfect, as is typical with most real-world data. A second very useful diagnostic plot for a linear regression is the so-called **residual plot**. This is a plot of residuals against corresponding fitted values for the observations in the training data. In other words, this is a plot of the pairs ($\hat{y}_i$, e_i). There are two important properties of the residual plot that interest us in particular. Firstly, we would like to confirm our assumption of constant variance by checking whether the residuals are not larger on average for a range of fitted values and smaller in a different range. Secondly, we should verify that there isn't some sort of pattern in the residuals. If a pattern is observed, however, it may be an indication that the underlying model is nonlinear in terms of the features involved or that there are additional features missing from our model that we have not included. In fact, one way of discovering new features that might be useful for our model is to look for new features that are correlated with our model's residuals.

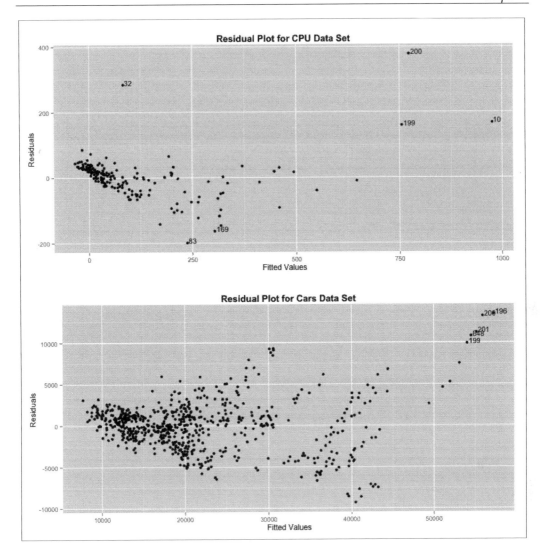

Both plots show a slight pattern of decreasing residuals in the left part of the graph. Slightly more worrying is the fact that the variance of the residuals seems to be a little higher for higher values of both output variables, which could indicate that the errors are not homoscedastic. This is more pronounced in the second plot for the cars data sets. In the preceding two residual plots, we have also labeled some of the larger residuals (in absolute magnitude). We'll see shortly that these are potential candidates for outliers. Another way to obtain a residual plot is to use the plot() function on the model produced by the lm() function itself. This generates four diagnostic plots, including the residual plot and the Q-Q plot.

Significance tests for linear regression

After scrutinizing the residual summaries, the next thing we should focus on is the table of coefficients that our models have produced. Here, every estimated coefficient is accompanied by an additional set of numbers, as well as a number of stars or a dot at the end. At first, this may seem confusing because of the barrage of numbers, but there is a good reason why all this information is included. When we collect measurements on some data and specify a set of features to build a linear regression model, it is often the case that one or more of these features are not actually related to the output we are trying to predict. Of course, this is something we are generally not aware of beforehand when we are collecting the data. Ideally, we would want our model to not only find the best values for the coefficients that correspond to the features that our output does actually depend on, but also tell us which of the features we don't need.

One possible approach for determining whether a particular feature is needed in our model is to train two models instead of one. The second model will have all the features of the first model, excluding the specific feature whose significance we are trying to ascertain. We can then test whether the two models are different by looking at their distributions of residuals. This is actually what R does for all of the features that we have specified in each model. For each coefficient, a **confidence interval** is constructed for the null hypothesis that its corresponding feature is unrelated to the output variable. Specifically, for each coefficient, we consider a linear model with all the other features included, except the feature that corresponds to this coefficient. Then, we test whether adding this particular feature to the model significantly changes the distribution of residual errors, which would be evidence of a linear relationship between this feature and the output and that its coefficient should be nonzero. R's `lm()` function automatically runs these tests for us.

In statistics, a confidence interval combines a point estimate with the precision of that estimate. This is done by specifying an interval in which the true value of the parameter that is being estimated is expected to lie under a certain degree of confidence. A 95 percent confidence interval for a parameter essentially tells us that if we were to collect 100 samples of data from the same experiment and construct a 95 percent confidence interval for the estimated parameter in each sample, the real value of the target parameter would lie within its corresponding confidence interval for 95 of these data samples. Confidence intervals that are constructed for point estimates with high variance, such as when the estimate is being made with very few data points, will tend to define a wider interval for the same degree of confidence than estimates made with low variance.

Let's look at a snapshot of the summary output for the CPU model, which shows the coefficient for the intercept and the MYCT feature in the CPU model:

```
            Estimate Std. Error t value Pr(>|t|)
(Intercept) -5.963e+01  8.861e+00  -6.730 2.43e-10 ***
MYCT         5.210e-02  1.885e-02   2.764 0.006335 **
```

Focusing on the MYCT feature for the moment, the first number in its row is the estimate of its coefficient, and this number is roughly 0.05 (5.210×10^{-2}). The **standard error** is the standard deviation of this estimate, and this is given next as 0.01885. We can gauge our confidence as to whether the value of our coefficient is really zero (indicating no linear relationship for this feature) by counting the number of standard errors between zero and our coefficient estimate. To do this, we can divide our coefficient estimate by our standard error, and this is precisely the definition of the **t-value**, the third value in our row:

```
> (q <- 5.210e-02 / 1.885e-02)
[1] 2.763926
```

So, our MYCT coefficient is almost three standard errors away from zero, which is a fairly good indicator that this coefficient is not likely to be zero. The higher the t-value, the more likely we should be including our feature in our linear model with a nonzero coefficient. We can turn this absolute value into a probability that tells us how likely it is that our coefficient should really be zero. This probability is obtained from Student's t-distribution and is known as the **p-value**. For the MYCT feature, this probability is 0.006335, which is small. We can obtain this value for ourselves using the pt() function:

```
> pt(q, df = 172, lower.tail = F) * 2
[1] 0.006333496
```

The pt() function is the distribution function for the t-distribution, which is symmetric. To understand why our p-value is computed this way, note that we are interested in the probability of the absolute value of the t-value being larger than the value we computed. To obtain this, we first obtain the probability of the upper or right tail of the t-distribution and multiply this by two in order to include the lower tail as well. Working with basic distribution functions is a very important skill in R, and we have included examples in our online tutorial chapter on R if this example seems overly difficult. The t-distribution is parameterized by the degrees of freedom.

> The number of degrees of freedom is essentially the number of variables that we can freely change when calculating a particular statistic, such as a coefficient estimate. In our linear regression context, this amounts to the number of observations in our training data minus the number of parameters in the model (the number of regression coefficients). For our CPU model, this number is $179 - 7 = 172$. For the cars model where we have more data points, this number is 664. The name comes from its relation to the number of independent dimensions or pieces or information that are applied as input to a system, and hence the extent to which the system can be freely configured without violating any constraints on the input.

As a general rule of thumb, we would like our p-values to be less than 0.05, which is the same as saying that we would like to have 95 percent confidence intervals for our coefficient estimates that do not include zero. The number of stars next to each coefficient provides us with a quick visual aid for what the confidence level is, and a single star corresponds to our 95 percent rule of thumb while two stars represent a 99 percent confidence interval. Consequently, every coefficient in our model summary that does not have any stars corresponds to a feature that we are not confident we should include in our model using our rule of thumb. In the CPU model, the CHMIN feature is the only feature that is suspect, with the other p-values being very small. The situation is different with the cars model. Here, we have four features that are suspect as well as the intercept.

It is important to properly understand the interpretation of p-values in the context of our linear regression model. Firstly, we cannot and should not compare p-values against each other in order to gauge which feature is the most important. Secondly, a high p-value does not necessarily indicate that there is no linear relationship between a feature and the output; it only suggests that in the presence of all the other model features, this feature does not provide any new information about the output variable. Finally, we should always remember that the 95 percent rule of thumb is not infallible and is only really useful when the number of features and hence coefficients is not very large. Under 95 percent confidence, if we have 1000 features in our model, we can expect to get the wrong result for 50 coefficients on average. Consequently, linear regression coefficient significance tests aren't as useful for problems in high dimensions.

The final test of significance actually appears at the very bottom of the summary of the `lm()` output and is on the last line. This line provides us with the **F statistic**, which gets its name from the F test that checks whether there is a statistical significance between the variances of two (ideally normal) distributions. The F statistic in this case tries to assess whether the variance of the residuals from a model in which all coefficients are zero is significantly different to the variance of the residuals from our trained model.

Put differently, the F test will tell us whether the trained model explains some of the variance in the output, and hence we know that at least one of the coefficients must be nonzero. While not as useful when we have many coefficients, this tests the significance of coefficients together and doesn't suffer from the same problem as the t-test on the individual coefficients. The summary shows a tiny p-value for this, so we know that at least one of our coefficients is nonzero. We can reproduce the F test that was run using the anova() function, which stands for **analysis of variance**. This test compares the **null model**, which is the model built with just an intercept and none of the features, with our trained model. We'll show this here for the CPU data set:

```
> machine_model_null <- lm(PRP ~ 1, data = machine_train)
> anova(machine_model_null, machine_model1)
Analysis of Variance Table

Model 1: PRP ~ 1
Model 2: PRP ~ MYCT + MMIN + MMAX + CACH + CHMIN + CHMAX
  Res.Df      RSS Df Sum of Sq      F    Pr(>F)
1    178 5130399
2    172  646479  6   4483919 198.83 < 2.2e-16 ***
---
Signif. codes:  0 '***' 0.001 '**' 0.01 '*' 0.05 '.' 0.1 ' ' 1
```

Note that the formula of the null model is PRP ~ 1, where the 1 represents the intercept.

Performance metrics for linear regression

The final details in our summary are concerned with the performance of the model as a whole and the degree to which the linear model fits the data. To understand how we assess a linear regression fit, we should first point out that the training criterion of the linear regression model is to minimize the MSE on the data. In other words, fitting a linear model to a set of data points amounts to finding a line whose slope and position minimizes the sum (or average) of the squared distances from these points. As we refer to the error between a data point and its predicted value on the line as the residual, we can define the **Residual Sum of Squares (RSS)** as the sum of all the squared residuals:

$$RSS = \sum_{i=1}^{n} e_i^2$$

In other words, RSS is just the Sum of Squared Errors (SSE), so we can relate to the MSE with which we are familiar via this simple equation:

$$MSE = \frac{1}{n} \cdot RSS$$

Beyond certain historic reasons, RSS is an important metric to be aware of because it is related to another important metric, known as the RSE, which we will talk about next. For this, we'll need to first build up an intuition about what happens when we train linear regression models. If we run our simple linear regression experiment with artificial data a number of times, each time changing the random seed so that we get a different random sample, we'll see that we will get a number of regression lines that are likely to be very close to the true population line, just as our single run showed us. This illustrates the fact that linear models are characterized by low variance in general. Of course, the unknown function we are trying to approximate may very well be nonlinear and as a result, even the population regression line is not likely to be a good fit to the data for nonlinear functions. This is because the linearity assumption is very strict, and consequently, linear regression is a method with high bias.

We define a metric known as the **Residual Standard Error (RSE)**, which estimates the standard deviation of our model compared to the target function. That is to say, it measures roughly how far away from the population regression line on average our model will be. This is measured in the units of the output variable and is an absolute value. Consequently, it needs to be compared against the values of y in order to gauge whether it is high or not for a particular sample. The general RSE for a model with k input features is computed as follows:

$$RSE = \sqrt{\frac{RSS}{n-k-1}}$$

For simple linear regression, this is just with $k = 1$:

$$RSE = \sqrt{\frac{RSS}{n-2}}$$

We can compute the RSE for our two models using the preceding formula, as follows:

```
> n_machine <- nrow(machine_train)
> k_machine <- length(machine_model1$coefficients) - 1
> sqrt(sum(machine_model1$residuals ^ 2) / (n_machine - k_machine - 1))
[1] 61.30743

> n_cars <- nrow(cars_train)
> k_cars <- length(cars_model2$coefficients) - 1
> sqrt(sum(cars_model2$residuals ^ 2) / (n_cars - k_cars - 1))
[1] 2946.98
```

To interpret the RSE values for our two models, we need to compare them with the mean of our output variables:

```
> mean(machine_train$PRP)
[1] 109.4804
> mean(cars_train$Price)
[1] 21320.2
```

Note that in the car model, the RSE of 61.3 is quite small compared to the RSE of the cars model, which is roughly 2947. When we look at these numbers in terms of how close they are to the means of their respective output variables, however, we learn that actually it is the cars model RSE that shows a better fit.

Now, although the RSE is useful as an absolute value in that one can compare it to the mean of the output variable, we often want a relative value that we can use to compare across different training scenarios. To this end, when evaluating the fit of linear regression models, we often also look at the **R² statistic**. In the summary, this is denoted as multiple R-squared. Before we provide the equation, we'll first present the notion of the **Total Sum of Squares (TSS)**. The total sum of squares is proportional to the total variance in the output variable, and is designed to measure the amount of variability intrinsic to this variable before we perform our regression. The formula for TSS is:

$$TSS(y) = n \cdot Var(y) = \sum_{i=1}^{n}(y_i - \overline{y})^2$$

The idea behind the R^2 statistic is that if a linear regression model is a close fit to the true population model, it should be able to completely capture all the variance in the output. In fact, we often refer to the R^2 statistic as the relative amount that shows us what proportion of the output variance is explained by the regression. When we apply our regression model to obtain an estimate of the output variable, we see that the errors in our observations are called residuals and the RSS is essentially proportional to the variance that is left between our prediction and the true values of the output function. Consequently, we can define the R^2 statistic, which is the amount of variance in our output y that our linear regression model explains, as the difference between our starting variance (TSS) and our ending variance (RSS) relative to our starting variance (TSS). As a formula, this is nothing other than:

$$R^2 = \frac{TSS - RSS}{TSS} = 1 - \frac{RSS}{TSS}$$

From this equation, we can see that R^2 ranges between 0 and 1. A value close to 1 is indicative of a good fit as it means that most of the variance in the output variable has been explained by the regression model. A low value, on the other hand, indicates that there is still significant variance in the errors in the model, indicating that our model is not a good fit. Let's see how the R^2 statistic can be computed manually for our two models:

```
compute_rsquared <- function(x, y) {
    rss <- sum((x - y) ^ 2)
    tss <- sum((y - mean(y)) ^ 2)
    return(1 - (rss / tss))
}

> compute_rsquared(machine_model1$fitted.values, machine_train$PRP)
[1] 0.8739904
> compute_rsquared(cars_model2$fitted.values, cars_train$Price)
[1] 0.9119826
```

We used the `fitted.values` attribute of the model trained by `lm()`, which are the predictions the model makes on the training data. Both values are quite high, with the cars model again indicating a slightly better fit. We've now seen two important metrics to assess a linear regression model, namely RSE and the R^2 statistic. At this point, we might consider whether there is a more general measure of the linear relationship between two variables that we could also apply to our case. From statistics, we might recall that the notion of correlation describes exactly that.

The **correlation** between two random variables, X and Y, is given by:

$$Cor(X,Y) = \frac{Cov(X,Y)}{\sqrt{Var(X)} \cdot \sqrt{Var(Y)}} = \frac{\sum_{i=1}^{n}(x_i - \bar{x})(y_i - \bar{y})}{\sqrt{\sum_{i=1}^{n}(x_i - \bar{x})^2} \sqrt{\sum_{i=1}^{n}(y_i - \bar{y})^2}}$$

It turns out that in the case of simple regression, the square of the correlation between the output variable and the input feature is the same as the R^2 statistic, a result that further bolsters the importance of the latter as a useful metric.

Comparing different regression models

When we want to compare between two different regression models that have been trained on the same set of input features, the R^2 statistic can be very useful. Often, however, we want to compare two models that don't have the same number of input features. For example, during the process of feature selection, we may want to know whether including a particular feature in our model is a good idea. One of the limitations of the R^2 statistic is that it tends to be higher for models with more input parameters.

The **adjusted R^2** attempts to correct the fact that R^2 always tends to be higher for models with more input features and hence is susceptible to overfitting. The adjusted R^2 is generally lower than R^2 itself, as we can verify by checking the values in our model summaries. The formula for the adjusted R^2 is:

$$R^2_{adjusted} = 1 - (1 - R^2) \cdot \frac{n-1}{n-k-1}$$

The definitions of n and k are the same as those for the R^2 statistic. Now, let's implement this function in R and compute the adjusted R^2 for our two models:

```
compute_adjusted_rsquared <- function(x, y, k) {
    n <- length(y)
    r2 <- compute_rsquared(x, y)
    return(1 - ((1 - r2) * (n - 1) / (n - k - 1)))
}

> compute_adjusted_rsquared(machine_model1$fitted.values,
                            machine_train$PRP, k_machine)
[1] 0.8695947
> compute_adjusted_rsquared(cars_model2$fitted.values,
                            cars_train$Price, k_cars)
[1] 0.9101407
```

There are several other commonly used metrics of performance designed to compare models with a different number of features. The **Akaike Information Criterion (AIC)** uses an information theoretic approach to assess the relative quality of a model by balancing the model complexity and accuracy. For our linear regression models trained by minimizing the squared error, this is proportional to another well-known statistic, **Mallow's C$_p$**, so these can be used interchangeably. A third metric is the **Bayesian Information Criterion (BIC)**. This tends to penalize models with more variables more heavily compared to the previous metrics.

Test set performance

So far, we've looked at the performance of our models in terms of the training data. This is important in order to gauge whether a linear model can fit the data well, but doesn't give us a good sense of predictive accuracy over unseen data. For this, we turn to our test data sets. To use our model to make predictions, we can use the predict() function. This is a general function in R that many packages extend. With models trained with lm(), we simply need to provide the model and a data frame with the observations that we want to predict:

```
> machine_model1_predictions <- predict(machine_model1,
                                         machine_test)
> cars_model2_predictions <- predict(cars_model2, cars_test)
```

Next, we'll define our own function for computing the MSE:

```
compute_mse <- function(predictions, actual) {
    mean( (predictions - actual) ^ 2 )
}
> compute_mse(machine_model1$fitted.values, machine_train$PRP)
[1] 3611.616
> compute_mse(machine_model1_predictions, machine_test$PRP)
[1] 2814.048
>
> compute_mse(cars_model2$fitted.values, cars_train$Price)
[1] 8494240
> compute_mse(cars_model2_predictions, cars_test$Price)
[1] 7180150
```

For each model, we've used our `compute_mse()` function to return the training and test MSE. It happens that in this case both test MSE values are smaller than the train MSE values. Whether the test MSE is slightly larger or smaller than the train MSE is not particularly important. The important issue is that the test MSE is not significantly larger than the train MSE as this would indicate that our model is overfitting the data. Note that, especially for the CPU model, the number of observations in the original data set is very small and this has resulted in a test set size that is also very small. Consequently, we should be conservative with our confidence in the accuracy of these estimates for the predictive performance of our models on unseen data, because predictions made using a small test set size will have a higher variance.

Problems with linear regression

In this chapter, we've already seen some examples where trying to build a linear regression model might run into problems. One big class of problems that we've talked about is related to our model assumptions of linearity, feature independence, and the homoscedasticity and normality of errors. In particular we saw methods of diagnosing these problems either via plots, such as the residual plot, or by using functions that identify dependent components. In this section, we'll investigate a few more issues that can arise with linear regression.

Multicollinearity

As part of our preprocessing steps, we were diligent to remove features that were linearly related to each other. In doing this we were looking for an exact linear relationship and this is an example of **perfect collinearity**. **Collinearity** is the property that describes when two features are approximately in a linear relationship. This creates a problem for linear regression as we are trying to assign separate coefficients to variables that are almost linear functions of each other. This can result in a situation where the coefficients of two highly collinear features have high p-values that indicate they are not related to the output variable, but if we remove one of these and retrain a model, the one left in has a low p-value. Another classic indication of collinearity is an unusual sign on one of the coefficients; for example a negative coefficient on educational background for a linear model that predicts income. Collinearity between two features can be detected through pairwise correlation. One way to deal with collinearity is to combine two features into a new one (e.g. by averaging); another is by simply discarding one of the features.

Multicollinearity occurs when the linear relationship involves more than two features. A standard method for detecting this is to calculate the **variance inflation factor (VIF)** for every input feature in a linear model. In a nutshell, the VIF tries to estimate the increase in variance that is observed in the estimate of a particular coefficient that is a direct result of that feature being collinear with other features. This is typically done by fitting a linear regression model in which we treat one of the features as the output feature and the remaining features as regular input features. We then compute the R^2 statistic for this linear model and from this, the VIF for our chosen feature using the formula $1 / (1 - R^2)$. In R, the `car` package contains the `vif()` function, which conveniently calculates the VIF value for every feature in a linear regression model. A rule of thumb here is that the VIF score of 4 or more for a feature is suspect, and a score in excess of 10 indicates strong likelihood of multicollinearity. Since we saw that our cars data had linearly dependent features that we had to remove, let's investigate whether we have multicollinearity in those that remain:

```
> library("car")
> vif(cars_model2)
    Mileage    Cylinder       Doors      Cruise       Sound
   1.010779    2.305737    4.663813    1.527898    1.137607
    Leather       Buick    Cadillac       Chevy     Pontiac
   1.205977    2.464238    3.158473    4.138318    3.201605
       Saab convertible   hatchback       sedan
   3.515018    1.620590    2.481131    4.550556
```

We are seeing three values here that are slightly above 4 but no values above that. As an example, the following code shows how the VIF value for sedan was calculated:

```
> sedan_model <- lm(sedan ~ .-Price -Saturn, data = cars_train)
> sedan_r2 <- compute_rsquared(sedan_model$fitted.values,
  cars_train$sedan)
> 1 / (1-sedan_r2)
[1] 4.550556
```

Outliers

When we looked at the residuals of our two models, we saw that there were certain observations that had a significantly higher residual than others. For example, referring to the residual plot for the CPU model, we can see that the observation 200 has a very high residual. This is an example of an **outlier**, an observation whose predicted value is very far from its actual value. Due to the squaring of residuals, outliers tend to have a significant impact on the RSS, giving us a sense that we don't have a good model fit. Outliers can occur due to measurement errors and detecting them may be important, as they may signify data that is inaccurate or invalid. On the other hand, outliers may simply be the result of not having the right features or building the wrong kind of model.

As we generally won't know whether an outlier is an error or a genuine observation during data collection, handling outliers can be very tricky. Sometimes, especially when we have very few outliers, a common recourse is to remove them, because including them frequently has the effect of changing the predicted model coefficients significantly. We say that outliers are often points with high **influence**.

> Outliers are not the only observations that can have high influence. **High leverage points** are observations that have an extreme value for at least one of their features and thus, lie far away from most of the other observations. **Cook's distance** is a typical metric that combines the notions of outlier and high leverage to identify points that have high influence on the data. For a more thorough exploration of linear regression diagnostics, a wonderful reference is *An R Companion to Applied Regression, John Fox, Sage Publications*.

To illustrate the effect of removing an outlier, we will create a new CPU model by using our training data without observation number 200. Then, we will see whether our model has an improved fit on the training data. Here, we've shown the steps taken and a truncated model summary with only the final three lines:

```
> machine_model2 <- lm(PRP ~ ., data = machine_ train[!(
    rownames(machine_train)) %in% c(200),])
> summary(machine_model2)
...
Residual standard error: 51.37 on 171 degrees of freedom
Multiple R-squared:  0.8884,  Adjusted R-squared:  0.8844
F-statistic: 226.8 on 6 and 171 DF,  p-value: < 2.2e-16
```

As we can see from the reduced RSE and improved R^2, we have a better fit on our training data. Of course, the real measure of model accuracy is the performance on the test data, and there are no guarantees that our decision to label observation 200 as a spurious outlier was the right one.

```
> machine_model2_predictions <- predict(machine_model2,
                                         machine_test)
> compute_mse(machine_model2_predictions, machine_test$PRP)
[1] 2555.355
```

We have a lower test MSE than before, which is usually a good sign that we made the right choice. Again, because we have a small test set, we cannot be certain of this fact despite the positive indication from the MSE.

Feature selection

Our CPU model only came with six features. Often, we encounter real-world data sets that have a very large number of features arising from a diverse array of measurements. Alternatively, we may have to come up with a large number of features when we aren't really sure what features will be important in influencing our output variable. Moreover, we may have categorical variables with many possible levels from which we are forced to create a large number of new indicator variables, as we saw in *Chapter 1, Gearing Up for Predictive Modeling*. When our scenario involves a large number of features, we often find that our output only depends on a subset of these. Given k input features, there are 2^k distinct subsets that we can form, so for even a moderate number of features, the space of subsets is too large for us to fully explore by fitting a model on each subset.

One easy way to understand why there are 2^k possible feature subsets is this: we can assign a unique identifying code to every subset as a string of binary digits of length k, where the digit at a certain position i is 1 if we chose to include the ith feature (features can be ordered arbitrarily) in the subset. For example, if we have three features, the string 101 corresponds to the subset that only includes the first and third features. In this way, we have formed all possible binary strings from a string of k zeros to a string of k ones, thus we have all the numbers from 0 to 2^{k-1} and 2^k total subsets.

Feature selection refers to the process by which a subset of features in a model is chosen in order to form a new model with fewer features. This removes features that we deem unrelated to the output variable and consequently results in a simpler model, which is easier to train as well as interpret. There are a number of methods designed to do this, and they generally do not involve exhaustively searching the space of possible subsets but performing a guided search through this space instead.

One such method is **forward selection**, which is an example of **stepwise regression** that performs feature selection in a series of steps. With forward selection, the idea is to start out with an empty model that has no features selected. We then perform k simple linear regressions (one for every feature that we have) and pick the best one. Here, we are comparing models that have the same number of features so that we can use the R^2 statistic to guide our choice, although we can use metrics such as AIC as well. Once we have chosen our first feature to add, we then pick another feature to add from the remaining $k-1$ features. Therefore, we now run $k-1$ multiple regressions for every possible pair of features, where one of the features in the pair is the feature that we picked in the first step. We continue adding in features like this until we have evaluated the model with all the features included and stop. Note that in every step, we make a hard choice about which feature to include for all future steps. For example, models that have more than one feature in them that do not include the feature we chose in the first step of this process are never considered. Therefore, we do not exhaustively search our space. In fact, if we take into account that we also assess the null model, we can compute the total number of models we perform a linear regression on as follows:

$$1+\left(k+\left(k-1\right)+\cdots+1\right)=1+\sum_{i=1}^{k}i=1+\frac{k\left(k+1\right)}{2}$$

The order of magnitude of this computation is on the scale of k^2, which for even small values of k is already considerably less than 2^k. At the end of the forward selection process, we have to choose between $k+1$ models, corresponding to the subsets we obtained at the end of every step of the process. As the final part of the process involves comparing models with different numbers of features, we usually use a criterion such as the AIC or the adjusted R^2 to make our final choice of model. We can demonstrate this process for our CPU data set by running the following commands:

```
> machine_model3 <- step(machine_model_null, scope =
  list(lower = machine_model_null, upper = machine_model1),
  direction = "forward")
```

The `step()` function implements the process of forward selection. We first provide it with the null model obtained by fitting a linear model with no features on our training data. For the `scope` parameter, we specify that we want our algorithm to step through from the null model all the way to our full model consisting of all six features. The effect of issuing these commands in R is an output that demonstrates which feature subset is specified at every step of the iteration. To conserve space, we present the results in the following table, along with the value of the AIC for each model. Note that the lower the AIC value, the better the model.

Step	Features in subset	AIC value
0	{ }	1839.13
1	{MMAX}	1583.38
2	{MMAX, CACH}	1547.21
3	{MMAX, CACH, MMIN}	1522.06
4	{MMAX, CACH, MMIN, CHMAX}	1484.14
5	{MMAX, CACH, MMIN, CHMAX, MYCT}	1478.36

The `step()` function uses an alternative specification for forward selection, which is to terminate when there is no feature from those remaining that can be added to the current feature subset that would improve our score. For our data set, only one feature was left out from the final model, as adding it did not improve the overall score. It is interesting and somewhat reassuring that this feature was CHMIN, which was the only variable whose relatively high p-value indicated that we weren't confident that our output variable is related to this feature in the presence of the other features.

One might wonder whether we could perform variable selection in the opposite direction by starting off with a full model and removing features one by one based on which feature, when removed, will make the biggest improvement in the model score. This is indeed possible, and the process is known either as **backward selection** or **backward elimination**. This can be done in R with the `step()` function by specifying `backward` as the direction and starting from the full model. We'll show this on our cars data set and save the result into a new cars model:

```
> cars_model_null <- lm(Price ~ 1, data = cars_train)
> cars_model3 <- step(cars_model2, scope = list(
    lower=cars_model_null, upper=cars_model2), direction = "backward")
```

The formula for the final linear regression model on the cars data set is:

```
Call:
lm(formula = Price ~ Mileage + Cylinder + Doors + Leather + Buick
   + Cadillac + Pontiac + Saab + convertible + hatchback + sedan,
     data = cars_train)
```

As we can see, the final model has thrown away the Cruise, Sound, and Chevy features. Looking at our previous model summary, we can see that these three features had high p-values. The previous two approaches are examples of a **greedy algorithm**. This is to say that once a choice about whether to include a variable has been made, it becomes final and cannot be undone later. To remedy this, a third method of variable selection known as **mixed selection** or **bidirectional elimination** starts as forward selection with forward steps of adding variables, but also includes backward steps when these can improve the AIC. Predictably, the step() function does this when the direction is specified as both.

Now that we have two new models, we can see how they perform on the test sets:

```
> machine_model3_predictions <- predict(
  machine_model3, machine_test)
> compute_mse(machine_model3_predictions, machine_test$PRP)
[1] 2805.762
>
> cars_model3_predictions <- predict(cars_model3, cars_test)
> compute_mse(cars_model3_predictions, cars_test$Price)
[1] 7262383
```

For the CPU model, we perform marginally better on the test set than our original model. A suitable next step might be to investigate whether this reduced set of features works better in combination with the removal of our outlier; this is left as an exercise for the reader. In contrast, for the cars model, we see that the test MSE has increased slightly as a result of removing all these features.

Regularization

Variable selection is an important process, as it tries to make models simpler to interpret, easier to train, and free of spurious associations by eliminating variables unrelated to the output. This is one possible approach to dealing with the problem of overfitting. In general, we don't expect a model to completely fit our training data; in fact, the problem of overfitting often means that it may be detrimental to our predictive model's accuracy on unseen data if we fit our training data too well. In this section on **regularization**, we'll study an alternative to reducing the number of variables in order to deal with overfitting. Regularization is essentially a process of introducing an intentional bias or constraint in our training procedure that prevents our coefficients from taking large values. As this is a process that tries to shrink the coefficients, the methods we'll look at are also known as **shrinkage methods**.

Ridge regression

When the number of parameters is very large, particularly compared to the number of available observations, linear regression tends to exhibit very high variance. This is to say that small changes in a few of the observations will cause the coefficients to change substantially. **Ridge regression** is a method that introduces bias through its constraint but is effective at reducing the model's variance. Ridge regression tries to minimize the sum of the residual sum of squares and a term that involves the sum of the squares of the coefficients multiplied by a constant for which we'll use the Greek letter λ. For a model with k parameters, not counting the constant term β_0, and a data set with n observations, ridge regression minimizes the following quantity:

$$RSS + \lambda \sum_{j=1}^{k} \beta_j^2 = \sum_{i=1}^{n} \left(y_i - \hat{y}_i \right)^2 + \lambda \sum_{j=1}^{k} \beta_j^2$$

We are still minimizing the RSS but the second term is the penalty term, which is high when any of the coefficients is high. Thus, when minimizing, we are effectively pushing the coefficients to smaller values. The λ parameter is known as a **meta parameter**, which we need to select or tune. A very large value of λ will mask the RSS term and just push the coefficients to zero. An overly small value of λ will not be as effective against overfitting and a λ parameter of 0 just performs regular linear regression.

When performing ridge regression, we often want to scale by dividing the values of all our features by their variance. This was not the case with regular linear regression because if one feature is scaled by a factor of ten, then the coefficient will simply be scaled by a factor of a tenth to compensate. With ridge regression, the scale of a feature affects the computation of all other features through the penalty term.

Least absolute shrinkage and selection operator (lasso)

The **lasso** is an alternative regularization method to ridge regression. The difference appears only in the penalty term, which involves minimizing the sum of the absolute values of the coefficients.

$$RSS + \lambda \sum_{j=1}^{k} \left| \beta_j \right| = \sum_{i=1}^{n} \left(y_i - \hat{y}_i \right)^2 + \lambda \sum_{j=1}^{k} \left| \beta_j \right|$$

It turns out that this difference in the penalty term is very significant, as the lasso combines both shrinkage and selection because it shrinks some coefficients to exactly zero, which is not the case with ridge regression. Despite this, there is no clear winner between these two. Models that depend on a subset of the input features will tend to perform better with lasso; models that have a large spread in coefficients across many different variables will tend to perform better with ridge regression. It is usually worth trying both.

The penalty in ridge regression is often referred to as an l_2 penalty, whereas the penalty term in lasso is known as an l_1 penalty. This arises from the mathematical notion of a **norm** of a vector. A norm of a vector is a function that assigns a positive number to that vector to represent its length or size. There are many different types of norms. Both the l_1 and l_2 norms are examples of a family of norms known as **p-norms** that have the following general form for a vector v with n components:

$$\sqrt[p]{\sum_{i=1}^{n}|v_i|^{p}}$$

Implementing regularization in R

There are a number of different functions and packages that implement ridge regression, such `lm.ridge()` from the `MASS` package and `ridge()` from the `genridge` package. For the lasso there is also the `lars` package. In this chapter, we are going to work with the `glmnet()` function from the `glmnet` package due to its consistent and friendly interface. The key to working with regularization is to determine an appropriate value of λ to use. The approach that the `glmnet()` function uses is to use a grid of different λ values and train a regression model for each value. Then, one can either pick a value manually or use a technique to estimate the best lambda. We can specify the sequence of λ values to try via the `lambda` parameter; otherwise, a default sequence with 100 values will be used. The first parameter to the `glmnet()` function must be a matrix of features, which we can build using the `model.matrix()` function.

The second parameter is a vector with the output variable. Finally, the `alpha` parameter is a switch between ridge regression (0) and lasso (1). We're now ready to train some models on the cars data set:

```
> library(glmnet)
> cars_train_mat <- model.matrix(Price ~ .-Saturn, cars_train)[,-1]
> lambdas <- 10 ^ seq(8, -4, length = 250)
> cars_models_ridge <-
  glmnet(cars_train_mat, cars_train$Price, alpha = 0, lambda = lambdas)
> cars_models_lasso <-
  glmnet(cars_train_mat, cars_train$Price, alpha = 1, lambda = lambdas)
```

As we provided a sequence of 250 λ values, we've actually trained 250 ridge regression models and another 250 lasso models. We can see the value of λ from the `lambda` attribute of the object that is produced by `glmnet()` and apply the `coef()` function on this object to retrieve the corresponding coefficients for the 100th model, as follows:

```
> cars_models_ridge$lambda[100]
[1] 1694.009
> coef(cars_models_ridge)[,100]
   (Intercept)        Mileage       Cylinder          Doors
  6217.5498831     -0.1574441   2757.9937160    371.2268405
        Cruise          Sound        Leather          Buick
  1694.6023651    100.2323812   1326.7744321   -358.8397493
       Cadillac          Chevy        Pontiac           Saab
 11160.4861489  -2370.3268837  -2256.7482905   8416.9209564
    convertible      hatchback          sedan
 10576.9050477  -3263.4869674  -2058.0627013
```

We can use the `plot()` function to obtain a plot showing how the values of the coefficients change as the logarithm of λ changes. It is very helpful to show the corresponding plot for ridge regression and lasso side by side:

```
> layout(matrix(c(1, 2), 1, 2))
> plot(cars_models_ridge, xvar = "lambda", main = "Ridge
  Regression\n")
> plot(cars_models_lasso, xvar = "lambda", main = "Lasso\n")
```

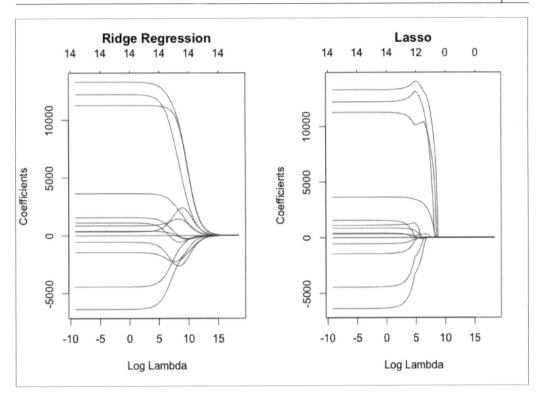

The key difference between these two graphs is that lasso forces many coefficients to fall to zero exactly, whereas in ridge regression, they tend to drop off smoothly and only become zero altogether at extreme values of λ. This is further evident by reading the values of the numbers on the top horizontal axis of both graphs, which show the number of non-zero coefficients as λ varies. In this way, the lasso has a significant advantage in that it can often be used to perform feature selection (because a feature with a zero coefficient is essentially not included in the model) as well as providing regularization to minimize the issue of overfitting. We can obtain other useful plots by changing the value supplied to the `xvar` parameter. The value `norm` plots the l_1 norm of the coefficients on the x-axis and `dev` plots the percentage deviance explained. We will learn about deviance in the next chapter.

To deal with the issue of finding a good value for λ, the `glmnet()` package offers the `cv.glmnet()` function. This uses a technique known as cross-validation (we'll study this in *Chapter 5, Support Vector Machines*) on the training data to find an appropriate λ that minimizes the MSE:

```
> ridge.cv <- cv.glmnet(cars_train_mat, cars_train$Price, alpha = 0)
> lambda_ridge <- ridge.cv$lambda.min
> lambda_ridge
```

```
[1] 641.6408

> lasso.cv <- cv.glmnet(cars_train_mat, cars_train$Price, alpha = 1)
> lambda_lasso <- lasso.cv$lambda.min
> lambda_lasso
[1] 10.45715
```

If we plot the result produced by the `cv.glmnet()` function, we can see how the MSE changes over the different values of lambda:

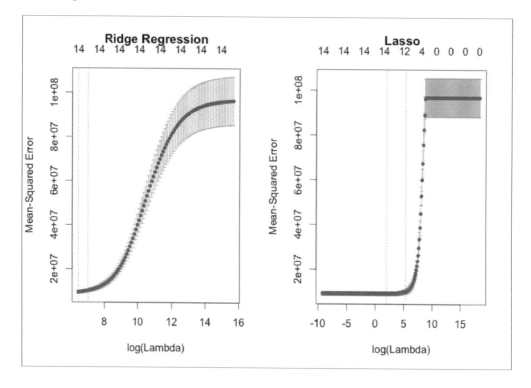

The bars shown above and below each dot are the error bars showing one standard deviation above and below the estimate of the MSE for each plotted value of lambda. The plots also show two vertical dotted lines. The first vertical line shown corresponds to the value of `lambda.min`, which is the optimal value proposed by cross-validation. The second vertical line to the right is the value in the attribute `lambda.1se`. This corresponds to a value that is 1 standard error away from `lambda.min` and produces a more regularized model.

With the `glmnet` package, the `predict()` function now operates in a variety of contexts. We can, for example, obtain the coefficients of a model for a lambda value that was not in our original list. For example, we have this:

```
> predict(cars_models_lasso, type = "coefficients", s = lambda_lasso)
15 x 1 sparse Matrix of class "dgCMatrix"
                            1
(Intercept)   -521.3516739
Mileage         -0.1861493
Cylinder      3619.3006985
Doors         1400.7484461
Cruise         310.9153455
Sound          340.7585158
Leather        830.7770461
Buick         1139.9522370
Cadillac     13377.3244020
Chevy         -501.7213442
Pontiac      -1327.8094954
Saab         12306.0915679
convertible  11160.6987522
hatchback    -6072.0031626
sedan        -4179.9112364
```

Note that it seems that the lasso has not forced any coefficients to zero in this case, indicating that based on the MSE, it is not suggesting to remove any of them for the cars data set. Finally, using the `predict()` function again, we can make predictions with a regularized model using the `newx` parameter to provide a matrix of features for observations on which we want to make predictions:

```
> cars_test_mat <- model.matrix(Price ~ . -Saturn, cars_test)[,-1]
> cars_ridge_predictions <- predict(cars_models_ridge, s =
                              lambda_ridge, newx = cars_test_mat)
> compute_mse(cars_ridge_predictions, cars_test$Price)
[1] 7609538
> cars_lasso_predictions <- predict(cars_models_lasso, s =
                              lambda_lasso, newx = cars_test_mat)
> compute_mse(cars_lasso_predictions, cars_test$Price)
[1] 7173997
```

The lasso model performs best, and unlike ridge regression in this case, also slightly outperforms the regular model on the test data.

Summary

In this chapter, we studied linear regression, a method that allows us to fit a linear model in a supervised learning setting where we have a number of input features and a single numeric output. Simple linear regression is the name given to the scenario where we have only one input feature, and multiple linear regression describes the case where we have multiple input features. Linear regression is very commonly used as a first approach to solving a regression problem. It assumes that the output is a linear weighted combination of the input features in the presence of an irreducible error component that is normally distributed and has zero mean and constant variance. The model also assumes that the features are independent. The performance of linear regression can be assessed by a number of different metrics from the more standard MSE to others, such as the R^2 statistic. We explored several model diagnostics and significance tests designed to detect problems from violated assumptions to outliers. Finally, we also discussed how to perform feature selection with stepwise regression and perform regularization using ridge regression and lasso.

Linear regression is a model with several advantages, which include fast and cheap parameter computation and a model that, by virtue of its simple form, is very easy to interpret and draw inferences from. There is a plethora of tests available to diagnose problems with the model fit and perform hypothesis testing to check the significance of the coefficients. In general, as a method, it is considered to be low variance because it is robust to small errors in the data. On the negative side, because it makes very strict assumptions, notably that the output function must be linear in the model parameters, it introduces a high degree of bias, and for general functions that are complex or highly nonlinear this approach tends to fare poorly. In addition, we saw that we cannot really rely on significance testing for coefficients when we move to a high number of input features. This fact, coupled with the independence assumption between features, renders linear regression a relatively poor choice to make when working in a higher dimensional feature space.

In the next chapter, we will study logistic regression, which is an important method used in classification problems.

3

Logistic Regression

For regression tasks where the goal is to predict a numerical output, such as price or temperature, we've seen that linear regression can potentially be a good starting point. It is simple to train and easy to interpret even though, as a model, it makes strict assumptions about the data and the underlying target function. Before studying more advanced techniques to tackle regression problems, we'll introduce **logistic regression**. Despite its somewhat misleading name, this is actually our first model for performing classification. As we learned in *Chapter 1, Gearing Up for Predictive Modeling*, in classification problems, our output is qualitative and is thus comprised of a finite set of values, which we call classes. We'll begin by thinking about the binary classification scenario, where we are trying to distinguish between two classes, which we'll arbitrarily label as 0 and 1, and later on, we'll extend this to distinguishing between multiple classes.

Classifying with linear regression

Even though we know classification problems involve qualitative outputs, it seems natural to ask whether we could use our existing knowledge of linear regression and apply it to the classification setting. We could do this by training a linear regression model to predict a value in the interval [0,1], remembering that we've chosen to label our two classes as 0 and 1. Then, we could apply a threshold to the output of our model in such a way that if the model outputs a value below 0.5, we would predict class 0; otherwise, we would predict class 1. The following graph demonstrates this concept for a simple linear regression with a single input feature X_1 and for a binary classification problem. Our output variable y is either 0 or 1, so all the data lies on two horizontal lines. The solid line shows the output of the model, and the dashed line shows the decision boundary, which arises when we put a threshold on the model's predicted output at the value 0.5. Points to the left of the dashed line are predicted as belonging to class 0, and points to the right are predicted as belonging to class 1.

The model is clearly not perfect, but it does seem to correctly classify a large proportion of the data.

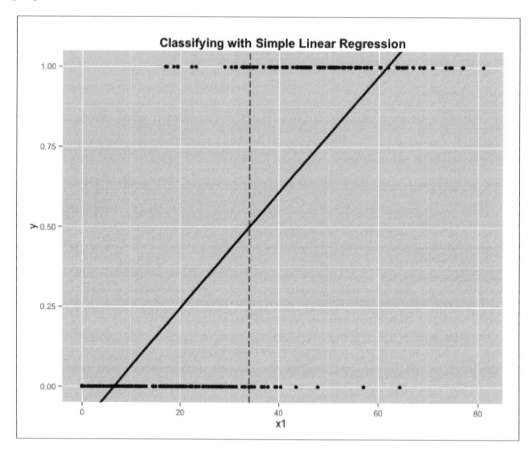

While a good approximation in this case, this approach doesn't feel right for a number of reasons. Firstly, although we know beforehand that our output variable is limited to the interval [0,1] because we have just two classes, the raw output from the linear regression predicts values outside this range. We can see this from the graph for values of input feature X_1 that are either very low or very high. Secondly, linear regression is designed to solve the problem of minimizing the MSE, which does not seem appropriate for us in this case. Our goal is really to find a way to separate the two classes, not to minimize the mean squared error against a line of best fit. As a consequence of this fact, the location of the decision boundary is very sensitive to the presence of high leverage points. As we discussed in *Chapter 2, Linear Regression*, high leverage points are points that lie far away from most of the data because they have extreme values for at least one of their input features.

The following plot demonstrates the effect of high leverage points on our classifier:

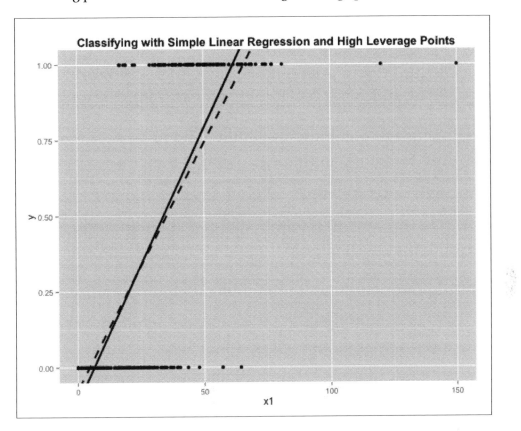

Here, the data is exactly the same as before, except that we have added two new observations for class 1 that have relatively high values for feature X_1 and thus appear far to the right of the graph. Now ideally, because these two newly added observations are well into the area of the graph where we predict class 1, they should not impact our decision boundary so heavily. Due to the fact that we are minimizing the MSE, the old linear regression line (shown as a solid line) has now shifted to the right (shown as a dashed line). Consequently, the point at which our new linear regression line crosses 0.5 on the y axis has moved to the right. Thus, our decision boundary has noticeably moved to the right as a result of adding only two new points.

Logistic regression addresses all of these points by providing an output that is bounded by the interval [0,1] and is trained using an entirely different optimization criterion than linear regression, so we are no longer fitting a function by minimizing the MSE, as we'll now see.

Introduction to logistic regression

In logistic regression, input features are linearly scaled just as with linear regression; however, the result is then fed as an input to the **logistic function**. This function provides a nonlinear transformation on its input and ensures that the range of the output, which is interpreted as the probability of the input belonging to class 1, lies in the interval [0,1]. The form of the logistic function is as follows:

$$f(x) = \frac{e^x}{e^x + 1} = \frac{e^{-x}}{e^{-x}} \cdot \frac{e^x}{(e^x + 1)} = \frac{1}{1 + e^{-x}}$$

Here is a plot of the logistic function:

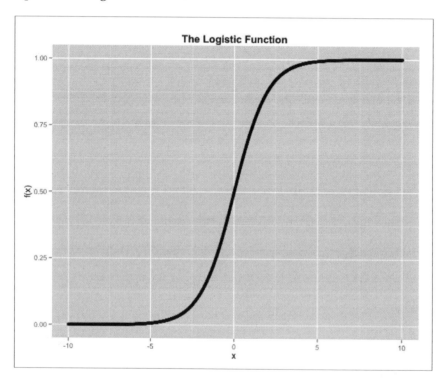

When $x = 0$, the logistic function takes the value 0.5. As x tends to $+\infty$, the exponential in the denominator vanishes and the function approaches the value 1. As x tends to $-\infty$, the exponential, and hence the denominator, tends to move toward infinity and the function approaches the value 0. Thus, our output is guaranteed to be in the interval [0,1], which is necessary for it to be a probability.

Generalized linear models

Logistic regression belongs to a class of models known as **generalized linear models (GLMs)**. Generalized linear models have three unifying characteristics. The first of these is that they all involve a linear combination of the input features, thus explaining part of their name. The second characteristic is that the output is considered to have an underlying probability distribution belonging to the family of exponential distributions. These include the normal distribution, the Poisson and the binomial distribution. Finally, the mean of the output distribution is related to the linear combination of input features by way of a function, known as the **link function**. Let's see how this all ties in with logistic regression, which is just one of many examples of a GLM. We know that we begin with a linear combination of input features, so for example, in the case of one input feature, we can build up an x term as follows:

$$x = \beta_0 + \beta_1 X_1$$

Note that in the case of logistic regression, we are modeling the probability that the output belongs to class 1, rather than modeling the output directly as we were in linear regression. As a result, we do not need to model the error term because our output, which is a probability, directly incorporates the inherent randomness of our model.

Next, we apply the logistic function to this term in order to produce our model's output:

$$P\left(Y = 1 \mid X\right) = \frac{e^{\beta_0 + \beta_1 X_1}}{e^{\beta_0 + \beta_1 X_1} + 1}$$

Here, the left term tells us directly that we are computing the probability that our output belongs to class 1, based on our evidence of seeing the value of the input feature X_1. For logistic regression, the underlying probability distribution of the output is the Bernoulli distribution. This is the same as the binomial distribution with a single trial, and is the distribution we would obtain in an experiment with only two possible outcomes having constant probability, such as a coin flip. The mean of the Bernoulli distribution, μ_y, is the probability of the (arbitrarily chosen) outcome for success, in this case, class 1. Consequently, the left-hand side in the previous equation is also the mean of our underlying output distribution. For this reason, the function that transforms our linear combination of input features is sometimes known as the **mean function**, and we just saw that this function is the logistic function for logistic regression.

Now, to determine the link function for logistic regression, we can perform some simple algebraic manipulations in order to isolate our linear combination of input features.

$$\mu_y = P(Y=1|X) = \frac{e^{\beta_0+\beta_1 X}}{e^{\beta_0+\beta_1 X}+1}$$

$$P(Y=1|X)\cdot\left(e^{\beta_0+\beta_1 X}+1\right) = e^{\beta_0+\beta_1 X}$$

$$P(Y=1|X)\cdot e^{\beta_0+\beta_1 X} + P(Y=1|X) = e^{\beta_0+\beta_1 X}$$

$$P(Y=1|X) = e^{\beta_0+\beta_1 X} - P(Y=1|X)\cdot e^{\beta_0+\beta_1 X}$$

$$\frac{P(Y=1|X)}{1-P(Y=1|X)} = e^{\beta_0+\beta_1 X}$$

$$ln\left(\frac{P(Y=1|X)}{1-P(Y=1|X)}\right) = \beta_0+\beta_1 X$$

The term on the left-hand side is known as the **log-odds** or **logit function** and is the link function for logistic regression. The denominator of the fraction inside the logarithm is the probability of the output being class 0 given the data. Consequently, this fraction represents the ratio of probability between class 1 and class 0, which is also known as the **odds ratio**.

[A good reference for logistic regression along with examples of other GLMs such as Poisson regression is *Extending the Linear Model with R, Julian J. Faraway, CRC Press.*]

Interpreting coefficients in logistic regression

Looking at the right-hand side of the last equation, we can see that we have almost exactly the same form that we had for simple linear regression, barring the error term. The fact that we have the logit function on the left-hand side, however, means we cannot interpret our regression coefficients in the same way that we did with linear regression. In logistic regression, a unit increase in feature X_i results in multiplying the odds ratio by an amount, e^{β_i}. When a coefficient β_i is positive, then we multiply the odds ratio by a number greater than 1, so we know that increasing the feature X_i will effectively increase the probability of the output being labeled as class 1.

Similarly, increasing a feature with a negative coefficient shifts the balance toward predicting class 0. Finally, note that when we change the value of an input feature, the effect is a multiplication on the odds ratio and not on the model output itself, which we saw is the probability of predicting class 1. In absolute terms, the change in the output of our model as a result of a change in the input is not constant throughout, but depends on the current value of our input features. This is, again, different from linear regression, where no matter what the values of the input features, the regression coefficients always represent a fixed increase in the output per unit increase of an input feature.

Assumptions of logistic regression

Logistic regression makes fewer assumptions about the input than linear regression. In particular, the nonlinear transformation of the logistic function means that we can model more complex input-output relationships. We still have a linearity assumption, but in this case, it is between the features and the log-odds. We no longer require a normality assumption for residuals and nor do we need the homoscedastic assumption. On the other hand, our error terms still need to be independent. Strictly speaking, the features themselves no longer need to be independent but in practice, our model will still face issues if the features exhibit a high degree of multicollinearity. Finally, we'll note that just as with unregularized linear regression, feature scaling does not affect the logistic regression model. This means that centering and scaling a particular input feature will simply result in an adjusted coefficient in the output model, without any repercussions on the model performance. It turns out that for logistic regression, this is the result of a property known as the **invariance property of maximum likelihood**. Maximum likelihood is the method used to select the coefficients and will be the focus of the next section. It should be noted, however, that centering and scaling features might still be a good idea if they are on very different scales. This is done to assist the optimization procedure during training. In short, we should turn to feature scaling only if we run into model convergence issues.

Maximum likelihood estimation

When we studied linear regression, we found our coefficients by minimizing the sum of squared error terms. For logistic regression, we do this by maximizing the **likelihood** of the data. The likelihood of an observation is the probability of seeing that observation under a particular model.

In our case, the likelihood of seeing an observation X for class 1 is simply given by the probability $P(Y=1 \mid X)$, the form of which was given earlier in this chapter. As we only have two classes, the likelihood of seeing an observation for class 0 is given by $1 - P(Y=1 \mid X)$. The overall likelihood of seeing our entire data set of observations is the product of all the individual likelihoods for each data point as we consider our observations to be independently obtained. As the likelihood of each observation is parameterized by the regression coefficients β_i, the likelihood function for our entire data set is also, therefore, parameterized by these coefficients. We can express our likelihood function as an equation, as shown in the following equation:

$$l\left(\beta_0, \beta_1 \cdots \beta_p\right) = \prod_{i:y_i=1} P\left(y_i = 1 \mid x_i\right) \cdot \prod_{j:y_j=0} 1 - P\left(y_j = 1 \mid x_j\right)$$

Now, this equation simply computes the probability that a logistic regression model with a particular set of regression coefficients could have generated our training data. The idea is to choose our regression coefficients so that this likelihood function is maximized. We can see that the form of the likelihood function is a product of two large products from the two big π symbols. The first product contains the likelihood of all our observations for class 1, and the second product contains the likelihood of all our observations for class 0. We often refer to the **log likelihood** of the data, which is computed by taking the logarithm of the likelihood function. Using the fact that the logarithm of a product of terms is the sum of the logarithm of each term we can write:

$$ll\left(\beta_0, \beta_1 \cdots \beta_p\right) = \sum_{i:y_i=1} log\left(P\left(y_i = 1 \mid x_j\right)\right) + \sum_{i:y_i=0} log\left(1 - P\left(y_j = 1 \mid x_j\right)\right)$$

We can simplify this even further using a classic trick to form just a single sum:

$$ll\left(\beta_0, \beta_1 \cdots \beta_p\right) = \sum_i y_i \cdot log\left(P\left(y_i = 1 \mid x_j\right)\right) + \left(1 - y_i\right) \cdot log\left(1 - P\left(y_i = 1 \mid x_j\right)\right)$$

To see why this is true, note that for the observations where the actual value of the output variable y is 1, the right term inside the summation is zero, so we are effectively left with the first sum from the previous equation. Similarly, when the actual value of y is 0, then we are left with the second summation from the previous equation. Understanding the form of the log likelihood is important, and we'll get some practice with this when we start working with R to train a logistic regression model in the next section. Note that maximizing the likelihood is equivalent to maximizing the log likelihood; both approaches will yield the same parameters.

Maximum likelihood estimation is a fundamental technique of parameter fitting, and we will encounter it in other models in this book. Despite its popularity, it should be noted that maximum likelihood is not a panacea. Alternative training criteria on which to build a model do exist, and there are some well-known scenarios under which this approach does not lead to a good model, as we shall see in subsequent chapters. Finally, note that the details of the actual optimization procedure, which finds the values of the regression coefficients for maximum likelihood are beyond the scope of this book and in general, we can rely on R to implement this for us.

Predicting heart disease

We'll put logistic regression for the binary classification task to the test with a real-world data set from the UCI Machine Learning Repository. This time, we will be working with the *Statlog (Heart) data set*, which we will refer to as the *heart data set* henceforth for brevity. The data set can be downloaded from the UCI Machine Repository's website at http://archive.ics.uci.edu/ml/datasets/ Statlog+%28Heart%29. The data contain 270 observations for patients with potential heart problems. Of these, 120 patients were shown to have heart problems, so the split between the two classes is fairly even. The task is to predict whether a patient has a heart disease based on their profile and a series of medical tests. First, we'll load the data into a data frame and rename the columns according to the website:

```
> heart <- read.table("heart.dat", quote = "\"")
> names(heart) <- c("AGE", "SEX", "CHESTPAIN", "RESTBP", "CHOL",
  "SUGAR", "ECG", "MAXHR", "ANGINA", "DEP", "EXERCISE", "FLUOR",
  "THAL", "OUTPUT")
```

The following table contains the definitions of our input features and the output:

Column name	Type	Definition
AGE	Numerical	Age (years)
SEX	Binary	Gender
CHESTPAIN	Categorical	4-valued chest pain type
RESTBP	Numerical	Resting blood pressure (beats per minute)
CHOL	Numerical	Serum cholesterol (mg/dl)
SUGAR	Binary	Is the fasting blood sugar level > 120 mg/dl?
ECG	Categorical	3-valued resting electrocardiographic results
MAXHR	Numerical	Maximum heart rate achieved (beats per minute)
ANGINA	Binary	Was angina induced by exercise?

Column name	Type	Definition
DEP	Numerical	ST depression induced by exercise relative to rest
EXERCISE	Ordered categorical	Slope of the peak exercise ST segment
FLUOR	Numerical	The number of major vessels colored by fluoroscopy
THAL	Categorical	3-valued Thal
OUTPUT	Binary	Presence or absence of a heart disease

Before we train a logistic regression model for these data, there are a couple of preprocessing steps that we should perform. A common pitfall when working with numerical data is the failure to notice when a feature is actually a categorical variable and not a numerical variable when the levels are coded as numbers. In the heart data set, we have four such features. The CHESTPAIN, THAL, and ECG features are all categorical features. The EXERCISE variable, although an ordered categorical variable, is nonetheless a categorical variable, so it will have to be coded as a factor as well:

```
> heart$CHESTPAIN = factor(heart$CHESTPAIN)
> heart$ECG = factor(heart$ECG)
> heart$THAL = factor(heart$THAL)
> heart$EXERCISE = factor(heart$EXERCISE)
```

In *Chapter 1, Gearing Up for Predictive Modeling*, we saw how we can transform categorical features with many levels into a series of binary valued indicator variables. By doing this, we can use them in a model such as linear or logistic regression, which requires all the inputs to be numerical. As long as the relevant categorical variables in a data frame have been coded as factors, R will automatically apply a coding scheme when performing logistic regression. Concretely, R will treat one of the *k* factor levels as a reference level and create *k-1* binary features from the other factor levels. We'll see visual evidence of this when we study the summary output of the logistic regression model that we'll train.

Next, we should observe that the OUTPUT variable is coded so that class 1 corresponds to the absence of heart disease and class 2 corresponds to the presence of heart disease. As a final change, we'll want to recode the OUTPUT variable so that we will have the familiar class labels of 0 and 1, respectively. This is done by simply subtracting 1:

```
> heart$OUTPUT = heart$OUTPUT - 1
```

Our data frame is now ready. Before we train our model, however, we will split our data frame into two parts, for training and testing, exactly as we did for linear regression. Once again, we'll use an 85-15 split:

```
> library(caret)
> set.seed(987954)
> heart_sampling_vector <-
  createDataPartition(heart$OUTPUT, p = 0.85, list = FALSE)
> heart_train <- heart[heart_sampling_vector,]
> heart_train_labels <- heart$OUTPUT[heart_sampling_vector]
> heart_test <- heart[-heart_sampling_vector,]
> heart_test_labels <- heart$OUTPUT[-heart_sampling_vector]
```

We now have 230 observations in our training set and 40 observations in our test set. To train a logistic regression model in R, we use the `glm()` function, which stands for generalized linear model. This function can be used to train various generalized linear models, but we'll focus on the syntax and usage for logistic regression here. The call is as follows:

```
> heart_model <-
  glm(OUTPUT ~ ., data = heart_train, family = binomial("logit"))
```

Note that the format is very similar to what we saw with linear regression. The first parameter is the model formula, which identifies the output variable and which features we want to use (in this case, all of them). The second parameter is the data frame and the final `family` parameter is used to specify that we want to perform logistic regression. We can use the `summary()` function to find out more about the model we just trained, as follows:

```
> summary(heart_model)

Call:
glm(formula = OUTPUT ~ ., family = binomial("logit"), data =
  heart_train)

Deviance Residuals:
    Min       1Q    Median       3Q      Max
-2.7137  -0.4421  -0.1382   0.3588   2.8118

Coefficients:
            Estimate Std. Error z value Pr(>|z|)
(Intercept) -7.946051   3.477686  -2.285 0.022321 *
AGE         -0.020538   0.029580  -0.694 0.487482
SEX          1.641327   0.656291   2.501 0.012387 *
```

```
CHESTPAIN2    1.308530    1.000913    1.307 0.191098
CHESTPAIN3    0.560233    0.865114    0.648 0.517255
CHESTPAIN4    2.356442    0.820521    2.872 0.004080 **
RESTBP        0.026588    0.013357    1.991 0.046529 *
CHOL          0.008105    0.004790    1.692 0.090593 .
SUGAR        -1.263606    0.732414   -1.725 0.084480 .
ECG1          1.352751    3.287293    0.412 0.680699
ECG2          0.563430    0.461872    1.220 0.222509
MAXHR        -0.013585    0.012873   -1.055 0.291283
ANGINA        0.999906    0.525996    1.901 0.057305 .
DEP           0.196349    0.282891    0.694 0.487632
EXERCISE2     0.743530    0.560700    1.326 0.184815
EXERCISE3     0.946718    1.165567    0.812 0.416655
FLUOR         1.310240    0.308348    4.249 2.15e-05 ***
THAL6         0.304117    0.995464    0.306 0.759983
THAL7         1.717886    0.510986    3.362 0.000774 ***
---
Signif. codes:  0 '***' 0.001 '**' 0.01 '*' 0.05 '.' 0.1 ' ' 1

(Dispersion parameter for binomial family taken to be 1)

    Null deviance: 315.90  on 229  degrees of freedom
Residual deviance: 140.36  on 211  degrees of freedom
AIC: 178.36

Number of Fisher Scoring iterations: 6
```

Assessing logistic regression models

The summary of the logistic regression model produced with the `glm()` function has a similar format to that of the linear regression model produced with the `lm()` function. This shows us that for our categorical variables, we have one fewer binary feature than the number of levels in the original variable, so for example, the three-valued THAL input feature produced two binary variables labeled THAL6 and THAL7. We'll begin by looking first at the regression coefficients that are predicted with our model. These are presented with their corresponding **z-statistic**. This is analogous to the t-statistic that we saw in linear regression, and again, the higher the absolute value of the z-statistic, the more likely it is that this particular feature is significantly related to our output variable. The p-values next to the z-statistic express this notion as a probability and are annotated with stars and dots, as they were in linear regression, indicating the smallest confidence interval that includes the corresponding p-value.

Due to the fact that logistic regression models are trained with the maximum likelihood criterion, we use the standard normal distribution to perform significance tests on our coefficients. For example, to reproduce the p-value for the THAL7 feature that corresponds to the listed z-value of 3.362, we can write the following (set the lower.tail parameter to T when testing negative coefficients):

```
> pnorm(3.362 , lower.tail = F) * 2
[1] 0.0007738012
```

 An excellent reference for learning about the essential concepts of distributions in statistics is *All of Statistics, Larry Wasserman, Springer.*

From the model summary, we see that FLUOR, CHESTPAIN4, and THAL7 are the strongest feature predictors for heart diseases. A number of input features have relatively high p-values. This indicates that they are probably not good indicators of heart disease in the presence of the other features. We'll stress once again the importance of interpreting this table correctly. The table does not say that heart age, for example, is not a good indicator for heart disease; rather, it says that in the presence of the other input features, age does not really add much to the model. Furthermore, note that we almost definitely have some degree of collinearity in our features as the regression coefficient of age is negative, whereas we would expect that the likelihood of heart disease increases with age. Of course, this assumption is valid only in the absence of all other input features. Indeed, if we retrain a logistic regression model with only the AGE variable, we get a positive regression coefficient as well as a low p-value, both of which support our belief that the features are collinear:

```
> heart_model2 <- glm(OUTPUT ~ AGE, data = heart_train, family =
  binomial("logit"))
> summary(heart_model2)

Call:
glm(formula = OUTPUT ~ AGE, family = binomial("logit"),
  data = heart_train)

Deviance Residuals:
    Min      1Q   Median      3Q      Max
-1.5027  -1.0691  -0.8435   1.2061   1.6759

Coefficients:
            Estimate Std. Error z value Pr(>|z|)
```

```
(Intercept)  -2.71136    0.86348  -3.140   0.00169 **
AGE           0.04539    0.01552   2.925   0.00344 **
---
Signif. codes:  0 '***' 0.001 '**' 0.01 '*' 0.05 '.' 0.1 ' ' 1

(Dispersion parameter for binomial family taken to be 1)

    Null deviance: 315.90  on 229  degrees of freedom
Residual deviance: 306.89  on 228  degrees of freedom
AIC: 310.89

Number of Fisher Scoring iterations: 4
```

Note that the AIC value of this simpler model is higher than what we obtained with the full model, so we would expect this simple model to be worse.

Model deviance

To understand the remainder of the model summary, we need to introduce an important concept known as **deviance**. In linear regression, our residuals were defined simply as the difference between the predicted value and the actual value of the output that we are trying to predict. Logistic regression is trained using maximum likelihood, so it is natural to expect that an analogous concept to the residual would involve the likelihood. There are several closely-related definitions of the concept of deviance. Here, we will use the definitions that the glm() function uses in order to explain the model's output. The deviance of an observation can be computed as the -2 times the log likelihood of that observation. The deviance of a data set is just the sum of all the observation deviances. The **deviance residual** of an observation is derived from the deviance itself and is analogous to the residual of a linear regression. It can be computed as follows:

$$dr_i = d_i \cdot sign\left(\hat{y}_i - P\left(y_i = 1 \mid x_i\right)\right)$$

For an observation i, dr_i represents the deviance residual and d_i represents the deviance. Note that squaring a deviance residual effectively eliminates the sign function and produces just the deviance of the observation. Consequently, the sum of squared deviance residuals is the deviance of the data set, which is just the log likelihood of the data set scaled by the constant -2. Consequently, maximizing the log likelihood of the data is the same as minimizing the sum of the squared deviance residuals, so our analogy with linear regression is complete.

In order to reproduce the results that are shown in the model summary, and to understand how deviance is computed, we'll write some of our own functions in R. We'll begin by computing the log likelihood for our data set using the equation for the log likelihood that we saw earlier on in this chapter. From the equation, we'll create two functions. The `log_likelihoods()` function computes a vector of log likelihoods for all the observations in a data set, given the probabilities that the model predicts and the actual target labels, and `dataset_log_likelihood()` sums these up to produce the log likelihood of a data set:

```
log_likelihoods <- function(y_labels, y_probs) {
    y_a <- as.numeric(y_labels)
    y_p <- as.numeric(y_probs)
    y_a * log(y_p) + (1 - y_a) * log(1 - y_p)
}

dataset_log_likelihood <- function(y_labels, y_probs) {
    sum(log_likelihoods(y_labels, y_probs))
}
```

Next, we can use the definition of deviance to compute two analogous functions, `deviances()` and `dataset_deviance()`. The first of these computes a vector of observation deviances, and the second sums these up for the whole data set:

```
deviances <- function(y_labels, y_probs) {
    -2 * log_likelihoods(y_labels, y_probs)
}

dataset_deviance <- function(y_labels, y_probs) {
    sum(deviances(y_labels, y_probs))
}
```

Given these functions, we can now create a function that will compute the deviance of a model. To do this, we need to use the `predict()` function in order to compute the model's probability predictions for the observations in the training data. This works just as with linear regression, except that by default, it returns probabilities on the logit scale. To ensure that we get actual probabilities, we need to specify the value of `response` for the `type` parameter:

```
model_deviance <- function(model, data, output_column) {
    y_labels = data[[output_column]]
    y_probs = predict(model, newdata = data, type = "response")
    dataset_deviance(y_labels, y_probs)
}
```

To check whether our function is working, let's compute the model deviance, also known as the residual deviance, for our heart model:

```
> model_deviance(heart_model, data = heart_train, output_column =
            "OUTPUT")
[1] 140.3561
```

Reassuringly, this is the same value as that listed in our model summary. One way to evaluate a logistic regression model is to compute the difference between the model deviance and the deviance of the null model, which is the model trained without any features. The deviance of the null model is known as **null deviance**. The null model predicts class 1 via a constant probability, as it has no features. This probability is estimated via the proportion of the observations of class 1 in the training data, which we can obtain by simply averaging the OUTPUT column:

```
null_deviance <- function(data, output_column) {
    y_labels <- data[[output_column]]
    y_probs <- mean(data[[output_column]])
    dataset_deviance(y_labels, y_probs)
}
```

```
> null_deviance(data = heart_training, output_column = "OUTPUT")
[1] 314.3811
```

Once again, we see that we have reproduced the value that R computes for us in the model summary. The residual deviance and null deviance are analogous to the Residual Sum of Squares (RSS) and the True Sum of Squares (TSS) that we saw in linear regression. If the difference between these two is high, the interpretation is similar to the notion of the residual sum of squares in linear regression *explaining away* the variance observed by the output variable. Continuing with this analogy, we can define a **pseudo R^2** value for our model using the same equation that we used to compute the R^2 for linear regression but substituting in the deviances. We implement this in R as follows:

```
model_pseudo_r_squared <- function(model, data, output_column) {
    1 - ( model_deviance(model, data, output_column) /
        null_deviance(data, output_column) )
}
```

```
> model_pseudo_r_squared(heart_model, data = heart_train,
                    output_column = "OUTPUT")
[1] 0.5556977
```

Our logistic regression model is said to explain roughly 56 percent of the null deviance. This is not particularly high; most likely, we don't have a rich enough feature set to make accurate predictions with a logistic model. Unlike linear regression, it is possible for the pseudo R^2 to exceed 1, but this only happens under problematic circumstances where the residual deviance exceeds the null deviance. If this happens, we should not trust the model and proceed with feature selection methods, or try out alternative models.

Besides the pseudo R^2, we may also want a statistical test to check whether the difference between the null deviance and the residual deviance is significant. The absence of a p-value next to the residual deviance in the model summary indicates that R has not created any test. It turns out that the difference between the residual and null deviances is approximately and asymptotically distributed with a χ_2 (pronounced *CHI squared*) distribution. We'll define a function to compute a p-value for this difference but state that this is only an approximation.

First, we need the difference between the null deviance and the residual deviance. We also need the degrees of freedom for this difference, which are computed simply by subtracting the number of degrees of freedom of our model from those of the null model. The null model only has an intercept, so the number of degrees of freedom is the total number of observations in our data set minus 1. For the residual deviance, we are computing a number of regression coefficients, including the intercept, so we need to subtract this number from the total number of observations. Finally, we use the `pchisq()` function to obtain a p-value, noting that we are creating an upper tail computation and hence need to set the `lower.tail` parameter to FALSE. The code is as follows:

```
model_chi_squared_p_value <-  function(model,
  data, output_column) {
    null_df <- nrow(data) - 1
    model_df <- nrow(data) - length(model$coefficients)
    difference_df <- null_df - model_df
    null_deviance <- null_deviance(data, output_column)
    m_deviance <- model_deviance(model, data, output_column)
    difference_deviance <- null_deviance - m_deviance
    pchisq(difference_deviance, difference_df,lower.tail = F)
}

> model_chi_squared_p_value(heart_model, data = heart_train,
                            output_column = "OUTPUT")
[1] 7.294219e-28
```

The p-value that we obtain is tiny, so we feel certain that our model produces predictions that are better than average guessing. In our original model summary we also saw a summary of the deviance residuals. Using the definition of deviance residual that we gave earlier, we'll define a function to compute the vector of deviance residuals:

```
model_deviance_residuals <- function(model, data, output_column) {
    y_labels = data[[output_column]]
    y_probs = predict(model, newdata = data, type = "response")
    residual_sign = sign(y_labels - y_probs)
    residuals = sqrt(deviances(y_labels, y_probs))
    residual_sign * residuals
}
```

Finally, we can use the `summary()` function on the deviance residuals that we obtain with our `model_deviance_residuals()` function to obtain a table:

```
> summary(model_deviance_residuals(heart_model, data =
        heart_train, output_column = "OUTPUT"))
    Min.   1st Qu.   Median     Mean   3rd Qu.     Max.
-2.71400  -0.44210  -0.13820  -0.02765  0.35880  2.81200
```

Once again, we can verify that we obtain the correct result. Our model summary provides us with one final diagnostic; name the fisher scoring iterations, which we have not yet discussed. This number is typically in the range of 4 to 8 and is a convergence diagnostic. If the optimization procedure that R uses to train the logistic model has not converged, we expect to see a number that is high. If this happens, our model is suspect and we may not be able to use it to make predictions. In our case, we are within the expected range.

Test set performance

We've seen how we can use the `predict()` function to compute the output of our model. This output is the probability of the input belonging to class 1. We can perform binary classification by applying a threshold. We'll do this with both our training and test data and compare them with our expected outputs to measure the classification accuracy:

```
> train_predictions <- predict(heart_model, newdata = heart_train,
                                type = "response")
> train_class_predictions <- as.numeric(train_predictions > 0.5)
> mean(train_class_predictions == heart_train$OUTPUT)
[1] 0.8869565
```

```
> test_predictions = predict(heart_model, newdata = heart_test,
                             type = "response")
> test_class_predictions = as.numeric(test_predictions > 0.5)
> mean(test_class_predictions == heart_test$OUTPUT)
[1] 0.9
```

The classification accuracies on the training and test sets are very similar and are close to 90 percent. This is a very good starting point for a modeler to work from. The coefficients table in our model showed us that several features did not seem to be significant, and we also saw a degree of collinearity that means we could now proceed with variable selection and possibly look for more features, either through computation or by obtaining additional data about our patients. The pseudo R^2 computation showed us that we did not explain enough of the deviance in our model, which also supports this.

Regularization with the lasso

In the previous chapter on linear regression, we used the `glmnet` package to perform regularization with ridge regression and the lasso. As we've seen that it might be a good idea to remove some of our features, we'll try applying lasso to our data set and assess the results. First, we'll train a series of regularized models with `glmnet()` and then we will use `cv.glmnet()` to estimate a suitable value for λ. Then, we'll examine the coefficients of our regularized model using this λ:

```
> library(glmnet)
> heart_train_mat <- model.matrix(OUTPUT ~ ., heart_train)[,-1]
> lambdas <- 10 ^ seq(8, -4, length = 250)
> heart_models_lasso <- glmnet(heart_train_mat,
  heart_train$OUTPUT, alpha = 1, lambda = lambdas, family = "binomial")
> lasso.cv <- cv.glmnet(heart_train_mat, heart_train$OUTPUT,
              alpha = 1,lambda = lambdas, family = "binomial")
> lambda_lasso <- lasso.cv$lambda.min
> lambda_lasso
[1] 0.01057052

> predict(heart_models_lasso, type = "coefficients", s = lambda_lasso)
19 x 1 sparse Matrix of class "dgCMatrix"
                        1
(Intercept) -4.980249537
AGE              .
SEX          1.029146139
CHESTPAIN2   0.122044733
```

```
CHESTPAIN3    .
CHESTPAIN4    1.521164330
RESTBP        0.013456000
CHOL          0.004190012
SUGAR        -0.587616822
ECG1          .
ECG2          0.338365613
MAXHR        -0.010651758
ANGINA        0.807497991
DEP           0.211899820
EXERCISE2     0.351797531
EXERCISE3     0.081846313
FLUOR         0.947928099
THAL6         0.083440880
THAL7         1.501844677
```

We see that a number of our features have effectively been removed from the model because their coefficients are zero. If we now use this model to measure the classification accuracy on our training and test sets, we observe that in both cases, we get slightly better performance. Even if this difference is small, remember that we have achieved this using three fewer features:

```
> lasso_train_predictions <- predict(heart_models_lasso,
  s = lambda_lasso, newx = heart_train_mat, type = "response")
> lasso_train_class_predictions <-
  as.numeric(lasso_train_predictions > 0.5)
> mean(lasso_train_class_predictions == heart_train$OUTPUT)
[1] 0.8913043
> heart_test_mat <- model.matrix(OUTPUT ~ ., heart_test)[,-1]
> lasso_test_predictions <- predict(heart_models_lasso,
  s = lambda_lasso, newx = heart_test_mat, type = "response")
> lasso_test_class_predictions <-
  as.numeric(lasso_test_predictions > 0.5)
> mean(lasso_test_class_predictions == heart_test$OUTPUT)
[1] 0.925
```

Classification metrics

Although we looked at the test set accuracy for our model, we know from *Chapter 1, Gearing Up for Predictive Modeling*, that the binary confusion matrix can be used to compute a number of other useful performance metrics for our data, such as precision, recall, and the *F* measure.

We'll compute these for our training set now:

```
> (confusion_matrix <- table(predicted =
  train_class_predictions, actual = heart_train$OUTPUT))
        actual
predicted   0   1
        0 118  16
        1  10  86
> (precision <- confusion_matrix[2, 2] / sum(confusion_matrix[2,]))
[1] 0.8958333
> (recall <- confusion_matrix[2, 2] / sum(confusion_matrix[,2]))
[1] 0.8431373
> (f = 2 * precision * recall / (precision + recall))
[1] 0.8686869
```

Here, we used the trick of bracketing our assignment statements to simultaneously assign the result of an expression to a variable and print out the value assigned. Now, recall is the ratio of correctly identified instances of class 1, divided by the total number of observations that actually belong to class 1. In a medical context such as ours, this is also known as **sensitivity**, as it is an effective measure of a model's ability to detect or be sensitive to a particular condition. Recall is also known as the true positive rate. There is an analogous measure known as **specificity**, which is the false negative rate. This involves the mirror computation of recall for class 0, that is, the correctly identified members of class 0 over all the observations of class 0 in our data set. In our medical context, for example, the interpretation of specificity is that it measures the model's ability to reject observations that do not have the condition represented by class 1 (in our case, heart disease). We can compute the specificity of our model as follows:

```
> (specificity <- confusion_matrix[1,1]/sum(confusion_matrix[1,]))
[1] 0.880597
```

In computing these metrics, we begin to see the importance of setting the threshold at 0.5. If we were to choose a different threshold, it should be clear that all of the preceding metrics would change. In particular, there are many circumstances, our current medical context being a prime example, in which we may want to adjust our threshold to be biased toward identifying members of class 1. For example, suppose our model was being used by a clinician to determine whether to have a patient undergo a more detailed and expensive examination for heart disease. We would probably consider that mislabeling a patient with a heart condition as healthy is a more serious mistake to make than asking a healthy patient to undergo further tests because they were deemed unhealthy. To achieve this bias, we could lower our classification threshold to 0.3 or 0.2, for example.

Ideally, what we would like is a visual way to assess the effect of changing the threshold on our performance metrics, and the precision recall curve is one such useful plot. In R, we can use the ROCR package to obtain precision-recall curves:

```
> library(ROCR)
> train_predictions <- predict(heart_model, newdata = heart_train,
  type = "response")
> pred <- prediction(train_predictions, heart_training$OUTPUT)
> perf <- performance(pred, measure = "prec", x.measure = "rec")
```

We can then plot the perf object to obtain our precision recall curve.

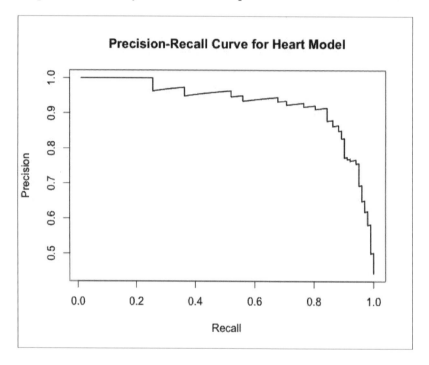

The graph shows us, for example, that to obtain values of recall above 0.8, we'll have to sacrifice precision quite abruptly. To fine-tune our threshold, we'll want to see individual thresholds that were used to compute this graph. A useful exercise is to create a data frame of cutoff values, which are the threshold values for which the precision and recall change in our data, along with their corresponding precision and recall values. We can then subset this data frame to inspect individual thresholds that interest us.

For example, suppose we want to find a suitable threshold so that we have at least 90 percent recall and 80 percent precision. We can do this as follows:

```
> thresholds <- data.frame(cutoffs = perf@alpha.values[[1]], recall =
  perf@x.values[[1]], precision = perf@y.values[[1]])
> subset(thresholds,(recall > 0.9) & (precision > 0.8))
      cutoffs    recall precision
112 0.3491857 0.9019608 0.8288288
113 0.3472740 0.9019608 0.8214286
114 0.3428354 0.9019608 0.8141593
115 0.3421438 0.9019608 0.8070175
```

As we can see, a threshold of roughly 0.35 will satisfy our requirements.

You may have noticed that we used the @ symbol to access some of the attributes of the perf object. This is because this object is a special type of object known as an S4 class. S4 classes are used to provide object-oriented features in R. A good reference to learn about S4 classes and object-orientated programming in R more generally is *Advanced R, Hadley Wickham, Chapman and Hall*.

Extensions of the binary logistic classifier

So far, the focus of this chapter has been on the binary classification task where we have two classes. We'll now turn to the problem of multiclass prediction. In *Chapter 1, Gearing Up for Predictive Modeling*, we studied the iris data set, where the goal is to distinguish between three different species of iris, based on features that describe the external appearance of iris flower samples. Before presenting additional examples of multiclass problems, we'll state an important caveat. The caveat is that several other methods for classification that we will study in this book, such as neural networks and decision trees, are both more natural and more commonly used than logistic regression for classification problems involving more than two classes. With that in mind, we'll turn to multinomial logistic regression, our first extension of the binary logistic classifier.

Multinomial logistic regression

Suppose our target variable is comprised of K classes. For example, in the iris data set, $K = 3$. **Multinomial logistic regression** tackles the multiclass problem by fitting K-1 independent binary logistic classifier models. This is done by arbitrarily choosing one of the output classes as a reference class and fitting K-1 regression models that compare each of the remaining classes to this one. For example, if we have two features, X_1 and X_2, and three classes, which we could call 0, 1, and 2, we construct the following two models:

$$ln\left(\frac{P(Y=1|X)}{P(Y=0|X)}\right) = \beta_{10} + \beta_{11}X_1 + \beta_{12}X_2$$

$$ln\left(\frac{P(Y=2|X)}{P(Y=0|X)}\right) = \beta_{20} + \beta_{21}X_1 + \beta_{22}X_2$$

Here we used class 0 as the baseline and built two binary regression models. In the first, we compare class 1 against class 0 and in the second, we compare class 2 against class 0. Note that because we now have more than one binary regression model, our model coefficients have two subscripts. The first subscript identifies the model and the second subscript pairs the coefficient with a feature. For example, β_{12} is the coefficient of feature X_2 in the first model. We can write a general expression for the probability that our combined model predicts class k when there are K classes in total, numbered from 0 to K-1, and class 0 is chosen as the reference class:

$$P(Y=k|X) = \begin{cases} \dfrac{1}{1+\sum_{j=1}^{K-1} e^{f_j(x)}}, & k=0 \\[4mm] \dfrac{e^{f_j(x)}}{1+\sum_{j=1}^{K-1} e^{f_j(x)}}, & k>0 \end{cases}$$

$$f_j(x) = \beta_{j0} + \beta_{j1}X_1 + \cdots + \beta_{jp}X_p$$

The reader should verify that the sum of all the output class probabilities is 1, as required. This particular mathematical form of an exponential divided by a sum of exponentials is known as the **softmax** function. For our three class problem discussed previously, we simply substitute $K=3$ in the preceding equations. At this point, we should mention some important characteristics of this approach.

To begin with, we are training one fewer model than the total number of classes in our output variable, and as a result, it should be easy to see that this approach does not scale very well when we have a large number of output classes from which to choose. The fact that we are building and training so many models also means that we tend to need a much larger data set to produce results with reasonable accuracy. Finally, as we independently compare each output class to a reference class, we make an assumption, known as the **Independence of Irrelevant Alternatives (IIA)** assumption.

The IIA assumption, in a nutshell, states that the odds of predicting one particular output class over another do not depend on whether we increase the number of possible output classes *k* by adding new classes. To illustrate this, suppose for simplicity that we model our iris data set using multinomial logistic regression, and the odds of the output classes are 0.33 : 0.33 : 0.33 for the three different species so that every species is in a 1 : 1 ratio with every other species. The IIA assumption states that if we refit a model that includes samples of a new type of iris, for example, ensata (the Japanese iris), the odds ratio between the previous three iris species is maintained. A new overall odds ratio of 0.2 : 0.2 : 0.2 : 0.4 between the four species (where the 0.4 corresponds to species ensata) would be valid, for example, because the 1 : 1 ratios between the old three species are maintained.

Predicting glass type

In this section, we'll demonstrate how we can train multinomial logistic regression models in R by way of an example data set. The data we'll examine is from the field of forensic science. Here, our goal is to examine properties of glass fragments found in crime scenes and predict the source of these fragments, for example, headlamps. The *glass identification data set* is hosted by the UCI Machine Learning Repository at http://archive.ics.uci.edu/ml/datasets/Glass+Identification. We'll first load the data in a data frame, rename the columns using information from the website, and throw away the first column that is a unique identifier for each sample, as this has been arbitrarily assigned and not needed by our model:

```
> glass <- read.csv("glass.data", header = FALSE)
> names(glass) <- c("id","RI","Na", "Mg", "Al", "Si", "K", "Ca",
                    "Ba", "Fe", "Type")
> glass <- glass[,-1]
```

Next, we'll look at a table showing what each column in our data frame represents.

Column name	Type	Definition
RI	Numerical	Refractive index
Na	Numerical	Percentage of Sodium Oxide by weight
Mg	Numerical	Percentage of Magnesium Oxide by weight
Al	Numerical	Percentage of Aluminium Oxide by weight
Si	Numerical	Percentage of Silicon Oxide by weight
K	Numerical	Percentage of Potassium Oxide by weight
Ca	Numerical	Percentage of Calcium Oxide by weight
Ba	Numerical	Percentage of Barium Oxide by weight
Fe	Numerical	Percentage of Iron Oxide by weight
Type	Categorical	Type of glass (1: float processed building windows, 2: nonfloat processed building windows, 3: float processed vehicle windows, 4: nonfloat processed vehicle windows, 5: containers, 6: tableware, 7: headlamps)

As usual, we'll proceed by preparing a training and test set for our glass data:

```
> set.seed(4365677)
> glass_sampling_vector
    <- createDataPartition(glass$Type, p = 0.80, list = FALSE)
> glass_train <- glass[glass_sampling_vector,]
> glass_test <- glass[-glass_sampling_vector,]
```

Now, to perform multinomial logistic regression, we will use the nnet package. This package also contains functions that work with neural networks, so we will revisit this package in the next chapter as well. The multinom() function is used for multinomial logistic regression. This works by specifying a formula and a data frame, so it has a familiar interface. In addition, we can also specify the maxit parameter that determines the maximum number of iterations for which the underlying optimization procedure will run. Sometimes, we may find that training a model returns an error that convergence was not reached. In this case, one possible approach is to increase this parameter and allow the model to train over a larger number of iterations. In doing so, however, we should be aware of the fact that the model may take longer to train:

```
> library(nnet)
> glass_model <- multinom(Type ~ ., data = glass_train, maxit = 1000)
> summary(glass_model)
```

```
Call:
multinom(formula = Type ~ ., data = glass_train, maxit = 1000)

Coefficients:
  (Intercept)          RI          Na          Mg          Al
2    52.259841   229.29126  -3.3704788   -5.975435   0.07372541
3   596.591193  -237.75997  -1.2230210   -2.435149  -0.65752347
5    -1.107583   -22.94764  -0.7434635   -4.244450   8.39355868
6    -7.493074   -11.83462  11.7893062   -6.383788  35.54561277
7   -55.888124   442.23590  -2.5269178  -10.479849   1.35983136
          Si           K          Ca          Ba           Fe
2  -4.0428142   -3.4934439  -4.6096363   -6.319183    3.2295218
3  -2.6703131   -4.1221815  -1.7952780   -3.910554    0.2818498
5   0.6992306   -0.2149109  -0.8790202   -4.642283    4.3379314
6  -2.2672275 -138.1047925   0.9011624 -161.700857 -200.9598019
7  -6.5363409   -7.5444163  -8.5710078   -4.087614  -67.9907347
```

```
Std. Errors:
  (Intercept)          RI          Na          Mg          Al          Si
2  0.03462075  0.08068713   0.5475710   0.7429120   1.282725   0.1392131
3  0.05425817  0.08750688   0.7339134   0.9173184   1.544409   0.1805758
5  0.06674926  0.11759231   1.0866157   1.4062285   2.738635   0.3225212
6  0.17049665  0.28791033  17.2280091   4.9726046   2.622643   4.3385330
7  0.06432732  0.10522206   2.2561142   1.5246356   3.244288   0.4733835
           K          Ca          Ba          Fe
2  1.98021049   0.4897356  1.473156e+00  2.45881312
3  2.35233054   0.5949799  4.222783e+00  3.45835575
5  2.78360034   0.9807043  5.471887e+00  5.52299959
6  0.02227295   7.2406622  1.656563e-08  0.01779519
7  3.25038195   1.7310334  4.381655e+00  0.28562065
```

```
Residual Deviance: 219.2651
AIC: 319.2651
```

Our model summary shows us that we have five sets of coefficients. This is because our TYPE output variable has six levels, which is to say that we are choosing to predict one of six different sources of glass. There are no examples in the data where Type takes the value 4. The model also shows us standard errors but no significance tests. In general, testing for coefficient significance is a lot trickier than with binary logistic regression, and this is one of the weaknesses of this approach. Often, we resort to independently testing the significance of coefficients for each of the binary models that we trained.

We won't dwell on this any further, but will instead check the overall accuracy on our training data to give us a sense of the overall quality of fit:

```
> glass_predictions <- predict(glass_model, glass_train)
> mean(glass_predictions == glass_train$Type)
[1] 0.7209302
```

Our training accuracy is 72 percent, which is not especially high. Here is the confusion matrix:

```
> table(predicted = glass_predictions, actual = glass_train$Type)
          actual
predicted  1  2  3  5  6  7
        1 46 17  8  0  0  0
        2 13 40  6  2  0  1
        3  0  0  0  0  0  0
        5  0  1  0  7  0  0
        6  0  0  0  0  7  0
        7  0  0  0  0  0 24
```

The confusion matrix reveals certain interesting facts. The first of these is that it seems that the model does not distinguish well between the first two classes, as many of the errors that are made involve these two. Part of the reason for this, however, is that these two classes are the most frequent in the data. The second problem that we are seeing is that the model never predicts class 3. In fact, it completely confuses this class with the first two classes. The seven examples of class 6 are perfectly distinguished, and accuracy for class 7 is also near perfect, with only 1 mistake out of 25. Overall, 72 percent accuracy on training data is considered mediocre, but given the fact that we have six output classes and only 172 observations in our training data, this is to be expected with this type of model. Let's repeat this for the test data set:

```
> glass_test_predictions <- predict(glass_model, glass_test)
> mean(glass_test_predictions == glass_test$Type)
[1] 0.6428571
> table(predicted = glass_test_predictions, actual =
        glass_test$Type)
          actual
predicted  1  2  3  5  6  7
        1  7  2  2  0  0  0
        2  4 15  1  2  0  0
        3  0  0  0  0  0  0
        5  0  0  0  1  0  2
        6  0  0  0  0  2  0
        7  0  1  0  1  0  2
```

As we can see, the confusion matrix paints a fairly similar picture to what we saw in training. Again, our model never predicts class 3 and the first two classes are still hard to distinguish. The number of observations in our test set is only 42, so this is very small. The test set accuracy is only 64 percent, somewhat less than we saw in training. If our sample sizes were larger, we may suspect that our model suffers from overfitting, but in this case, the variance of our test set performance is high due to the small sample size.

With multinomial logistic regression, we assumed that there was no natural ordering to the output classes. If our output variable is an ordinal, also known as an **ordered factor**, we can train a different model known as **ordinal logistic regression**. This is our second extension of the binary logistic regression model and is presented in the next section.

Ordinal logistic regression

Ordered factors are very common in a number of scenarios. For example, human responses to surveys are often on subjective scales with scores ranging from 1 to 5 or using qualitative labels with an intrinsic ordering such as *disagree*, *neutral*, and *agree*. We can try to treat these problems as regression problems, but we will still face similar issues as we did with treating the binary classification problem as a regression problem. Instead of trying to train *K-1* binary logistic regression models as with multinomial logistic regression, ordinal logistic regression trains a single model with multiple thresholds on the output. In order to achieve this, it makes an important assumption known as the assumption of **proportional odds**. If we have *K* classes and want to put a threshold on the output of a single binary logistic regression model, we will need *K-1* thresholds or cutoff points. The proportional odds assumption is that in the logit scale, all of these thresholds lie on a straight line. Put differently, the model uses a single set of β_i coefficients determining the slope of the straight line, but there are *K-1* intercept terms. For a model with *p* features and an output variable with *K* classes numbered from 0 to *K-1*, our model predicts:

$$\ln\left(\frac{P(Y \leq k \mid X)}{P(Y > k \mid X)}\right) = \beta_k + \beta_1 X_1 + \cdots + \beta_p X_p, \quad \forall k \in \{0, \ldots K-1\}$$

This assumption may be a little hard to visualize and is perhaps best understood by way of an example. Suppose that we are trying to predict the results of a survey on the opinions of the public on a particular government policy, based on demographic data about survey participants.

The output variable is an ordered factor that ranges from *strongly disagree* to *strongly agree* on a five-point scale (also known as a **Likert** scale). Suppose that l_0 is the log-odds of the probabilities of strongly disagreeing versus disagreeing or better, l_1 is the log-odds of the probabilities of disagreeing or strongly disagreeing versus at least being neutral, and so on until l_3. These four log-odds l_0 to l_3 form an arithmetic sequence, which means that the distance between consecutive numbers is a constant.

Even though the proportional odds model is the most frequently cited logistic regression model that handles ordered factors, there are alternative approaches. A good reference that discusses the proportional odds model as well as other related models, such as the adjacent-category logistic model, is *Applied Logistic Regression Third Edition, Hosmer Jr., Lemeshow, and Sturdivant*, published by *Wiley*.

Predicting wine quality

The data set for our ordinal logistic regression example is the *wine quality data set* from the *UCI Machine Learning Repository*. The observations in this data set consist of wine samples taken from both red and white wines of the Portuguese Vinho Verde variety. The wine samples have been rated on a scale from 1 to 10 by a number of wine experts. The goal of the data set is to predict the rating that an expert will give to a wine sample, using a range of physiochemical properties, such as acidity and alcohol composition. The website is `https://archive.ics.uci.edu/ml/datasets/Wine+Quality`. The data is split into two files, one for red wines and one for white wines. We will use the white wine data set, as it contains a larger number of samples. In addition, for simplicity and because the distribution of wine samples by score is sparse, we will contract our original output variable to a three point scale from 0 to 2. First, let's load and process our data:

```
> wine <- read.csv("winequality-white.csv", sep = ";")
> wine$quality <- factor(ifelse(wine$quality < 5, 0,
                         ifelse(wine$quality > 6, 2, 1)))
```

The following table shows our input features and output variables:

Column name	Type	Definition
`fixed.acidity`	Numerical	Fixed Acidity (g(tartaric acid)/dm$_3$)
`volatile.acidity`	Numerical	Volatile acidity (g(acetic acid)/dm$_3$)
`citric.acid`	Numerical	Citric acid (g/dm$_3$)
`residual.sugar`	Numerical	Residual sugar (g/dm$_3$)
`chlorides`	Numerical	Chlorides (g(sodium chloride)/dm$_3$)

Column name	Type	Definition
free.sulfur.dioxide	Numerical	Free Sulfur Dioxide (mg/dm$_3$)
total.sulfur.dioxide	Numerical	Total Sulfur Dioxide (mg/dm$_3$)
density	Numerical	Density (g/cm$_3$)
pH	Numerical	PH
sulphates	Numerical	Sulphates (g(potassium sulphate)/dm$_3$)
alcohol	Numerical	Alcohol (% vol.)
quality	Categorical	Wine quality (1 = Poor, 2 = Average, 3 = Good)

First, we'll prepare a training and test set:

```
> set.seed(7644)
> wine_sampling_vector <- createDataPartition(wine$quality, p =
                      0.80, list = FALSE)
> wine_train <- wine[wine_sampling_vector,]
> wine_test <- wine[-wine_sampling_vector,]
```

Next, we'll use the `polr()` function from the MASS package to train a proportional odds logistic regression model. Just as with the other model functions we have seen so far, we first need to specify a formula and a data frame with our training data. In addition, we must specify the Hess parameter to TRUE in order to obtain a model that includes additional information, such as standard errors on the coefficients:

```
> library(MASS)
> wine_model <- polr(quality ~ ., data = wine_train, Hess = T)
> summary(wine_model)
Call:
polr(formula = quality ~ ., data = wine_train, Hess = T)

Coefficients:
                          Value Std. Error     t value
fixed.acidity          4.728e-01   0.055641      8.4975
volatile.acidity      -4.211e+00   0.435288     -9.6741
citric.acid            9.896e-02   0.353466      0.2800
residual.sugar         3.386e-01   0.009835     34.4248
chlorides             -2.891e+00   0.116025    -24.9162
free.sulfur.dioxide    1.176e-02   0.003234      3.6374
total.sulfur.dioxide  -1.618e-04   0.001384     -0.1169
density               -7.534e+02   0.625157  -1205.1041
pH                     3.107e+00   0.301434     10.3087
sulphates              2.199e+00   0.338923      6.4873
```

```
alcohol                 2.883e-02    0.041479      0.6951

Intercepts:
     Value      Std. Error t value
1|2  -736.9784     0.6341 -1162.3302
2|3  -731.4177     0.6599 -1108.4069

Residual Deviance: 4412.75
AIC: 4438.75
```

Our model summary shows us that we have three output classes, and we have two intercepts. Now, in this data set, we have many wines that were rated average (either 5 or 6) and as a result, this class is the most frequent. We'll use the `table()` function to count the number of samples by the output score and then apply `prop.table()` to express these as relative frequencies:

```
> prop.table(table(wine$quality))

         1          2          3
0.03736219 0.74622295 0.21641486
```

Class 2, which corresponds to average wines, is by far the most frequent. In fact, a simple baseline model that always predicts this category would be correct 74.6 percent of the time. Let's see whether our model does better than this. We'll begin by looking at the fit on the training data and the corresponding confusion matrix:

```
> wine_predictions <- predict(wine_model, wine_train)
> mean(wine_predictions == wine_train$quality)
[1] 0.7647359
> table(predicted = wine_predictions,actual = wine_train$quality)
          actual
predicted    1    2    3
        1    4    1    0
        2  141 2764  619
        3    2  159  229
```

Our model performs only marginally better on the training data than our baseline model. We can see why this is the case—it predicts the average class (2) very often and almost never predicts class 1. Repeating with the test set reveals a similar situation:

```
> wine_test_predictions <- predict(wine_model, wine_test)
> mean(wine_test_predictions == wine_test$quality)
[1] 0.7681307
> table(predicted = wine_test_predictions,
              actual = wine_test$quality)
```

```
             actual
predicted    1    2    3
        1    2    2    0
        2   33  693  155
        3    1   36   57
```

It seems that our model is not a particularly good choice for this data set. As we know, there are a number of possible reasons ranging from having chosen the wrong type of model to having insufficient features or the wrong kind of features. One aspect of the ordinal logistic regression model that we should always try to check is whether the proportional odds assumption is valid. There is no universally accepted way to do this, but a number of different statistical tests have been proposed in the literature. Unfortunately, it is very difficult to find reliable implementations of these tests in R. One simple test that is easy to do, however, is to train a second model using multinomial logistic regression. Then, we can compare the AIC value of our two models. Let's do this:

```
> wine_model2 <- multinom(quality ~ ., data = wine_train,
                          maxit = 1000)
> wine_predictions2 <- predict(wine_model2, wine_test)
> mean(wine_predictions2 == wine_test$quality)
[1] 0.7630235
> table(predicted = wine_predictions2, actual = wine_test$quality)
             actual
predicted    1    2    3
        1    2    2    0
        2   32  682  149
        3    2   47   63
```

The two models have virtually no difference in the quality of the fit. Let's check their AIC values:

```
> AIC(wine_model)
[1] 4438.75
> AIC(wine_model2)
[1] 4367.448
```

The AIC is lower in the multinomial logistic regression model, which suggests that we might be better off working with that model. Another possible avenue for improvement on this data set would be to carry out feature selection. The step() function that we saw in the previous chapter, for example, also works on models trained with the polr() function. We'll leave this as an exercise for the reader to verify that we can, in fact, get practically the same level of performance by removing some of the features. Unsatisfied with the results of logistic regression on this latest data set, we will revisit it in subsequent chapters in order to see whether more sophisticated classification models can do better.

Summary

Logistic regression is the prototypical method for solving classification problems, just as linear regression was the prototypical example of a model to solve regression problems. In this chapter, we demonstrated why logistic regression offers a better way of approaching classification problems compared to linear regression with a threshold, by showing that the least squares criterion is not the most appropriate criterion to use when trying to separate two classes. We presented the notion of likelihood and its maximization as the basis for training a model. This is a very important concept that features time and again in various machine learning contexts. Logistic regression is an example of a generalized linear model. This is a model that relates the output variable to a linear combination of input features via a link function, which we saw was the logit function in this case. For the binary classification problem, we used R's glm() function to perform logistic regression on a real-world data set and studied the model diagnostics to evaluate our model's performance. We discovered parallels with linear regression, in that the model produces deviance residuals that are analogous to least squared error residuals and that we can compute a pseudo R^2 statistic that is analogous to the R^2 statistic, which measures the goodness of fit in linear regression. We also saw that we can apply regularization techniques to logistic regression models. Our tour of binary classification with the logistic regression model ended by studying precision-recall curves in order to choose appropriate model thresholds, an exercise that is very important when the cost of misclassifying an observation is not symmetric for the two classes involved. Finally, we investigated two possible extensions of the binary logistic regression model to handle outputs with many class labels. These were the multinomial logistic regression model and the ordinal logistic regression model, which can be useful when the output classes are ordered.

It turns out that logistic regression is not a great choice for multiclass settings in general. In the next chapter, we'll introduce neural networks, which are a nonlinear model used to solve both regression and classification problems. We'll also see how neural networks are able to handle multiple class labels in a natural way.

4
Neural Networks

So far, we've looked at two of the most well-known methods used for predictive modeling. Linear regression is probably the most typical starting point for problems where the goal is to predict a numerical quantity. The model is based on a linear combination of input features. Logistic regression uses a nonlinear transformation of this linear feature combination in order to restrict the range of the output in the interval [0,1]. In so doing, it predicts the probability that the output belongs to one of two classes. Thus, it is a very well-known technique for classification.

Both methods share the disadvantage that they are not robust when dealing with many input features. In addition, logistic regression is typically used for the binary classification problem. In this chapter, we will introduce the concept of **neural networks**, a nonlinear approach to solving both regression and classification problems. They are significantly more robust when dealing with a higher dimensional input feature space, and for classification, they possess a natural way to handle more than two output classes.

Neural networks are a biologically inspired model, the origins of which date back to the 1940s. Interest in neural networks has fluctuated greatly over the years as the first models proved to be quite limited compared to the expectations at the time. Additionally, training a large neural network requires substantial computational resources. Recently, there has been a huge surge in interest in neural networks as distributed on-demand computing resources are now widespread and an important area of machine learning, known as **deep learning**, is already showing great promise. For this reason, it is a great time to be learning about this type of model.

The biological neuron

Neural network models draw their analogy from the organization of neurons in the human brain, and for this reason they are also often referred to as **artificial neural networks (ANNs)** to distinguish them from their biological counterparts. The key parallel is that a single biological neuron acts as a simple computational unit, but when a large number of these are combined together, the result is an extremely powerful and massively distributed processing machine capable of complex learning, known more commonly as the human brain. To get an idea of how neurons are connected in the brain, the following image shows a simplified picture of a human neural cell:

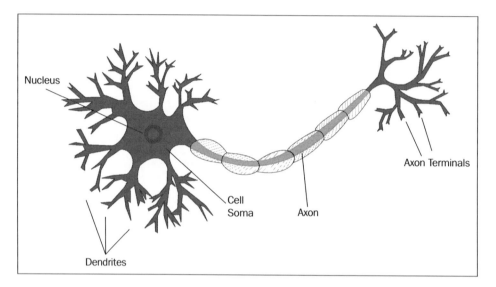

In a nutshell, we can think of a human neuron as a computational unit that takes in a series of parallel electrical signal inputs known as **synaptic neurotransmitters** coming in from the **dendrites**. The dendrites transmit signal chemicals to the **soma** or body of the neuron in response to the received synaptic neurotransmitters. This conversion of an external input signal to a local signal can be thought of as a process in which the dendrites apply a **weight** (which can be negative or positive depending on whether the chemicals produced are **inhibitors** or **activators** respectively) to their inputs.

The soma of the neuron, which houses the **nucleus** or central processor, mixes these input signals in a process that can be thought of as summing up all the signals. Consequently, the original dendrite inputs are basically transformed into a single linear weighted sum. This sum is sent to the **axon** of the neuron, which is the transmitter of the neuron. The weighted sum of electrical inputs creates an electric potential in the neuron, and this potential is processed in the axon by means of an **activation function**, which determines whether the neuron will fire.

Typically, the activation function is modeled as a switch that requires a minimum electrical potential, known as the **bias**, to be reached before it is turned on. Thus, the activation function essentially determines whether the neuron will output an electrical signal or not, and if so, the signal is transported through the axon and propagated to other neurons through the **axon terminals**. These, in turn, connect to the dendrites of neighboring neurons and the electrical signal output becomes an input to subsequent neural processing.

This description is, of course, a simplification of what happens in our neurons, but the goal here is to explain what aspects of the biological process have been used to inspire the computational model of a neural network.

The artificial neuron

Using our biological analogy, we can construct a model of a computational neuron, and this model is known as the **McCulloch-Pitts model** of a neuron:

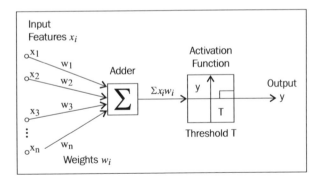

Warren McCulloch and *Walter Pitts* proposed this model of a neural network as a computing machine in a paper titled *A logical calculus of the ideas immanent in nervous activity*, published by the *Bulletin of Mathematical Biophysics* in 1943.

This computational neuron is the simplest example of a neural network. We can construct the output function, *y*, of our neural network directly from following our diagram:

$$y = g\left(w_0 + \sum_{i=1}^{p} w_i x_i \right)$$

The function g() in our neural network is the activation function. Here, the specific activation function that is chosen is the **step function**:

$$g(x) = \begin{cases} -1, & x < 0 \\ 1, & x \geq 0 \end{cases}$$

When the linear weighted sum of inputs exceeds zero, the step function outputs 1, and when it does not, the function outputs -1. It is customary to create a dummy input feature x_0 which is always taken to be 1, in order to merge the bias or threshold w_0 into the main sum as follows:

$$y = g\left(\sum_{i=0}^{p} w_i x_i \right)$$

Using our experience with logistic regression, it should be very easy to conclude that we could construct a simple classifier using this setup for the binary classification problem. The only difference is that in logistic regression, we would choose the logistic function as the activation function. In fact, in 1957, Frank Rosenblatt proposed a supervised learning algorithm for training the McCulloch-Pitts model of neurons to perform binary classification, and this algorithm along with the learning model produced is known as the **Rosenblatt perceptron**.

We've thus far presented linear and logistic regression as models that can solve supervised learning problems and showed the criteria that are used to train them without actually going into the optimization details of the training algorithms involved. This was done intentionally to allow us to focus our attention on understanding the models themselves, and how to apply them in R.

Now that we have built up some experience with classification and regression, this chapter is going to be different, in that we will look at some of the details of how predictive models are trained, as this too is an important process that adds to our overall understanding of a model. In addition, neural networks differ substantially from previous models we have seen so far, in that training a neural network is often more time consuming and involves adjusting a number of parameters, many of which arise from the optimization procedure itself. Thus, it helps to understand the role these parameters play during training and how they can affect the final model.

Before we present a training algorithm for the perceptron, we'll first have to learn one of the most fundamental techniques used in solving optimization problems.

Stochastic gradient descent

In the models we've seen so far, such as linear regression, we've talked about a criterion or objective function that the model must minimize while it is being trained. This criterion is also sometimes known as the **cost function**. For example, the least squares cost function for a model can be expressed as:

$$\frac{1}{2n}\sum_{i=1}^{n}\left(\hat{y}_i - y_i\right)^2$$

We've added a constant term of ½ in front of this for reasons that will become apparent shortly. We know from basic differentiation that when we are minimizing a function, multiplying the function by a constant factor does not alter the value of the minimum value of the function. In linear regression, just as with our perceptron model, our model's predicted $\hat{y}_i$ is just the sum of a linear weighted combination of the input features. If we assume that our data is fixed and that the weights are variable and must be chosen so as to minimize our criterion, we can treat the cost function as being a function of the weights:

$$J\left(\vec{w}\right) = \frac{1}{2n}\sum_{i=1}^{n}\left(\left(\sum_{j=1}^{p}w_j x_j\right) - y_i\right)^2$$

We have used the letter w to represent the model weights here for the more general case, though in linear regression we've seen that it is customary to use the Greek letter β instead. As our model variables are the weights, we can consider that our function is a function of a weight vector, $\vec{w}$. To find the minimum of this function, we just need to take the partial derivative of our cost function with respect to this weight vector. For a specific weight w_k, this partial derivative is given by:

$$\frac{\partial J(\vec{w})}{\partial w_k} = \frac{1}{n} \sum_{i=1}^{n} \left(\left(\sum_{j=1}^{p} w_j x_j \right) - y_i \right) x_{ik}$$

Note that the coefficient of one half has usefully cancelled out the 2 from the derivative. We now have three different subscripts, so it is a good idea to take a step back and try to understand this equation. The innermost sum is still computing $\hat{y}_i$, which is the model's predicted output. Let's replace this into the equation to simplify things a bit:

$$\frac{\partial J(\vec{w})}{\partial w_k} = \frac{1}{n} \sum_{i=1}^{n} (\hat{y}_i - y_i) x_{ik}$$

Now we should be in a better position to understand this equation. It says that the partial derivative of the cost function that we are trying to minimize for a specific weight, w_k, in our model is just the difference between the predicted output of the model and the actual labeled output, multiplied by x_{ik} (for the ith observation, the value of the input feature that corresponds to our weight w_k), and averaged over all the n observations in our data set.

If you are not familiar with partial differentiation but are familiar with differentiation, you already know everything you need to in order to understand this equation. We use partial differentiation to explicitly identify the variable that we will be differentiating with respect to an equation that has more than one variable. When we do this, we treat all other variables as constants and the differentiation is carried out normally.

To find the optimal weights, we need to solve this equation for every weight in our weight vector. Note that through the predicted output term, all the weights in the model appear in the partial derivative of every individual weight. Put differently, this produces a complete system of linear equations that is often very large, so solving this directly is often prohibitively expensive, computationally speaking.

Instead, many model implementations use iterative optimization procedures that are designed to gradually approach the correct solution. One such method is **gradient descent**. For a particular value of the weight vector, gradient descent finds the direction in which the gradient of the cost function is steepest, and adjusts the weights in that direction by a small amount, which is determined by a parameter known as the **learning rate**. Thus, the update equation is:

$$w_k \leftarrow w_k - \eta \frac{1}{n} \sum_{i=1}^{n} \left(\hat{y}_i - y_i \right) x_{ik}$$

In the previous equation, the learning rate is denoted by the Greek letter η. Setting the learning rate to an appropriate value is a very important aspect of optimizing with gradient descent. If we choose a value that is too small, the algorithm will update the weights by a very small amount each time, and thus it will take too long to finish. If we use a value that is too large, we may cause the weights to change too drastically, oscillating between values, and so again the learning algorithm will either take too long to converge or oscillate continuously.

There are various sophisticated methods to estimate an appropriate learning rate, the details of which we won't discuss here. Instead, we'll try to find an appropriate learning rate through trial and error, and this often works just fine in practice. One way to keep track of whether our chosen learning rate is decent is to plot the cost function we are trying to minimize versus time (represented by the number of iterations made through the data set). We should be seeing a decreasing (or at least non-increasing) change in the cost function over time if we have chosen a good value for the learning rate.

A variant of the gradient descent method is **stochastic gradient descent**, which does a similar computation but takes the observations one at a time instead of all together. The key idea is that, on average, the gradient of the cost function computed for a particular observation will equal that of the gradient computed across all observations. This is, of course, an approximation, but it does mean that we can process individual observations one at a time, which is very useful, especially if we want to perform online learning. Stochastic gradient descent updates a particular weight, w_k, when processing the ith observation in the data set according to the following equation:

$$w_k \leftarrow w_k - \eta \left(\hat{y}_i - y_i \right) x_{ik}$$

An excellent resource for some of the tricks that are useful when training a model with stochastic gradient descent is a book chapter by *Leo Bottou*, titled *Stochastic Gradient Descent Tricks*. A version of this can be found online at http://research.microsoft.com/pubs/192769/tricks-2012.pdf.

Gradient descent and local minima

Gradient descent methods rely on the idea that the cost function that is being minimized is a **convex function**. We'll skip the mathematical details of this and just say that a convex function is a function that has, at most, a single global minimum. Let's look at an example of a non-convex cost function in terms of a single weight w:

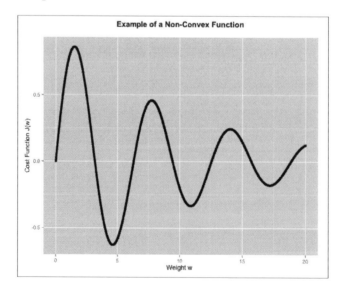

The global minimum of this function is the first trough on the left for a value of w, close to 4.5. If our initial guess for the weight w is 1, the gradient of the cost function points towards the global minimum, and we will progressively approach it until we reach it. If our initial guess of the weight is 12, then the gradient of the cost function will point downwards towards the trough near the value 10.5. Once we reach the second trough, the gradient of the cost function will be 0 and consequently, we will not be able to make any progress towards our global minimum because we have landed in a local minimum.

Detecting and avoiding local minima can be very tricky, especially if there are many of them. One way to do this is to repeat the optimization with different starting points and then pick the weights that produce the lowest value of the cost function across the different times the optimization is run. This procedure works well if the number of local minima is small and they are not too close together. Thankfully, the squared error cost function that we saw in the previous section is a convex function and so gradient descent methods are guaranteed to find the global minimum, but it is good to be aware that there are other examples of cost functions that we will encounter that are non-convex.

The perceptron algorithm

Without further ado, we'll present our first training algorithm for classification with neural networks. This is a variation of the perceptron learning algorithm and is known as the **pocket perceptron algorithm**.

Inputs:

- x: A two-dimensional matrix, where the rows are the observations and the columns are the input features.
- y: A vector with the class label (-1 or 1) for all the observations in x.
- learning_rate: A number that controls the learning rate of the algorithm.
- max_iterations: The maximum number of cycles through our data that our algorithm is allowed to perform while learning.

Outputs:

- w: The learned weights of the perceptron.
- converged: Whether the algorithm converged (true or false).
- iterations: The actual number of iterations through the data performed during learning.

> **Method:**
>
> 1. Randomly initialize the weights w.
>
> 2. Select an observation in x, and call it x_i.
>
> 3. Compute the predicted class, $\hat{y}_i$, using the current values of the weights w and the equation for the output of the perceptron.
>
> 4. If the predicted class, $\hat{y}_i$, is not the same as the actual class, y_i, then update the weights vector using stochastic gradient descent.
>
> 5. Repeat steps 2–4 for all the observations in our data set and count the number of errors made.
>
> 6. If the number of errors is zero, we have converged and the algorithm terminates.
>
> 7. If the number of errors made in the current iteration was less than the lowest numbers of errors ever made, store the weights vector as the best weights vector seen so far.
>
> 8. If we have reached the maximum number of iterations, stop and return the value of the best weights vector. Otherwise, begin a new iteration over the data set at *step 2*.

We'll see the R code for this directly and discuss the steps in detail:

```
step_function <- function(x) {
    if (x < 0) -1 else 1
}


pocket_perceptron <- function(x, y, learning_rate,
    max_iterations) {
  nObs = nrow(x)
  nFeatures = ncol(x)
  w = rnorm(nFeatures + 1, 0, 2) # Random weight initialization
  current_iteration = 0
  has_converged = F
  best_weights = w
  # Start by assuming you get all the examples wrong
  best_error = nObs
  while ((has_converged == F) &
          (current_iteration < max_iterations)) {
    # Assume we are done unless we misclassify an observation
    has_converged = T
    # Keep track of misclassified observations
    current_error = 0
    for (i in 1:nObs) {
```

```
    xi = c(1, x[i,]) # Append 1 for the dummy input feature x0
    yi = y[i]
    y_predicted = step_function(sum(w * xi))
    if (yi != y_predicted) {
      current_error = current_error + 1
      # We have at least one misclassified example
      has_converged = F
      w = w - learning_rate * sign(y_predicted - yi) * xi
    }
  }
  if (current_error < best_error) {
    best_error = current_error
    best_weights = w
  }
  current_iteration = current_iteration+1
}
model <- list("weights" = best_weights,
              "converged" = has_converged,
              "iterations" = current_iteration)
model
}
```

The first function we define is the step function, which we know will produce either the value -1 or the value 1 corresponding to the two classes in our data set. We then define our main function, which we call pocket_perceptron(). The job of this function is to learn the weights for our perceptron so that our model classifies our training data correctly.

Note that we have not introduced any regularization in our algorithm, so as to keep things simple, and so we will likely end up with a model that will overfit our data, as we are shooting for 100 percent training accuracy. Proceeding with our algorithm description, we begin our function by initializing the weights vector to small randomly generated numbers. In practice, it is a good idea to make sure that weights are not set to 0 and are not symmetric, and this method is a good way to avoid this.

We will also set our starting best guess of the weights to be our initial vector and our starting best error rate to be the total number of observations, which is the worst possible error rate on a data set.

The main while loop of the function controls the number of iterations over which our algorithm will run. We will only begin a new iteration when we have not converged and when we have not hit our maximum number of iterations. Inside the while loop, we use a for loop to iterate over the observations in our data set and classify these using the current version of our weight vector.

Every time we make a mistake in classification, we update our error rate, note that we have not converged in this iteration, and update our weight vector according to the stochastic gradient descent update rule for least squares that we saw in the previous section. Although the cost function for the perceptron is not differentiable because of the step function used to threshold the output, it turns out that we can, in fact, still use the same update rule for the weights.

At the end of a complete iteration through our data set, also known as an **epoch**, we check whether we need to update our best weights vector and update the number of iterations. We update our best weights vector only if the performance in the current iteration on the training data was the best performance we have seen thus far across all completed iterations. When the algorithm terminates, we return the best weights we found, whether or not we converged, and the total number of completed iterations.

 The definitive textbook on neural networks, and one that explains perceptron learning in more detail, including proof of why the algorithm works, is *Neural Networks and Learning Machines 3rd Edition, Simon Haykin, Prentice Hall*

We can put our model to the test by generating some artificial data. We'll do this by sampling values from two uniform distributions in order to create two input features: x_1 and x_2. We'll then separate these data points into two different classes according to a linear decision boundary that we've chosen randomly:

$$y = \begin{cases} -1, & -0.89 + 2.07x_1 - 3.09x_2 < 0 \\ 1, & otherwise \end{cases}$$

Once we have the data and the computed class labels, we can run our perceptron algorithm on it. The following code generates the test data and builds our model:

```
> set.seed(4910341)
> x1 <- runif(200, 0, 10)
> set.seed(2125151)
> x2 <- runif(200, 0, 10)
> x <- cbind(x1, x2)
> y <- sign(-0.89 + 2.07 * x[,1] - 3.09 * x[,2])
> pmodel <- pocket_perceptron(x, y, 0.1, 1000)
> pmodel
$weights
                  x1          x2
-1.738271   4.253327  -6.360326

$converged
```

```
[1]  TRUE

$iterations
[1]  32
```

We can see that after 32 iterations, our perceptron algorithm has converged. If we divide our weights vector by 2 (this does not alter our decision boundary), we can see more clearly that we have a decision boundary that is very close to the one that was used when classifying the data:

```
> model$weights / 2
                    x1          x2
 -0.8741571   2.1420697  -3.2122627
```

The following plot shows that the model's decision boundary is virtually indistinguishable from the population line. For our artificially generated data set, this is because the two classes are so close together. If the classes were further apart, we would more likely see a noticeable difference between the population decision boundary and the model's decision boundary. This is because the space of possible lines (or planes when we are dealing with more than two features) that can separate the data would be larger.

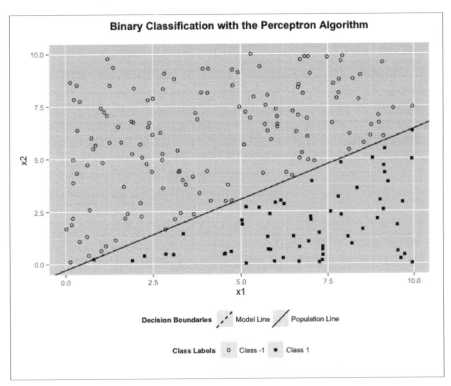

Linear separation

The data that we generated had a particular property that ensured that the perceptron algorithm would converge — it was **linearly separable**. When two classes are linearly separable in terms of a set of features, it means that it is possible to find a linear combination of these features as a decision boundary that will allow us to classify the two classes with 100 percent accuracy.

If we consider plotting the data points belonging to the two classes in the *p*-dimensional feature space, then linear separation means that there is a plane (or line for 2 dimensions, as we saw in our example) that can be drawn to separate the two classes. There is a theorem, known as the **perceptron convergence theorem**, which states that for linearly separable classes, the perceptron learning algorithm will always converge to a solution that correctly classifies all the data given enough time.

The logistic neuron

The perceptron is also known as a **binary threshold neuron**. We can create different types of neurons by changing the activation function. For example, if we remove the threshold function completely, we end up with a **linear neuron**, which essentially performs the same task as linear regression. By changing the activation function to a logistic function, we can create a **logistic neuron**.

A logistic neuron performs the same task as logistic regression, by taking a linear combination of inputs and applying the logistic function to predict a value in the interval [0,1]. Stochastic gradient descent can be applied in order to learn the weights of linear neurons as well as logistic neurons. Hence, it can also be applied to learn the weights for logistic and linear regression. The general form of the stochastic gradient descent weight update rule is:

$$w_k \leftarrow w_k - \eta \frac{\partial J(\vec{w})}{\partial w_k}$$

Here, the derivative is computing the gradient of the cost function at the particular observation. We saw the simple form for linear regression and the linear neuron in the previous section. If we perform differentiation on the cost function for logistic regression, we will discover that the update rule for stochastic gradient descent for the logistic neuron appears to be exactly the same as with the linear neuron:

$$w_k \leftarrow w_k - \eta (\hat{y}_i - y_i) x_{ik}$$

The subtle difference here is that the form of $\hat{y}_i$ is completely different as it now includes the weights inside the logistic function, whereas this was not the case in linear regression. Logistic neurons are very important because they are the most common type of neuron used when building networks of many neurons connected together. As we'll see in the next section, we generally build neural networks in layers. The layer containing the neurons that produce our outputs is known as the **output layer**. The **input layer** is comprised of our data features that are the inputs to network.

Layers in between the input and output layers are known as **hidden layers**. Logistic neurons are the most common hidden layer neuron. Additionally, we use logistic neurons as output layer neurons when our task is classification, and linear neurons when our task is regression.

Multilayer perceptron networks

Multilayer neural networks are models that chain many neurons in order to create a neural architecture. Individually, neurons are very basic units, but when organized together, we can create a model significantly more powerful than the individual neurons.

As touched upon in the previous section, we build neural networks in layers and we distinguish between different kinds of neural networks primarily on the basis of the connections that exist between these layers and the types of neurons used. The following diagram shows the general structure of a **multilayer perceptron (MLP)** neural network, shown here for two hidden layers:

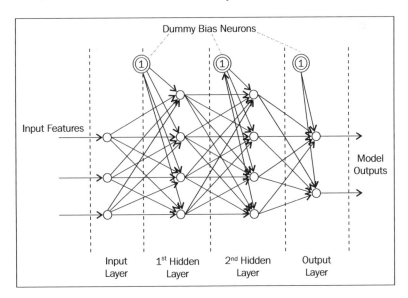

The first characteristic of the MLP network is that the information flows in a single direction from input layer to output layer. Thus, it is known as a **feedforward neural network**. This is in contrast to other neural network types, in which there are cycles that allow information to flow back to earlier neurons in the network as a feedback signal. These networks are known as **feedback neural networks** or **recurrent neural** networks. Recurrent neural networks are generally very difficult to train and often do not scale well with the number of inputs. Nonetheless, they do find a number of applications, in particular with problems involving a time component such as forecasting and signal processing.

Returning to the MLP architecture shown in the diagram, we note that the first group of neurons on the left are known as the input neurons and form the input layer. We always have as many input neurons as there are input features. The input neurons are said to produce the values of our input features as outputs. For this reason, we often don't refer to them as input neurons, but rather as input sources or input nodes. At the far right of the diagram, we have the output layer with the output neurons. We usually have as many output neurons as outputs that we are modeling. Thus, our neural network can naturally learn to predict more than one thing at a time. One exception to this rule is that when we are modeling a multiclass classification problem, we usually have one binary output neuron for every class. In this case, all the output neurons are a dummy encoding of a single multiclass factor output.

Between the input and output layers, we have the hidden layers. Neurons are organized into layers depending on how many neurons are between them and an input neuron. For example, neurons in the first hidden layer are directly connected to at least one neuron in the input layer, whereas neurons in the second hidden layer are directly connected to one or more neurons in the first hidden layer. Our diagram is an example of a 4-4 architecture, which means that there are two hidden layers with four neurons each. Even though they are not neurons themselves, the diagram explicitly shows the bias units for all the neurons. We saw in our equation for the output of a single neuron that we can treat the bias unit as a dummy input feature with a value of 1 that has a weight on it that corresponds to the bias or threshold.

Not all the neurons in the architecture are assumed to have the same activation function. In general, we pick the activation function for the neurons in the hidden layers separately from that of the output layer. The activation function for the output layer we've already seen is chosen based on what type of output we would like, which in turn depends on whether we are performing regression or classification.

The activation function for the hidden layer neurons is generally nonlinear, because chaining together linear neurons can be algebraically simplified to a single linear neuron with different weights and so this does not add any power to the network. The most common activation function is the logistic function, but others such as the hyperbolic tangent function are also used.

The output of the neural network can be calculated by successively computing the outputs of the neurons of each layer. The output of the units of the first hidden layer can be computed using the equations for the output of a neuron that we have seen thus far. These outputs become inputs to the neurons of the second hidden layer and thus, are effectively the new features with respect to that layer.

One of the strengths of neural networks is this power to learn new features through the learning of weights in the hidden layers. This process repeats for every layer in the neural network until the final layer, where we obtain the output of the neural network as a whole. This process of propagating the signals from the input to the output layer is known as **forward propagation**.

Training multilayer perceptron networks

Multilayer perceptron networks are more complicated to train than a single perceptron. The famous algorithm used to train them — that has been around since the 1980s — is known as the **backpropagation algorithm**. We'll give a sketch of how this algorithm works here, but the reader interested in neural networks is strongly encouraged to read up on this algorithm in more depth.

There are two very important insights to understand about this algorithm. The first is that for every observation, it proceeds in two steps. The forward propagation step begins at the input layer and ends at the output layer, and computes the predicted output of the network for this observation. This is relatively straightforward to do using the equation for the output of each neuron, which is just the application of its activation function on the linear weighted sum of its inputs.

The backward propagation step is designed to modify the weights of the network when the predicted output does not match the desired output. This step begins at the output layer, computing the error on the output nodes and the necessary updates to the weights of the output neurons. Then, it moves backwards through the network, updating the weights of each hidden layer in reverse until it reaches the first hidden layer, which is processed last. Thus, there is a forward pass through the network, followed by a backward pass.

The second important insight to understand is that updating the weights of the neurons in the hidden layer is substantially trickier than updating the weights in the output layer. To see this, consider that when we want to update the weights of neurons in the output layer, we know precisely what the desired output for that neuron should be for a given input. This is because the desired outputs of the output neurons are the outputs of the network itself, which are available to us in our training data. By contrast, at first glance, we don't actually know what the right output of a neuron in a hidden layer should be for a particular input. Additionally, this output is distributed to all the neurons of the next layer in the network and hence impacts all of their outputs as well.

The key insight here is that we propagate the error made in the output neurons back to the neurons in the hidden layers. We do this by finding the gradient of the cost function to adjust the weights of the neurons in the direction of the greatest error reduction and apply the chain rule of differentiation to express this gradient in terms of the output of the individual neuron we are interested in. This process results in a general formula for updating the weights of any neuron in the network, known as the **delta update rule**:

$$w_{ji}^{(n)} \leftarrow w_{ji}^{(n)} + \eta \cdot \delta_j^{(n)} \cdot y_i^{(n)}$$

Let's understand this equation by assuming that we are currently processing the weights for all the neurons in layer l. This equation tells us how to update the weight between the jth neuron in layer l and the ith neuron in the layer before it (layer l-1). The (n) superscripts all denote the fact that we are currently updating the weight as a result of processing the nth observation in our data set. We will drop these from now on, and assume they are implied.

In a nutshell, the delta rule tells us that to obtain the new value of the neuron weight, we must add a product of three terms to the old value. The first of these terms is the learning rate η. The second is known as the local gradient, δ_j, and is the product of the error, e_j, of neuron j and the gradient of its activation function, $g()$:

$$\delta_j = e_j \cdot g'(z_j)$$

Here, we denote the output of neuron j before applying its activation function by z_j, so that the following relation holds:

$$y_j = g(z_j)$$

It turns out that the local gradient is also the gradient of the cost function of the network computed with respect to z_j. Finally, the third term in the delta update rule is the input to neuron j from neuron i, which is just the output of neuron i, y_i. The only term that differs between output layer neurons and hidden layer neurons is the local gradient term. We'll see an illustrative example for neural networks that perform classification using logistic neurons throughout. When neuron j is an output neuron, the local gradient is given by:

$$\delta_j = \left(t_j - y_j\right) \cdot y_j \cdot \left(1 - y_j\right)$$

The first term in brackets is just the known error of the output neuron, this being the difference between the target output, t_j, and the actual output, y_j. The other two terms arise from the differentiation of the logistic activation function. When neuron j is a hidden layer neuron, the gradient of the logistic activation function is the same, but the error term is computed as the weighted sum of the local gradients of the k neurons in the next layer that receive input from neuron j:

$$\delta_j = \left(\sum_k \delta_k \cdot w_{kj}\right) \cdot y_j \cdot \left(1 - y_j\right)$$

Predicting the energy efficiency of buildings

In this section, we will investigate how neural networks can be used to solve a real-world regression problem. Once again, we turn to the UCI Machine Learning Repository for our data set. We've chosen to try out the *energy efficiency data set* available at `http://archive.ics.uci.edu/ml/datasets/Energy+efficiency`. The prediction task is to use various building characteristics, such as surface area and roof area, in order to predict the energy efficiency of a building, which is expressed in the form of two different metrics—heating load and cooling load.

This is a good example for us to try out as we can demonstrate how neural networks can be used to predict two different outputs with a single network. The full attribute description of the data set is given in the following table:

Column name	Type	Definition
relCompactness	Numerical	Relative compactness
surfArea	Numerical	Surface area
wallArea	Numerical	Wall area
roofArea	Numerical	Roof area
height	Numerical	Overall height
orientation	Numerical	Building orientation (factor)
glazArea	Numerical	Glazing area
glazAreaDist	Numerical	Glazing area distribution (factor)
heatLoad	Numerical	Heating load (first output)
coolLoad	Numerical	Cooling load (second output)

The data was generated using a simulator called *Ecotect*. Each observation in the data set corresponds to a simulated building. All the buildings have the same volume, but other attributes that impact their energy efficiency, such as their glazing area, are modified.

This data set is described in the paper *Accurate quantitative estimation of energy performance of residential buildings using statistical machine learning tools*, Athanasios Tsanas and *Angeliki Xifara*, published in *Energy and Buildings*, Vol. 49, in 2012.

The data on the website comes in Microsoft Excel format. To load this into R, we can use the R package xlsx, which can read and understand Microsoft Excel files:

```
> library(xlsx)
> eneff <- read.xlsx2("ENB2012_data.xlsx", sheetIndex = 1,
                      colClasses = rep("numeric", 10))
> names(eneff) <- c("relCompactness", "surfArea", "wallArea",
  "roofArea", "height", "orientation", "glazArea",
  "glazAreaDist", "heatLoad", "coolLoad")
> eneff <- eneff[complete.cases(eneff),]
```

The import adds a number of empty observations at the end of the data frame, so the last line removes these. Now, by referring to the paper in which the data set was presented, we discover that two of our attributes are actually factors. In order for our neural network to work with these, we will need to convert them into dummy variables. To do this, we will use the dummyVars() function from the caret package:

```
> library(caret)
> eneff$orientation <- factor(eneff$orientation)
> eneff$glazAreaDist <- factor(eneff$glazAreaDist)
> dummies <- dummyVars(heatLoad + coolLoad ~ ., data = eneff)
> eneff_data <- cbind(as.data.frame(predict(dummies, newdata =
                                    eneff)), eneff[,9:10])
> dim(eneff_data)
[1] 768  18
```

The dummyVars() function takes in a formula and a data frame. From these, it identifies the input features and performs dummy encoding on those that are factors in order to produce new binary columns. There are as many columns created for a factor as there are levels in that factor. Just as with the preProcess() function that we've been using, we actually obtain the columns themselves after using the predict() function. Next, we'll do an 80-20 split between the training and test data:

```
> set.seed(474576)
> eneff_sampling_vector <- createDataPartition(eneff_data$heatLoad, p
  = 0.80, list = FALSE)
> eneff_train <- eneff_data[eneff_sampling_vector, 1:16]
> eneff_train_outputs <- eneff_data[eneff_sampling_vector, 17:18]
> eneff_test <- eneff_data[-eneff_sampling_vector, 1:16]
> eneff_test_outputs <- eneff_data[-eneff_sampling_vector, 17:18]
```

One of the most important preprocessing steps to perform when training neural networks is to scale input features and outputs. One good reason to perform input scaling is in order to avoid **saturation** which occurs when the optimization procedure reaches a point where the gradient of the error function is very small in absolute value. This is usually the result of very large or very small inputs to the nonlinear neuron activation functions. Saturation causes the optimization procedure to terminate, thinking we have converged.

Depending on the particular neural network implementation, for regression tasks it may also make sense to scale the outputs as some implementations of linear neurons are designed to produce an output in the interval [-1,1]. Scaling can also help convergence. Consequently, we will use `caret` to scale all our data dimensions to the unit interval, noting that this has no effect on the binary columns produced earlier:

```
> eneff_pp <- preProcess(eneff_train, method = c("range"))
> eneff_train_pp <- predict(eneff_pp, eneff_train)
> eneff_test_pp <- predict(eneff_pp, eneff_test)

> eneff_train_out_pp <- preProcess(eneff_train_outputs, method =
                        c("range"))
> eneff_train_outputs_pp <-
  predict(eneff_train_out_pp, eneff_train_outputs)
> eneff_test_outputs_pp <-
  predict(eneff_train_out_pp, eneff_test_outputs)
```

Several different packages implement neural networks in R, each with their various merits and strengths. For this reason, it helps to be familiar with more than one package and in this chapter we will investigate three of these, the first being `neuralnet`:

```
> library("neuralnet")
> n <- names(eneff_data)
> f <- as.formula(paste("heatLoad + coolLoad ~", paste(n[!n %in%
                  c("heatLoad", "coolLoad")], collapse = " + ")))
> eneff_model <- neuralnet(f,
  data = cbind(eneff_train_pp, eneff_train_outputs_pp), hidden = 10)
> eneff_model
Call: neuralnet(formula = f, data = cbind(eneff_train_pp, eneff_train_
outputs_pp),     hidden = 10)

1 repetition was calculated.

        Error Reached Threshold Steps
1 0.3339635783    0.009307995429  9998
```

The `neuralnet()` function trains a neural network based on the information provided in its arguments. The first argument we provide is a formula and the format is similar to the formulae that we've seen with the `lm()` and `glm()` functions in previous chapters. One interesting difference here is that we have specified two outputs, `heatLoad` and `coolLoad`. Another difference is that currently we are unable to use the dot (.) notation to imply that all the remaining columns in our data frame can be used as features, so we need to specify them explicitly.

Note that with the formula, we have effectively defined the input and output layers of the neural network and so what remains to be specified is the structure of the hidden layers. This is specified with the `hidden` parameter, which either takes in a scalar for a single layer, or a vector of scalars that specify the number of hidden units in each layer, starting from the layer just after the input layer, and ending with the layer just before the output layer.

In the example we saw earlier, we've used a single layer with 10 nodes. We can actually visualize our neural network as the package provides us with the ability to plot the model directly (the numbered circles are dummy bias neurons):

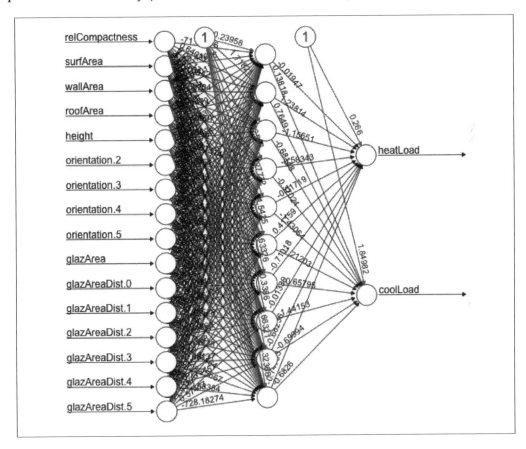

The call to `neuralnet()` also allows us to specify what type of activation function we would like to use for our neurons through the parameter string `act.fct`. By default, this is set to the logistic activation function and so we have not changed this. Another very important parameter is `linear.output`, which can be either TRUE or FALSE. This specifies whether we should apply the activation function to the neurons in the output layer. The default value of TRUE that we used means that we do not apply the activation function and so we can observe a linear output. For regression type problems, this is what is appropriate. This is because, if we were to apply a logistic activation function our output would be bounded in the interval [0,1]. Finally, we can specify a differentiable error function through the `err.fct` parameter to use as part of our optimization strategy. As we are doing regression, we use the default value of `sse`, which corresponds to the sum of squared error.

As there is a random component in neural network training, namely the initialization of the weights, we may want to specify that we should retrain the same model a number of times in order for us to pick the best possible model that we get (using criteria such as the SSE to rank these). This can be done by specifying an integer value for the `rep` parameter. Let's rewrite our original call to explicitly show the default values we are using:

```
> eneff_model <- neuralnet(f,
  data = cbind(eneff_train_pp, eneff_train_outputs_pp), hidden =
  10, act.fct = "logistic", linear.output = TRUE, err.fct =
  "sse", rep = 1)
```

The model's output provides us with some information about the performance of the neural network and what is shown depends on its configuration. As we have specified the SSE as our error metric, the error shown is the SSE that was obtained. The threshold figure is just the value of the partial derivative of the error function when the model stopped training. Essentially, instead of terminating when the gradient is 0 exactly, we specify a very small value below which the error gradient needs to fall before the algorithm terminates. The default value for this is 0.01 and can be changed by supplying a number for the threshold parameter in the `neuralnet()` function. Reducing this value will generally result in longer training times. The model output also shows us the number of training steps that were performed. Finally, if we had used the `rep` parameter to repeat this process multiple times, we would see a row for each model trained. Our output shows us that we trained only one model.

As the neural network contains a random component in the form of the initialization of weight vectors, reproducing our code will likely not give the exact same results. If, when running the examples, R outputs a message that the model has not converged, try running the code again.

Evaluating multilayer perceptrons for regression

The package `neuralnet` provides us with a neat way to use our model to perform predictions through the `compute()` function. Essentially, it provides us with not only the predicted output for a data frame of observations, but also shows us the output values of all the neurons in the model's architecture. To evaluate the performance of the model, we are interested in the outputs of the neural network on our test set:

```
> test_predictions <- compute(eneff_model, eneff_test_pp)
```

We can access the predicted outputs of the neural network using the `net.result` attribute of the `test_predictions` object as follows:

```
> head(test_predictions$net.result)
           [,1]            [,2]
7   0.38996108769 0.39770348145
8   0.38508402576 0.46726904682
14  0.29555228848 0.24157156896
21  0.49912349400 0.51244876337
23  0.50036257800 0.47436990729
29  0.01133684342 0.01815294595
```

As this is a regression problem, we would like to be able to use the MSE in order to evaluate the performance of our model on both target outputs. In order to do that, we need to transform our predicted outputs back onto their original scale for a fair assessment to be made. The scaling constants we used on our data are stored in the `ranges` attribute of the `eneff_train_out_pp` object:

```
> eneff_train_out_pp$ranges
      heatLoad coolLoad
[1,]      6.01    10.90
[2,]     42.96    48.03
```

The first row contains the minimum values of the original data, and the second row contains the maximum values. We'll now write a function that will take in a scaled vector and another vector that contains the original minimum and maximum values, and will return the original unscaled vector:

```
reverse_range_scale <- function(v, ranges) {
    return( (ranges[2] - ranges[1]) * v + ranges[1] )
}
```

Next, we'll use this to obtain the unscaled predicted outputs for our test set:

```
> output_ranges <- eneff_train_out_pp$ranges
> test_predictions_unscaled <- sapply(1:2, function(x)
  reverse_range_scale(test_predictions[,x], output_ranges[,x]))
```

We can also define a simple function to compute the MSE and use it to check the performance on our two tasks:

```
mse <- function(y_p, y) {
   return(mean((y - y_p) ^ 2))
}

> mse(test_predictions_unscaled[,1], eneff_test_outputs[,1])
[1] 0.2940468477
> mse(test_predictions_unscaled[,2], eneff_test_outputs[,2])
[1] 1.440127075
```

These values are very low, indicating that we have very good prediction accuracy. We can also investigate correlation, which is scale independent, and we could have used it on the unscaled outputs as well:

```
> cor(test_predictions_unscaled[,1], eneff_test_outputs[,1])
[1] 0.9986655316
> cor(test_predictions_unscaled[,2], eneff_test_outputs[,2])
[1] 0.9926735348
```

These values are extremely high, indicating that we have near-perfect performance, something very rare to see with real-world data. If the accuracy were not this high, we would experiment by making the architecture more complicated. We could, for example, build a model with an additional layer by setting `hidden=c(10,5)` so that we would have an additional layer of five neurons before the output layer.

Predicting glass type revisited

In *Chapter 3, Logistic Regression*, we analyzed the glass identification data set, whose task is to identify the type of glass comprising a glass fragment found at a crime scene. The output of this data set is a factor with several class levels corresponding to different types of glass. Our previous approach was to build a one-versus-all model using multinomial logistic regression. The results were not very promising, and one of the main points of concern was a poor model fit on the training data.

In this section, we will revisit this data set and see whether a neural network model can do better. At the same time, we will demonstrate how neural networks can handle classification problems as well:

```
> glass <- read.csv("glass.data", header = FALSE)
> names(glass) <- c("id", "RI", "Na", "Mg", "Al", "Si", "K", "Ca",
                    "Ba", "Fe", "Type")
> glass$id <- NULL
```

Our output is a multiclass factor and so we will want to dummy-encode this into binary columns. With the `neuralnet` package, we would normally need to do this manually as a preprocessing step before we can build our model.

In this section, we will look at a second package that contains functions for building neural networks, `nnet`. This is actually the same package that we used for multinomial logistic regression. One of the benefits of this package is that for multiclass classification, the `nnet()` function that trains the neural network will automatically detect outputs that are factors and perform the dummy encoding for us. With that in mind, we will prepare a training and test set:

```
> glass$Type <- factor(glass$Type)
> set.seed(4365677)
> glass_sampling_vector <- createDataPartition(glass$Type, p =
                            0.80, list = FALSE)
> glass_train <- glass[glass_sampling_vector,]
> glass_test <- glass[-glass_sampling_vector,]
```

Next, just as with our previous data set, we will normalize our input data:

```
> glass_pp <- preProcess(glass_train[1:9], method = c("range"))
> glass_train <- cbind(predict(glass_pp, glass_train[1:9]),
  Type = glass_train$Type)
> glass_test  <- cbind(predict(glass_pp, glass_test[1:9]),
  Type = glass_test$Type)
```

We are now ready to train our model. Whereas the neuralnet package is able to model multiple hidden layers, the nnet package is designed to model neural networks with a single hidden layer. As a result, we still specify a formula as before, but this time, instead of a hidden parameter that can be either a scalar or a vector of integers, we specify a size parameter that is an integer representing the number of nodes in the single hidden layer of our model.

Also, the default neural network model in the nnet package is for classification, as the output layer uses a logistic activation function. It is really important when working with different packages for training the same type of model, such as multilayer perceptrons, to check the default values for the various model parameters, as these will be different from package to package. One other difference between the two packages that we will mention here is that nnet currently does not offer any plotting capabilities. Without further ado, we will now train our model:

```
> glass_model <- nnet(Type ~ ., data = glass_train, size = 10)
# weights:  166
initial  value 343.685179
iter  10 value 265.604188
iter  20 value 220.518320
iter  30 value 194.637078
iter  40 value 192.980203
iter  50 value 192.569751
iter  60 value 192.445198
iter  70 value 192.421655
iter  80 value 192.415382
iter  90 value 192.415166
iter 100 value 192.414794
final  value 192.414794
stopped after 100 iterations
```

From the output, we can see that the model has not converged, stopping after the default value of 100 iterations. To converge, we can either rerun this code a number of times or we can increase the number of allowed iterations to 1,000 using the maxit parameter:

```
> glass_model <- nnet(Type ~ ., data = glass_train, size = 10, maxit =
    1000)
```

Let's first investigate the accuracy of our model on the training data in order to assess the quality of fit. To compute predictions, we use the `predict()` function and specify the type parameter to be `class`. This lets the `predict()` function know that we want the class with highest probability to be selected. If we want to see the probabilities of each class, we can specify the value `response` for the `type` parameter. Finally, remember that we must pass in a data frame without the outputs to the `predict()` function, and thus the need to subset the training data frame:

```
> train_predictions <- predict(glass_model, glass_train[,1:9],
                               type = "class")
> mean(train_predictions == glass_train$Type)
[1]  0.7183908046
```

Our first attempt shows us that we are getting the same quality of fit as with our multinomial logistic regression model. To improve upon this, we'll increase the complexity of the model by adding more neurons in our hidden layer. We will also increase our `maxit` parameter to `10,000` as the model is more complex and might need more iterations to converge:

```
> glass_model2 <- nnet(Type ~ ., data = glass_train, size = 50, maxit =
                       10000)
> train_predictions2 <- predict(glass_model2, glass_train[,1:9],
                                type = "class")
> mean(train_predictions2 == glass_train$Type)
[1]  1
```

As we can see, we have now achieved 100 percent training accuracy. Now that we have a decent model fit, we can investigate our performance on the test set:

```
> test_predictions2 <- predict(glass_model2, glass_test[,1:9],
                               type = "class")
> mean(test_predictions2 == glass_test$Type)
[1]  0.6
```

Even though our model fits the training data perfectly, we see that the accuracy on the test set is only 60 percent. Even factoring in that the data set is very small, this discrepancy is a classic signal that our model is overfitting on the training data. When we looked at linear and logistic regression, we saw that there are shrinkage methods, such as the lasso, which are designed to combat overfitting by restricting the size of the coefficients in the model.

An analogous technique known as **weight decay** exists for neural networks. With this approach, the product of a decay constant and the sum of the squares of all the network weights is added to the cost function. This limits any weights from taking overly large values and thus performs regularization on the network. Whereas there is currently no option for regularization with `neuralnet()`, `nnet()` uses the `decay` parameter:

```
> glass_model3 <- nnet(Type~., data = glass_train, size = 10, maxit =
                       10000, decay = 0.01)
> train_predictions3 <- predict(glass_model3, glass_train[,1:9],
                               type = "class")
> mean(train_predictions3 == glass_train$Type)
[1] 0.9367816092
> test_predictions3 <- predict(glass_model3, glass_test[,1:9],
                              type = "class")
> mean(test_predictions3 == glass_test$Type)
[1] 0.775
```

With this model, the fit on our training data is still very high, and substantially higher than we achieved with multinomial logistic regression. On the test set, the performance is still worse than on the training set, but much better than we had before.

We won't spend any more time on the glass identification data. Instead, we will reflect on a few lessons learned before moving on. The first of these is that achieving good performance with a neural network, and sometimes even just reaching convergence, might be tricky. Training the model involves a random initialization of network weights and the final result is often quite sensitive to these starting conditions. We can convince ourselves of this fact by training the different model configurations we have seen so far a number of times and noticing that certain configurations on some runs might not converge, and the performance on our training and test set does tend to differ from one run to the next.

Another insight is that training a neural network involves tuning a diverse range of parameters, from the number and arrangement of hidden neurons to the value of the `decay` parameter. Others that we did not experiment with include the choice of nonlinear activation function to use with the hidden layer neurons, the criteria for convergence, and the particular cost function we use to fit our model. For example, instead of using least squares, we could use a criterion known as **entropy**.

Before settling on a final choice of model, therefore, it pays to try out as many different combinations of these as possible. A good place to experiment with different parameter combinations is the train() function of the caret package. It provides a unified interface for both neural network packages we have seen and, in conjunction with expand.grid(), allows the simultaneous training and evaluation of several different neural network configurations. We'll provide just a vignette here, and the interested reader can use this to continue their investigation further:

```
> library(caret)
> nnet_grid <- expand.grid(.decay = c(0.1, 0.01, 0.001, 0.0001),
                           .size = c(50, 100, 150, 200, 250))
> nnetfit <- train(Type ~ ., data = glass_train, method = "nnet",
  maxit = 10000, tuneGrid = nnet_grid, trace = F, MaxNWts = 10000)
```

Predicting handwritten digits

Our final application for neural networks will be the handwritten digit prediction task. In this task, the goal is to build a model that will be presented with an image of a numerical digit (0–9) and the model must predict which digit is being shown. We will use the *MNIST* database of handwritten digits from http://yann.lecun.com/exdb/mnist/.

From this page, we have downloaded and unzipped the two training files train-images-idx3-ubyte.gz and train-images-idx3-ubyte.gz. The former contains the data from the images and the latter contains the corresponding digit labels. The advantage of using this website is that the data has already been preprocessed by centering each digit in the image and scaling the digits to a uniform size. To load the data, we've used information from the website about the IDX format to write two functions:

```
read_idx_image_data <- function(image_file_path) {
  con <- file(image_file_path, "rb")
  magic_number <- readBin(con, what = "integer", n = 1, size = 4,
                          endian = "big")
  n_images <- readBin(con, what = "integer", n = 1, size = 4,
                      endian="big")
  n_rows <- readBin(con, what = "integer", n = 1, size = 4,
                    endian = "big")
  n_cols <- readBin(con, what = "integer", n = 1, size = 4,
                    endian = "big")
  n_pixels <- n_images * n_rows * n_cols
  pixels <- readBin(con, what = "integer", n = n_pixels, size = 1,
                    signed = F)
```

```
    image_data <- matrix(pixels, nrow = n_images, ncol = n_rows *
                         n_cols, byrow = T)
    close(con)
    return(image_data)
}

read_idx_label_data <- function(label_file_path) {
    con <- file(label_file_path, "rb")
    magic_number <- readBin(con, what = "integer", n = 1, size = 4,
                            endian = "big")
    n_labels <- readBin(con, what = "integer", n = 1, size = 4,
                        endian = "big")
    label_data <- readBin(con, what = "integer", n = n_labels, size = 1,
                          signed = F)
    close(con)
    return(label_data)
}
```

We can then load our two data files by issuing the following two commands:

```
> mnist_train <- read_idx_image_data("train-images-idx3-ubyte")
> mnist_train_labels <- read_idx_label_data("train-labels-idx1-
                                             ubyte")
> str(mnist_train)
 int [1:60000, 1:784] 0 0 0 0 0 0 0 0 0 0 ...
> str(mnist_train_labels)
 int [1:60000] 5 0 4 1 9 2 1 3 1 4 ...
```

Each image is represented by a 28-pixel by 28-pixel matrix of grayscale values in the range 0 to 255, where 0 is white and 255 is black. Thus, our observations each have $28^2 = 784$ feature values. Each image is stored as a vector by rasterizing the matrix from right to left and top to bottom. There are 60,000 images in the training data, and our mnist_train object stores these as a matrix of 60,000 rows by 78 columns so that each row corresponds to a single image. To get an idea of what our data looks like, we can visualize the first seven images:

To analyze this data set, we will introduce our third and final R package for training neural network models, RSNNS. This package is actually an R wrapper around the **Stuttgart Neural Network Simulator** (**SNNS**), a popular software package containing standard implementations of neural networks in C created at the University of Stuttgart.

The package authors have added a convenient interface for the many functions in the original software. One of the benefits of using this package is that it provides several of its own functions for data processing, such as splitting the data into a training and test set. Another is that it implements many different types of neural networks, not just MLPs. We will begin by normalizing our data to the unit interval by dividing by 255 and then indicating that our output is a factor with each level corresponding to a digit:

```
> mnist_input <- mnist_train / 255
> mnist_output <- as.factor(mnist_train_labels)
```

Although the MNIST website already contains separate files with test data, we have chosen to split the training data file as the models already take quite a while to run. The reader is encouraged to repeat the analysis that follows with the supplied test files as well. To prepare the data for splitting, we will randomly shuffle our images in the training data:

```
> set.seed(252)
> mnist_index <- sample(1:nrow(mnist_input), nrow(mnist_input))
> mnist_data <- mnist_input[mnist_index, 1:ncol(mnist_input)]
> mnist_out_shuffled <- mnist_output[mnist_index]
```

Next, we must dummy-encode our output factor as this is not done automatically for us. The decodeClassLabels() function from the RSNNS package is a convenient way to do this. Additionally, we will split our shuffled data into an 80–20 training and test set split using splitForTrainingAndTest(). This will store the features and labels for the training and test sets separately, which will be useful for us shortly.

Finally, we can also normalize our data using the normTrainingAndTestSet() function. To specify unit interval normalization, we must set the type parameter to 0_1:

```
> library("RSNNS")
> mnist_out <- decodeClassLabels(mnist_out_shuffled)
> mnist_split <- splitForTrainingAndTest(mnist_data, mnist_out,
                                          ratio = 0.2)
> mnist_norm <- normTrainingAndTestSet(mnist_split, type = "0_1")
```

For comparison, we will train two MLP networks using the mlp() function. By default, this is configured for classification and uses the logistic function as the activation function for hidden layer neurons. The first model will have a single hidden layer with 100 neurons; the second model will use 300.

The first argument to the `mlp()` function is the matrix of input features and the second is the vector of labels. The `size` parameter plays the same role as the `hidden` parameter in the `neuralnet` package. That is to say, we can specify a single integer for a single hidden layer, or a vector of integers specifying the number of hidden neurons per layer when we want more than one hidden layer.

Next, we can use the `inputsTest` and `targetsTest` parameters to specify the features and labels of our test set beforehand, so that we can be ready to observe the performance on our test set in one call. The models we will train will take several hours to run. If we want to know how long each model took to run, we can save the current time using `proc.time()` before training a model and comparing it against the time when the model completes. Putting all this together, here is how we trained our two MLP models:

```
> start_time <- proc.time()
> mnist_mlp <- mlp(mnist_norm$inputsTrain,
  mnist_norm$targetsTrain, size = 100, inputsTest =
  mnist_norm$inputsTest, targetsTest = mnist_norm$targetsTest)
> proc.time() - start_time
   user   system  elapsed
2923.936   5.470 2927.415


> start_time <- proc.time()
> mnist_mlp2 <- mlp(mnist_norm$inputsTrain,
  mnist_norm$targetsTrain, size = 300, inputsTest =
  mnist_norm$inputsTest, targetsTest = mnist_norm$targetsTest)
> proc.time() - start_time
   user   system  elapsed
7141.687   7.488 7144.433
```

As we can see, the models take quite a long time to run (the values are in seconds). For reference, these were trained on a 2.5 GHz Intel Core i7 Apple MacBook Pro with 16 GB of memory. The model predictions on our test set are saved in the `fittedTestValues` attribute (and for our training set, they are stored in the `fitted.values` attribute). We will focus on test set accuracy. First, we must decode the dummy-encoded network outputs by selecting the binary column with the maximum value. We must also do this for the target outputs. Note that the first column corresponds to the digit 0.

```
> mnist_class_test <-
  (0:9)[apply(mnist_norm$targetsTest, 1, which.max)]
> mlp_class_test <-
  (0:9)[apply(mnist_mlp$fittedTestValues, 1, which.max)]
> mlp2_class_test <-
  (0:9)[apply(mnist_mlp2$fittedTestValues, 1, which.max)]
```

Now we can check the accuracy of our two models, as follows:

```
> mean(mnist_class_test == mlp_class_test)
[1] 0.974
> mean(mnist_class_test == mlp2_class_test)
[1] 0.981
```

The accuracy is very high for both models, with the second model slightly outperforming the first. We can use the confusionMatrix() function to see the errors made in detail:

```
> confusionMatrix(mnist_class_test, mlp2_class_test)
         predictions
targets    0    1    2    3    4    5    6    7    8    9
      0 1226    0    0    1    1    0    1    1    3    1
      1    0 1330    5    3    0    0    0    3    0    1
      2    3    0 1135    3    2    1    1    5    3    0
      3    0    0    6 1173    0   11    1    5    6    1
      4    0    5    0    0 1143    1    5    5    0   10
      5    2    2    1   12    2 1077    7    3    5    4
      6    3    0    2    1    1    3 1187    0    1    0
      7    0    0    7    1    3    1    0 1227    1    4
      8    5    4    3    5    1    4    4    0 1110    5
      9    1    0    0    6    8    5    0   11    6 1164
```

As expected, we see quite a bit of symmetry in this matrix because certain pairs of digits are often harder to distinguish than others. For example, the most common pair of digits that the model confuses is the pair (3,5). The test data available on the website contains some examples of digits that are harder to distinguish from others.

By default, the mlp() function allows for a maximum of 100 iterations, via its maxint parameter. Often, we don't know the number of iterations we should run for a particular model; a good way to determine this is to plot the training and testing error rates versus iteration number. With the RSNNS package, we can do this with the plotIterativeError() function.

The following graphs show that for our two models, both errors plateau after 30 iterations:

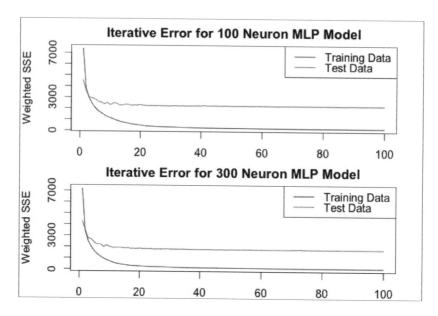

Receiver operating characteristic curves

In *Chapter 3*, *Logistic Regression*, we studied the precision-recall graph as an example of an important graph showing the trade-off between two important performance metrics of a binary classifier—precision and recall. In this chapter, we will present another related and commonly used graph to show binary classification performance, the **receiver operating characteristic (ROC)** curve.

This curve is a plot of the true positive rate on the y axis and the false positive rate on the x axis. The true positive rate, as we know, is just the recall or, equivalently, the sensitivity of a binary classifier. The false positive rate is just 1 minus the specificity. A random binary classifier will have a true positive rate equal to the false positive rate and thus, on the ROC curve, the line $y = x$ is the line showing the performance of a random classifier. Any curve lying above this line will perform better than a random classifier.

A perfect classifier will exhibit a curve from the origin to the point (0,1), which corresponds to a 100 percent true positive rate and a 0 percent false positive rate. We often talk about the **ROC Area Under the Curve (ROC AUC)** as a performance metric. The area under the random classifier is just 0.5 as we are computing the area under the line $y = x$ on a unit square. By convention, the area under a perfect classifier is 1 as the curve passes through the point (0,1). In practice, we obtain values between these two. For our MNIST digit classifier, we have a multiclass problem, but we can use the `plotROC()` function of the RSNNS package to study the performance of our classifier on individual digits. The following plot shows the ROC curve for digit 1, which is almost perfect:

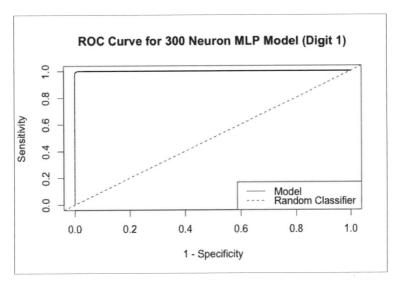

Summary

In this chapter, we saw neural networks as a nonlinear method capable of solving both regression and classification problems. Motivated by the biological analogy to human neurons, we first introduced the simplest neural network, the perceptron. This is able to solve binary classification problems only when the two classes are linearly separable, something that we very rarely rely upon in practice.

By changing the function that transforms the linear weighted combination of inputs, namely the activation function, we discovered how to create different types of individual neurons. A linear activation function creates a neuron that performs linear regression, whereas the logistic activation function creates a neuron that performs logistic regression. By organizing and connecting neurons into layers, we can create multilayer neural networks that are powerful models for solving nonlinear problems.

The idea behind having hidden layers of neurons is that each hidden layer learns a new set of features from its inputs. As the most common type of multilayer neural network, we introduced the multilayer perceptron and saw that it can naturally learn multiple outputs with the same network. In addition, we experimented on real-world data sets for both regression and classification tasks, including a multiclass classification problem that we saw is also handled naturally. R has a number of packages for implementing neural networks, including `neuralnet`, `nnet`, and `RSNNS`, and we experimented with each of these in turn. Each has its respective advantages and disadvantages and there isn't a clear winner for every circumstance.

An important benefit of working with neural networks is that they can be very powerful in solving highly complex nonlinear problems of regression and classification alike without making any significant assumptions about the relationships between the input features. On the other hand, neural networks can often be quite tricky to train. Scaling input features is important. It is also important to be aware of the various parameters affecting the convergence of the model, such as the learning rate and the error gradient tolerance. Another crucial decision to make is the number and distribution of hidden layer neurons. As the complexity of the network, the number of input features, or the size of the training data increases, the training time often becomes quite long compared to other supervised learning methods.

We also saw in our regression example that because of the flexibility and power of neural networks, they can be prone to overfitting the data, thus overestimating the model's accuracy. Regularization approaches, such as weight decay, exist to mitigate this problem to a certain extent. Finally, one clear disadvantage that deserves mention is that the neural weights have no direct interpretation, unlike regression coefficients, and even though the neural network topology may learn features, these are difficult to explain or interpret.

Our next chapter continues our foray into the world of supervised learning and presents support vector machines, our third nonlinear modeling tool, which is primarily used for dealing with classification problems.

5
Support Vector Machines

In this chapter, we are going to take a fresh look at nonlinear predictive models by introducing support vector machines. Support vector machines, often abbreviated as SVMs, are very commonly used for classification problems, although there are certainly ways to perform function approximation and regression tasks with them. In this chapter, we will focus on the more typical case of their role in classification. To do this, we'll first present the notion of maximal margin classification, which presents an alternative formulation of how to choose between many possible classification boundaries and differs from approaches such as maximum likelihood, which we have seen thus far. We'll introduce the related idea of support vectors and how, together with maximal margin classification, we can obtain a linear model in the form of a support vector classifier. Finally, we'll present how we can generalize these ideas in order to introduce nonlinearity through the use of certain functions known as kernels to finally arrive at our destination, the support vector machine.

Maximal margin classification

We'll begin this chapter by returning to a situation that should be very familiar by now: the binary classification task. Once again, we'll be thinking about the problem of how to design a model that will correctly predict whether an observation belongs to one of two possible classes. We've already seen that this task is simplest when the two classes are linearly separable, that is, when we can find a *separating hyperplane* (a plane in a multidimensional space) in the space of our features so that all the observations on one side of the hyperplane belong to one class and all the observations that lie on the other side belong to the second class. Depending on the structure, assumptions, and optimizing criterion that our particular model uses, we could end up with one of infinitely many such hyperplanes.

Let's visualize this scenario using some data in a two-dimensional feature space, where the separating hyperplane is just a separating line:

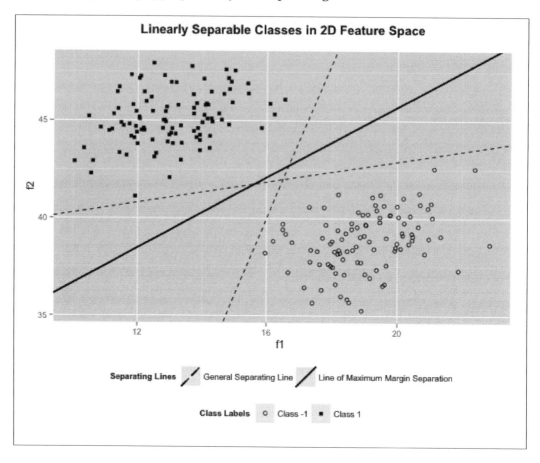

In the preceding diagram, we can see two clusters of observations, each of which belongs to a different class. We've used different symbols for the two classes to denote this explicitly. Next, we show three different lines that could serve as the decision boundary of a classifier, all of which would generate 100 percent classification accuracy on the entire data set. We'll remind ourselves that the equation of a hyperplane can be expressed as a linear combination of the input features, which are the dimensions of the space in which the hyperplane resides:

$$y = \beta_0 + \sum_{k=1}^{p} \beta_k x_k$$

A separating hyperplane has this property:

$$\beta_0 + \sum_{k=1}^{p} \beta_k x_{ik} > 0 \ \textit{if} \ y_i = 1$$

$$\beta_0 + \sum_{k=1}^{p} \beta_k x_{ik} < 0 \ \textit{if} \ y_i = -1$$

The first equation simply says that the data points that belong to class 1 all lie above the hyperplane, and the second equation says that the data points that belong to class -1 all lie below the hyperplane. The subscript i is used to index observations, and the subscript k is used to index features so that x_{ik} means the value of the kth feature in the ith observation. We can combine these two equations into a single equation for simplicity, as follows:

$$y_i \cdot \left(\beta_0 + \sum_{k=1}^{p} \beta_k x_{ik} \right) > 0, \forall i$$

To see why this simplification works, consider an observation of the class -1 ($y_i = -1$). This observation will lie below the separating hyperplane, so the linear combination in brackets will produce a negative value. Multiplying this with its y_i value of -1 results in a positive value. A similar argument works for observations of class 1.

Looking back at our diagram, note that the two dashed lines come quite close to certain observations. The solid line intuitively feels better than the other two lines as a decision boundary, as it separates the two classes without coming too close to either, by traversing the center of the space between them. In this way, it distributes the space between the two classes equally. We can define a quantity known as the **margin** that a particular separating hyperplane generates, as the smallest perpendicular distance from any point in the data set to the hyperplane. In two dimensions and two classes, we will always have at least two points that lie at a perpendicular distance equal to the margin from the separating line, one on each side of the line. Sometimes, as is the case with our data, we may have more than two points whose perpendicular distance from the separating line equals the margin.

The next plot shows the margin of the solid line from the previous plot, demonstrating that we have three points at a distance equal to the margin from this separating line:

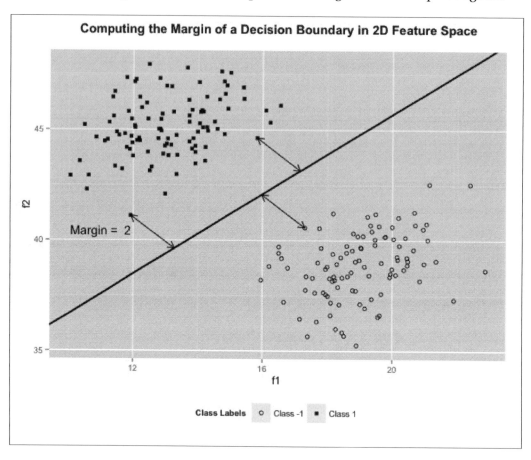

Now that we have the definition of the margin under our belt, we have a way to codify our intuition that led us to choose the solid line as the better decision boundary among the three lines that we saw in the first plot. We can go a step further and define the **maximal margin hyperplane** as the hyperplane whose margin is the largest amongst all possible separating hyperplanes. In our 2D example, we are essentially looking for the line that will separate the two classes while at the same time being as far away from the observations as possible. It turns out that the solid line from our example is actually the maximal margin line so that there is no other line that can be drawn with a higher margin than 2 units. This explains why we chose to label it as the line of maximum margin separation in our first plot.

In order to understand how we found the maximal margin hyperplane in our simple example, we need to formalize the problem as an optimization problem with p features using the following equations:

$$Select\ \beta_0, \beta_1 \ldots \beta_p\ that\ maximize\ M$$

$$such\ that : \sum_{k=1}^{p} \beta_k^2 = 1$$

$$and\ \forall i : y_i \cdot \left(\beta_0 + \sum_{k=1}^{p} \beta_k x_{ik} \right) \geq M$$

Together, these two constraints in our optimization problem express the idea that observations in our data need to not only be correctly classified, but also lie at least M units away from the separating hyperplane. The goal is to maximize this distance M by appropriately choosing the coefficients β_i. Thus, we need an optimization procedure that handles this type of problem. The details of how the optimization is actually implemented in practice are beyond the scope of this book, but we will see them in action later on when we do some programming with R.

We have a natural way forward now, which is to start looking at how the situation changes when our data is not linearly separable, something that we know by now is the typical scenario for a real-world data set. Let us take a step back before doing this. We've already studied two different methods for estimating the parameters of a model, namely maximum likelihood estimation and the least squared error criterion for linear regression. For example, when we looked at classification with logistic regression, we considered the idea of maximizing the likelihood of our data. This takes into account all of the available data points. This is also the case when classifying with multilayer perceptrons. With the maximum margin classifier, however, the construction of our decision boundary is only supported by the points that lie on the margin. Put differently, with the data in our 2D example, we can freely adjust the position of any observation except the three on the margin, and as long as the adjustment does not result in the observation falling inside the margin, our separating line will stay exactly in the same position. For this reason, we define the perpendicular vectors from the points that lie on the margin to the separating hyperplane as the **support vectors**. Thus, we've seen that our 2D example has three support vectors. The fact that only a subset of all the points in our data essentially determines the placement of the separating hyperplane means that we have the potential to overfit our training data.

On the other hand, this approach does yield a couple of nice properties. We split the space between the two classes equally between them without applying any bias toward either. Points that clearly lie well inside the area of space occupied by a particular class do not play such a big role in the model compared to points on the fringes, which is where we need to place our decision boundary.

Support vector classification

We need our data to be linearly separable in order to classify with a maximal margin classifier. When our data is not linearly separable, we can still use the notion of support vectors that define a margin, but this time, we will allow some examples to be misclassified. Thus, we essentially define a **soft margin** in that some of the observations in our data set can violate the constraint that they need to be at least as far as the margin from the separating hyperplane. It is also important to note that sometimes, we may want to use a soft margin even for linearly separable data. The reason for this is in order to limit the degree of overfitting the data. Note that the larger the margin, the more confident we are about our ability to correctly classify new observations, because the classes are further apart from each other in our training data. If we achieve separation using a very small margin, we are less confident about our ability to correctly classify our data and we may, instead, want to allow a few errors and come up with a larger margin that is more robust. Study the following plot:

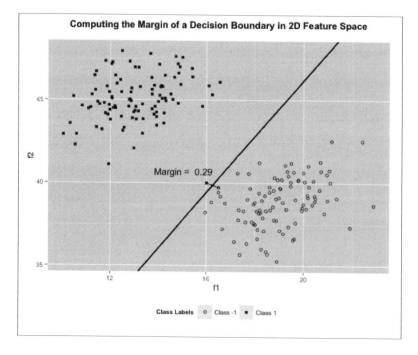

In order to get a firmer grasp of the reason why a soft margin may be preferable to a hard margin even for linearly separable data, we've changed our data slightly. We used the same data that we had previously, but we added an extra observation to class 1 and placed it close to the boundary of class -1. Note that with the addition of this single new data point, with feature values f_1=16 and f_2=40, our maximal margin line has moved drastically! The margin has been reduced from 2 units to 0.29 units. Looking at this graph, we are tempted to feel that the new point might either be an outlier or a mislabeling in our data set. If we were to allow our model to make one single misclassification using a soft margin, we would go back to our previous line, which separates the two classes with a much wider margin and is less likely to have overfit the data. We formalize the notion of our soft classifier by modifying our optimization problem setup.

$$Select\ \beta_0, \beta_1 \ldots \beta_p\ that\ maximize\ M$$

$$such\ that: \sum_{k=1}^{p} \beta_k^2 = 1$$

$$and\ \forall i: y_i \cdot \left(\beta_0 + \sum_{k=1}^{p} \beta_k x_{ik} \right) \geq M \left(1 - \xi_i \right)$$

$$and\ \forall i: \xi_i \geq 0, \sum_{i=1}^{n} \xi_i \leq C$$

Under this new setup, we've introduced a new set of variables ξ_i known as the **slack variables**. There is one slack variable for every observation in our data set and the value of the ξ_i slack variable depends on where the ith observation falls with respect to the margin. When an observation is on the correct side of the separating hyperplane and outside the margin, the slack variable for that observation takes the value 0. This is the ideal situation that we have seen for all observations under a hard boundary. When an observation is correctly classified but falls at a distance within the margin, the corresponding slack variable takes a small positive value less than 1. When an observation is actually misclassified, thus falling on the wrong side of the hyperplane altogether, then its associated slack variable takes a value greater than 1. In summary, take a look at the following:

$$\xi_i = 0, \qquad x_i\ is\ correctly\ classified, and\ outside\ the\ margin$$
$$0 < \xi_i \leq 1, \quad x_i\ is\ correctly\ classified, but\ falls\ inside\ the\ margin$$
$$\xi_i > 1 \qquad\quad x_i\ is\ incorrectly\ correctly\ classified$$

When an observation is incorrectly classified, the magnitude of the slack variables is proportional to the distance between that observation and the boundary of the separating hyperplane. The fact that the sum of the slack variables must be less than a constant C means that we can think of this constant as an error budget that we are prepared to tolerate. As a misclassification of a single particular observation results in a slack variable taking at least the value 1, and our constant C is the sum of all the slack variables, setting a value of C less than 1 means that our model will tolerate a few observations falling inside the margin but no misclassifications. A high value of C often results in many observations either falling inside the margin or being misclassified, and as these are all support vectors, we end up having a greater number of support vectors. This results in a model that has a lower variance, but because we have shifted our boundary in a way that has increased tolerance to margin violations and errors, we may have a higher bias. By contrast, depending on fewer support vectors caused by having a much stricter model and hence a lower value of C, may result in a lower bias in our model. These support vectors, however, will individually affect the position of our boundary to a much higher degree. Consequently, we will experience a higher variance in our model performance across different training sets. Once again, the interplay between model bias and variance resurfaces in the design decisions that we must make as predictive modelers.

Inner products

The exact details of how the parameters of the support vector classifier model are computed are beyond the scope of this book. However, it turns out that the model itself can be simplified into a more convenient form that uses the **inner products** of the observations. An inner product of two vectors, v_1 and v_2, of identical length is computed by first computing the element-wise multiplication of the two vectors and then taking the sum of the resulting elements. In R, we obtain an element-wise multiplication of two vectors by simply using the multiplication symbol, so we can compute the inner product of two vectors as follows:

```
> v1 <- c(1.2, 3.3, -5.6, 4.5, 0, 9.0)
> v2 <- c(-3.5, 0.1, -0.2, 1.0, -8.7, 0)
> v1 * v2
[1] -4.20  0.33  1.12  4.50  0.00  0.00
> inner_product <- sum(v1 * v2)
> inner_product
[1] 1.75
```

In mathematical terms, we use triangular brackets to denote the inner product operation, and we represent the process as follows:

$$\langle v_1, v_2 \rangle = \sum_{i=1}^{p} v_{1i} \cdot v_{2i}$$

In the preceding equation, for the two vectors v_1 and v_2, the index i is iterating over the p features or dimensions. Now, here is the original form of our support vector classifier:

$$y = \beta_0 + \sum_{i=1}^{p} \beta_k x_k$$

This is just the standard equation for a linear combination of the input features. It turns out that for the support vector classifier, the model's solution can be expressed in terms of the inner product between the x observation that we are trying to classify and all other x_i observations that are in our training data set. More concretely, the form of our support vector classifier can also be written as:

$$y(x) = \beta_0 + \sum_{i=1}^{n} \alpha_i \langle x, x_i \rangle$$

For this equation, we have explicitly indicated that our model predicts y as a function of an input observation x. The summing function now computes a weighted sum of all the inner products of the current observation with every other observation in the data set which is why we are now summing across the n observations. We want to make it very clear that we haven't changed anything in the original model itself; we have simply written two different representations of the same model. Note that we cannot assume that a linear model takes this form in general; this is only true for the support vector classifier. Now, in a real-world scenario, the number of observations in our data set, n, is typically much greater than the number of parameters, p, so the number of a coefficients is seemingly larger than the number of β coefficients. Additionally, whereas in the first equation we were considering observations independently of each other, the form of the second equation shows us that to classify all our observations, we need to consider all possible pairs and compute their inner product. There are $^nC_2$ such pairs, which is of the order of n^2. Thus, it would seem like we are introducing complexity rather than producing a representation that is simpler. It turns out, however, that all a coefficients are zero for all observations in our data set, except those that are support vectors.

The number of support vectors in our data set is typically much smaller than the total number of observations. Thus, we can simplify our new representation by explicitly showing that we sum over elements from the set of support vectors, S, in our data set.

$$y(x) = \beta_0 + \sum_{s \in S} \alpha_s \langle x, x_s \rangle$$

Kernels and support vector machines

So far, we've introduced the notion of maximum margin classification under linearly separable conditions and its extension to the support vector classifier, which still uses a hyperplane as the separating boundary but handles data sets that are not linearly separable by specifying a budget for tolerating errors. The observations that are on or within the margin, or are misclassified by the support vector classifier are support vectors. The critical role that these play in the positioning of the decision boundary was also seen in an alternative model representation of the support vector classifier that uses inner products.

What is common in the situations that we have seen so far in this chapter is that our model is always linear in terms of the input features. We've seen that the ability to create models that implement nonlinear boundaries between the classes to be separated is far more flexible in terms of the different kinds of underlying target functions that they can handle. One way to introduce nonlinearity in our model that uses our new representation involving inner products is to apply a nonlinear transformation to this result. We can define a general function K, which we'll call a **kernel function** that operates on two vectors and produces a scalar result. This allows us to generalize our model as follows:

$$y(x) = \beta_0 + \sum_{s \in S} \alpha_s K \langle x, x_s \rangle$$

Our model now has as many features as there are support vectors, and each feature is defined as the result of a kernel acting upon the current observation and one of the support vectors. For the support vector classifier, the kernel we applied is known as the **linear kernel** as this just uses the inner product itself, producing a linear model.

$$K_{linear}(x_i, x_j) = \sum_{k=1}^{p} x_{ik} x_{jk}$$

Kernel functions are also known as similarity functions as we can consider the output they produce as a measure of the similarity between the two input vectors provided. We introduce nonlinearity in our model using nonlinear kernels, and when we do this, our model is now known as a **support vector machine**. There are a number of different types of nonlinear kernels. The two most common ones are the **polynomial kernel** and the **radial basis function kernel**. The polynomial kernel uses a power expansion of the inner product between two vectors. For a polynomial of degree d, the form of the polynomial kernel is:

$$K_{polynomial}\left(x_i, x_j\right) = \left(1 + \sum_{k=1}^{p} x_{ik} x_{jk}\right)^d$$

Using this kernel, we are essentially transforming our feature space into a higher dimensional space. Computing the kernel applied to the inner product is much more efficient than first transforming all the features into a high-dimensional space and then trying to fit a linear model into that space. This is especially true when we use the **radial basis function kernel**, often referred to simply as the **radial kernel**, where the number of dimensions of the transformed feature space is actually infinite due to the infinite number of terms in the expansion. The form of the radial kernel is:

$$K_{radial}\left(x_i, x_j\right) = e^{-\frac{1}{2\sigma^2}\sum_{k=1}^{p}\left(x_{ik} - x_{jk}\right)^2}$$

Upon close inspection, we should be able to spot that the radial kernel does not use the inner product between two vectors. Instead, the summation in the exponent is just the square of the Euclidean distance between these two vectors. The radial kernel is often referred to as a **local kernel**, because when the Euclidean distance between the two input vectors is large, the resulting value that the kernel computes is very small because of the negative sign in the exponent. Consequently, when we use a radial kernel, only vectors close to the current observation for which we want to get a prediction play a significant role in the computation. We're now ready to put all this to practice with some real-world data sets.

Predicting chemical biodegration

In this section, we are going to use R's e1071 package to try out the models we've discussed on a real-world data set. As our first example, we have chosen the *QSAR biodegration data set*, which can be found at https://archive.ics.uci.edu/ml/datasets/QSAR+biodegradation#. This is a data set containing 41 numerical variables that describe the molecular composition and properties of 1055 chemicals. The modeling task is to predict whether a particular chemical will be biodegradable based on these properties. Example properties are the percentages of carbon, nitrogen, and oxygen atoms as well as the number of heavy atoms in the molecule. These features are highly specialized and sufficiently numerous, so a full listing won't be given here. The complete list and further details
of the quantities involved can be found on the website. For now, we've downloaded the data into a bdf data frame:

```
> bdf <- read.table("biodeg.csv", sep = ";", quote = "\"")
> head(bdf, n = 3)
      V1     V2 V3 V4 V5 V6 V7   V8 V9 V10 V11 V12    V13
1 3.919 2.6909  0  0  0  0  0 31.4  2   0   0   0 3.106
2 4.170 2.1144  0  0  0  0  0 30.8  1   1   0   0 2.461
3 3.932 3.2512  0  0  0  0  0 26.7  2   4   0   0 3.279
     V14    V15 V16    V17    V18 V19 V20 V21    V22 V23 V24
1 2.550  9.002   0 0.960 1.142   0   0   0 1.201   0   0
2 1.393  8.723   1 0.989 1.144   0   0   0 1.104   1   0
3 2.585  9.110   0 1.009 1.152   0   0   0 1.092   0   0
  V25 V26    V27    V28    V29 V30    V31 V32 V33 V34 V35
1   0   0 1.932  0.011   0   0 4.489   0   0   0   0
2   0   0 2.214 -0.204   0   0 1.542   0   0   0   0
3   0   0 1.942 -0.008   0   0 4.891   0   0   0   1
     V36    V37 V38    V39 V40 V41 V42
1 2.949 1.591   0 7.253   0   0  RB
2 3.315 1.967   0 7.257   0   0  RB
3 3.076 2.417   0 7.601   0   0  RB
```

The final column, V42, contains the output variable, which takes the value NRB for chemicals that are not biodegradable and RB for those that are. We'll recode this into the familiar labels of 0 and 1:

```
> levels(bdf$V42) <- c(0, 1)
```

Now that we have our data ready, we'll begin, as usual, by splitting them into training and testing sets, with an 80-20 split.

```
> library(caret)
> set.seed(23419002)
> bdf_sampling_vector <- createDataPartition(bdf$V42, p = 0.80,
                                             list = FALSE)
> bdf_train <- bdf[bdf_sampling_vector,]
> bdf_test <- bdf[-bdf_sampling_vector,]
```

There are a number of packages available in R that implement support vector machines. In this chapter, we'll explore the use of the `e1071` package, which provides us with the `svm()` function. If we examine our training data, we'll quickly notice that on the one hand, the scales of the various features are quite different, and on the other hand, many features are sparse features, which means that for many entries they take a zero value. It is a good idea to scale features as we did with neural networks, especially if we want to work with radial kernels. Fortunately for us, the `svm()` function has a `scale` parameter, which is set to TRUE by default. This normalizes the input features so that they have zero mean and unit variance before the model is trained. This circumvents the need for us to manually carry out this preprocessing step. The first model that we will investigate will use a linear kernel:

```
> library(e1071)
> model_lin <- svm(V42 ~ ., data = bdf_train, kernel = "linear", cost
  = 10)
```

The call to the `svm()` function follows the familiar paradigm of first providing a formula, then providing the name of the data frame, and finally, other parameters relevant to the model. In our case, we want to train a model where the final V42 column is the predictor column and all other columns are to be used as features. For this reason, we can just use the simple formula V42 ~ . instead of having to fully enumerate all the other columns. After specifying our data frame, we then specify the type of kernel we will use, and in this case, we've opted for a linear kernel. We'll also specify a value for the `cost` parameter, which is related to the error budget C in our model:

```
> model_lin

Call:
svm(formula = V42 ~ ., data = biodeg_training2, kernel =
  "linear", cost = 10)
Parameters:
   SVM-Type:  C-classification
 SVM-Kernel:  linear
       cost:  10
      gamma:  0.02439024

Number of Support Vectors:  272
```

Our model doesn't provide us with too much information on its performance beyond the details of the parameters that we specified. One interesting piece of information is the number of data points that were support vectors in our model; in this case, 272. If we use the str() function to examine the structure of the fitted model, however, we will find that it contains a number of useful attributes. For example, the fitted attribute contains the model's predictions on the training data. We'll use this to gauge the quality of model fit by computing the accuracy of the training data and the confusion matrix:

```
> mean(bdf_train[,42] == model_lin$fitted)
[1] 0.8887574
> table(actual = bdf_train[,42], predictions = model_lin$fitted)
      predictions
actual   0   1
     0 519   41
     1  53 232
```

We have a training accuracy of just under 89 percent, which is a decent start. Next, we'll examine the performance of the test data using the predict() function to see whether we can get a test accuracy close to this or whether we have ended up overfitting the data:

```
> test_predictions <- predict(model_lin, bdf_test[,1:41])
> mean(bdf_test[,42] == test_predictions)
[1] 0.8619048
```

We do have a slightly lower test accuracy than we'd expect, but we are sufficiently close to the training accuracy we obtained earlier in order to be relatively confident that we are not in a position where we are overfitting the training data. Now, we've seen that the cost parameter plays an important role in our model, and that choosing this involves a trade-off in model bias and variance. Consequently, we want to try different values of our cost parameter before settling on a final model. After manually repeating the preceding code for a few values of this parameter, we obtained the following set of results:

```
> linearPerformances
               0.01   0.1     1      10    100    1000
training      0.858  0.888  0.883  0.889  0.886  0.886
test          0.886  0.876  0.876  0.862  0.862  0.862
```

Sometimes, when building a model, we may see a warning informing us that the maximum number of iterations has been reached. If this happens, we should be doubtful of the model that we produced, as it may be an indication that a solution was not found and the optimization procedure did not converge. In such a case, it is best to experiment with a different cost value and/or kernel type.

These results show that for most values of the `cost` parameter, we are seeing a very similar level of quality of fit on our training data, roughly 88 percent. Ironically, the best performance on the test data was obtained using the model whose fit on the training data was the worst, using a cost of 0.01. In short, although we have reasonable performance on our training and test data sets, the low variance in the results shown in the table essentially tells us that we are not going to get a significant improvement in the quality of fit by tweaking the `cost` parameter on this particular data set.

Now let's try using a radial kernel to see whether introducing some nonlinearity can allow us to improve our performance. When we specify a radial kernel, we must also specify a positive `gamma` parameter. This corresponds to the $1/2\sigma^2$ parameter in the equation of a radial kernel. The role that this parameter plays is that it controls the locality of the similarity computation between its two vector inputs. A large `gamma` means that the kernel will produce values that are close to zero unless the two vectors are very close together. A smaller `gamma` results in a smoother kernel and takes into account pairs of vectors that are farther away. Again, this choice boils down to a trade-off between bias and variance, so just as with the `cost` parameter, we'll have to try out different values of `gamma`. For now, let's see how we can create a support vector machine model using a radial kernel with a specific configuration:

```
> model_radial <- svm(V42 ~ ., data = bdf_train, kernel = "radial",
                       cost = 10, gamma = 0.5)
> mean(bdf_train[,42] == model_radial$fitted)
[1] 0.9964497
> test_predictions <- predict(model_radial, bdf_test[,1:41])
> mean(bdf_test[,42] == test_predictions)
[1] 0.8047619
```

Note that the radial kernel under these settings is able to fit the training data much more closely, as indicated by the near 100 percent training accuracy, but when we see the performance on the test data set, the result is substantially lower than what we obtained on the training data. Consequently, we have a very clear indication that this model is overfitting the data. To get around this problem, we will manually experiment with a few different settings of the `gamma` and `cost` parameters to see whether we can improve the fit:

```
> radialPerformances
          [,1]  [,2]  [,3]  [,4]  [,5]  [,6]  [,7]  [,8]  [,9]
cost      0.01  0.1   1     10    100   0.01  0.1   1     10
gamma     0.01  0.01  0.01  0.01  0.01  0.05  0.05  0.05  0.05
training  0.663 0.824 0.88  0.916 0.951 0.663 0.841 0.918 0.964
test      0.662 0.871 0.89  0.89  0.886 0.662 0.848 0.89  0.89
```

	[,10]	[,11]	[,12]	[,13]	[,14]	[,15]	[,16]	[,17]
cost	100	0.01	0.1	1	10	100	0.01	0.1
gamma	0.05	0.1	0.1	0.1	0.1	0.1	0.5	0.5
training	0.989	0.663	0.815	0.937	0.985	0.995	0.663	0.663
test	0.838	0.662	0.795	0.886	0.867	0.824	0.662	0.662
	[,18]	[,19]	[,20]	[,21]	[,22]	[,23]	[,24]	[,25]
cost	1	10	100	0.01	0.1	1	10	100
gamma	0.5	0.5	0.5	1	1	1	1	1
training	0.98	0.996	0.998	0.663	0.663	0.991	0.996	0.999
test	0.79	0.805	0.805	0.662	0.662	0.748	0.757	0.757

As we can see, the combination of the two parameters, cost and gamma, yields a much wider range of results using the radial kernel. From the data frame we built previously, we can see that some combinations, such as *cost = 1* and *gamma = 0.05*, have brought our accuracy up to 89 percent on the test data while still maintaining an analogous performance on our training data. Also, in the data frame, we see many examples of settings in which the training accuracy is nearly 100 percent, but the test accuracy is well below this.

As a result, we conclude that using a nonlinear kernel, such as the radial kernel, needs to be done with care in order to avoid overfitting. Nonetheless, radial kernels are very powerful and can be quite effective at modeling a highly nonlinear decision boundary, often allowing us to achieve higher rates of classification accuracy than a linear kernel. At this point in our analysis, we would usually want to settle on a particular value for the cost and gamma parameters and then retrain our model using the entire data available before deploying it in the real world.

Unfortunately, after using the test set to guide our decision on what parameters to use, it no longer represents an unseen data set that would enable us to predict the model's accuracy in the real world. One possible solution to this problem is to use a validation set, but this would require us to set aside some of our data resulting in smaller training and test set sizes. The next section will propose a way out of this dilemma.

Cross-validation

We've seen that many times in the real world, we come across a situation where we don't have an available test data set that we can use in order to measure the performance of our model on unseen data. The most typical reason is that we have very few data overall and want to use all of it to train our model. Another situation is that we want to keep a sample of the data as a validation set to tune some model meta parameters such as cost and gamma for SVMs with radial kernels, and as a result, we've already reduced our starting data and don't want to reduce it further.

Whatever the reason for the lack of a test data set, we already know that we should never use our training data as a measure of model performance and generalization because of the problem of overfitting. This is especially relevant for powerful and expressive models such as the nonlinear models of neural networks and SVMs with radial kernels that are often capable of approximating the training data very closely but may end up failing to generalize well on unseen data. In this section, we introduce the notion of **cross-validation**, which is perhaps best explained by a diagram:

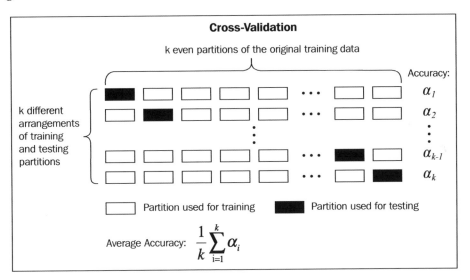

There is actually more than one variant of cross-validation, but in the previous diagram, we show the most common one, which is known as **k-fold cross-validation**. Under this scheme, we split our training data into *k* equally sized and nonoverlapping partitions. We then train a model using *k-1* of these partitions and use the remaining partition as a test set. This is done *k* times in total, once for every partition that is left out and used as a test set. Finally, we compute a global estimate of the accuracy of our method on unseen data by aggregating all estimates that we obtained across the *k* different test sets. For example, for classification problems where we compute the classification accuracy, we can obtain a global test set classification accuracy by taking the average classification accuracy across all the different test sets.

As an example, suppose that we want to train a binary classification model with a training data set of only 500 observations, and we want to do 10-fold cross validation. We produce 10 partitions of 50 observations each. Then, we train 10 models, each of which is trained with 9 of these partitions for a training set size of 450 observations and tested with the remaining partition of 50 observations. For each of these models, we will measure the classification accuracy on the partition set aside for testing, and take the average of these 10 measurements in order to obtain a global estimate of the model's classification accuracy on unseen data. Individually, the test set accuracy of one of these models may be inaccurate due to the randomness of the sampling of the training data and the relatively small size of the testing data. The averaging process at the end is instrumental in smoothing out these irregularities that might occur for individual models.

Choosing a good value for *k* is an important design decision. Using a small number for *k* results in models that are trained on a small proportion of the input data, which introduces a significant bias in the model. For example, if we were to use a value of 2 for *k*, we would end up training a model on only half of the training data. This is yet another example of the bias-variance trade-off that constantly crops up in statistical modeling. If, instead, we choose to have a large value of *k*, each time we train a model we will be using most of the training data and thus our bias will be kept low. However, because we are essentially using almost the same training data each time and testing it on a small-sized test set, we will observe a large variance in our prediction of the model's accuracy on unseen data. In the limit, we can actually set the value of *k* to be the total number of observations in our training data. When this happens, each time we train a model, our test set will consist of only one observation that is left out. For this reason, this process is referred to as **leave-one-out cross validation**.

Note that we train as many models as the value of *k*. At the same time, the size of the training data also increases with the value of *k* so when *k* is high, we also end up having a large overall training time. Sometimes, this may also be a factor in choosing an appropriate value of *k*, especially when the training time of an individual model is high. A good rule of thumb is to choose a value of 10 for *k*.

Returning to the analysis we performed in the previous section, remember that we manually tried out different `gamma` and `cost` parameters on the same test set because we didn't want to set aside a validation set to do this. The `e1071` package provides us with a `tune()` function that can carry out k-fold cross-validation to determine appropriate values for model meta parameters, such as the SVM cost. To do this, it receives an input called `ranges`, which is a list of vectors that contain values for all the parameters that we want to vary across the different runs of cross validation. In this case, we have two parameters, `cost` and `gamma`, so we provide it with two vectors:

```
> set.seed(2002)
> bdf_radial_tune <- tune(svm, V42 ~ ., data = bdf_train,
  kernel = "radial", ranges = list(cost = c(0.01, 0.1, 1, 10, 100),
  gamma = c(0.01, 0.05, 0.1, 0.5, 1)))
> bdf_radial_tune

Parameter tuning of 'svm':

- sampling method: 10-fold cross validation

- best parameters:
 cost gamma
    1  0.05


- best performance: 0.1194818
```

As we can see, our *k*-fold cross-validation predicts that the best parameter combination to use is a cost of 1 and a gamma of 0.05, which in this case, turns out to be consistent with what we found earlier using performance on a held out test set. This, of course, will not always be the case in general and in fact, our cross-validation indicates that the expected performance is actually closer to 88 percent rather than the 89 percent that we found earlier using these parameters. We deduced this from the output by noting that the best performance that is listed in the tuning results is actually the lowest average error obtained across the 10 data folds using the training data.

A very readable book on support vector machines is *An Introduction to Support Vector Machines and Other Kernel-based Learning Methods* by *Nello Christiani* and *John Shawe-Taylor*. Another good reference that presents an insightful link between SVMs and a related type of neural network known as a **Radial Basis Function Network** is *Neural Networks and Learning Machines* by *Simon Haykin*, which we also referenced in *Chapter 4, Neural Networks*.

Predicting credit scores

In this section, we will explore another data set; this time, in the field of banking and finance. The particular data set in question is known as the *German Credit Dataset* and is also hosted by the UCI Machine Learning Repository. The link to the data is https://archive.ics.uci.edu/ml/datasets/Statlog+%28German+Credit+Data%29.

The observations in the data set are loan applications made by individuals at a bank. The goal of the data is to determine whether an application constitutes a high credit risk.

Column name	Type	Definition
checking	Categorical	The status of the existing checking account
duration	Numerical	The duration in months
creditHistory	Categorical	The applicant's credit history
purpose	Categorical	The purpose of the loan
credit	Numerical	The credit amount
savings	Categorical	Savings account/bonds
employment	Categorical	Present employment since
installmentRate	Numerical	The installment rate (as a percentage of disposable income)
personal	Categorical	Personal status and gender
debtors	Categorical	Other debtors/guarantors
presentResidence	Numerical	Present residence since
property	Categorical	The type of property
Age	Numerical	The applicant's age in years
otherPlans	Categorical	Other installment plans
housing	Categorical	The applicant's housing situation
existingBankCredits	Numerical	The number of existing credits at this bank
Job	Categorical	The applicant's job situation
dependents	Numerical	The number of dependents
telephone	Categorical	The status of the applicant's telephone
foreign	Categorical	Foreign worker
risk	Binary	Credit risk (1 = good, 2 = bad)

First, we will load the data into a data frame called german_raw and provide it with column names that match the previous table:

```
> german_raw <- read.table("german.data", quote = "\"")
> names(german_raw) <- c("checking", "duration", "creditHistory",
  "purpose", "credit", "savings", "employment", "installmentRate",
  "personal", "debtors", "presentResidence", "property", "age",
  "otherPlans", "housing", "existingBankCredits", "job",
  "dependents", "telephone", "foreign", "risk")
```

Note from the table describing the features that we have a lot of categorical features to deal with. For this reason, we will employ dummyVars() once again to create dummy binary variables for these. In addition, we will record the risk variable, our output, as a factor with level 0 for good credit and level 1 for bad credit:

```
> library(caret)
> dummies <- dummyVars(risk ~ ., data = german_raw)
> german <- data.frame(predict(dummies, newdata = german_raw),
                       risk = factor((german_raw$risk - 1)))
> dim(german)
[1] 1000    62
```

As a result of this processing, we now have a data frame with 61 features because several of the categorical input features had many levels. Next, we will partition our data into training and test sets:

```
> set.seed(977)
> german_sampling_vector <- createDataPartition(german$risk,
                                p = 0.80, list = FALSE)
> german_train <- german[german_sampling_vector,]
> german_test <- german[-german_sampling_vector,]
```

One particularity of this data set that is mentioned on the website is that these data comes from a scenario where the two different types of errors have different costs. Specifically, the cost of misclassifying a high-risk customer as a low-risk customer is five times more expensive for the bank than misclassifying a low-risk customer as a high-risk customer. This is understandable, as in the first case, the bank stands to lose a lot of money from a loan it gives out that cannot be repaid, whereas in the second case, the bank misses out on an opportunity to give out a loan that will yield interest for the bank.

The svm() function has a class.weights parameter, which we use to specify the cost of misclassifying an observation to each class. This is how we will incorporate our asymmetric error cost information into our model. First, we'll create a vector of class weights, noting that we need to specify names that correspond to the output factor levels. Then, we will use the tune() function to train various SVM models with a radial kernel:

```
> class_weights <- c(1, 5)
> names(class_weights) <- c("0", "1")
> class_weights
0 1
1 5
```

```
> set.seed(2423)
> german_radial_tune <- tune(svm,risk ~ ., data = german_train,
  kernel = "radial", ranges = list(cost = c(0.01, 0.1, 1, 10, 100),
  gamma = c(0.01, 0.05, 0.1, 0.5, 1)), class.weights = class_weights)
> german_radial_tune$best.parameters
   cost gamma
9   10  0.05
> german_radial_tune$best.performance
[1] 0.26
```

The suggested best model has *cost* = *10* and *gamma* = *0.05* and achieves 74 percent training accuracy. Let's see how this model fares on our test data set:

```
> german_model <- german_radial_tune$best.model
> test_predictions <- predict(german_model, german_test[,1:61])
> mean(test_predictions == german_test[,62])
[1] 0.735
> table(predicted = test_predictions, actual = german_test[,62])
          actual
predicted   0    1
        0 134   47
        1   6   13
```

The performance on our test set is 73.5 percent and very close to what we saw in training. As expected, our model tends to make many more errors that misclassify a low risk customer as a high risk customer. Predictably, this takes a toll on the overall classification accuracy, which just computes the ratio of correctly classified observations to the overall number of observations. In fact, were we to remove this cost imbalance, we would actually select a different set of parameters for our model and our performance, from the perspective of the unbiased classification accuracy, would be better:

```
> set.seed(2423)
> german_radial_tune_unbiased <- tune(svm,risk ~ .,
  data = german_train, kernel = "radial", ranges = list(
  cost = c(0.01, 0.1, 1, 10, 100), gamma = c(0.01, 0.05, 0.1, 0.5, 1)))
> german_radial_tune_unbiased$best.parameters
   cost gamma
3    1  0.01
> german_radial_tune_unbiased$best.performance
[1] 0.23875
```

Of course, this last model will tend to make a greater number of costly misclassifications of high-risk customers as low-risk customers, which we know is very undesirable. We'll conclude this section with two final thoughts. Firstly, we have used relatively small ranges for the `gamma` and `cost` parameters. It is left as an exercise for the reader to rerun our analysis with a greater spread of values for these two in order to see whether we can get even better performance. This will, however, necessarily result in longer training times. Secondly, this particular data set is quite challenging in that its baseline accuracy is actually 70 percent. This is because 70 percent of the customers in the data are low-risk customers (the two output classes are not balanced). For this reason, computing the Kappa statistic, which we saw in *Chapter 1, Gearing Up for Predictive Modeling*, might be a better metric to use instead of classification accuracy.

Multiclass classification with support vector machines

Just like with logistic regression, we've seen that the basic premise behind the support vector machine is that it is designed to handle two classes. Of course, we often have situations where we would like to be able to handle a greater number of classes, such as when classifying different plant species based on a variety of physical characteristics. One way to do this is the **one versus all** approach. Here, if we have *K* classes, we create *K* SVM classifiers, and for each classifier, we are attempting to distinguish one particular class from all the rest. To determine the best class to pick, we assign the class for which the observation produces the highest distance from the separating hyperplane, thus lying farthest away from all other classes. More formally, we pick the class for which our linear feature combination has a maximum value across all the different classifiers.

An alternative approach is known as the (balanced) **one versus one** approach. We create a classifier for all possible pairs of output classes. We then classify our observation with every one of these classifiers and tally up the totals for every winning class. Finally, we pick the class that has the most votes. This latter approach is actually what is implemented by the `svm()` function in the `e1071` package. We can, therefore, use this function when we have a problem with multiple classes.

Summary

In this chapter, we presented the maximal margin hyperplane as a decision boundary that is designed to separate two classes by finding the maximum distance from either of them. When the two classes are linearly separable, this creates a situation where the space between the two classes is evenly split.

We've seen that there are circumstances where this is not always desirable, such as when the classes are close to each other because of a few observations. An improvement to this approach is the support vector classifier that allows us to tolerate a few margin violations, or even misclassifications, in order to obtain a more stable result. This also allows us to handle classes that aren't linearly separable. The form of the support vector classifier can be written in terms of inner products between the observation that is being classified and the support vectors. This transforms our feature space from p features into as many features as we have support vectors. Using kernel functions on these new features, we can introduce nonlinearity in our model and thus obtain a support vector machine.

In practice, we saw that training a support vector classifier, which is a support vector machine with a linear kernel, involves adjusting the `cost` parameter. The performance we obtain on our training data can be close to what we get in our test data. By contrast, we saw that by using a radial kernel, we have the potential to fit our training data much more closely, but we are far more likely to fall into the trap of overfitting.

To deal with this, it is useful to try different combinations of the `cost` and the `gamma` parameters. To do this efficiently and without requiring us to sacrifice data for use as a validation set, we introduced the idea of cross-validation. Effectively, we try out many different splits of the original training data into training and test sets and average the test set accuracy across all the splits. We then use this accuracy to decide on values for the parameters that interest us, and use our original test data set to estimate the performance on unseen data using a model that has been trained with our chosen parameter values.

In the next chapter, we are going to explore another cornerstone of machine learning: tree-based models. Also known as decision trees, they can handle regression and classification problems with many classes, are highly interpretable, and have a built-in way of handling missing data.

6
Tree-based Methods

In this chapter, we are going to present one of the most intuitive ways to create a predictive model—using the concept of a tree. Tree-based models, often also known as decision tree models, are successfully used to handle both regression and classification type problems. We'll explore both scenarios in this chapter, and we'll be looking at a range of different algorithms that are effective in training these models. We will also learn about a number of useful properties that these models possess, such as their ability to handle missing data and the fact that they are highly interpretable.

The intuition for tree models

A **decision tree** is a model with a very straightforward structure that allows us to make a prediction on an output variable, based on a series of rules arranged in a tree-like structure. The output variable that we can model can be categorical, allowing us to use a decision tree to handle classification problems. Equally, we can use decision trees to predict a numerical output, and in this way we'll also be able to tackle problems where the predictive task is a regression task.

Decision trees consist of a series of split points, often referred to as **nodes**. In order to make a prediction using a decision tree, we start at the top of the tree at a single node known as the **root node**. The root node is a decision or split point, because it places a condition in terms of the value of one of the input features, and based on this decision we know whether to continue on with the left part of the tree or with the right part of the tree. We repeat this process of choosing to go left or right at each **inner node** that we encounter until we reach one of the **leaf nodes**. These are the nodes at the base of the tree, which give us a specific value of the output to use as our prediction.

To illustrate this, let's look at a very simple decision tree in terms of two features, *x1* and *x2*.

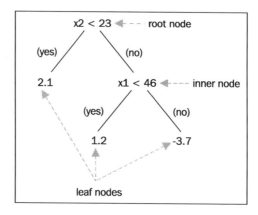

Note that the tree is a recursive structure, in that the left and right parts of the tree that lie beneath a particular node are themselves trees. They are referred to as the **left subtree** and the **right subtree** respectively, and the nodes that they lead to are the **left child** and **right child**. To understand how we go about using a decision tree in practice, we can try a simple example. Suppose we want to use our tree to predict the output for an observation where the value of *x1* is 96.0 and the value of *x2* is 79.9. We start at the root and make a decision as to which subtree to follow. Our value of *x2* is larger than 23, so we follow the right branch and come to a new node with a new condition to check. Our value of *x1* is larger than 46, so we once again take the right branch and arrive at a leaf node. Thus, we output the value indicated by the leaf node, which is -3.7. This is the value that our model predicts given the pair of inputs that we specified.

One way of thinking about decision trees is that they are in fact encoding a series of if-then rules leading to distinct outputs. For every leaf node, we can write a single rule (using the Boolean AND operator if necessary to join together multiple conditions) that must hold true for the tree to output that node's value. We can extract all of these if-then rules by starting at the root node and following every path down the tree that leads to a leaf node. For example, our small regression tree leads to the following three rules, one for each of its leaf nodes:

- ```If (x2 < 23) Then Output 2.1```
- ```If (x2 > 23) AND (x1 < 46) Then Output 1.2```
- ```If (x2 > 23) AND (x1 > 46) Then Output -3.7```

Note that we had to join together two conditions for each one of the last two rules using the AND operator, as the corresponding paths leading down to a leaf node included more than one decision node (counting the root node).

Another way to think about decision trees is that they partition the feature space into a series of rectangular regions in two dimensions, cubes in three dimensions, and hypercubes in higher dimensions. Remember that the number of dimensions in the feature space is just the number of features. So the feature space for our example regression tree has two dimensions and we can visualize how this space is split up into rectangular regions as follows:

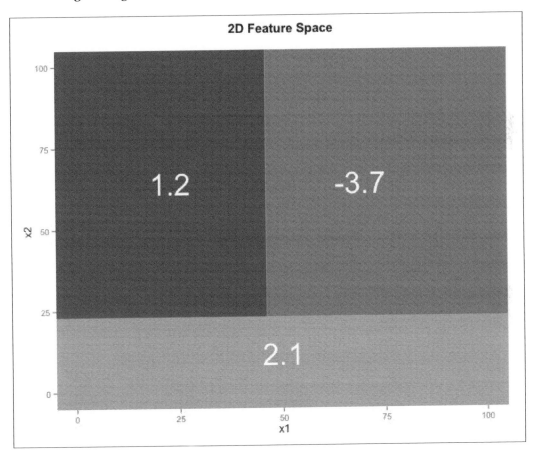

The rule-based interpretation and the space partitioning interpretation are equivalent views of the same model. The space partitioning interpretation in particular is very useful in helping us appreciate one particular characteristic of decision trees, which is that they must have complete coverage over all possible combinations of input features. Put differently, there should be no particular input for which there is no path to a leaf node in the decision tree. Every time we are given a value for our input features, we should always be able to return an answer. Our feature space partitioning interpretation of a decision tree essentially tells us that there is no point or space of points that doesn't belong to a particular partition with an assigned value. Similarly, with our if-then ruleset view of a decision tree, we are saying that there is always one rule that can be used for any input feature combination, and therefore we can reorganize our rules into an equivalent if-then-else structure where the last rule is an `else` statement.

Algorithms for training decision trees

Now that we have understood how a decision tree works, we'll want to address the issue of how we can train one using some data. There are several algorithms that have been proposed to build decision trees, and in this section we will present a few of the most well-known. One thing we should bear in mind is that whatever tree-building algorithm we choose, we will have to answer four fundamental questions:

- For every node (including the root node), how should we choose the input feature to split on and, given this feature, what is the value of the split point?
- How do we decide whether a node should become a leaf node or if we should make another split point?
- How deep should our tree be allowed to become?
- Once we arrive at a leaf node, what value should we predict?

A great introduction to decision trees is *Chapter 3 of Machine Learning, Tom Mitchell*. This book was probably the first comprehensive introduction to machine learning and is well worth reading. Although published in 1997, much of the material in the book remains relevant today. Furthermore, according to the book's website at `http://www.cs.cmu.edu/~tom/mlbook.html`, there is a planned second edition in the works.

Classification and regression trees

The **Classification and Regression Tree (CART)** methodology, to which we will henceforth refer simply as CART, is one of the earliest proposed approaches to building tree-based models. As the name implies, the methodology encompasses both an approach to building regression trees and an approach to building classification trees.

CART regression trees

For regression trees, the key intuition with the CART approach is that at any given point in the tree, we choose both the input feature to split on and the value of the split point within that feature, by finding which combination of these maximizes the reduction in the Sum of Squared Error (SSE). For every leaf node in a regression tree built using CART, the predicted value is simply the average value of the output predicted by all the data points that are assigned to that particular leaf node. To determine whether a new split point should be made or whether the tree should grow a leaf node, we simply count the number of data points that are currently assigned to a node, and if this value is less than a predetermined threshold, we create a new leaf node.

For any given node in the tree, including the root node, we begin by having some data points assigned to that node. At the root node, all the data points are assigned, but once we make a split, some of the data points are assigned to the left child and the remaining points are assigned to the right child. The starting value of the SSE is just the sum of squared error computed using the average value $\bar{y}$ of the output variable y_i for the n data points assigned to the current node:

$$SSE = \sum_{i=1}^{n}\left(y_i - \bar{y}\right)^2$$

If we split these data points into two groups of size n_1 and n_2 so that $n_1 + n_2 = n$, and we compute the new SSE for all the data points as the sum of the SSE values for each of the two new groups, we have:

$$SSE = \sum_{j=1}^{n_1}\left(y_j - \bar{y}_1\right)^2 + \sum_{k=1}^{n_2}\left(y_k - \bar{y}_2\right)^2$$

Here, the first sum iterates over j, which are the new indices of the data points in the first group corresponding to the left child, and the second sum iterates over k, which are the new indices of the data points inside the second group belonging to the right child. The idea behind CART is that we find a way to form these two groups of data points by considering every possible feature and every possible split point within that feature so that this new quantity is minimized. Thus, we can think of our error function in CART as the SSE.

One of the natural advantages of CART and tree-based models in general, is that they are capable of handling various input types, from numerical inputs (both discrete and continuous) to binary inputs as well as categorical inputs. Numerical inputs can be ordered in a natural way by sorting them in ascending order, for example. When we do this, we can see that if we have k distinct numbers, there are $k-1$ distinct ways to split these into two groups so that all the numbers in one group are smaller than all the numbers in the second group, and both groups have at least one element. This is simply done by picking the numbers themselves as split points and not counting the smallest number as a split point (which would produce an empty group). So if we have a feature vector x with the numbers $\{5.6, 2.8, 9.0\}$, we first sort these into $\{2.8, 5.6, 9.0\}$. Then, we take each number except the smallest (2.8) to form a split point and a corresponding rule that checks whether the input value is smaller than the split point. In this way, we produce the only two possible groupings for our feature vector:

- `Group1 = {2.8}, Group2 = {5.6, 9.0} IF x < 5.6 THEN Group1 ELSE Group2`

- `Group1 = {2.8, 5.6}, Group2 = {9.0} IF x < 9.0 THEN Group1 ELSE Group2`

Note that it is important to have at least one element in each group, otherwise we haven't actually split our data. Binary input features can also be handled by simply using the split point that corresponds to putting all data points that have this feature take the first value in the first group, and the remaining data points that have the second value of this feature in the second group.

Handling unordered categorical input features (factors) is substantially harder because there is no natural order. As a result, any combination of levels can be assigned to the first group and the remainder to the second group. If we are dealing with a factor that has k distinct levels, then there are $2^{k-1}-1$ possible ways to form two groups with at least one level assigned to each group.

So, a binary-valued feature has one possible split, as we know, and a three-valued feature has three possible splits. With the numerical feature vector containing the numbers {5.6, 2.8, 9.0}, we've already seen two possible splits. The third possible split that could arise if these numbers were labels, is the one in which one group has data points with this feature taking the value 5.6, and another group with the two values 2.8 and 9.0. Clearly, this is not a valid split when we treat the feature as numerical.

As a final note, we always have the option of a one-versus-all approach for categorical input features, which is essentially the same as considering splits in which one group always consists of a single element. This is not always a good idea as it may turn out that a particular subset of the levels when taken together are more predictive of an output compared to a single level. If this is the case, the resulting tree will probably be more complex, having a greater number of node splits.

There are various ways to deal with the large increase in complexity associated with finding and evaluating all the different split points for categorical input features, but we won't go into further detail right now. Instead, let's write some R code to see how we might find the split point of a numerical input feature using the SSE criterion that CART uses:

```
compute_SSE_split <- function(v, y, split_point) {
  index <- v < split_point
  y1 <- y[index]
  y2 <- y[!index]
  SSE <- sum((y1 - mean(y1)) ^ 2) + sum((y2 - mean(y2)) ^ 2)
  return(SSE)
}

compute_all_SSE_splits <- function(v, y) {
  sapply(unique(v), function(sp) compute_SSE_split(v, y, sp))
}
```

The first function, `compute_SSE_split()`, takes in a feature vector v, an output vector y, and a specific value for the feature vector that we want to split on, namely `split_point`. It uses these to compute the SSE value for that split. To do this, it first creates an indexing vector, identifying all the elements of the feature vector whose value is less than the `split_point` value. This is then used to split the output vector into two groups, y1 and y2; the former contains elements identified by the indexing vector and the latter contains the remaining elements. Finally, the SSE is computed as the sum of the SSE of the two groups using the familiar formula of the sum of squared distances from the group mean.

The second function, `compute_all_SSE_splits()`, takes in a feature vector v, and an output vector y, and uses all the unique elements of the feature vector as potential split points (for simplicity, we are ignoring the fact that we should not be splitting on the smallest value of the feature vector).

In order to demonstrate how splitting works in CART, we will generate a small artificial data set. The following code snippet generates twenty random observations of two input features and stores the result in a data frame, `rcart_df`:

```
> set.seed(99)
> x1 <- rbinom(20, 1, 0.5)
> set.seed(100)
> x2 <- round(10 + rnorm(20, 5, 5), 2)
> set.seed(101)
> y <- round((1 + (x2 * 2 / 5) + x1 - rnorm(20, 0, 3)), 2)
> rcart_df <- data.frame(x1, x2, y)
> rcart_df
     x1    x2     y
1     1 12.49  7.97
2     0 15.66  5.61
3     1 14.61  9.87
4     1 19.43  9.13
5     1 15.58  7.30
6     1 16.59  5.11
7     1 12.09  4.98
8     0 18.57  8.77
9     0 10.87  2.60
10    0 13.20  6.95
11    1 15.45  6.60
12    1 15.48 10.58
13    0 13.99  2.31
14    1 18.70 13.88
15    1 15.62  8.96
16    1 14.85  8.52
17    0 13.06  8.77
18    0 17.55  7.84
19    0 10.43  7.63
20    0 26.55 17.77
```

In practice, twenty data points might be a suitable number to use as a threshold for building a leaf node, but for this example, we will simply suppose that we wanted to make a new split using these data. We have two input features, x1 and x2. The former is a binary input feature that we have coded using the numerical labels 0 and 1. This allows us to reuse the functions we just wrote to compute the possible splits. The latter is a numerical input feature. By applying our `compute_all_SSE_splits()` function on each feature separately, we can compute all the possible split points for each feature and their SSE. The following two plots show these SSE values for each feature in turn:

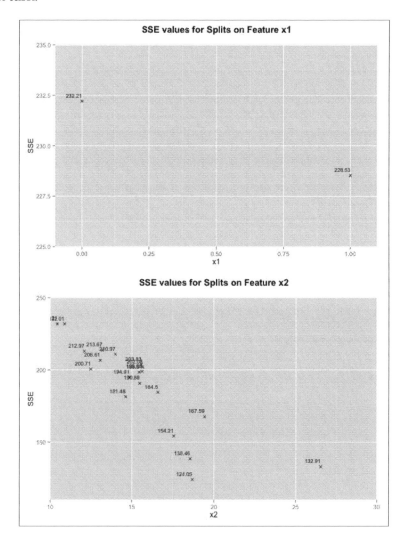

Looking at both plots, we can see that the best possible split produces an SSE value of 124.05 and this can be achieved by splitting on the feature $x2$ at the value 18.7. Consequently, our regression tree would contain a node with the following splitting rule:

```
If x2 < 18.7
```

The CART methodology always applies the same logic to determine whether to make a new split at each node as well as how to pick which feature and value to split on. This recursive approach of splitting up the data points at each node to build the regression tree is why this process is also known as **recursive partitioning**.

Tree pruning

If we were to allow the recursive partitioning process to repeat indefinitely, we would eventually terminate by having leaf nodes with a single data point each, because that is when we cannot split the data any further. This model would fit the training data perfectly, but it is highly unlikely that its performance would generalize on unseen data. Thus, tree-based models are susceptible to overfitting. To combat this, we need to control the depth of our final decision tree.

The process of removing nodes from the tree to limit its size and complexity is known as **pruning**. One possible pruning method is to impose a threshold for the smallest number of data points that can be used in order to create a new split in the tree instead of creating a leaf node. This will create leaf nodes earlier on in the procedure and the data points that are assigned to them may not all have the same output. In this case, we can simply predict the average value for regression (and the most popular class for classification). This is an example of **pre-pruning**, as we are pruning the tree while building it and before it is fully constructed.

Intuitively, we should be able to see that the larger the depth of the tree and the fewer the average number of data points assigned to leaf nodes, the greater the degree of overfitting. Of course, if we have fewer nodes in the tree, we probably aren't being granular enough in our modeling of the underlying data.

The question of how large a tree should be allowed to grow is thus effectively a question of how to model our data as closely as possible while controlling the degree of overfitting. In practice, using pre-pruning is tricky as it is difficult to find an appropriate threshold.

Another regularization process that is used by the CART methodology to prune trees is known as **cost-complexity tuning**. In effect, trees are often allowed to grow fully using the recursive partitioning approach described in the previous section. Once this completes, we prune the resulting tree, that is to say, we start removing split points and merging leaf nodes to shrink the tree according to a certain criterion. This is known as **post-pruning**, as we prune the tree after it has been built. When we construct the original tree, the error function that we use is the SSE. To prune the tree, we use a penalized version of the SSE for minimizing:

$$SSE_{penalized} = SSE + \alpha \cdot T_p$$

Here, a is a complexity parameter controlling the degree of regularization and T_p is the number of nodes in the tree, which is a way to model the size of the tree. Similar to the way in which the lasso limits the size of regression coefficients in generalized linear models, this regularization procedure limits the size of the resulting tree. A very small value of a results in a small degree of pruning, which in the limit of a taking the value of 0 corresponds to no pruning at all. On the other hand, using a high value for this parameter results in trees that are much shorter, which, at its limit, can result in a zero-sized tree with no splits at all, which predicts a single average value of the output for all possible inputs.

It turns out that every particular value of a corresponds to a unique tree structure that minimizes this penalized form of the SSE for that particular value. Put differently, given a particular value for a, there is a unique and predictable way to prune a tree in order to minimize the penalized SSE, but the details of this procedure are beyond the scope of this book. For now, we can simply assume that every value of a is associated with a single tree.

This particular feature is very useful, as we don't have any ambiguity in picking a tree once we settle on a value for the complexity parameter a. It does not, however, give us a way to determine what actual value we should use. Cross-validation, which we saw in *Chapter 5, Support Vector Machines*, is a commonly used approach designed to estimate an appropriate value of this parameter. Cross-validation applied to this problem would involve partitioning the data into k folds. We then train and prune k trees by using all the data excluding a single fold and repeating this for each of the k folds. Finally, we measure the SSE on the folds held out for testing and average the results. We can repeat our cross-validation procedure for different values of a. Another approach when more data is available is to use a validation data set for evaluating models that have been trained on the same training data set but with different values of a.

Missing data

One characteristic of decision trees is that they have a natural way of handling missing data during training. For example, when we consider which feature to split on at a particular node, we can ignore data points that have a missing value for a particular feature and compute the potential reduction in our error function (deviance, SSE, and so on) using the remaining data points. Note that while this approach is handy, it could potentially increase the bias of the model substantially, especially if we are ignoring a large portion of our available training data because of missing values.

One might wonder whether we are able to handle missing values during prediction for unseen data points. If we are at a particular node in the tree that is splitting on a feature, for which our test data point has a missing value, we are seemingly stuck. In practice, this situation can be dealt with via the use of **surrogate splits**. The key notion behind these is that for every node in the tree, apart from the feature that was optimally chosen to split on, we keep track of a list of other features that produce similar splits in the data as the feature we actually chose. In this way, when our testing data point has a missing value for a feature that we need in order to make a prediction, we can refer to a node's surrogate splits instead, and use a different feature for this node.

Regression model trees

One of the potential drawbacks of regression trees built with CART is that even though we limit the number of data points that are assigned to a particular leaf node, these may still have significant variations in the output variable among themselves. When this happens, taking the average value and using this as a single prediction for that leaf node may not be the best idea.

Regression model trees attempt to overcome this limitation by using the data points at the leaf nodes to construct a linear model to predict the output. The original regression model tree algorithm was developed by *J. Ross Quinlan* and is known as **M5**. The M5 algorithm computes a linear model at each node in the tree. For a test data point, we first compute the decision path traversed from the root node to the leaf node. The prediction that is then made is the output of the linear model associated with that leaf node.

M5 also differs from the algorithm used in CART in that it employs a different criterion to determine which feature to split on. This criterion is the weighted reduction in standard deviation:

$$\sigma_{reduced} = \sigma_{initial} - \sum_{i=1}^{p} \frac{n_i}{n} \cdot \sigma_i$$

This general equation assumes that we split the data into p partitions (as we have seen for trees, p is typically 2). For each partition i, we compute the standard deviation σ_i. Then we compute the weighted average of these standard deviations using the relative size of each partition (n_i/n) as the weights. This is subtracted from the initial standard deviation of the unpartitioned data.

The idea behind this criterion is that splitting a node should produce groups of data points that within each group display less variability with respect to the output variable than all the data points when grouped together. We'll have a chance to see M5 trees as well as CART trees in action later on in this chapter.

CART classification trees

Building classification trees using the CART methodology continues the notion of recursively splitting up groups of data points in order to minimize some error function. Our first guess for an appropriate error function is the classification accuracy. It turns out that this is not a particularly good measure to use to build a classification tree.

What we would actually like to use is a measure for node purity that would score nodes based on whether they contain data points primarily belonging to one of the output classes. This is a very intuitive idea because what we are effectively aiming for in a classification tree is to eventually be able to group our training data points into sets of data points at the leaf nodes, so that each leaf node contains data points belonging to only one of the classes. This will mean that we can confidently predict this class if we arrive at that leaf node during prediction.

One possible measure of node purity, which is frequently used with CART for classification trees is the **Gini index**. For an output variable with K different classes, the Gini index G is defined as follows:

$$G = \sum_{k=1}^{K} \hat{p}_k \cdot \left(1 - \hat{p}_k\right)$$

To calculate the Gini index, we compute an estimate of the probability of every class and multiply this with the probability of not being that class. We then add up all these products. For a binary classification problem, it should be easy to see that the Gini index evaluates to $2\,\hat{p}\,(1-\hat{p})$, where $\hat{p}$ is the estimated probability of one of the classes.

To compute the Gini index at a particular node in a tree, we can simply use the ratio of the number of data points labeled as class *k* over the total number of data points as an estimate for the probability of a data point belonging to class *k* at the node in question. Here is a simple R function to compute the Gini index:

```
gini_index <- function(v) {
  t <- table(v)
  probs <- t / sum(t)
  terms <- sapply(probs, function(p) p * (1 - p) )
  return(sum(terms))
}
```

To compute the Gini index, our `gini_index()` function first tabulates all the entries in a vector. It divides each of these frequency counts with the total number of counts to transform them into probability estimates. Finally, it computes the product $\hat{p}(1-\hat{p})$ for each of these and sums up all the terms. Let's try a few examples:

```
> gini_index(v = c(0, 0, 0, 1, 1, 1))
[1] 0.5
> gini_index(v = c(0, 0, 0, 1, 1, 1, 1, 1, 1))
[1] 0.4444444
> gini_index(v = c(0, 0, 0, 1, 1, 1, 2, 2, 2))
[1] 0.6666667
> gini_index(v = c(1, 1, 1, 1, 1, 1))
[1] 0
```

Note how the Gini index for a completely pure node (a node with only one class) is 0. For a binary output with equal proportions of the two classes, the Gini index is 0.5. Similar to the standard deviation in regression trees, we use the weighted reduction in Gini index, where we weigh each partition by its relative size, to determine appropriate split points:

$$Gini_{reduced} = Gini_{initial} - \sum_{i=1}^{p} \frac{n_i}{n} \cdot Gini_i$$

Another commonly used criterion is deviance. When we studied logistic regression, we saw that this is just the constant -2 multiplied by the log-likelihood of the data. In a classification tree setting, we compute the deviance of a node in a classification tree as:

$$D = -2\sum_{k=1}^{K} n_k \cdot \log\left(\hat{p}_k\right)$$

Unlike the Gini index, the total number of observations n_k at a node affects the value of deviance. All nodes that have the same proportion of data points across different classes will have the same value of the Gini index, but if they have different numbers of observations, they will have different values of deviance. In both splitting criteria, however, a completely pure node will have a value of 0 and a positive value otherwise.

Aside from using a different splitting criterion, the logic to build a classification tree using the CART methodology is exactly parallel to that of building a regression tree. Missing values are handled in the same way and the tree is pre-pruned in the same way using a threshold on the number of data points left to build leaf nodes. The tree is also post-pruned using the same cost-complexity approach outlined for regression trees, but after replacing the SSE as the error function with either the Gini index or the deviance.

C5.0

The **C5.0** algorithm developed by *Ross Quinlan* is an algorithm to build a decision tree for classification. This algorithm is the latest in a chain of successively improved versions starting from an algorithm known as **ID3**, which developed into **C4.5** (and an open source implementation in the Java programming language known as **J48**) before culminating in C5.0. There are a good many acronyms used for decision trees, but thankfully many of them are related to each other. The C5.0 chain of algorithms has several differences from the CART methodology, most notably in the choice of splitting criterion as well as in the pruning procedure.

The splitting criterion used with C5.0 is known as **entropy** or the **information statistic**, and has its roots in information theory. Entropy is defined as the average number of binary digits (bits) needed to communicate information via a message as a function of the probabilities of the different symbols used. Entropy also has roots in statistical physics, where it is used to represent the degree of chaos and uncertainty in a system. When the symbols or components of a system have equal probabilities, there is a high degree of uncertainty, but entropy is lower when one symbol is far likelier than the others. This observation renders the definition of entropy very useful in measuring node purity. The formal definition of entropy in bits for the multiclass scenario with K classes is:

$$Entropy = -\sum_{k=1}^{K} p_k \cdot \log_2 p_k$$

In the binary case, the equation simplifies to (where p arbitrarily refers to the probability of one of the two classes):

$$Binary\,Class\,Entropy = -\left[p \cdot \log_2 p + (1-p) \cdot \log_2 (1-p)\right]$$

We can compare entropy to the Gini index for binary classification in the following plot:

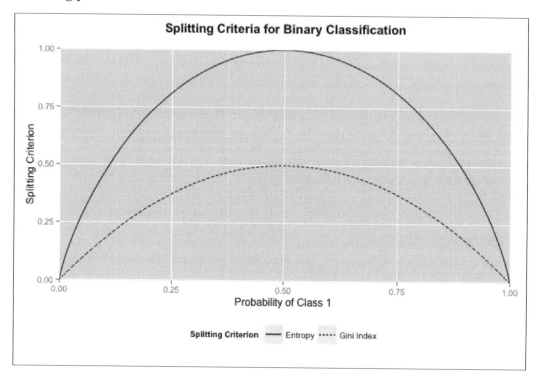

From the plot, we can see that both functions have the same general shape for the binary class problem. Recall that the lower the entropy, the lower the uncertainty we have about the distribution of our classes and hence we have higher node purity. Consequently, we want to minimize the entropy as we build our tree. In ID3, the splitting criterion that is used is the weighted entropy reduction, which is also known as the **information gain**:

$$Information\,Gain = Entropy_{initial} - \sum_{i=1}^{p} \frac{n_i}{n} \cdot Entropy_i$$

It turns out that this criterion suffers from **selection bias**, in that it tends to favor categorical variables because of the large number of possible groupings compared to the linear range of splits we find with continuous features. To combat this, from C4.5 onwards, the criterion was refined into the **information gain ratio**. This is a normalized version of the information gain, where we normalize with respect to a quantity known as the **split information value**.

This in turn represents the potential increase in information that we can get just by the size of the partitions themselves. A high split information value occurs when we have evenly sized partitions and a low value occurs when most of the data points are concentrated in a small number of the partitions. In summary, we have this:

$$Information\,Gain\,Ratio = \frac{Information\,Gain}{Split\,Information\,Value}$$

$$Split\,Information\,Value = -\sum_{i=1}^{p} \frac{n_i}{n} \cdot \log_2\left(\frac{n_i}{n}\right)$$

The C5.0 chain of algorithms also incorporate alternative methods to prune a tree that go beyond simple elimination of nodes and sub-trees. For example, inner nodes may be removed before leaf nodes so that the nodes beneath the removed node (the sub-tree) are pushed up (raised) to replace the removed node. C5.0, in particular, is a very powerful algorithm that also contains improvements to speed, memory usage, native boosting (covered in the next chapter) abilities, as well as the ability to specify a cost matrix so that the algorithm can avoid making certain types of misclassifications over others, just as we saw with support vector machines in the previous chapter.

We'll demonstrate how to build trees with C5.0 in R in a subsequent section.

Predicting class membership on synthetic 2D data

Our first example showcasing tree-based methods in R will operate on a synthetic data set that we have created. The data set can be generated using commands in the companion R file for this chapter, available from the publisher. The data consists of 287 observations of two input features, x1 and x2.

The output variable is a categorical variable with three possible classes: a, b, and c. If we follow the commands in the code file, we will end up with a data frame in R, mcdf:

```
> head(mcdf, n = 5)
          x1        x2 class
1 18.58213 12.03106     a
2 22.09922 12.36358     a
3 11.78412 12.75122     a
4 23.41888 13.89088     a
5 16.37667 10.32308     a
```

This problem is actually very simple because on the one hand, we have a very small data set with only two features, and on the other because the classes happen to be quite well separated in the feature space, something that is very rare. Nonetheless, our objective in this section is to demonstrate the construction of a classification tree on *well-behaved* data before we get our hands (or keyboards) dirty on a real-world data set in the next section.

To build a classification tree for this data set, we will use the tree package, which provides us with the tree() function that trains a model using the CART methodology. As is the norm, the first parameter to be provided is a formula and the second parameter is the data frame. The function also has a split parameter that identifies the criterion to be used for splitting. By default, this is set to deviance for the deviance criterion, for which we observed better performance on this data set. We encourage readers to repeat these experiments by setting the split parameter to gini for splitting on the Gini index.

Without further ado, let us train our first decision tree:

```
> library(tree)
> d2tree <- tree(class ~ ., data = mcdf)
> summary(d2tree)

Classification tree:
tree(formula = class ~ ., data = mcdf)
Number of leaf nodes:  5
Residual mean deviance:  0.03491 = 9.844 / 282
Misclassification error rate: 0.003484 = 1 / 287
```

We invoke the `summary()` function on our trained model to get some useful information about the tree we built. Note that for this example, we won't be splitting our data into a training and test set, as our goal is to discuss the quality of the model fit first. From the provided summary, we seem to have only misclassified a single example in our entire data set. Ordinarily, this would raise suspicion that we are overfitting; however, we already know that our classes are well separated in the feature space. We can use the `plot()` function to plot the shape of our tree as well as the `text()` function to display all the relevant labels so we can fully visualize the classifier we have built:

```
> plot(d2tree)
> text(d2tree, all = T)
```

This is the plot that is produced:

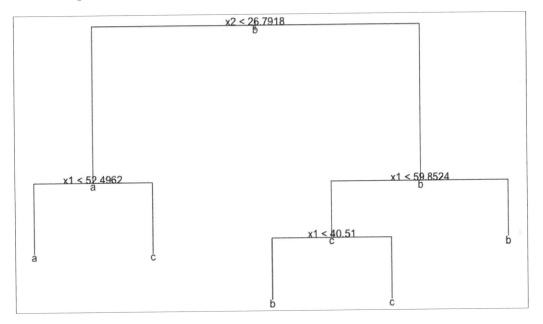

Note that our plot shows a predicted class for every node, including non-leaf nodes. This simply allows us to see which class is predominant at every step of the tree. For example, at the root node, we see that the predominant class is class b, simply because this is the most commonly represented class in our data set. It is instructive to be able to see the partitioning of our 2D space that our decision tree represents.

For one and two features, the `tree` package allows us to use the `partition.tree()` function to visualize our decision tree. We have done this and superimposed our original data over it in order to see how the classifier has partitioned the space:

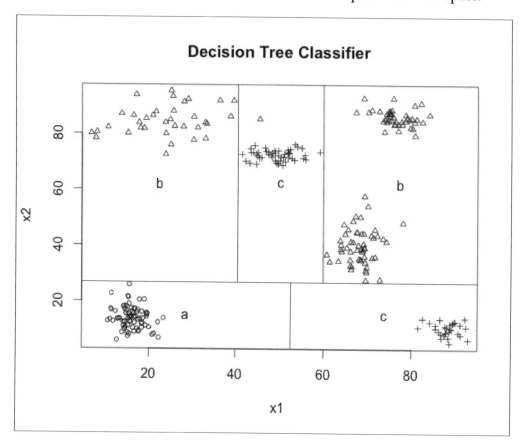

Most of us would probably identify six clusters in our data; however, the clusters on the top-right of the plot are both assigned to class b and so the tree classifier has identified this entire region of space as a single leaf node. Finally, we can spot the misclassified point belonging to class b that has been assigned to class c (it is the triangle in the middle of the top part of the graph).

Another interesting observation to make is how efficiently the space has been partitioned into rectangles in this particular case (only five rectangles for a data set with six clusters). On the other hand, we can expect this model to have some instabilities because several of the boundaries of the rectangles are very close to data points in the data set (and thus close to the edges of a cluster). Consequently, we should also expect to obtain a lower accuracy with unseen data that is generated from the same process that generated our training data.

In the next section, we will build a tree model for a real-world classification problem.

Predicting the authenticity of banknotes

In this section, we will study the problem of predicting whether a particular banknote is genuine or whether it has been forged. The *banknote authentication data set* is hosted at https://archive.ics.uci.edu/ml/datasets/banknote+authentication. The creators of the data set have taken specimens of both genuine and forged banknotes and photographed them with an industrial camera. The resulting grayscale image was processed using a type of time-frequency transformation known as a **wavelet transform**. Three features of this transform are constructed, and along with the image entropy, they make up the four features in total for this binary classification task.

Column name	Type	Definition
waveletVar	Numerical	Variance of the wavelet-transformed image
waveletSkew	Numerical	Skewness of the wavelet-transformed image
waveletCurt	Numerical	Curtosis of the wavelet-transformed image
entropy	Numerical	Entropy of the image
class	Binary	Authenticity (output of 0 means genuine and output of 1 means forged)

First, we will split our 1,372 observations into training and test sets:

```
> library(caret)
> set.seed(266)
> bnote_sampling_vector <- createDataPartition(bnote$class, p =
                          0.80, list = FALSE)
> bnote_train <- bnote[bnote_sampling_vector,]
> bnote_test <- bnote[-bnote_sampling_vector,]
```

Next, we will introduce the C50 R package that contains an implementation of the C5.0 algorithm for classification. The C5.0() function that belongs to this package also takes in a formula and a data frame as its minimum required input. Just as before, we can use the summary() function to examine the resulting model. Instead of reproducing the entire output of the latter, we'll focus on just the tree that is built:

```
> bnote_tree <- C5.0(class ~ ., data = bnote_train)
> summary(bnote_tree)
waveletVar > 0.75896:
:...waveletCurt > -1.9702: 0 (342)
:   waveletCurt <= -1.9702:
:   :...waveletSkew > 4.9228: 0 (128)
```

```
    :           waveletSkew <= 4.9228:
    :           :...waveletVar <= 3.4776: 1 (34)
    :               waveletVar > 3.4776: 0 (2)
waveletVar <= 0.75896:
:...waveletSkew > 5.1401:
    :...waveletVar <= -3.3604: 1 (31)
    :   waveletVar > -3.3604: 0 (93/1)
    waveletSkew <= 5.1401:
    :...waveletVar > 0.30081:
        :...waveletCurt <= 0.35273: 1 (25)
        :   waveletCurt > 0.35273:
        :   :...entropy <= 0.71808: 0 (24)
        :       entropy > 0.71808: 1 (3)
        waveletVar <= 0.30081:
        :...waveletCurt <= 3.0423: 1 (241)
            waveletCurt > 3.0423:
            :...waveletSkew > -1.8624: 0 (21/1)
                waveletSkew <= -1.8624:
                :...waveletVar <= -0.69572: 1 (146)
                    waveletVar > -0.69572:
                    :...entropy <= -0.73535: 0 (2)
                        entropy > -0.73535: 1 (6)
```

As we can see, it is perfectly acceptable to use a feature more than once in the tree in order to make a new split. The numbers in brackets to the right of the leaf nodes in the tree indicate the number of observations from each class that are assigned to that node. As we can see, the vast majority of the leaf nodes in the tree are pure nodes, so that only observations from one class are assigned to them.

Only two leaf nodes have a single observation each from the minority class for that node, and with this we can infer that we only made two mistakes in our training data using this model. To see if our model has overfit the data or whether it really can generalize well, we'll test it on our test set:

```
> bnote_predictions <- predict(bnote_tree, bnote_test)
> mean(bnote_test$class == bnote_predictions)
[1] 0.9890511
```

The test accuracy is near perfect, a rare sight and the last time in this chapter that we'll be done so easily! As a final note, C50() also has a costs parameter, which is useful for dealing with asymmetric error costs.

Predicting complex skill learning

In this section, we'll have a chance to explore data from an innovative and recent project known as *SkillCraft*. The interested reader can find out more about this project on the Web by going to http://skillcraft.ca/. The key premise behind the project is that by studying the performance of players in a **real-time strategy** (**RTS**) game that involves complex resource management and strategic decisions, we can study how humans learn complex skills and develop speed and competence in dynamic resource allocation scenarios. To achieve this, data has been collected from players playing the popular real-time strategy game, *Starcraft 2*, developed by *Blizzard*.

In this game, players compete against each other on one of many fixed maps and starting locations. Each player must choose a fictional race from three available choices and start with six worker units, which are used to collect one of two game resources. These resources are needed in order to build military and production buildings, military units unique to each race, research technologies, and build more worker units. The game involves a mix of economic advancement, military growth, and military strategy in real-time engagements.

Players are pitted against each other via an online matching algorithm that groups players into leagues according to their perceived level of skill. The algorithm's perception of a player's skill changes over time on the basis of that player's performance across the games in which the player participates. There are eight leagues in total, which are uneven in population in that the lower leagues tend to have more players and the upper leagues have fewer players.

Having a basic understanding of the game, we can download the SkillCraft1 Master Table data set from the UCI Machine Learning repository by going to https://archive.ics.uci.edu/ml/datasets/SkillCraft1+Master+Table+Dataset. The rows of this data set are individual games that are played and the features of the games are metrics of a player's playing speed, competence, and decision-making. The authors of the data set have used both standard performance metrics familiar to players of the game, as well as other metrics such as **Perception Action Cycles** (**PACs**), which attempt to quantify a player's actions at the fixed location on the map at which a player is looking during a particular time window.

The task at hand is to predict which of the eight leagues a player is currently assigned to on the basis of these performance metrics. Our output variable is an ordered categorical variable because we have eight distinct leagues ordered from 1 to 8, where the latter corresponds to the league with players of the highest skill.

One possible way to deal with ordinal outputs is to treat them as a numeric variable, modeling this as a regression task, and build a regression tree. The following table describes the features and output variables that we have in our data set:

Feature name	Type	Description
Age	Numeric	Player's age
HoursPerWeek	Numeric	Reported hours spent playing per week
TotalHours	Numeric	Reported total hours ever spent playing
APM	Numeric	Game actions per minute
SelectByHotkeys	Numeric	Number of unit or building selections made using hotkeys per timestamp
AssignToHotkeys	Numeric	Number of units or buildings assigned to hotkeys per timestamp
UniqueHotkeys	Numeric	Number of unique hotkeys used per timestamp
MinimapAttacks	Numeric	Number of attack actions on minimap per timestamp
MinimapRightClicks	Numeric	Number of right-clicks on minimap per timestamp
NumberOfPACs	Numeric	Number of PACs per timestamp
GapBetweenPACs	Numeric	Mean duration in milliseconds between PACs
ActionLatency	Numeric	Mean latency from the onset of a PAC to their first action in milliseconds
ActionsInPAC	Numeric	Mean number of actions within each PAC
TotalMapExplored	Numeric	The number of 24x24 game coordinate grids viewed by the player per timestamp
WorkersMade	Numeric	Number of worker units trained per timestamp
UniqueUnitsMade	Numeric	Unique units made per timestamp
ComplexUnitsMade	Numeric	Number of complex units trained per timestamp
ComplexAbilitiesUsed	Numeric	Abilities requiring specific targeting instructions used per timestamp
LeagueIndex	Numeric	Bronze, Silver, Gold, Platinum, Diamond, Master, GrandMaster, and Professional leagues coded 1-8 (output)

If the reader has never played a real-time strategy game like *Starcraft 2* on a computer before, it is likely that many of the features used by the data set will sound arcane. If one simply takes it on board that these features represent various aspects of a player's level of performance in the game, it will still be possible to follow all the discussion surrounding the training and testing of our regression tree without any difficulty.

To start with, we load this data set onto the data frame `skillcraft`. Before beginning to work with the data, we will have to do some preprocessing. Firstly, we'll drop the first column. This simply has a unique game identifier that we don't need and won't use. Secondly, a quick inspection of the imported data frame will show that three columns have been interpreted as factors because the input data set contains a question mark to denote a missing value. To deal with this, we first need to convert these columns to numeric columns, a process that will introduce missing values in our data set.

Next, although we've seen that trees are quite capable of handling these missing values, we are going to remove the few rows that have them. We will do this because we want to be able to compare the performance of several different models in this chapter and in the next, not all of which support missing values. Here is the code for the preprocessing steps just described:

```
> skillcraft <- read.csv("SkillCraft1_Dataset.csv")
> skillcraft <- skillcraft[-1]
> skillcraft$TotalHours <- as.numeric(
   levels(skillcraft$TotalHours))[skillcraft$TotalHours]
Warning message:
NAs introduced by coercion
> skillcraft$HoursPerWeek <- as.numeric(
   levels(skillcraft$HoursPerWeek))[skillcraft$HoursPerWeek]
Warning message:
NAs introduced by coercion
> skillcraft$Age <- as.numeric(
   levels(skillcraft$Age))[skillcraft$Age]
Warning message:
NAs introduced by coercion
> skillcraft <- skillcraft[complete.cases(skillcraft),]
```

As usual, the next step will be to split our data into training and test sets:

```
> library(caret)
> set.seed(133)
> skillcraft_sampling_vector <- createDataPartition(
   skillcraft$LeagueIndex, p = 0.80, list = FALSE)
> skillcraft_train <- skillcraft[skillcraft_sampling_vector,]
> skillcraft_test <- skillcraft[-skillcraft_sampling_vector,]
```

This time, we will use the `rpart` package in order to build our decision tree (along with the `tree` package, these two are the most commonly used packages for building tree-based models in R). This package provides us with an `rpart()` function to build our tree. Just as with the `tree()` function, we can build a regression tree using the default behavior by simply providing a formula and our data frame:

```
> library(rpart)
> regtree <- rpart(LeagueIndex ~ ., data = skillcraft_train)
```

We can plot our regression tree to see what it looks like:

```
> plot(regtree, uniform = TRUE)
> text(regtree, use.n = FALSE, all = TRUE, cex = .8)
```

This is the plot that is produced:

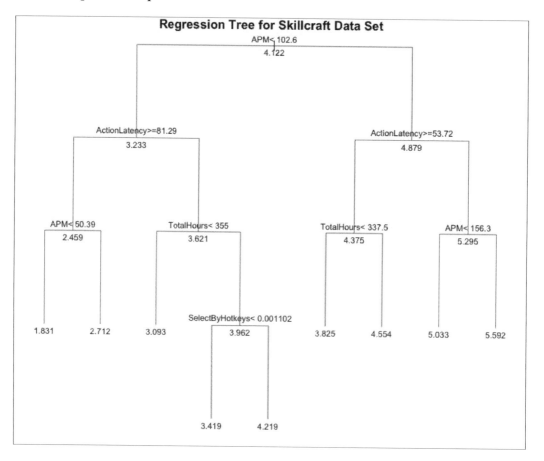

To get a sense of the accuracy of our regression tree, we will compute predictions on the test data and then measure the SSE. This can be done with the help of a simple function that we will define, `compute_SSE()`, which calculates the sum of squared error, when given a vector of target values and a vector of predicted values:

```
compute_SSE <- function(correct, predictions) {
    return(sum((correct - predictions) ^ 2))
}

> regtree_predictions <- predict(regtree, skillcraft_test)
> (regtree_SSE <- compute_SSE(regtree_predictions,
    skillcraft_test$LeagueIndex))
[1]  740.0874
```

Tuning model parameters in CART trees

So far, all we have done is use default values for all the parameters of the recursive partitioning algorithm for building the tree. The `rpart()` function has a special `control` parameter to which we can provide an object containing the values of any parameters we wish to override. To build this object, we must use the special `rpart.control()` function. There are a number of different parameters that we could tweak, and it is worth studying the help file for this function to learn more about them.

Here we will focus on three important parameters that affect the size and complexity of our tree. The `minsplit` parameter holds the minimum number of data points that are needed in order for the algorithm to attempt a split before it is forced to create a leaf node. The default value is 30. The `cp` parameter is the complexity parameter we have seen before and the default value of this is 0.01. Finally, the `maxdepth` parameter limits the maximum number of nodes between a leaf node and the root node. The default value of 30 is quite liberal here, allowing for fairly large trees to be built. We can try out a different regression tree by specifying some values for these that are different from their default. We'll do this, and see if this affects the SSE performance on our test set:

```
> regtree.random <- rpart(LeagueIndex ~ ., data = skillcraft_train,
    control = rpart.control(minsplit = 20, cp = 0.001, maxdepth = 10))
> regtree.random_predictions <- predict(regtree.random,
    skillcraft_test)
> (regtree.random_SSE <- compute_SSE(regtree.random_predictions,
    skillcraft_test$LeagueIndex))
[1]  748.6157
```

Using these values we are trying to limit the tree to a depth of 10, while making it easier to force a split by needing 20 or more data points at a node. We are also lowering the effect of regularization by setting the complexity parameter to 0.001. This is a completely random choice that happens to give us a worse SSE value on our test set. In practice, what is needed is a systematic way to find appropriate values of these parameters for our tree by trying out a number of different combinations and using cross-validation as a way to estimate their performance on unseen data.

Essentially, we would like to tune our regression tree training and in *Chapter 5, Support Vector Machines,* we met the `tune()` function inside the `e1071` package, which can help us do just that. We will use this function with `rpart()` and provide it with ranges for the three parameters we just discussed:

```
> library(e1071)
> rpart.ranges <- list(minsplit = seq(5, 50, by = 5), cp = c(0,
  0.001, 0.002, 0.005, 0.01, 0.02, 0.05, 0.1, 0.2,0.5), maxdepth =
  1:10)
> (regtree.tune <- tune(rpart,LeagueIndex ~ .,
    data = skillcraft_train, ranges = rpart.ranges))

Parameter tuning of 'rpart':

- sampling method: 10-fold cross validation

- best parameters:
 minsplit      cp maxdepth
       35 0.002        6


- best performance: 1.046638
```

Running the preceding tasks will likely take several minutes to complete, as there are many combinations of parameters. Once the procedure completes, we can train a tree with the suggested values:

```
> regtree.tuned <- rpart(LeagueIndex ~ ., data = skillcraft_train,
    control = rpart.control(minsplit = 35, cp = 0.002, maxdepth = 6))
> regtree.tuned_predictions <- predict(regtree.tuned,
    skillcraft_test)
> (regtree.tuned_SSE <- compute_SSE(regtree.tuned_predictions,
    skillcraft_test$LeagueIndex))
[1] 701.3386
```

Indeed, we have a lower SSE value with these settings on our test set. If we type in the name of our new regression tree model, `regree.tuned`, we'll see that we have many more nodes in our tree, which is now substantially more complex.

Variable importance in tree models

For large trees such as this, plotting is less useful as it is very hard to make the plot readable. One interesting plot that we can obtain is a plot of **variable importance**. For every input feature, we keep track of the reduction in the optimization criterion (for example, deviance or SSE) that occurs every time it is used anywhere in the tree. We can then tally up this quantity for all the splits in the tree and thus obtain relative amounts of variable importance.

Intuitively, features that are highly important will tend to have been used early to split the data (and hence appear higher up in the tree, closer to the root node) as well as more often. If a feature is never used, then it is not important and in this way we can see that we have a built-in feature selection.

Note that this approach is sensitive to correlation in the features. When trying to determine what feature to split on, we may randomly end up picking between two highly correlated features resulting in the model using more features than necessary and as a result, the importance of these features is lower than if either had been chosen on its own. It turns out that variable importance is automatically computed by rpart() and stored in the variable.importance attribute on the tree model that is returned. Plotting this using barplot() produces the following:

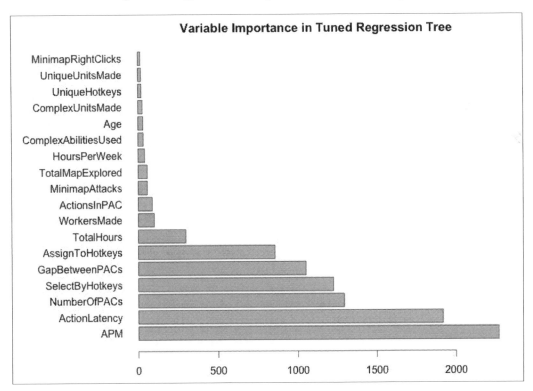

To an experienced player of the RTS genre, this graph looks quite reasonable and intuitive. The biggest separator of skill according to this graph is the average number of game actions that a player makes in a minute (APM). Experienced and effective players are capable of making many actions whereas less experienced players will make fewer.

At first glance, this may seem to be simply a matter of acquiring so-called muscle memory and developing faster reflexes, but in actuality it is knowing which actions to carry out, and playing with strategy and planning during the game (a characteristic of better players) that also significantly increases this metric.

Another speed-related attribute is the `ActionLatency` feature, which essentially measures the time between choosing to focus the map on a particular location on the battlefield and executing the first action at that location. Better players will spend less time looking at a map location and will be faster at selecting units, giving orders, and deciding what to do given an image of a situation in the game.

Regression model trees in action

We'll wrap up the experiments in this chapter with a very short demonstration of how to run a regression model tree in R. We can do this very easily using the RWeka package, which contains the `M5P()` function. This follows the typical convention of requiring a formula and a data frame with the training data:

```
> library("RWeka")
> m5treee <- M5P(LeagueIndex ~ ., data = skillcraft_train)
> m5tree_predictions <- predict(m5tree, skillcraft_test)
> m5tree_SSE <- compute_SSE(m5tree_predictions,
                             skillcraft_test$LeagueIndex)
> m5tree_SSE
[1] 714.8785
```

Note that we get almost comparable performance to our tuned CART tree using the default settings. We'll leave the readers to explore this function further, but we will be revisiting this data set once again in the next chapter on ensemble methods.

 A good reference on regression model trees containing several case studies is the original paper by *Quinlan*, titled *Learning with continuous cases*, from the proceedings of the *Australian Joint Conference on Artificial Intelligence* (1992).

Summary

In this chapter, we learned how to build decision trees for regression and classification tasks. We saw that although the idea is simple, there are several decisions that we have to make in order to construct our tree model, such as what splitting criterion to use, as well as when and how to prune our final tree.

In each case, we considered a number of viable options and it turns out that there are several algorithms that are used to build decision tree models. Some of the best qualities of decision trees are the fact that they are typically easy to implement and very easy to interpret, while making no assumptions about the underlying model of the data. Decision trees have native options for performing feature selection and handling missing data, and are very capable of handling a wide range of feature types.

Having said that, we saw that from a computational perspective, finding a split for categorical variables is quite expensive due to the exponential growth of the number of possible splits. In addition, we saw that categorical features can often tend to impose selection bias in splitting criteria such as information gain, because of this large number of potential splits.

Another drawback of using decision tree models is the fact that they can be unstable in the sense that small changes in the data can potentially alter a splitting decision high up in the tree and consequently we can end up with a very different tree after that. Additionally, and this is particularly relevant to regression problems, because of the finite number of leaf nodes, our model may not be sufficiently granular in its output. Finally, although there are several different approaches to pruning, we should note that decision trees can be vulnerable to overfitting.

In the next chapter, we are not going to focus on a new type of model. Instead, we are going to look at different techniques to combine multiple models together, such as bagging and boosting. Collectively, these are known as ensemble methods. These methods have been demonstrated to be quite effective in improving the performance of simpler models, and overcoming some of the limitations just discussed for tree-based models, such as model instability and susceptibility to overfitting.

We'll present a well-known algorithm, AdaBoost, which can be used with a number of models that we've seen so far. In addition, we will also introduce random forests, as a special type of ensemble model specifically designed for decision trees. Ensemble methods in general are typically not easy to interpret, but for random forests we can still use the notion of variable importance that we saw in this chapter in order to get an overall idea of which features our model relies upon the most.

7

Ensemble Methods

In this chapter, we take a step back from learning new models and instead think about how several trained models can work together as an ensemble, in order to produce a single model that is more powerful than the individual models involved.

The first type of ensemble that we will study uses different samples of the same data set in order to train multiple versions of the same model. These models then vote on the correct answer for a new observation and an average or majority decision is made, depending on the type of problem. This process is known as bagging, which is short for bootstrap aggregation. Another approach to combine models is boosting. This essentially involves training a chain of models and assigning weights to observations that were incorrectly classified or fell far from their predicted value so that successive models are forced to prioritize them.

As methods, bagging and boosting are fairly general and have been applied with a number of different types of models. Decision trees, studied in *Chapter 6, Tree-based Methods*, are particularly suited to ensemble methods. So much so, that a particular type of tree-based ensemble model has its own name—the random forest. Random forests offer significant improvements over the single decision tree and are generally considered to be very powerful and flexible models, as we shall soon discover. In this chapter, we'll revisit some of the data sets we analyzed in previous chapters and see if we can improve performance by applying some of the principles we learn here.

Bagging

The focus of this chapter is on combining the results from different models in order to produce a single model that will outperform individual models on their own. **Bagging** is essentially an intuitive procedure for combining multiple models trained on the same data set, by using majority voting for classification models and average value for regression models. We'll present this procedure for the classification case, and later show how this is easily extended to handle regression models.

Bagging procedure for binary classification

Inputs:

- *data*: The input data frame containing the input features and a column with the binary output label
- *M*: An integer, representing the number of models that we want to train

Output:

- *models*: A set of M trained binary classifier models

Method:

1. Create a random sample of size n, where n is the number of observations in the original data set, with replacement. This means that some of the observations from the original training set will be repeated and some will not be chosen at all. This process is known as **bootstrapping, bootstrap sampling,** or **bootstrap resampling.**

2. Train a classification model using this sampled data set. Typically, we opt not to use regularization or shrinkage methods designed to reduce overfitting in this step, because the aggregating process used at the end will be used to smooth out overfitting.

3. For each observation in the sampled data set, record the class assigned by the model.

4. Repeat this process M times in order to train M models.

5. For every observation in the original training data set, compute the predicted class via a majority vote across the different models. For example, suppose M = 61 and through bootstrap sampling a particular observation appears in the training data for 50 of the models. If 37 of these predict class 1 for this observation and 13 predict class -1, by majority vote the overall prediction will be class 1.

6. Compute the model's accuracy using the labels provided by the training set.

In a nutshell, all we are effectively doing is training the same model on M different versions of the input training set (created through sampling with replacement) and averaging the result.

A legitimate question to ask would be: "How many distinct observations do we get each time we sample with replacement?" On average, we end up with 63 percent of the distinct observations in every sample that we make. To understand where this comes from, consider that because we are sampling with replacement, the probability of not picking out a particular observation, x_1, during sampling is just the result of n failed Bernoulli trials: $\left(1-\frac{1}{n}\right)^n$. This number also happens to be the average proportion of observations that are not selected across the entire training data set because we multiply and divide the previous expression by n to compute this quantity. The numerical result of this expression can be approximated by e^{-1}, which is roughly 37 percent. Consequently, the average proportion of observations that are selected is around 63 percent. This number is just an average, of course, and is more accurate for larger values of n.

Margins and out-of-bag observations

Let's imagine that for a particular observation, x_1, 85 percent of our models predict the correct class and the remaining 15 percent predict the incorrect class. Let's also imagine that we have another observation, x_2, for which the analogous percentages are 53 percent and 47 percent. Clearly, our intuition suggests that we should be more confident about the classification of the former observation compared to the latter observation. Put differently, the difference between the classification proportions, also known as the **margin** (similar to but not to be confused with the margin used for support vector machines) is a good indicator of the confidence of our classification.

The 70 percent margin of observation x_1 is much larger than the 6 percent margin of observation x_2 and thus, we believe more strongly in our ability to correctly classify the former observation. In general, what we are hoping for is a classifier that has a large margin for all the observations. We are less optimistic about the generalization abilities of a classifier that has a small margin for more than a handful of observations.

One thing the reader may have noticed here is that in generating the set of predicted values for each model, we are using the same data on which the model was trained. If we look closely at *step 3* of the procedure, we are classifying the same sampled data that we used in *step 2* to train the model. Even though we are eventually relying on using an averaging process at the end in order to obtain the estimated accuracy of the bagged classifier for unseen data, we haven't actually used any unseen data at any step of the way.

Remember that in *step 1* we constructed a sample of the training data with which to train our model. From the original data set, we refer to the observations that were not chosen for a particular iteration of the procedure as the **out-of-bag** (**OOB**) observations. These observations are therefore not used in the training of the model at that iteration. Consequently, instead of relying on the observations used to train the models at every step, we can actually use the OOB observations to record the accuracy of a particular model.

In the end, we average over all the OOB accuracy rates to obtain an average accuracy. This average accuracy is far more likely to be a realistic and objective estimate of the performance of the bagged classifier on unseen data. For a particular observation, the assigned class is thus decided as the majority vote over all classifiers for which the observation was not picked in their corresponding training sample.

The samples generated from sampling the original data set with replacement, known as **bootstrapped samples**, are similar to drawing multiple samples from the same distribution. As we are trying to estimate the same target function using a number of different samples instead of just one, the averaging process reduces the variance of the result. To see this, consider trying to estimate the mean of a set of observations drawn from the same distribution and all mutually independent of each other. More formally, these are known as **independent and identically distributed (iid)** observations. The variance of the mean of these observations is σ^2 / n.

This shows that as the number of observations increases, the variance decreases. Bagging tries to achieve the same behavior for the function we are trying to model. We don't have truly independent training samples, and are instead forced to use bootstrapped samples, but this thought experiment should be enough to convince us that, in principle, bagging has the potential to reduce the variance of the model. At the same time, this averaging process is a form of smoothing over any localized bumps in the function that we are trying to estimate. Assuming that the target regression function or classification boundary that we are trying to estimate is actually smooth, then bagging may also reduce the bias of our model.

Predicting complex skill learning with bagging

Bagging and boosting are both very popular with the tree-based models that we studied in *Chapter 6, Tree-based Methods*. There are many notable implementations to apply these approaches to methodologies like CART for building trees.

The `ipred` package, for example, contains an implementation to build a bagged predictor for trees built with `rpart()`. We can experiment with the `bagging()` function that this package provides. To do this, we specify the number of bagged trees to make using the `nbagg` parameter (default is 25) and indicate that we want to compute accuracy using the out-of-bag (OOB) samples by setting the `coob` parameter to `TRUE`.

We will do this for our complex skill learning data set from the previous chapter, using the same training data frame:

```
> baggedtree <- bagging(LeagueIndex ~ ., data = skillcraft_train,
                        nbagg = 100, coob = T)
> baggedtree_predictions <- predict(baggedtree, skillcraft_test)
> (baggedtree_SSE <- compute_SSE(baggedtree_predictions,
                                 skillcraft_test$LeagueIndex))
[1] 646.3555
```

As we can see, the SSE on the test set is less than the lowest SSE that we saw when tuning a single tree. Increasing the number of bagged iterations, however, does not seem to improve this performance substantially. We will revisit this data set again later.

Predicting heart disease with bagging

The prototypical use case for bagging is the decision tree; however, it is important to remember that we can use this method with a variety of different models. In this section, we will show how we can build a bagged logistic regression classifier. We built a logistic regression classifier for the Statlog Heart data set in *Chapter 3, Logistic Regression*. Now, we will repeat that experiment but use bagging in order to see if we can improve our results. To begin with, we'll draw our samples with replacement and use these to train our models:

```
> M <- 11
> seeds <- 70000 : (70000 + M - 1)
> n <- nrow(heart_train)
> sample_vectors <- sapply(seeds, function(x) { set.seed(x);
  return(sample(n, n, replace = T)) })
```

In our code, the data frames `heart_train` and `heart_test` are referring to the same data frames that we prepared in *Chapter 3, Logistic Regression*. We begin by deciding on the number of models that we will train and setting the appropriate value of `M`. Here, we have used an initial value of `11`.

Note that it is a good idea to use an odd number of models with bagging, so that during the majority voting process there can never be a tie with binary classification. For reproducibility, we set a vector of seeds that we will use. This is simply a counter from an arbitrarily chosen starting seed value of 70,000. The `sample_vectors` matrix in our code contains a matrix where the columns are the indexes of randomly selected rows from the training data with replacement. Note that the rows are numbered 1 through 230 in the training data, making the sampling process easy to code.

Next, we'll define a function that creates a single logistic regression model given a sampling vector of indices to use with our training data frame:

```
train_1glm <- function(sample_indices) {
    data <- heart_train[sample_indices,];
    model <- glm(OUTPUT ~ ., data = data, family = binomial("logit"));
    return(model)
}


> models <- apply(sample_vectors, 2, train_1glm)
```

In the last line of the preceding code, we iterate through the columns of the `sample_vectors` matrix we produced earlier and supply them as an input to our logistic regression model training function, `train_1glm()`. The resulting models are then stored in our final list variable, `models`. This now contains 11 trained models.

As the first method of evaluating our models, we are going to use the data on which each individual model was trained. To that end, we'll construct the `bags` variable that is a list of these data frames, this time with unique indexes, as we don't want to use any duplicate rows from the bootstrap sampling process in the evaluation. We'll also add a new column called `ID` to these data frames that stores the original row names from the `heart_train` data frame. We'll see why we do this shortly.

```
get_1bag <- function(sample_indices) {
    unique_sample <- unique(sample_indices);
    df <- heart_train[unique_sample, ];
    df$ID <- unique_sample;
    return(df)
}


> bags <- apply(sample_vectors, 2, get_1bag)
```

We now have a list of models and a list of data frames that they were trained on, the latter without duplicate observations. From these two, we can create a list of predictions. For each training data frame, we will tack on a new column called PREDICTIONS {m}, where {m} will be the number of the model being used to make the predictions. Consequently, the first data frame in the bags list will have a predictions column called PREDICTIONS 1. The second data frame will have a predictions column called PREDICTIONS 2, the third will have one called PREDICTIONS 3, and so on.

The following call produces a new set of data frames as just described, but only keeping the PREDICTIONS{m} and ID columns, and these data frames are stored as a list in the variable training_predictions:

```
glm_predictions <- function(model, data, model_index) {
    colname <- paste("PREDICTIONS", model_index);
    data[colname] <- as.numeric(
                    predict(model, data, type = "response") > 0.5);
    return(data[,c("ID", colname), drop = FALSE])
}


> training_predictions <-
        mapply(glm_predictions, models, bags, 1 : M, SIMPLIFY = F)
```

Next, we want to merge all of these data frames onto a single data frame, where the rows are the rows of the original data frame (and thus, correspond to the observations in the data set) and the columns are the predictions made by each model on the observations. Where a particular row (observation) was not selected by the sampling process to train a particular model, it will have an NA value in the column corresponding to the predictions that that model makes.

Just to be clear, recall that each model is making predictions only on the observations that were used to train it and so the number of predictions that each model makes is smaller than the total number of observations available in our starting data.

As we have stored the original row numbers of the heart_train data frame in the ID column of every data frame created in the previous step, we can merge using this column. We use the Reduce() function along with the merge() function in order to merge all the data frames in our training_predictions variable into one new data frame. Here is the code:

```
> train_pred_df <- Reduce(function(x, y) merge(x, y, by = "ID",
                        all = T), training_predictions)
```

Let's have a look at the first few lines and columns of this aggregated data frame:

```
> head(training_prediction_df[, 1:5])
  ID PREDICTIONS 1 PREDICTIONS 2 PREDICTIONS 3 PREDICTIONS 4
1  1             1            NA             1            NA
2  2             0            NA            NA             0
3  3            NA             0             0            NA
4  4            NA             1             1             1
5  5             0             0             0            NA
6  6             0             1             0             0
```

The first column is the ID row that was used to merge the data frame. The numbers in this column are the row numbers of the observations from the starting training data frame. The PREDICTIONS 1 column contains the predictions that the first model makes. We can see that this model had rows 1, 2, 5, and 6 as part of its training data. For the first row, the model predicts class 1 and for the other three rows, it predicts class 0. Rows 3 and 4 were not part of its training data and so there are two NA values. This reasoning can be used to understand the remaining columns, which correspond to the next three models trained.

With this data frame constructed, we can now produce our training data predictions for the whole bagged model using a majority vote across each row of the preceding data frame. Once we have these, we merely need to match the predictions with the labeled values of the corresponding rows of the original heart_train data frame and compute our accuracy:

```
> train_pred_vote <- apply(train_pred_df[,-1], 1,
               function(x) as.numeric(mean(x, na.rm = TRUE) > 0.5))
> (training_accuracy <- mean(train_pred_vote ==
               heart_train$OUTPUT[as.numeric(train_pred_df$ID)]))
[1] 0.9173913
```

We now have our first accuracy measure for our bagged model—91.7 percent. This is analogous to measuring the accuracy on our training data. We will now repeat this process using the out-of-bag observations for each model to compute the out-of-bag accuracy.

There is one caveat here, however. In our data, the ECG column is a factor with three levels, one of which, level 1, is very rare. As a result of this, when we draw bootstrap samples from the original training data, we may encounter samples in which this factor level never appears. When that happens, the glm() function will think this factor only takes two levels, and the resulting model will be unable to make predictions when it encounters an observation with a value for the ECG factor that it has never seen before.

To handle this situation, we need to replace the level 1 value of this factor with an NA value for the out-of-bag observations, if the model they correspond to did not have at least one observation with an ECG factor level of 1 in its training data. Essentially, for simplicity, we will just not attempt to make a prediction for these problematic observations when they arise. With this in mind, we will define a function to compute the out-of-bag observations for a particular sample and then use this to find the out-of-bag observations for all our samples:

```
get_loo_bag <- function(sample_indices) {
    unique_sample <- setdiff(1 : n, unique(sample_indices));
    df <- heart_train[unique_sample,];
    df$ID <- unique_sample;
    if (length(unique(heart_train[sample_indices,]$ECG)) < 3)
        df[df$ECG == 1,"ECG"] = NA;
    return(df)
}

> oo_bags <- apply(sample_vectors, 2, get_loo_bag)
```

Next, we will use our `glm_predictions()` function to compute predictions using our out-of-bag samples. The remainder of the process is identical to what we did earlier:

```
> oob_predictions <- mapply(glm_predictions, models, oo_bags,
                            1 : M, SIMPLIFY = F)
> oob_pred_df <- Reduce(function(x, y) merge(x, y, by = "ID",
                        all = T), oob_predictions)
> oob_pred_vote <- apply(oob_pred_df[,-1], 1,
                        function(x) as.numeric(mean(x, na.rm = TRUE) > 0.5))

> (oob_accuracy <- mean(oob_pred_vote ==
                heart_train$OUTPUT[as.numeric(oob_pred_df$ID)],
            na.rm = TRUE))
[1] 0.8515284
```

As expected, we see that our out-of-bag accuracy, which is a better measure of performance on unseen data, is lower than the training data accuracy. In the last line of the previous code sample, we excluded NA values when computing the out-of-bag accuracy. This is important because it is possible that a particular observation may appear in all the bootstrap samples and therefore never be available for an out-of-bag prediction.

Equally, our fix for the rare level of the ECG factor means that even if an observation is not selected by the sampling process, we may still not be able to make a prediction for it. The reader should verify that only one observation happens to produce an NA value because of the combination of the two phenomena just described.

Finally, we'll repeat this process a third time using the `heart_test` data frame to obtain the test set accuracy:

```
get_1test_bag <- function(sample_indices) {
    df <- heart_test;
    df$ID <- row.names(df);
    if (length(unique(heart_train[sample_indices,]$ECG)) < 3)
        df[df$ECG == 1,"ECG"] = NA;
    return(df)
}


> test_bags <- apply(sample_vectors, 2, get_1test_bag)
> test_predictions <- mapply(glm_predictions, models, test_bags,
                          1 : M, SIMPLIFY = F)
> test_pred_df <- Reduce(function(x, y) merge(x, y, by = "ID",
                      all = T), test_predictions)
> test_pred_vote <- apply(test_pred_df[,-1], 1,
                function(x) as.numeric(mean(x, na.rm = TRUE) > 0.5))
> (test_accuracy <- mean(test_pred_vote ==
                heart_test[test_pred_df$ID,"OUTPUT"], na.rm = TRUE))
[1] 0.8
```

The accuracy on the test set seems lower than what we found without a bagged model. This is not necessarily bad news for us, since the test set is very small. In fact, the difference between the performance of this bagged model and the original model trained in *Chapter 3, Logistic Regression*, is 32/40 compared to 36/40, which is to say it is only worse by four observations in 40.

In a real-world situation, we generally want to have a much larger test set to estimate our unseen accuracy. In fact, because of this, we are more inclined to believe our out-of-bag accuracy measurement, which is done over a larger number of observations and averaged over many models.

Bagging is actually very useful for us in this scenario as it gives us a model for which we can have a better estimate of the test accuracy, using the out-of-bag observations because the test set is so small. As a final demonstration, we run the previous code a number of times with different values of M and store the results in a data frame:

```
> heart_bagger_df
     M Training Accuracy Out-of-bag Accuracy Test Accuracy
1   11         0.9173913           0.8515284         0.800
2   51         0.9130435           0.8521739         0.800
3  101         0.9173913           0.8478261         0.800
4  501         0.9086957           0.8521739         0.775
5 1001         0.9130435           0.8565217         0.775
```

This table shows us that the test accuracy fluctuates around 80 percent. This isn't that surprising given the small size of our test set of only 40 observations. For the training accuracy, we see that we are fluctuating around 91 percent. The OOB accuracy, which is far more stable as an accuracy measure, shows us that the expected performance of the model is around 85 percent. As the number of models increases, we don't see much of an improvement over 11 models, though for most real-world data sets, we would usually see some improvement before tapering off.

Although our example focused exclusively on bagging for classification problems, the move to regression problems is relatively straightforward. Instead of using majority votes for a particular observation, we use the average value of the target function predicted by the individual models. Bagging is not always guaranteed to provide a performance improvement on a model. For starters, we should note that it makes sense to use bagging only when we have a nonlinear model. As the bagging process is performing an average (a linear operation) over the models generated, we will not see any improvements with linear regression, for example, because we aren't increasing the expressive power of our model. The next section talks about some other limitations of bagging.

 For more information on bagging, consult the original paper of *Leo Breiman* titled *Bagging Predictors*, published in 1996 in the journal *Machine Learning*.

Limitations of bagging

So far, we've only explored the upside of using bagging, but in some cases it may turn out not to be a good idea. Bagging involves taking the average across predictions made by several models, which are trained on bootstrapped samples of the training data. This averaging process smoothens the overall output, which may reduce bias when the target function is smooth. Unfortunately, if the target function is not smooth, we may actually introduce bias by using bagging.

Another way that bagging introduces bias is when one of the output classes is very rare. Under those circumstances, the majority voting system tends to be biased towards the more common class. Other problems may arise in relation to the sampling process itself. As we have already learned, when some categorical features include values that are rare, these may not appear at all in some of the bootstrap samples. When this happens, the models built for these samples will be unable to make a prediction when they encounter this new feature level in their test set.

High leverage points, which are highly influential in determining the model's output function compared to other points, can also be a problem. If a bootstrap sample is drawn that does not include one or more high leverage points, the resulting trained model will be quite different compared to when they are included. Therefore, bagging performance depends on how often these particular observations are sampled in order to win the majority vote. Due to this fact, our ensemble model will have a high variance in the presence of high leverage points. For a given data set, we can often predict if we are in this situation by looking for outliers and highly skewed features.

We must also remember that the different models we build are not truly independent of each other in the strict sense because they still use the same set of input features. The averaging process would have been more effective if the models were independent. Also, bagging does not help when the type of model that we are using predicts a functional form that is very far from the true form of the target function. When this happens, training multiple models of this type merely reproduces the systematic errors across the different models. Put differently, bagging works better when we have low bias and high variance models as the averaging process is primarily designed to reduce the variance.

Finally, and this applies to ensemble models in general, we tend to lose the explanative power of our model. We saw an example of explanative power in linear regression where each model parameter (regression coefficient) corresponded to the amount of change in the output, for a unit increase in the corresponding feature. Decision trees are another example of a model with high explanatory power. Using bagging loses this benefit because of the majority voting process and so we cannot directly relate our inputs to the predicted output.

Boosting

Boosting offers an alternative take on the problem of how to combine models together to achieve greater performance. In particular, it is especially suited to **weak learners**. Weak learners are models that produce an accuracy that is better than a model that randomly guesses, but not by much. One way to create a weak learner is to use a model whose complexity is configurable.

For example, we can train a multilayer perceptron network with a very small number of hidden layer neurons. Similarly, we can train a decision tree but only allow the tree to comprise a single node, resulting in a single split in the input data. This special type of decision tree is known as a **stump**.

When we looked at bagging, the key idea was to take a set of random bootstrapped samples of the training data and then train multiple versions of the same model using these different samples. In the classical boosting scenario, there is no random component, as all the models use all of the training data.

For classification, boosting works by building a model on the training data and then measuring the classification accuracy on that training data. The individual observations that were misclassified by the model are given a larger weight than those that were correctly classified, and then the model is retrained again using these new weights. This is then repeated multiple times, each time adjusting the weights of individual observations based on whether they were correctly classified or not in the last iteration.

To combat overfitting, the ensemble classifier is built as a weighted average of all the models trained in this sequence, with the weights usually being proportional to the classification accuracy of each individual model. As we are using the entire training data, there are no out-of-bag observations and so the accuracy in each case is measured using the training data itself. Regression with boosting is usually done by adjusting the weights of observation based on some measure of the distance between the predicted value and the labeled value.

AdaBoost

Continuing our focus on classification problems, we now introduce **AdaBoost**, which is short for **adaptive boosting**. In particular, we will focus on **Discrete AdaBoost**, as it makes predictions on binary classes. We will use -1 and 1 as the class labels. **Real AdaBoost** is an extension of AdaBoost, in which the outputs are the class probabilities. In our version of AdaBoost, all of the training data is used; however, there are other versions of AdaBoost in which the training data is also sampled. There are also multiclass extensions of AdaBoost as well as extensions that are suited to regression-type problems.

AdaBoost for binary classification

Inputs:

- *data*: The input data frame containing the input features and a column with the binary output label
- *M*: An integer, representing the number of models that we want to train

Output:

- *models*: A series of *M* trained models
- *alphas*: A vector of *M* model weights

Method:

1. Initialize a vector of observation weights, *w*, of length *n* with entries $w_i = 1/n$. This vector will be updated in every iteration.

2. Using the current value of the observation weights and all the data in the training set, train a classifier model G_m.

3. Compute the weighted error rate as the sum of all misclassified observations multiplied by their observation weights, divided by the sum of the weight vector. Following our usual convention of using x_i as an observation and y_i as its label, we can express this using the following equation:

$$err_m = \frac{\sum_{i=1}^{n} w_i I(y_i \neq G_m(x_i))}{\sum_{i=1}^{n} w_i}$$

4. We then set the model weight for this model, a_m, as the logarithm of the ratio between the accuracy and error rates. In a formula, this is:

$$\alpha_m = \frac{1}{2} \log_e \left(\frac{1 - err_m}{err_m} \right)$$

5. We then update the observation weights vector, *w*, for the next iteration. Incorrectly classified observations have their weight multiplied by e^{a_m}, thereby increasing their weight for the next iteration. Correctly classified observations have their weight multiplied by e^{-a_m}, thereby reducing their weight for the next iteration.

6. Renormalize the weights vector so that the sum of the weights is 1.

7. Repeat steps two through six *M* times in order to produce *M* models.

8. Define our ensemble classifier as the sign of the weighted sum of the outputs of all the boosted models:

$$G(x) = sign\left(\sum_{m=1}^{M} \alpha_m G_m(x) \right)$$

Predicting atmospheric gamma ray radiation

In order to study boosting in action, in this section we'll introduce a new prediction problem from the field of atmospheric physics. More specifically, we will analyze the patterns made by radiation on a telescope camera in order to predict whether a particular pattern came from gamma rays leaking into the atmosphere, or from regular background radiation.

Gamma rays leave distinctive elliptical patterns and so we can create a set of features to describe these. The data set we will use is the *MAGIC Gamma Telescope data set*, hosted by the *UCI Machine Learning* repository at `http://archive.ics.uci.edu/ml/datasets/MAGIC+Gamma+Telescope`. Our data consists of 19,020 observations of the following attributes:

Column name	Type	Definition
FLENGTH	Numerical	The major axis of the ellipse (mm)
FWIDTH	Numerical	The minor axis of the ellipse (mm)
FSIZE	Numerical	Logarithm to the base ten of the sum of the content of all pixels in the camera photo
FCONC	Numerical	Ratio of the sum of the two highest pixels over FSIZE
FCONC1	Numerical	Ratio of the highest pixel over FSIZE
FASYM	Numerical	Distance from the highest pixel to the center, projected onto the major axis (mm)
FM3LONG	Numerical	Third root of the third moment along the major axis (mm)
FM3TRANS	Numerical	Third root of the third moment along the minor axis (mm)
FALPHA	Numerical	Angle of the major axis with the vector to the origin (degrees)
FDIST	Numerical	Distance from the origin to the center of the ellipse (mm)
CLASS	Binary	Gamma rays (*g*) or Background Hadron Radiation (*b*)

First, we will load the data into a data frame called `magic`, recoding the `CLASS` output variable to use classes `1` and `-1` for gamma rays and background radiation respectively:

```
> magic <- read.csv("magic04.data", header = FALSE)
> names(magic) <- c("FLENGTH", "FWIDTH", "FSIZE", "FCONC", "FCONC1",
  "FASYM", "FM3LONG", "FM3TRANS", "FALPHA", "FDIST", "CLASS")
> magic$CLASS <- as.factor(ifelse(magic$CLASS =='g', 1, -1))
```

Next, we'll split our data frame into a training data and a test data frame using our typical 80-20 split:

```
> library(caret)
> set.seed(33711209)
> magic_sampling_vector <- createDataPartition(magic$CLASS,
                            p = 0.80, list = FALSE)
> magic_train <- magic[magic_sampling_vector, 1:10]
> magic_train_output <- magic[magic_sampling_vector, 11]
> magic_test <- magic[-magic_sampling_vector, 1:10]
> magic_test_output <- magic[-magic_sampling_vector, 11]
```

The model that we are going to use with boosting is a simple multilayer perceptron with a single hidden layer. Harkening back to *Chapter 4, Neural Networks*, we know that the `nnet` package is perfect for this task. With neural networks, we often get superior accuracy when we normalize the inputs and so before training any models, we will carry out this preprocessing step:

```
> magic_pp <- preProcess(magic_train, method = c("center",
                                               "scale"))
> magic_train_pp <- predict(magic_pp, magic_train)
> magic_train_df_pp <- cbind(magic_train_pp,
                           CLASS = magic_train_output)
> magic_test_pp <- predict(magic_pp, magic_test)
```

Boosting is designed to work best with weak learners, and for this reason, we are going to use a very small number of hidden neurons in our hidden layer. Concretely, we will begin with the simplest possible multilayer perceptron that uses a single hidden neuron. To understand the effect of using boosting, we will establish our baseline performance by training a single neural network and measuring its accuracy. We can do this as follows:

```
> library(nnet)
> n_model <- nnet(CLASS ~ ., data = magic_train_df_pp, size = 1)
> n_test_predictions <- predict(n_model, magic_test_pp,
                              type = "class")
> (n_test_accuracy <- mean(n_test_predictions ==
                        magic_test_output))
[1] 0.7948988
```

This establishes that we have a baseline accuracy of around 79.5 percent. This isn't too bad, but we are going to use boosting to see if we can improve it. To that end, we are going to write our own function, AdaBoostNN(), that will take as input a data frame, the name of the output variable, the number of single hidden layer neural network models we want to build, and finally the number of hidden units these neural networks will have. This function will then implement the AdaBoost algorithm that we previously described and finally return a list of models and their weights. Here is the function:

```
AdaBoostNN <- function(training_data, output_column, M,
                       hidden_units) {
  require("nnet")
  models <- list()
  alphas <- list()
  n <- nrow(training_data)
  model_formula <- as.formula(paste(output_column, '~ .', sep = ''))
  w <- rep((1/n), n)
  for (m in 1:M) {
    model <- nnet(model_formula, data = training_data,
                  size = hidden_units, weights = w)
    models[[m]] <- model
    predictions <- as.numeric(predict(model,
                   training_data[, -which(names(training_data) ==
                   output_column)], type = "class"))
    errors <- predictions != training_data[, output_column]
    error_rate <- sum(w * as.numeric(errors)) / sum(w)
    alpha <- 0.5 * log((1 - error_rate) / error_rate)
    alphas[[m]] <- alpha
    temp_w <- mapply(function(x, y) if (y) { x * exp(alpha) }
                     else { x * exp(-alpha)}, w, errors)
    w <- temp_w / sum(temp_w)
  }
  return(list(models = models, alphas = unlist(alphas)))
}
```

Before proceeding, we will work our way through the function to understand what each line is doing. We first initialize empty lists of models and model weights (alphas). We also compute the number of observations in our training data, storing this in the variable n. The name of the output column provided is then used to create a formula that describes the neural network that we will build.

In our data set, this formula will be CLASS ~ ., which means that the neural network will compute CLASS as a function of all the other columns as input features. We then initialize our weights vector, as we did in *step 1* of AdaBoost, and define our loop that will run for *M* iterations in order to build *M* models.

In every iteration, the first step is to use the current setting of the weights vector to train a neural network using as many hidden units as specified in the input, hidden_units. We then compute a vector of predictions that this model generates on the training data using the predict() function. By comparing these predictions to the output column of the training data, we calculate the errors that the current model makes on the training data. This then allows us to compute the error rate. According to *step 4* of the AdaBoost algorithm, this error rate is set as the weight of the current model. Finally, the observation weights to be used in the next iteration of the loop are updated according to whether each observation was correctly classified using *step 5* of the AdaBoost algorithm. The weight vector is then normalized and we are ready to begin the next iteration. After completing *M* iterations, we output a list of models and their corresponding model weights.

We now have a function that is able to train our ensemble classifier using AdaBoost but we also need a function to make predictions. This function will take in the output list produced by our training function, AdaBoostNN(), along with a test data set. We've called this function AdaBoostNN.predict() and it is shown here:

```
AdaBoostNN.predict <- function(ada_model, test_data) {
   models <- ada_model$models
   alphas <- ada_model$alphas
   prediction_matrix <- sapply(models, function (x)
               as.numeric(predict(x, test_data, type = "class")))
   weighted_predictions <- t(apply(prediction_matrix, 1,
               function(x) mapply(function(y, z) y * z, x, alphas)))
   final_predictions <- apply(weighted_predictions, 1,
               function(x) sign(sum(x)))
   return(final_predictions)
}
```

In this function, we first extract the models and the model weights from the list produced by our previous function. We then create a matrix of predictions, where each column corresponds to the vector of predictions made by a particular model. Thus, we will have as many columns in this matrix as models that we used for boosting.

We then multiply the predictions produced by each model with their corresponding model weight. For example, every prediction from the first model is in the first column of the prediction matrix and will have its value multiplied by the first model weight a_1. Finally, in the last step, we reduce our matrix of weighted observations into a single vector of observations by summing the weighted predictions for each observation and taking the sign of the result. This vector of predictions is then returned by our function.

As an experiment, we will train ten neural network models with a single hidden unit and see if boosting improves accuracy:

```
> ada_model <- AdaBoostNN(magic_train_df_pp, 'CLASS', 10, 1)
> predictions <- AdaBoostNN.predict(ada_model, magic_test_pp,
                                    'CLASS')
> mean(predictions == magic_test_output)
 [1]  0.804365
```

Boosting ten models seems to give us a marginal improvement in accuracy, but perhaps training more models might make more of a difference. We are also interested in the relationship between the complexity of our weak learner, as measured by the number of hidden neurons, and the performance benefits we can expect from boosting on this data set. The following plot shows the results of experimenting with our functions using different numbers of models as well as hidden neurons:

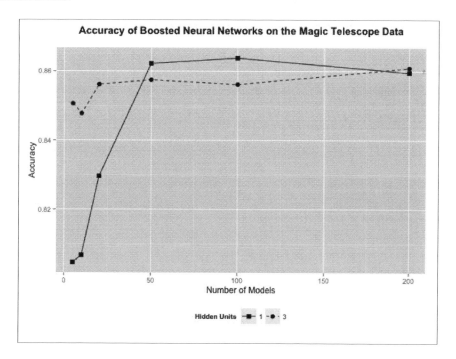

For the neural networks with one hidden unit, as the number of boosting models increases, we see an improvement in accuracy, but after 100 models, this tapers off and is actually slightly less for 200 models. The improvement over the baseline of a single model is substantial for these networks. When we increase the complexity of our learner by having a hidden layer with three hidden neurons, we get a much smaller improvement in performance. At 200 models, both ensembles perform at a similar level, indicating that at this point our accuracy is being limited by the type of model we are training.

The original AdaBoost algorithm was presented by *Freund* and *Schapire* in the journal of *Computer and System Sciences* in a 1997 paper titled *A Decision-theoretic generalization of on-line learning and an application to boosting*. This is a good place to start learning more about AdaBoost.

Predicting complex skill learning with boosting

We will revisit our Skillcraft data set in this section—this time in the context of another boosting technique known as **stochastic gradient boosting**. The main characteristic of this method is that in every iteration of boosting, we compute a gradient in the direction of the errors that are made by the model trained in the current iteration.

This gradient is then used in order to guide the construction of the model that will be added in the next iteration. Stochastic gradient boosting is commonly used with decision trees, and a good implementation in R can be found in the gbm package, which provides us with the gbm() function. For regression problems, we need to specify the distribution parameter to be gaussian. In addition, we can specify the number of trees we want to build (which is equivalent to the number of iterations of boosting) via the n.trees parameter, as well as a shrinkage parameter that is used to control the algorithm's learning rate.

```
> boostedtree <- gbm(LeagueIndex ~ ., data = skillcraft_train,
    distribution = "gaussian", n.trees = 10000, shrinkage = 0.1)
```

To learn more about how stochastic gradient boosting works, a good source to consult is the paper titled *Stochastic Gradient Boosting*. This was written by *Jerome H. Friedman* and appears in the February 2002 issue of the journal *Computational Statistics & Data Analysis*.

In order to make predictions with this setup, we need to use the `gbm.perf()` function, whose job it is to take the boosted model we built and pick out the optimal number of boosting iterations. We can then provide this to our `predict()` function in order to make predictions on our test data. To measure the SSE on our test set, we will use the `compute_SSE()` function that we wrote in *Chapter 6, Tree-based Methods*:

```
> best.iter <- gbm.perf(boostedtree, method = "OOB")
> boostedtree_predictions <- predict(boostedtree,
                                 skillcraft_test, best.iter)
> (boostedtree_SSE <- compute_SSE(boostedtree_predictions,
                            skillcraft_test$LeagueIndex))
[1] 555.2997
```

A bit of experimentation has revealed that we can't get substantially better results than this by allowing the algorithm to iterate over more trees. Despite this, we are already performing better using this method than both the single and bagged tree classifiers.

Limitations of boosting

Boosting is a very powerful technique that continues to receive a lot of attention and research, but it is not without its limitations. Boosting relies on combining weak learners together. In particular, we can expect to get the most out of boosting when the models that are used are not already complex models themselves. We already saw an example of this with neural networks, by noting that the more complex architecture of three hidden neurons gives a better learner to begin with than the simpler architecture of a single hidden neuron.

Combining weak learners may be a way to reduce overfitting, but this is not always effective. By default, boosting uses all of its training data and progressively tries to correct mistakes that it makes without any penalizing or shrinkage criterion (although the individual models trained may themselves be regularized). Consequently, boosting can sometimes overfit.

Finally, a very important limitation is that many boosting algorithms have a symmetric loss function. Specifically, there is no distinction that is made in classification between a false positive classification error and a false negative classification error. Every type of error is treated the same when the observation weights are updated.

In practice, this might not be desirable, in that one of the two errors may be more costly. For example, on the website for our MAGIC Telescope data set, the authors state that a false positive of detecting gamma rays where there are none, is worse than a false negative of misclassifying gamma rays as background radiation. Cost-sensitive extensions of boosting algorithms have been proposed, however.

Random forests

The final ensemble model that we will discuss in this chapter is unique to tree-based models and is known as the **random forest**. In a nutshell, the idea behind random forests stems from an observation on bagging trees. Let's suppose that the actual relationship between the features and the target variable can be adequately described with a tree structure. It is quite likely that during bagging with moderately sized bootstrapped samples, we will keep picking the same features to split on high up in the tree.

For example, in our Skillcraft data set, we expect to see APM as the feature that will be chosen at the top of most of the bagged trees. This is a form of tree correlation that essentially impedes our ability to derive the variance reduction benefits from bagging. Put differently, the different tree models that we build are not truly independent of each other because they will have many features and split points in common. Consequently, the averaging process at the end will be less successful in reducing the ensemble variance.

To counteract this effect, the random forest algorithm introduces an element of randomization in the tree construction process. Just as with bagging, random forests involve building a number of trees with bootstrapped samples and using the average of their predictions to form the ensemble prediction. When we construct individual trees, however, the random forest algorithm imposes a constraint.

At each node in the tree, we draw a random sample of size m_{try} from the total number of input features. Whereas in regular tree construction, we consider all the features at each node to determine which one to split on, with random forests, we only consider features from the sample we created for that node. We can often use a relatively small number for m_{try}.

The number of trees that we build, in combination with the fact that each tree has several nodes, is often enough to ensure that the more important features are sampled a sufficient number of times. Various heuristics have been proposed for choosing appropriate values for this parameter, such as one third or the square root of the total number of features available.

This sampling step effectively forces the structure of the bagged trees to be different from each other and offers a number of different benefits. Feature sampling allows us to consider input features that are successful in splitting the data for only a small range of the target variable. These locally relevant features are rarely chosen without the sampling constraint because we usually prefer features that form good overall splits of the data at a given node in the tree. Nonetheless, we may want to include these features in our model if we don't want to overlook local variations in the output.

Similarly, sampling input features is useful when we have correlated input features. Regular tree construction tends to favor only one of the features from a correlated set while ignoring the rest despite the fact that the resulting splits from even highly correlated features are not exactly the same. When we sample input features we are less likely to have correlated features compete with each other and so we can choose a wider range of features to use with our model.

In general, the randomized nature of the sampling process is designed to combat overfitting because we can think of this process as applying regularization on the impact of each input feature. Overfitting can still be a problem if we happen to have too many input features unrelated to the target variable compared to those that are related, but this is a fairly rare scenario. Random forests in general scale quite favorably with the number of input features, precisely because of this sampling process that doesn't require us to consider all the features when splitting at each node. In particular, this model is a good choice when the number of features exceeds the number of observations. Finally, the sampling process mitigates the cost of constructing a large number of trees again because we consider a subset of input features when deciding on how to split at each node. The number of trees is another tuning parameter that we must decide on in a random forest model; it is very common to build anywhere between several hundred and a few thousand trees.

In R, we can use the `randomForest` package in order to train random forest models. The `randomForest()` function takes in a formula and a training data frame, as well as a number of other optional parameters. Of particular interest is the `ntree` parameter, which controls the number of trees that will be built for the ensemble, and the `mtry` parameter, which is the number of features sampled for use at each node for splitting. These parameters should be tuned by trying out different configurations, and we can use the `tune()` function from the `e1071` package to do just that:

```
> library("randomForest")
> library("e1071")
> rf_ranges <- list(ntree = c(500, 1000, 1500, 2000), mtry = 3:8)
> rf_tune <- tune(randomForest, LeagueIndex ~ ., data =
                  skillcraft_train, ranges = rf_ranges)
> rf_tune$best.parameters
   ntree mtry
14  1000    6
> rf_best <- rf_tune$best.model
> rf_best_predictions <- predict(rf_best, skillcraft_test)
> (rf_best_SSE <- compute_SSE(rf_best_predictions,
                        skillcraft_test$LeagueIndex))
[1] 555.7611
```

The results show that on this data set, the best parameter combination is to train 1,000 trees and use a value of 6 for *mtry*. This last value corresponds to one third of the number of input features, which is the typical heuristic for regression problems. The SSE value on our test set is almost identical to what we obtained using gradient boosting.

The importance of variables in random forests

We already discussed the fact that ensemble models do not, in general, have explanative power. For random forests, it turns out that we can still measure variable importance scores for the different input features by tallying and keeping track of the reductions in our error function across all the trees in the ensemble. In this way, we can obtain an analogous plot to the one we obtained for a single tree when we looked at this data set in *Chapter 6, Tree-based Methods*.

To compute variable importance, we use the `importance()` function and plot the results:

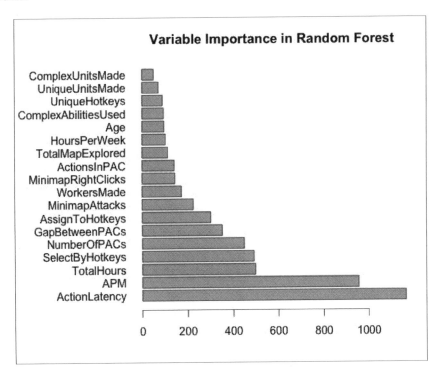

Looking at this plot, we can see that `APM` and `ActionLatency` are once again the most important features, but their order is reversed. We also see that `TotalHours` is now third in importance, significantly higher than what we saw before in a single tree.

We have explored the Skillcraft data set using a number of different methods, but each time we treated this as a regression problem and measured our accuracy using the SSE. Our target variable is the league index, which tells us the gaming league in which a player competes. As such, it is actually an ordered factor.

As we've already seen before, models whose output is an ordered factor can be tricky to train as well as assess. For example, perhaps a more appropriate method of assessing our model would be to first round our model's numerical output so that we obtain a prediction on an actual player league. Then, we could assess the model using a weighted classification error rate that more heavily penalizes a predicted league index that is very far from the actual league index. We leave this as an exercise for the reader.

One of the issues that we often face when we model the problem as a regression problem is that we have no way to force the output to predict across the full range of the original levels. In our particular data set, for example, we might never predict the lowest or highest league. For some suggestions on alternative ways to model ordered factors with regression trees, there is an insightful paper published in 2000 by *Kramer* and others, titled *Prediction of Ordinal Classes Using Regression Trees*. This appears in the *34th* issue of *Fundamentals Informaticae* by *IOS Press*.

> For random forests, the original reference is a 2001 paper by *Leo Breiman*, titled *Random Forests*, published in the journal *Machine Learning*. Besides this reference, a fantastic chapter with numerous examples appears in the book *Statistical Learning from a Regression Perspective*, Richard A. Derk, Springer.

Summary

In this chapter, we deviated from our usual pattern of learning a new type of model and instead focused on techniques to build ensembles of models that we have seen before. We discovered that there are numerous ways to combine models in a meaningful way, each with its own advantages and limitations. Our first technique for building ensemble models was bagging. The central idea behind bagging is that we build multiple versions of the same model using bootstrap samples of the training data. We then average the predictions made by these models in order to construct our overall prediction. By building many different versions of the model we can smooth out errors made due to overfitting and end up with a model that has reduced variance.

A different approach to building model ensembles uses all of the training data and is known as boosting. Here, the defining characteristic is to train a sequence of models but each time we weigh each observation with a different weight depending on whether we classified that observation correctly in the previous model. There are many variants of boosting and we presented two of the most well-known algorithms, AdaBoost and stochastic gradient boosting. The averaging process that operates over the predictions made by individual models to compute the final prediction often weighs each model by its performance.

Traditional texts that present bagging and boosting introduce them in the context of decision trees. There is good reason for this, as the decision tree is the prototypical model for which bagging and boosting have been applied. Boosting in particular works best on models that are weak learners and decision trees can easily be made into weak learners by significantly restricting their size and complexity during construction.

At the same time, however, this often leaves the reader with a view that ensemble methods only work for decision trees, or without any experience in how they can be applied to other methods. In this chapter, we emphasized how these techniques are general and how they can be used with a number of different types of models. Consequently, we applied these techniques to models that we have seen before, such as neural networks and logistic regression.

The final type of ensemble model that we studied was the random forest. This is a very popular and powerful algorithm based on bagging decision trees. The key breakthrough behind this model is the use of an input feature sampling procedure, which limits the choice of features that are available to split on during the construction of each tree. In doing this, the model reduces the correlation between trees, captures significant localized variations in the output and improves the degree of variance reduction in the final result. Another key benefit of this model is that it scales well with a larger number of input features. For our real-world Skillcraft data set, we discovered that random forests and stochastic gradient boosting produced the best performance.

In the next chapter, we will introduce another type of model with a distinct structure known as the probabilistic graphical model. These models use a graphical structure in order to explicitly represent the conditional independence between input features. Probabilistic graphical models find applications across a wide variety of predictive tasks from spam e-mail identification to DNA sequence labeling.

8
Probabilistic Graphical Models

Probabilistic graphical models, or simply graphical models as we will refer to them in this chapter, are models that use the representation of a graph to describe the conditional independence relationships between a series of random variables. This topic has received an increasing amount of attention in recent years and probabilistic graphical models have been successfully applied to tasks ranging from medical diagnosis to image segmentation. In this chapter, we'll present some of the necessary background that will pave the way to understanding the most basic graphical model, the Naïve Bayes classifier. We will then look at a slightly more complicated graphical model, known as the Hidden Markov Model, or HMM for short. To get started in this field, we must first learn about graphs and why they are useful.

A little graph theory

Graph theory is a branch of mathematics that deals with mathematical objects known as **graphs**. Here, a graph does not have the everyday meaning that we are more used to talking about, in the sense of a diagram or plot with an x and y axis. In graph theory, a graph consists of two sets. The first is a set of vertices, which are also referred to as **nodes**. We typically use integers to label and enumerate the vertices. The second set consists of **edges** between these vertices.

Thus, a graph is nothing more than a description of some points and the connections between them. The connections can have a direction so that an edge goes from the **source** or **tail vertex** to the **target** or **head vertex**. In this case, we have a **directed graph**. Alternatively, the edges can have no direction, so that the graph is **undirected**.

A common way to describe a graph is via the **adjacency matrix**. If we have V vertices in the graph, an adjacency matrix is a $V \times V$ matrix whose entries are 0 if the vertex represented by the row number is not connected to the vertex represented by the column number. If there is a connection, the entry is 1.

With undirected graphs, both nodes at each edge are connected to each other so the adjacency matrix is symmetric. For directed graphs, a vertex v_i is connected to a vertex v_j via an edge (v_i, v_j); that is, an edge where v_i is the tail and v_j is the head. Here is an example adjacency matrix for a graph with seven nodes:

```
> adjacency_m
  1 2 3 4 5 6 7
1 0 0 0 0 0 1 0
2 1 0 0 0 0 0 0
3 0 0 0 0 0 0 1
4 0 0 1 0 1 0 1
5 0 0 0 0 0 0 0
6 0 0 0 1 1 0 1
7 0 0 0 0 1 0 0
```

This matrix is not symmetric, so we know that we are dealing with a directed graph. The first 1 value in the first row of the matrix denotes the fact that there is an edge starting from vertex 1 and ending on vertex 6. When the number of nodes is small, it is easy to visualize a graph. We simply draw circles to represent the vertices and lines between them to represent the edges.

For directed graphs, we use arrows on the lines to denote the directions of the edges. It is important to note that we can draw the same graph in an infinite number of different ways on the page. This is because the graph tells us nothing about the positioning of the nodes in space; we only care about how they are connected to each other. Here are two different but equally valid ways to draw the graph described by the adjacency matrix we just saw:

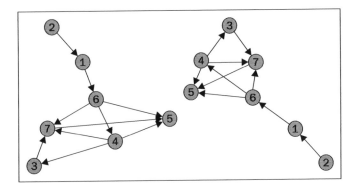

Two vertices are said to be connected with each other if there is an edge between them (taking note of the order when talking about directed graphs). If we can move from vertex v_i to vertex v_j by starting at the first vertex and finishing at the second vertex, by moving on the graph along the edges and passing through an arbitrary number of graph vertices, then these intermediate edges form a **path** between these two vertices. Note that this definition requires that all the vertices and edges along the path are distinct from each other (with the possible exception of the first and last vertex).

For example, in our graph, vertex 6 can be reached from vertex 2 by a path leading through vertex 1. Sometimes, there can be many such possible paths through the graph, and we are often interested in the shortest path, which moves through the fewest number of intermediary vertices. We can define the distance between two nodes in the graph as the length of the shortest path between them. A path that begins and ends at the same vertex is known as a **cycle**. A graph that does not have any cycles in it is known as an **acyclic graph**. If an acyclic graph has directed edges, it is known as a **directed acyclic graph**, which is often abbreviated to **DAG**.

 There are many excellent references on graph theory available. One such reference which is available online, is *Graph Theory, Reinhard Diestel, Springer*. This landmark reference is now in its 4th edition and can be found at http://diestel-graph-theory.com/.

It might not seem obvious at first, but it turns out that a large number of real world situations can be conveniently described using graphs. For example, the network of friendships on social media sites, such as Facebook, or followers on Twitter, can be represented as graphs. On Facebook, the friendship relation is reciprocal, and so the graph is undirected. On Twitter, the follower relation is not, and so the graph is directed.

Another graph is the network of websites on the Web, where links from one web page to the next form directed edges. Transport networks, communication networks, and electricity grids can be represented as graphs. For the predictive modeler, it turns out that a special class of models known as **probabilistic graphical models**, or **graphical models** for short, are models that involve a graph structure.

In a graphical model, the nodes represent random variables and the edges in between represent the dependencies between them. Before we can go into further detail, we'll need to take a short detour in order to visit Bayes' Theorem, a classic theorem in statistics that despite its simplicity has implications both profound and practical when it comes to statistical inference and prediction.

Bayes' Theorem

Suppose we are interested in two events, A and B. In this case, event A might represent the event that a patient has appendicitis and event B might represent a patient having a high white blood cell count. The **conditional probability** of event A given event B is essentially the probability that event A will occur when we know that event B has already happened.

Formally, we define the conditional probability of event A given event B as the joint probability of both events occurring divided by the probability of event B occurring:

$$P(A|B) = \frac{P(A \cap B)}{P(B)}$$

Note that this is consistent with the way in which we define statistical independence. Statistical independence occurs when the joint probability of two events occurring is just the product of the individual probabilities of the two events. If we substitute this in our previous equation, we have:

$$P_{independent\ events}(A|B) = \frac{P(A) \cdot P(B)}{P(B)} = P(A)$$

This makes sense intuitively because if we know that two events are independent of each other, knowing that event B has occurred does not change the probability of event A occurring. Now, we can rearrange our equation for conditional probability as follows, and note that we can switch over events A and B to get an alternative form:

$$P(A \cap B) = P(A \mid B) \cdot P(B) = P(B \mid A) \cdot P(A)$$

This last step allows us to state Bayes' Theorem in its simplest form:

$$P(A \mid B) = \frac{P(B \mid A) \cdot P(A)}{P(B)}$$

In the previous equation, $P(A)$ is referred to as the **prior probability** of event A, as it represents the probability of event A occurring prior to any new information. $P(A \mid B)$, which is the conditional probability of event A given that event B has occurred, is often also referred to as the **posterior probability** of A. It is the probability of event A occurring after receiving some new information; in this case, the fact that event B has occurred.

All of this might seem like algebraic trickery, but if we revisit our example of event A representing a patient having appendicitis and event B representing a patient having a high white blood cell count, the usefulness of Bayes' Theorem will be revealed. Knowing $P(A \mid B)$, the conditional probability of having appendicitis, given that we observe that a patient has a high white blood cell count (and similarly for other symptoms), is knowledge that would be very useful to doctors. This would allow them to make a diagnosis about something that isn't easily observable (appendicitis) using something that is (high white blood cell count).

Unfortunately, this is something that is very hard to estimate because a high white blood cell count might occur as a symptom of a host of other diseases or pathologies. The reverse probability, $P(B \mid A)$, however (namely, the conditional probability of having a high white blood cell count given that a patient already has appendicitis), is much easier to estimate. One simply needs to examine records of past cases with appendicitis and inspect the blood tests of those cases. Bayes' Theorem is a fundamental boon to predictive modeling because it allows us to estimate cause by observing effect.

Conditional independence

We know from statistics that the notion of statistical independence says that the joint probability of two random variables A and B is just the product of their (marginal) probabilities. Sometimes, two variables may not be statistically independent of each other to begin with, but observing a third variable, C, might result in them becoming independent of each other. In short, we say that events A and B are **conditionally independent** given C, and we can express this as:

$$P(A \cap B \mid C) = P(A \mid C) \cdot P(B \mid C)$$

For example, suppose that J represents the probability of being given a job offer at a particular company and G represents the probability of being accepted into graduate school at a particular university. Both of these might depend on a variable U, a person's performance on their undergraduate degree. This can be summarized in a graph as:

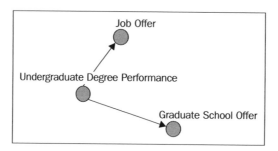

When we don't know U, a person's performance on their undergraduate degree, knowing that they were accepted into graduate school might increase our belief in their chances of getting a job and vice versa. This is because we are inclined to believe that they did well in their undergraduate degree, which influences that person's chances of getting a job. Thus, the two events J and G are not independent of each other.

If we are told the performance of a person on their undergraduate degree, however, we might assume that the person's chance of getting a job offer might be independent of their chance of getting into graduate school. This is because of other factors that might affect this, such as the person's job interview on a particular day or the quality of other potential candidates for the job, which are not influenced by the person's application to graduate school.

Bayesian networks

Bayesian networks are a type of graphical model that involves a directed acyclic graph structure. We often refer to the tail node of a directed edge in a graphical model as the **parent** and the head node as the **child** or **descendant**. In fact, we generalize this latter notion so that if there is a path from node A to node B in the model, node B is a descendant of node A. We can distinguish the special case of node A connected to node B by saying that the latter is a **direct descendant**.

The parent relationship and the descendant relationship are mutually exclusive in a Bayesian network because it has no cycles. Bayesian networks have the distinguishing property that given its parents, every node in the network is conditionally independent of all other nodes in the network that are not its descendants. This is sometimes referred to as the **local Markov property**. It is an important property because it means that we can easily factorize the joint probability function of all the random variables in the model by simply taking note of the edges in the graph.

To understand how this works, we will begin with the product rule of probability for three variables that says the following (taking G, J, and U as example variables):

$$P(G,J,U) = P(G \mid J,U) \cdot P(J,U) = P(G \mid J,U) \cdot P(J \mid U) \cdot P(U)$$

This rule is a general rule and always holds without any loss of generality. Let's return to our student applicant example. This is actually a simple Bayesian network where G and J have U as a parent. Using the local Markov property of Bayesian networks, we can simplify the equation for the joint probability distribution as follows:

$$P(G,J,U) = P(G \mid U) \cdot P(J \mid U) \cdot P(U)$$

The ability to factorize a probability distribution in this way is useful as it simplifies the computations we need to make. It can also allow us to represent the entire distribution in a more compact form. Suppose that the distribution of each random variable is discrete and takes on a finite set of values, for example, random variables G and J could each take on the two discrete values {yes, no}. To store a joint probability distribution without factorizing, and taking into account independence relations, we need to consider all possible combinations of every random variable.

By contrast, if the distribution factorizes into a product of simpler distributions as we saw earlier, the total number of random variable combinations we need to consider are far fewer. For networks with several random variables that take on many values, the savings are very substantial indeed.

Besides computation and storage, another significant benefit is that when we want to determine the joint probability distribution of our random variables given some data, it becomes much simpler to do so when we can factorize it because of known independence relations. We will see this in detail when, in the next section, we study an important example of a Bayesian network.

To wrap up this section, we'll note the factorization of the joint probability function of the Bayesian network, represented by the graph we saw in the first diagram in this chapter, and leave it as an exercise for the reader to verify:

$$P\left(A_1, A_2, A_3, A_4, A_5, A_6, A_7\right) =$$
$$P\left(A_2\right) \cdot P\left(A_1 \mid A_2\right) \cdot P\left(A_6 \mid A_1\right) \cdot P\left(A_4 \mid A_6\right) \cdot$$
$$P\left(A_3 \mid A_4\right) \cdot P\left(A_7 \mid A_3, A_4, A_6\right) \cdot P\left(A_5 \mid A_4, A_6, A_7\right)$$

The Naïve Bayes classifier

We now have the necessary tools to learn about our first and simplest graphical model, the **Naïve Bayes classifier**. This is a directed graphical model that contains a single parent node and a series of child nodes representing random variables that are dependent only on this node with no dependencies between them. Here is an example:

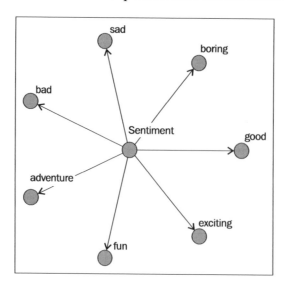

We usually interpret our single parent node as the causal node, so in our particular example, the value of the *Sentiment* node will influence the value of the *sad* node, the *fun* node, and so on. As this is a Bayesian network, the local Markov property can be used to explain the core assumption of the model. Given the *Sentiment* node, all other nodes are independent of each other.

In practice, we use the Naïve Bayes classifier in a context where we can observe and measure the child nodes and attempt to estimate the parent node as our output. Thus, the child nodes will be the input features of our model, and the parent node will be the output variable. For example, the child nodes may represent various medical symptoms and the parent node might be whether a particular disease is present.

To understand how the model works in practice, we make recourse to Bayes' Theorem, where C is the parent node and F_i are the children or feature nodes:

$$P\left(C \mid F_1,...,F_n\right) = \frac{P\left(C\right) \cdot P\left(F_1,...,F_n \mid C\right)}{P\left(F_1,...,F_n\right)}$$

We can simplify this using the conditional independence assumptions of the network:

$$P\left(C \mid F_1,...,F_n\right) = \frac{P\left(C\right) \cdot P\left(F_1 \mid C\right) \cdot ... \cdot P\left(F_n \mid C\right)}{P\left(F_1,...,F_n\right)}$$

To make a classifier out of this probability model, our objective is to choose the class C_i that maximizes the posterior probability $P(C_i \mid F_1...F_n)$; that is, the posterior probability of that class given the observed features. The denominator is the joint probability of the observed features, which is not influenced by the class that is chosen. Consequently, maximizing the posterior class probability amounts to maximizing the numerator of the previous equation:

$$Classify\ C_i : \underset{c}{\mathrm{argmax}}\ P\left(C\right) \cdot \prod_{i=1}^{n} P\left(F_i \mid C\right)$$

Given some data, we can estimate the probabilities, $P(F_i \mid C_j)$, for all the different values of the feature F_i as the relative proportion of the observations of class C_j that have each different value of feature F_i. We can also estimate $P(C_j)$ as the relative proportion of the observations that are assigned to class C_j. These are the maximum likelihood estimates. In the next section, we will see how the Naïve Bayes classifier works on a real example.

Predicting the sentiment of movie reviews

In a world of online reviews, forums, and social media, a task that has received, and continues to receive, a growing amount of interest is the task of **sentiment analysis**. Put simply, the task is to analyze a piece of text to determine the sentiment that is being expressed by the author. A typical scenario involves collecting online reviews, blog posts, or tweets and building a model that predicts whether the user is trying to express a positive or a negative feeling. Sometimes, the task can be framed to capture a wider variety of sentiments, such as a neutral sentiment or the degree of sentiment, such as mildly negative versus very negative.

In this section, we will limit ourselves to the simpler task of discerning positive from negative sentiments. We will do this by modeling sentiment, using a similar Bayesian network to the one that we saw in the previous section. The sentiment is our target output variable, which is either positive or negative. Our input features are all binary features that describe whether a particular word is present in a movie review. The key idea here is that users expressing a negative sentiment will tend to choose from a characteristic set of words in their review that is different from the characteristic set that users would pick from when writing a positive review.

By using the Naïve Bayes model, our assumption will be that if we know the sentiment being expressed, the presence of each word in the text is independent from all the other words. Of course, this is a very strict assumption to use and doesn't speak at all to the process of how real text is written. Nonetheless, we will show that even under these strict assumptions, we can build a model that performs reasonably well.

We will use the *Large Movie Review Data Set*, first presented in the paper titled *Learning Word Vectors for Sentiment Analysis, Andrew L. Maas, Raymond E. Daly, Peter T. Pham, Dan Huang, Andrew Y. Ng*, and *Christopher Potts*, published in *The 49th Annual Meeting of the Association for Computational Linguistics (ACL 2011)*. The data is hosted at http://ai.stanford.edu/~amaas/data/sentiment/ and is comprised of a training set of 25,000 movie reviews and a test set of another 25,000 movie reviews.

In order to demonstrate how the model works, we would like to keep the training time of our model low. For this reason, we are going to partition the original training set into a new training and test set, but the reader is very strongly encouraged to repeat the exercise with the larger test data set that is part of the original data. When downloaded, the data is organized into a train folder and a test folder. The train folder contains a folder called pos that has 12,500 positive movie reviews, each inside a separate text file, and similarly, a folder called neg with 12,500 negative movie reviews.

Our first task is to load all this information into R and perform some necessary preprocessing. To do this, we are going to install and use the tm package, which is a specialized package for performing text-mining operations. This package is very useful when working with text data and we will use it again in a subsequent chapter.

When working with the tm package, the first task is to organize the various sources of text into a **corpus**. In linguistics, this commonly refers to a collection of documents. In the tm package, it is just a collection of strings representing individual sources of text, along with some metadata that describes some information about them, such as the names of the files from which they were retrieved.

With the tm package, we build a corpus using the Corpus() function, to which we must provide a source for the various documents we want to import. We could create a vector of strings and pass this as an argument to Corpus() using the VectorSource() function. Instead, as our data source is a series of text files in a directory, we will use the DirSource() function. First, we will create two string variables that will contain the absolute paths to the aforementioned neg and pos folders on our machine (this will depend on where the data set is downloaded).

Then, we can use the Corpus() function twice to create two corpora for positive and negative reviews, which will then be merged into a single corpus.

```
> path_to_neg_folder <- "~/aclImdb/train/neg"
> path_to_pos_folder <- "~/aclImdb/train/pos"
> library("tm")
> nb_pos <- Corpus(DirSource(path_to_pos_folder),
                   readerControl = list(language = "en"))
> nb_neg <- Corpus(DirSource(path_to_neg_folder),
                   readerControl = list(language = "en"))
> nb_all <- c(nb_pos, nb_neg, recursive = T)
```

The second argument to the Corpus() function, readerControl, is a list of optional parameters. We used this to specify that the language of our text files is English. The recursive parameter in the c() function used to merge the two corpora is necessary to maintain the metadata information stored in the corpus objects.

Note that we can merge the two corpora without actually losing the sentiment label. Each text file representing a movie review is named using the format <counter>_<score>.txt, and this information is stored in the metadata portion of the corpus object created by the Corpus() function. We can see the metadata for the first review in our corpus using the meta() function:

```
> meta(nb_all[[1]])
Metadata:
  author       : character(0)
```

```
datetimestamp: 2015-04-19 09:17:48
description  : character(0)
heading      : character(0)
id           : 0_9.txt
language     : en
origin       : character(0)
```

The meta() function thus retrieves a metadata object for each entry in our corpus. The ID attribute in this object contains the name of the file. The score part of the name is a number between 0 and 10, where higher numbers denote positive reviews, and low numbers denote negative reviews. In the training data, we only have polar reviews; that is, reviews that are in the ranges 0-4 and 7-10. We can thus use this information to create a vector of document names:

```
> ids <- sapply( 1 : length(nb_all),
                 function(x) meta(nb_all[[x]], "id"))
> head(ids)
[1] "0_9.txt"     "1_7.txt"     "10_9.txt"     "100_7.txt"
[5] "1000_8.txt"  "10000_8.txt"
```

From this list of document names, we'll extract the score component using the sub() function with an appropriate regular expression. If the score of a movie review is less than or equal to 5, it is a negative review and if greater, it is a positive review:

```
> scores <- as.numeric(sapply(ids,
            function(x) sub("[0-9]+_([0-9]+)\\.txt", "\\1", x)))
> scores <- factor(ifelse(scores >= 5, "positive", "negative"))
> summary(scores)
negative positive
   12500    12500
```

The sub() function is just one of R's functions that uses regular expressions. For readers unfamiliar with the concept, a regular expression is essentially a pattern language for describing strings. Online tutorials for regular expressions are easy to find. An excellent resource for learning about regular expressions as well as text processing more generally is *Speech and Language Processing Second Edition, Jurafsky and Martin*.

The features of our model will be binary features that describe the presence or absence of specific words in the dictionary. Intuitively, we should expect that a movie review containing words such as *boring*, *cliché*, and *horrible* is likely to be a negative review. A movie review with words such as *inspiring*, *enjoyable*, *moving*, and *excellent* is likely to be a good review.

When working with text data, we almost always need to perform a series of preprocessing steps. For example, we tend to convert all the words to a lowercase format because we don't want to have two separate features for the words *Excellent* and *excellent*. We also want to remove anything from our text that will likely be uninformative as features. For this reason, we tend to remove punctuation, numbers, and **stop words**. Stop words are words like *the, and, in*, and *he*, which are very frequently used in the English language and are bound to appear in nearly all of the movie reviews. Finally, because we are removing words from sentences and creating repeated spaces, we will want to remove these in order to assist the process of tokenization (the process of splitting up the text into words).

The `tm` package has two functions, `tm_map()` and `content_transformer()`, which together can be used to apply text transformations to the content of every entry in our corpus:

```
> nb_all <- tm_map(nb_all, content_transformer(removeNumbers))
> nb_all <- tm_map(nb_all, content_transformer(removePunctuation))
> nb_all <- tm_map(nb_all, content_transformer(tolower))
> nb_all <- tm_map(nb_all, content_transformer(removeWords),
                      stopwords("english"))
> nb_all <- tm_map(nb_all, content_transformer(stripWhitespace))
```

Now that we have preprocessed our corpus, we are ready to compute our features. Essentially, what we need is a data structure known as a **document term matrix**. The rows of the matrix are the documents. The columns of the matrix are the words in our dictionary. Each entry in the matrix is a binary value, with `1` representing the fact that the word represented by the column number was found inside the review represented by the row number. For example, if the first column corresponds to the word `action`, the fourth row corresponds to the fourth movie review, and the value of the matrix at position (4,1) is `1`, this signifies that the fourth movie review contains the word `action`.

The `tm` package provides us with the `DocumentTermMatrix()` function that takes in a corpus object and builds a document term matrix. The particular matrix built has numerical entries that represent the total number of times a particular word is seen inside a particular text, so we will have to convert these into a binary factor afterwards.

```
> nb_dtm <- DocumentTermMatrix(nb_all)
> dim(nb_dtm)
[1]   25000 117473
```

Our document term matrix in this case has 117,473 columns, indicating that we have found this number of different words in the corpus. This matrix is very sparse, meaning that most of the entries are 0. This is a very typical scenario when building document term matrices for text documents, especially text documents that are as short as movie reviews. Any particular movie review will only feature a tiny fraction of the words in the vocabulary. Let's examine our matrix to see just how sparse it is:

```
> nb_dtm
<<DocumentTermMatrix (documents: 25000, terms: 117473)>>
Non-/sparse entries: 2493414/2934331586
Sparsity           : 100%
Maximal term length: 64
Weighting          : term frequency (tf)
```

From the ratio of non-sparse to sparse entries, we can see that of the 2,936,825,000 entries in the matrix (25000 × 117473), only 2,493,414 are nonzero. At this point, we should reduce the number of columns of this matrix for two reasons. On the one hand, because the words in our vocabulary will become the features in our model, we don't want to build a model that uses 117,473 features. This would take a very long time to train and at the same time is unlikely to provide us with a decent fit using only 25,000 data points.

Another significant reason for us to want to reduce the number of columns is that many words will appear only once or twice in the whole corpus, and will be as uninformative about the user's sentiment as words that occur in nearly all the documents. Given this, we have a natural way to reduce the dimensions of the document term matrix, namely by dropping the columns (that is, removing certain words from the feature set) that are the sparsest. We can remove all columns that have a certain percentage of sparse elements using the removeSparseTerms() function. The first argument that we must provide this with is a document term matrix, and the second is the maximum degree of column sparseness that we will allow. Choosing the degree of sparseness is tricky, because we don't want to throw away too many of the columns that will become our features. We will proceed by running our experiments with 99 percent sparseness, but encourage the reader to repeat with different values to see the effect this has on the number of features and model performance.

We have 25,000 rows in the matrix corresponding to the total number of documents in our corpus. If we allow a maximum of 99 percent sparseness, we are effectively removing words that do not occur in at least 1 percent of those 25,000 documents; that is, in at least 250 documents:

```
> nb_dtm <- removeSparseTerms(x = nb_dtm, sparse = 0.99)
> dim(nb_dtm)
[1] 25000  1603
```

We have now significantly reduced the number of columns down to 1,603. This is a substantially more reasonable number of features for us to work with. Next, we convert all entries to binary, using another function of tm, weightBin().

```
> nb_dtm <- weightBin(nb_dtm)
```

As the document term matrix is in general a very sparse matrix, R uses a compact data structure to store the information. To peek inside this matrix and examine the first few terms, we will use the inspect() function on a small slice of this matrix:

```
> inspect(nb_dtm[10:16, 1:6])
<<DocumentTermMatrix (documents: 7, terms: 6)>>
Non-/sparse entries: 2/40
Sparsity            : 95%
Maximal term length: 10
Weighting           : binary (bin)
```

```
                 Terms
Docs          ability able absolute absolutely absurd academy
   10004_8.txt       0    1        0          0      0       0
   10005_7.txt       0    0        0          0      0       0
   10006_7.txt       0    0        0          0      0       0
   10007_7.txt       0    0        0          0      0       0
   10008_7.txt       0    0        0          0      0       1
   10009_9.txt       0    0        0          0      0       0
   1001_8.txt        0    0        0          0      0       0
```

It looks like the word ability does not appear in the first six documents and the word able appears in the document 10004_8.txt. We now have both our features and our output vector. The next step is to convert our document term matrix into a data frame. This is needed by the function that will train our Naïve Bayes model. Then, before we train the model, we will split our data into a training set with 80 percent of the documents and a test set with 20 percent of the documents, as follows:

```
> nb_df <- as.data.frame(as.matrix(nb_dtm))
> library(caret)
> set.seed(443452342)
> nb_sampling_vector <- createDataPartition(scores, p = 0.80,
                                    list = FALSE)
> nb_df_train <- nb_df[nb_sampling_vector,]
> nb_df_test <- nb_df[-nb_sampling_vector,]
> scores_train = scores[nb_sampling_vector]
> scores_test = scores[-nb_sampling_vector]
```

To train a Naïve Bayes model, we will use the `naiveBayes()` function in the `e1071` package that we have seen earlier. The first argument we will provide it with is our feature data frame, and the second argument is our vector of output labels:

```
> library("e1071")
> nb_model <- naiveBayes(nb_dtm_train, scores_train)
```

We can use the `predict()` function to obtain predictions on our training data:

```
> nb_train_predictions <- predict(nb_model, nb_df_train)
> mean(nb_train_predictions == scores_train)
[1] 0.83015
> table(actual = scores_train, predictions = nb_train_predictions)
            predictions
actual      negative positive
  negative      8442     1558
  positive      1839     8161
```

We have hit over 83 percent training accuracy with our simple Naïve Bayes model, which, admittedly, is not bad for such a simple model with an independence assumption that we know is not realistic for our data. Let's repeat the same on our test data:

```
> nb_test_predictions <- predict(nb_model, nb_df_test)
> mean(nb_test_predictions == scores_test)
[1] 0.8224
> table(actual = scores_test, predictions = nb_test_predictions)
            predictions
actual      negative positive
  negative      2090      410
  positive       478     2022
```

The test accuracy of over 82 percent is comparable to what we saw on our training data. There are a number of potential avenues for improvement here. The first involves noticing that words such as *movie* and *movies* are treated differently, even though they are the same word but inflected. In linguistics, **inflection** is the process by which the base form or **lemma** of a word is modified to agree with another word on attributes such as tense, case, gender, and number. For example, in English, verbs must agree with their subject. The `tm` package supports **stemming**, a process of removing the inflected part of a word in order to keep just a stem or root word. This is not always the same as retrieving what is known as the **morphological lemma** of a word, which is what we look up in a dictionary, but is a rough approximation. The `tm` package uses the well-known **Porter Stemmer**.

Martin Porter, the author of the Porter Stemmer, maintains a website at http://tartarus.org/martin/PorterStemmer/, which is a great source of information on his famous algorithm.

To apply stemming to our corpus, we need to add a final transformation to our corpus using tm_map() and then recompute our document term matrix anew as the columns (the word features) are now word stems:

```
> nb_all <- tm_map(nb_all, stemDocument, language = "english")
> nb_dtm <- DocumentTermMatrix(nb_all)
> nb_dtm <- removeSparseTerms(x = nb_dtm, sparse = 0.99)
> nb_dtm <- weightBin(nb_dtm)
> nb_df_train <- nb_df[nb_sampling_vector,]
> nb_df_test <- nb_df[-nb_sampling_vector,]
> dim(nb_dtm)
[1] 25000  1553
```

Note that we have fewer columns that match our criterion of 99 percent maximum sparsity. We can use this new document term matrix to train another Naïve Bayes classifier and then measure the accuracy on our test set:

```
> nb_model_stem <- naiveBayes(nb_df_train, scores_train)
> nb_test_predictions_stem <- predict(nb_model_stem, nb_df_test)
> mean(nb_test_predictions_stem == scores_test)
[1] 0.8
> table(actual = scores_test, predictions =
                          nb_test_predictions_stem)
         predictions
actual     negative positive
  negative     2067      433
  positive      567     1933
```

The result, 80 percent, is slightly lower than what we observed without stemming, although we are using slightly fewer features than before. Stemming is not always guaranteed to be a good idea, as in some problems it may improve performance whereas in others it will make no difference or even make things worse. It is, however, a common transformation that is worth trying when working with text data.

A second possible improvement is to use **additive smoothing** (also known as **laplacian smoothing**) during the training of our Naïve Bayes model. This is actually a form of regularization and it works by adding a fixed number to all the counts of feature and class combinations during training. Using our original document term matrix, we can compute a Naïve Bayes model with additive smoothing by specifying the `laplace` parameter. For our particular data set, however, we did not witness any improvements by doing this.

There are a few more avenues of approach that we might try with a Naïve Bayes model, and we will propose them here for the reader to experiment with. The first of these is that it is often worth manually curating the list of words used as features for the model. When we study the terms selected by our document term matrix, we may find that some words are frequent in our training data but we do not expect them to be frequent in general, or representative of the overall population. Furthermore, we may only want to experiment with words that we know are suggestive of emotion and sentiment. This can be done by specifying a specific dictionary of terms to use when constructing our document term matrix. Here is an example:

```
> emotion_words <- c("good", "bad", "enjoyed", "hated", "like")
> nb_dtm <- DocumentTermMatrix(nb_all, list(dictionary =
                                            emotion_words))
```

It is relatively straightforward to find examples of such lists on the Internet. Another common preprocessing step that is used with a Naïve Bayes model is to remove correlations between features. One way of doing this is to perform PCA, as we saw in *Chapter 1, Gearing Up for Predictive Modeling*. Furthermore, this method also allows us to begin with a slightly more sparse document term matrix with a larger number of terms, as we know we will be reducing the overall number of features with PCA.

Potential model improvements notwithstanding, it is important to be aware of the limitations that the Naïve Bayes model imposes that impede our ability to train a highly accurate sentiment analyzer. Assuming that all the words in a movie review are independent of each other, once we know the sentiment involved, is quite an unrealistic assumption. Our model completely disregards sentence structure and word order. For example, the phrase *not bad* in a review might indicate a positive sentiment, but because we look at words in isolation, we will tend to correlate the word *bad* with a negative sentiment. Negation in general is one of the hardest problems to handle in text processing. Our model also cannot handle common patterns of language, such as sarcasm, irony, quoted passages that include other people's thoughts, and other such linguistic devices.

The next section will introduce a more powerful graphical model.

A good reference to study for the Naïve Bayes classifier is *An empirical study of the Naïve Bayes classifier, I. Rish*, presented in the 2001 IJCAI workshop on *Empirical Methods in AI*. For sentiment analysis, we recommend the slides from *Bing Liu's* AAAI 2011 tutorial at http://www.cs.uic.edu/~liub/FBS/ Sentiment-Analysis- tutorial-AAAI-2011.pdf.

Hidden Markov models

A **Hidden Markov model**, often abbreviated to **HMM**, which we will use here, is a Bayesian network with a repeating structure that is commonly used to model and predict sequences. In this section, we'll see two applications of this model: one to model DNA gene sequences, and another to model the sequences of letters that make up English text. The basic diagram for an HMM is shown here:

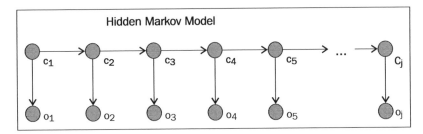

As we can see in the diagram, the sequence flows from left to right and we have a pair of nodes for every entry in the sequence that we are trying to model. Nodes labeled C_i are known as **latent states**, **hidden states**, or merely **states**, as they are typically nodes that are not observable. The nodes labeled O_i are **observed states** or **observations**. We will use the terms *states* and *observations*.

Now, as this is a Bayesian network, we can immediately identify some key properties. All the observations are independent of each other given their corresponding state. Also, every state is independent of every other state earlier on in the sequence history, given the state that preceded it (which is its parent in the network). The key idea behind an HMM, therefore, is that the model moves in a linear fashion from one state to the next state.

In each latent state, it produces an observation, which is also known as an **emitted symbol**. These symbols are the observed part of the sequence. Hidden Markov models are very common in natural language processing, and a good example is their application to **part of speech tagging**. The task of a part of speech tagger is to read a sentence and return the sequence of corresponding part of speech labels for the words in that sentence. For example, given the previous sentence, a part of speech tagger might return *determiner* for the word *The*, *singular noun* for the word *task*, and so on.

To model this using an HMM, we would have the words be the emitted symbols, and the part of speech tags be the latent states, as the former are observable and the latter are what we want to determine. There are many other sequence labeling tasks in natural language processing to which Hidden Markov models have been applied, such as **named entity recognition**, where the goal is to identify the words in a sentence that refer to names of individuals, locations, organizations, and other entities.

A Hidden Markov model is comprised of five core components. The first of these is the set of possible latent class labels. For the part of speech tagger example, this might be a list of all the part of speech tags that we will use. The second component is the set of all possible emitted symbols. For an English part of speech tagger, this is the dictionary of English words.

The next three components involve probabilities. The **starting probability vector** is a vector of probabilities that tells us the probability of starting in each latent state. For part of speech tagging, we may, for example, have a high probability of starting with a determiner such as *the*. The **transition probability matrix** is a matrix that tells us the probabilities of going to state C_j when the current state is C_i. Thus, this contains the probability of moving from a determiner to a noun for our part of speech example. Finally, the **emission probability matrix** tells us the probability of emitting every symbol in our dictionary for every state that we can be in. Note that some words (such as *bank*, which is both a noun and a verb) can be labeled with more than one part of speech tag, and so will have nonzero probabilities of being emitted from more than one state.

In circumstances such as part of speech tagging, we usually have a collection of labeled sequences so that our data contain both sequences of observations as well as their corresponding states. In this case, similar to the Naïve Bayes model, we use relative frequency counts to populate the probability components of our model.

For example, to find a suitable starting probability vector, we could tabulate the starting state for every sequence in our data set and use this to get the relative frequency of beginning in each state. When all we have are unlabeled sequences, the task is significantly harder because we might not even know how many states we need to include in our model. One method to assign states to unlabeled observation sequences in training data is known as the **Baum-Welch algorithm**.

Once we know the parameters of our model, the question becomes how to predict the most likely sequence of states behind a sequence of observations. Given an unlabeled sentence in English, a part of speech tagger based on an HMM must predict the sequence of part of speech labels. The most commonly used algorithm for this is based on a programming technique known as **dynamic programming** and is known as the **Viterbi algorithm**.

The algorithms we have discussed for the Hidden Markov model are beyond the scope of this book but are quite intuitive and well worth studying. Given a basic understanding of the core components of the model and its assumptions, our next goal is to see how we can apply them to some real-world situations. We will first see an example with labeled sequences and later an example with unlabeled sequences.

Perhaps the most definitive and thorough introduction to hidden Markov models is the seminal paper titled *A Tutorial on Hidden Markov Models and Selected Applications in Speech Recognition, L. R. Rabiner*, published in the *Proceedings of the IEEE 1989*. The *Jurafsky* and *Martin* textbook we mentioned earlier is also an ideal reference to learn more about HMMs, including details on the Baum-Welch and Viterbi algorithms as well as applications such as part of speech tagging and named entity recognition.

Predicting promoter gene sequences

The first application we will study in detail comes from the field of biology. There, we learn that the basic building blocks of DNA molecules are actually four fundamental molecules known as **nucleotides**. These are called *Thymine, Cytosine, Adenine*, and *Guanine*, and it is the order in which these molecules appear in a DNA strand that encodes the genetic information carried by the DNA.

An interesting problem in molecular biology is finding **promoter sequences** within a larger DNA strand. These are special sequences of nucleotides that play an important role in regulating a genetic process known as **gene transcription**. This is the first step in the mechanism by which information in the DNA is read.

The *molecular biology (promoter gene sequences) data set*, hosted by the UCI Machine Learning repository at `https://archive.ics.uci.edu/ml/datasets/Molecular+Biology+(Promoter+Gene+Sequences)` contains a number of gene sequences from DNA belonging to the bacterium *E. Coli*.

The predictive task at hand is to build a model that will discern promoter gene sequences from non-promoter gene sequences. We will approach this problem using HMMs. Specifically, we will build an HMM for promoters and an HMM for non-promoters, and we will pick the model that gives us the highest probability for a test sequence in order to label that sequence:

```
> promoters <- read.csv("promoters.data", header = F, dec = ",",
              strip.white = TRUE, stringsAsFactors = FALSE)
> promoters[1,]
  V1  V2                                                        V3
1  +  S10 tactagcaatacgcttgcgttcggtggttaagtatgtataatgcgcgggcttgtcgt
```

Note that it is important to strip whitespace using the `strip.white = TRUE` parameter setting in the call to `read.csv()` as some fields have leading tab characters. The first column in the data frame contains a + or - to denote promoters or non-promoters respectively. The second column is just an identifier for the particular sequence and the third column is the sequence of nucleotides itself. We'll begin by separating the data into positive and negative observations of promoter sequences using the first column:

```
> positive_observations <- subset(promoters, V1 == '+', 3)
> negative_observations <- subset(promoters, V1 == '-', 3)
```

In order to train our HMMs, we want to concatenate all the observations from each class into a single observation. We do, however, want to store information about the start and end of each sequence. Consequently, we will prepend each sequence with the character s to denote the start of a sequence and append each sequence with the character x to denote the end of a sequence:

```
> positive_observations <- sapply(positive_observations,
                           function(x) paste("S", x, "X", sep=""))
> negative_observations <- sapply(negative_observations,
                           function(x) paste("S", x, "X", sep=""))
> positive_observations[1]
[1] "StactagcaatacgcttgcgttcggtggttaagtatgtataatgcgcgggcttgtcgtX"
```

Next, we will split each observation from a string into a vector of characters using the `strsplit()` function, which takes a string to split as the first argument and the character to use as the split points. Here, we use an empty character on which to split, so that the whole string is broken up into single characters.

```
> positive_observations <- strsplit(positive_observations, "")
> negative_observations <- strsplit(negative_observations, "")
> head(positive_observations[[1]], n = 15)
 [1] "S" "t" "a" "c" "t" "a" "g" "c" "a" "a" "t" "a" "c" "g" "c"
```

Now we have to specify the probability matrices for the HMM models that we want to train. In this particular situation, the states have a one-to-one correspondence with the emitted symbols, so in fact this type of problem can be simplified to a visible Markov model, which in this case is just a Markov chain. Nonetheless, the process we will follow for modeling this problem as an HMM is the same we would follow in the more general case of having multiple symbols assigned to each state. We are going to assume that both positive and negative HMM models involve four states corresponding to the four nucleotides. Although both models will emit the same symbols in each state, they will differ in their transition probabilities from one state to the next.

Apart from the four states we mentioned earlier, we created a special terminating state at the end of each sequence using the symbol X. We also created a special starting state, which we called S, so that the starting probability of all the other states is 0. In addition, the emission probabilities are trivial to compute as only one symbol is emitted per state. Due to the one-to-one correspondence between states and symbols, we will use the same alphabet to represent the states and the symbols they emit:

```
> states <- c("S", "X", "a", "c", "g", "t")
> symbols <- c("S", "X", "a", "c", "g", "t")
> startingProbabilities <- c(1,0,0,0,0,0)
> emissionProbabilities <- diag(6)
> colnames(emissionProbabilities) <- states
> rownames(emissionProbabilities) <- symbols
> emissionProbabilities
  S X a c g t
S 1 0 0 0 0 0
X 0 1 0 0 0 0
a 0 0 1 0 0 0
c 0 0 0 1 0 0
g 0 0 0 0 1 0
t 0 0 0 0 0 1
```

Computing the transition probability matrix requires us to do a bit more work. Thus, we defined our own function for this: `calculateTransitionProbabilities()`. The input to this function is a single vector of training sequences concatenated with each other, along with a vector containing the names of the states.

The function first computes an empty transition probability matrix. By cycling over each consecutive pair of states, it tallies up counts of state transitions. After all the data have been traversed, we normalize the transition probability matrix by dividing each row of the matrix by the sum of the elements in that row. This is done because the rows of this matrix must sum to one. We use the `sweep()` function, which allows us to apply a function on every element of the matrix using a summary statistic. Here is `calculateTransitionProbabilities()`:

```
calculateTransitionProbabilities <- function(data, states) {

   transitionProbabilities <- matrix(0, length(states), length(states))
   colnames(transitionProbabilities) <- states
   rownames(transitionProbabilities) <- states

   for (index in 1:(length(data) - 1)) {
     current_state <- data[index]
     next_state <- data[index + 1]
     transitionProbabilities[current_state, next_state] <-
         transitionProbabilities[current_state, next_state] + 1
   }

   transitionProbabilities <- sweep(transitionProbabilities, 1,
         rowSums(transitionProbabilities), FUN = "/")
   return(transitionProbabilities)
}
```

Now we are ready to train our models. The key observation to make on this data set is that we have very few observations, just 53 of each class in fact. This data set is too small to set a portion aside for testing. Instead, we will implement leave-one-out cross validation to estimate the accuracy of our models. To do this, we will begin by leaving an observation out from the positive observations. This leaves all the negative observations available for computing the transition probability matrix for our negative HMM:

```
> negative_observation<-Reduce(function(x, y) c(x, y),
                        negative_observations, c())
> (transitionProbabilitiesNeg <-
    calculateTransitionProbabilities(negative_observation, states))
    S         X         a         c         g         t
S 0 0.00000000 0.2264151 0.2830189 0.1320755 0.3584906
X 1 0.00000000 0.0000000 0.0000000 0.0000000 0.0000000
a 0 0.02168022 0.2113821 0.2696477 0.2506775 0.2466125
c 0 0.01256983 0.2500000 0.1634078 0.2667598 0.3072626
g 0 0.01958225 0.3133159 0.2480418 0.1919060 0.2271540
t 0 0.01622971 0.1885144 0.2434457 0.2946317 0.2571785
```

When in the start state (s), we can randomly move to a nucleotide state, but have zero probability of moving to the stop state (x) or staying in the start state. When in the nucleotide states, we can randomly transition to any state except back to the start state. Finally, the only valid transition from a stop state is to the start state for a new sequence.

We now introduce the HMM package in R, which is for working with hidden Markov models, as the name implies. We can initialize an HMM with a specific set of parameters using the initHMM() function. As expected, this takes five inputs corresponding to the five components of a Hidden Markov model, which we discussed earlier.

```
> library("HMM")
> negative_hmm <- initHMM(states, symbols, startProbs =
  startingProbabilities, transProbs = transitionProbabilitiesNeg,
  emissionProbs = emissionProbabilities)
```

The next step is to build the positive HMM, but we will have to do this multiple times, leaving out one observation for testing. This test observation will then be processed by the negative HMM model we trained earlier and the positive HMM that was trained without that observation. If the positive HMM predicts a higher probability for the test observation than the negative HMM, our model will correctly classify the test observation. The following block of code performs a loop of these calculations for every positive observation:

```
> incorrect <- 0
> for (obs in 1 : length(positive_observations)) {

    positive_observation <- Reduce(function(x, y) c(x, y),
                      positive_observations[-obs], c())
    transitionProbabilitiesPos <-
    calculateTransitionProbabilities(positive_observation, states)
    positive_hmm <- initHMM(states, symbols,
                    startProbs = startingProbabilities,
                    transProbs = transitionProbabilitiesPos,
                    emissionProbs = emissionProbabilities)

    test_observation <- positive_observations[[obs]]
    final_index <- length(test_observation)

    pos_probs <- exp(forward(positive_hmm, test_observation))
    neg_probs <- exp(forward(negative_hmm, test_observation))
    pos_seq_prob <- sum(pos_probs[, final_index])
    neg_seq_prob <- sum(neg_probs[, final_index])

    if (pos_seq_prob < neg_seq_prob) incorrect <- incorrect + 1

}
```

We'll now walk through the previous code block. Firstly, we keep track of any mistakes we make using the `incorrect` variable. For every observation in our positive observations list, we'll train a positive HMM without this observation. This observation then becomes our test observation.

To find the probability of a particular sequence given a particular HMM, we used the `forward()` function, which computes a matrix containing the logarithm of all the forward probabilities for every step in the observation sequence. The final column in this matrix, whose numerical index is just the length of the sequence, contains the forward probability for the whole sequence. We compute the positive sequence probability using the positive HMM that we trained and use the `exp()` to undo the logarithm operation (although not strictly necessarily in this case, where we just need a comparison). We repeat this for the negative sequence probability using the negative HMM. As our test observation was one of the positive observations, we will misclassify only if the negative sequence probability is greater than the positive sequence probability. After our code block completes its execution, we can see how many mistakes we have made:

```
> incorrect
[1] 13
```

This means that out of the 53 positive observations, we misclassified 13 and correctly classified 40. We are not done yet, though, as we need to do a similar loop with the negative observations. This time, we will train a positive HMM once with all the positive observations:

```
> positive_observation <- Reduce(function(x, y) c(x, y),
                               positive_observations, c())
> transitionProbabilitiesPos  <-
  calculateTransitionProbabilities(positive_observation, states)
> positive_hmm = initHMM(states, symbols, startProbs =
  startingProbabilities, transProbs = transitionProbabilitiesPos,
  emissionProbs = emissionProbabilities)
```

Next, we are going to iterative over all the negative observations. We will train a negative model by leaving one observation out as the test observation. We will then process this observation with both the positive HMM we just trained and the negative HMM trained without this observation in its training data.

Finally, we will compare the predicted sequence probability for this test observation produced by the two HMM models and classify the test observation according to which model produced the higher probability. In essence, we are doing exactly the same process as we did earlier when we were iterating over the positive observations. The following code block will continue to update our incorrect variable and should be self-explanatory:

```
> for (obs in 1:length(negative_observations)) {

    negative_observation<-Reduce(function(x, y) c(x, y),
                    negative_observations[-obs], c())
    transitionProbabilitiesNeg <-
    calculateTransitionProbabilities(negative_observation, states)
    negative_hmm <- initHMM(states, symbols,
                  startProbs = startingProbabilities,
                  transProbs = transitionProbabilitiesNeg,
                  emissionProbs = emissionProbabilities)

    test_observation <- negative_observations[[obs]]
    final_index <- length(test_observation)

    pos_probs <- exp(forward(positive_hmm,test_observation))
    neg_probs <- exp(forward(negative_hmm,test_observation))
    pos_seq_prob <- sum(pos_probs[, final_index])
    neg_seq_prob <- sum(neg_probs[, final_index])

    if (pos_seq_prob > neg_seq_prob) incorrect <- incorrect+1

}
```

The overall number of misclassifications in the cross-validation is stored in the incorrect variable:

```
> incorrect
[1] 25
> (cross_validation_accuracy <- 1 - (incorrect/nrow(promoters)))
  [1] 0.7641509
```

Our overall cross-validation accuracy is roughly 76 percent. Given that we are using the leave-one-out approach, and that the overall size of the training data is so small, we expect this estimate to have a relatively high variance.

In our HMM model, the Markov property essentially makes the assumption that only the previous nucleotide determines the choice of the next nucleotide in the sequence. We can reasonably expect that there are longer-range dependencies at work and as a result we are limited in accuracy by the assumptions of our model. For this reason, there are models, such as the **Trigram HMM**, that take into account additional states in the past other than the current state.

In the next section, we will study an example where we train a hidden Markov model using unlabeled data. We will manually define the number of hidden states and use the Baum-Welch algorithm to train an HMM while estimating both state transitions and emissions.

Predicting letter patterns in English words

In this section, we will model the patterns of letters that form English words. Beyond having different words, and sometimes alphabets, languages differ from each other in the patterns of letters that are used to form words. English words have a characteristic distribution of letters and letter sequences, and in this section we will try to model the process of word formation in a very simplistic way by using a hidden Markov model.

The emitted symbols of our model will be the letters themselves, but this time we don't know what the states could be as we are using unlabeled data. For this reason, we are going to provide just the number of states that we want our model to have, and then use the Baum-Welch algorithm to train the parameters of our HMM.

All we need for this task is a corpus of text in English. Earlier in this chapter, we studied movie reviews with the Naïve Bayes classifier, so we will use these for convenience, although other sources of English text could be used as well. We shall begin by reloading our movie reviews and use the tm package to transform them all to lowercase:

```
> library("tm")
> nb_pos <- Corpus(DirSource(path_to_pos_folder),
                readerControl = list(language = "en"))
> nb_neg <- Corpus(DirSource(path_to_neg_folder),
                readerControl = list(language = "en"))
> nb_all <- c(nb_pos, nb_neg, recursive = T)
> nb_all <- tm_map(nb_all, content_transformer(tolower))
```

Next, we will the text from every review and collect these in a single vector:

```
> texts <- sapply(1 : length(nb_all), function(x) nb_all[[x]])
```

To simplify our task, aside from the individual letters, we will consider a category with all the whitespace characters (spaces, tabs, and so on) and represent these with the uppercase letter w. We will do the same for numerical digits with the uppercase character N, all punctuation marks with the uppercase character P, and use the uppercase character O for anything that is left. We use regular expressions for this:

```
> texts <- sapply(texts, function(x) gsub("\\s", "W", x))
> texts <- sapply(texts, function(x) gsub("[0-9]", "N", x))
> texts <- sapply(texts, function(x) gsub("[[:punct:]]", "P", x))
> texts <- sapply(texts, function(x) gsub("[^a-zWNP]", "O", x))
```

Once we have transformed all our text, we'll pick out a sample and split each review into characters. The sequences of characters from each review will then be concatenated with each other to create one long character sequence. This works quite well in this context as the corpus of reviews contain complete sentences and concatenating them amounts to joining up complete sentences. We've chosen to use a sample of 100 movie reviews. We can use more but the time taken to train the model will be longer.

```
> big_text_splits <- lapply(texts[1:100],
                            function(x) strsplit(x, ""))
> big_text_splits <- unlist(big_text_splits, use.names = F)
```

Next, we'll want to initialize our HMM. In this example, we'll consider a model with three states, which we'll arbitrarily name s1, s2, and s3. For emitted symbols, we have the lowercase alphabet and the four uppercase characters that as we saw earlier are being used to represent four special character categories such as numbers. R holds a vector of lowercase letters in the variable letters, which is very convenient for us:

```
> states <- c("s1", "s2", "s3")
> numstates <- length(states)
> symbols <- c(letters, "W", "N", "P", "O")
> numsymbols <- length(symbols)
```

Next, we'll create random starting, emission, and transmission probability matrices. We'll generate random entries in the [0,1] interval using the runif() function. We will need to normalize every row in these matrices in order to ensure that the entries correspond to probabilities. To achieve this, we'll use the sweep() function as we did earlier:

```
> set.seed(124124)
> startingProbabilities <- matrix(runif(numstates), 1, numstates)
> startingProbabilities <- sweep(startingProbabilities, 1,
                              rowSums(startingProbabilities), FUN = "/")
> set.seed(454235)
> transitionProbabilities <- matrix(runif(numstates * numstates),
```

```
                             numstates, numstates)
> transitionProbabilities <- sweep(transitionProbabilities, 1,
                    rowSums(transitionProbabilities), FUN = "/")
> set.seed(923501)
> emissionProbabilities <- matrix(runif(numstates * numsymbols),
                    numstates, numsymbols)
> emissionProbabilities <- sweep(emissionProbabilities, 1,
                    rowSums(emissionProbabilities), FUN = "/")
```

We now initialize and train the HMM using the large character sequence
we obtained earlier. This will take several minutes to run depending on the
computational resources available, and this is the main reason we drew only a
sample of the text earlier on.

```
> hmm <- initHMM(states, symbols,  startProbs =
    startingProbabilities, transProbs = transitionProbabilities,
    emissionProbs = emissionProbabilities)
> hmm_trained <- baumWelch(hmm, big_text_splits)
```

We trained our model in a completely unsupervised way by simply providing it
with character sequences. We don't have a meaningful test data set on which to
assess the performance of our model; rather, this exercise is worthwhile in that it
produces an HMM that has interesting properties. It is instructive to take a peek
at the symbol emission probabilities for each state. These are accessible via
the hmm$emissionProbs attribute on the hmm_trained object.

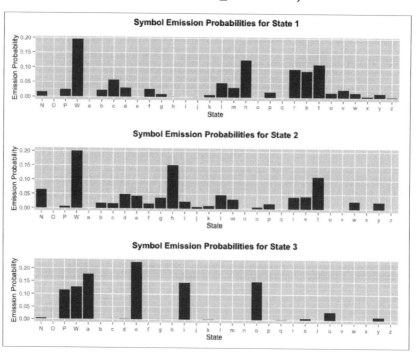

Let's examine these states carefully. All states have a relatively high probability of emitting a whitespace character. State 3 is very interesting, as besides whitespace, it seems to have grouped together punctuation and vowels. The HMM has successfully managed to group together the letters *a*, *e*, *i*, *o*, and *u* in the same category without any prior information about the English language.

This state also emits two consonants with a noticeable probability. The consonant *y* is emitted, which we know occasionally does behave like a vowel in words such as *rhythm* and *phylum*, for example. The consonant *s* is also emitted, and because it is often used to form the plural of nouns, we find this at the end of words just like punctuation marks. So, we see that this state seems to have grouped two main themes.

By contrast, state 1 tends to emit consonants and not vowels. In fact, only the vowel *u* seems to have a small probability of being emitted from this state. State 2 has a mix of vowels and consonants, but it is the only state in which the consonant *h* has a high probability. This is very interesting, as *h* is another letter of the alphabet that has vowel-like properties in pronunciation (it is often silent or part of a diphthong). We can learn more by examining the transition probabilities between the states:

```
> (trained_transition_probabilities <- hmm_trained$hmm$transProbs)
     to
from          s1            s2           s3
  s1 1.244568e-01 5.115204e-01 0.36402279
  s2 7.739387e-05 2.766151e-01 0.72330746
  s3 9.516911e-01 5.377194e-06 0.04830349
```

Again, we can discover a wealth of interesting properties. For example, when we are in state 3, the vowel state, we have a 95 percent chance of going to state 1, the consonant state. This is quite intuitive, in that English rarely has consecutive vowels. When we are in state 1, we have a 36 percent chance of going to the vowel state and a 51 percent chance of going to state 2.

Now we can begin to understand what state 2 represents. It primarily represents the state that emits the second consonant when we have two consecutive consonants. This is why the letter *h* has such a high probability in this state, as it participates in very common diphthongs, such as *ch*, *sh*, and *th*, the latter of course being found in very frequent words such as *the*. From this state, the most successor common state, with 72 percent probability, is the vowel state as expected after two consecutive consonants.

This experiment is worth repeating with different conditions. If we use different seeds or sample a different number of movie reviews, we may see different results, as the Baum-Welch algorithm is sensitive to initial conditions and is unsupervised. Specifically, our hidden Markov model might learn a completely different set of states.

For example, on some iterations, we noticed that all punctuation and numerical digits are grouped into one state, another state becomes the vowel state, and the third state is a pure consonant state. We can reproduce this behavior if in the previous code, we sample 40 texts and use the numbers 1816, 1817, and 1818 for the three seeds. There are many more possibilities—some of which are easier to interpret than others.

Another parameter that is worth varying here is the number of states. If we use two states, then the split tends to be between vowels and consonants. If we increase the number of states, we will often continue to find results that are interpretable for as many as ten states. Hidden Markov models are often also referred to as **generative models** because we can use them to generate examples of states and observations once they have been trained. We can do this with the simHMM() function by providing our model and the length of the sequence we want to generate:

```
> set.seed(987987)
> simHMM(hmm_trained$hmm, 30)
$states
 [1] "s2" "s3" "s1" "s3" "s3" "s1" "s3" "s3" "s1" "s1" "s2" "s3"
[13] "s3" "s1" "s2" "s3" "s1" "s2" "s2" "s2" "s3" "s1" "s2" "s2"
[25] "s3" "s1" "s2" "s3" "s1" "s2"


$observation
 [1] "h" "o" "P" "P" "a" "n" "W" "i" "r" "r" "h" "e" "i" "n" "h"
[16] "o" "n" "l" "W" "h" "e" "s" "t" "W" "e" "t" "c" "e" "P" "W"
```

As a final point, we can download and use the markovchain package, take our learned transition probability matrix, and find out over the long run how much time our model spends in each state. This is done using a **steady state calculation**, the mathematics of which we will not explore in this book. Thankfully, the markovchain package has a simple way to initialize a Markov chain when we know the probabilities that are involved. It does this by using the simpleMc() function, and we can use the steadyStates() function on our Markov chain to find out the steady state distribution:

```
> library("markovchain")
> simpleMc<-new("markovchain", states = c("s1", "s2", "s3"),
               transitionMatrix = trained_transition_probabilities,
               name = "simpleMc")
```

```
> steadyStates(simpleMc)
            s1        s2        s3
[1,] 0.3806541 0.269171 0.3501748
```

In the long term, we spend 38 percent of our time in state 1, the first consonant state; 27 percent in state 2, the second consonant state, and 35 percent of our time in state 3, the main vowel state.

Summary

In this chapter, we introduced ourselves to one of the very active areas of research in machine learning, namely the field of probabilistic graphical models. These models involve using a graphical structure to encode conditional independence relations between random variables. We saw how Bayes' Theorem, a very simple formula that essentially tells us how we can predicate cause by observing effect, can be used to build a simple classifier known as the Naïve Bayes classifier. This is a simple model where we are trying to predict an output class that best explains a set of observed features, all of which are assumed to be independent of each other given the output class.

We used this model to predict user sentiment on a set of movie reviews where the features were the words that were present in the reviews. Although we obtained reasonable accuracy, we found that the assumptions in our model are quite strict and prevent us from doing substantially better. Often, a Naïve Bayes model is built during the modeling process to provide us with a baseline performance that we know we should exceed with more sophisticated models.

We also studied Hidden Markov models, which are models typically used to label and predict sequences. Every position in the sequence is comprised of a hidden state and an observation emitted from that state. The key assumption of the model is that every state is independent of the entire sequence history, given the state that immediately preceded it. In addition, all observations are independent of each other as well as all other states in the sequence, given the state from which they were emitted.

When we have labeled sequences, we can train a hidden Markov model by using state transition and symbol emission counts obtained from the data themselves. It is also possible to train an unsupervised HMM using a very smart algorithm known as the Baum-Welch algorithm. Even though we did not dive into the algorithmic details, we saw an example of how this works in practice by training an HMM on sequences of characters in English words.

From this, we saw that the resulting model picked up on some interesting properties of language. Incidentally, even though we did not mention it, it is also possible to train a Naïve Bayes model with missing class labels, this time using the **EM algorithm**. Despite also having relatively strict independence assumptions, HMMs are quite powerful and have been successfully applied to a wide variety of applications from speech processing to molecular biology.

In the next chapter, we will look at analyzing and making predictions on time series. Many real-world applications involve taking measurements over a particular period of time and using them to make predictions about the future. For example, we might want to predict tomorrow's weather based on the weather today, or tomorrow's stock market index based on market fluctuations over the past few weeks.

9

Time Series Analysis

Many models that we come across involve observing a process of some sort over a period of time in order to learn to predict how that process will behave in the future. As we are dealing with a process that generates observations indexed by time, we refer to these models as time series models. Classic examples of time series are stock market indexes, volume of sales of a company's product over time, and changing weather attributes such as temperature and rainfall during the year.

In this chapter, we will focus on univariate time series, that is to say, time series that involve monitoring how a single variable fluctuates over time. To do this, we begin with some basic tools for describing time series, followed by an overview of a number of fundamental examples. It turns out that there is a wide variety of different approaches to modeling time series; in this chapter, we will focus primarily on ARIMA models, but we will also provide pointers on a few alternatives.

Fundamental concepts of time series

A **time series** is just a sequence of random variables, Y_1, Y_2, ..., Y_T, indexed by an evenly spaced sequence of points in time. Time series are ubiquitous in everyday life; we can observe the total amount of rainfall in millimeters over yearly periods for consecutive years, the average daytime temperature over consecutive days, the price of a particular share in the stock market at the close of every day of trading, or the total number of patients in a doctor's waiting room every half hour. As we can see, examples abound.

To analyze time series data, we use the concept of a **stochastic process**, which is just a sequence of random variables that are generated via an underlying mechanism that is stochastic or random, as opposed to deterministic. From the perspective of the predictive modeler, our goal is to study time series in order to build a model that best describes the behavior of a finite set of samples that we have obtained, in order for us to predict how the time series will behave in the future.

For example, if we have a vested interest in foreign currency exchange rates, we might want to study how the exchange rate between the Euro and the British Pound changed over a period of time in the past, in order for us to predict what the exchange rate might be in the near future. This could help us make a decision as to whether we should convert the Euros we have now into Pounds, or wait to convert them later if we expect the exchange rate to work in our favor in the near future.

At first glance, we might think that an approach to analyzing a time series would be to obtain the probability distribution of every variable in the sequence. In actuality, our time sequence can be quite large and this approach is impractical and unrealistic. Instead, we will begin by summarizing the main properties of the joint probability distribution of our random variables using the mean, covariance, and correlation functions.

Time series summary functions

From basic statistics, we are already familiar with the ideas of mean, variance, covariance, and correlation when it comes to two random variables. We can take these ideas and apply them in the context of time series by treating each point in time as a random variable. The **mean function** of a time series is the expected value of the time series at a particular time index, t:

$$\mu_t = E(Y_t)$$

In the general case, the mean of a time series at a particular time index t_1 is not the same as the mean of that time series at a different time index t_2. The **autocovariance function** and **autocorrelation function** are two important functions that measure the linear dependence between the random variables that make up the time series at different time points. The autocorrelation function is commonly abbreviated to the **ACF function**. For two time indexes, t_1 and t_2, we compute the autocovariance function as:

$$\gamma_{t_1,t_2} = Cov(Y_{t_1}, Y_{t_2}) = E\left[(Y_{t_1} - \mu_{t_1})(Y_{t_2} - \mu_{t_2})\right] = E(Y_{t_1} \cdot Y_{t_2}) - \mu_{t_1} \cdot \mu_{t_2}$$

When the two time indexes are the same, the autocovariance function is just the variance:

$$\gamma_{t_1,t_2} = Var(Y_{t_1}) = E\left[(Y_{t_1} - \mu_{t_1})^2\right] = E(Y_{t_1}^2) - \mu_{t_1}^2$$

The variance and autocovariance functions are measured in squared units of the original time series output units. Additionally, the autocovariance is a symmetric function, in that the same result is obtained if we switch the two time indexes in the computation. The ACF function is also symmetric, but it is unitless and its absolute value is bounded by the value 1. When the autocorrelation between two time indexes is 1 or -1, there is a perfect linear dependence or correlation, whereas when the value is 0, then the two time indexes are said to be uncorrelated. The ACF function is computed as follows:

$$\rho_{t_1,t_2} = Corr\left(Y_{t_1},Y_{t_2}\right) = \frac{Cov\left(Y_{t_1},Y_{t_2}\right)}{\sqrt{Var\left(Y_{t_1}\right)\cdot Var\left(Y_{t_2}\right)}}$$

It should be easy to spot from the previous equation that the ACF when computed on two identical time indexes just produces the value 1 since the covariance in the numerator just reduces to the variance. This result makes sense as any random variable is trivially perfectly correlated with itself.

Some fundamental time series

We will begin our study of time series by looking at two famous but very simple examples. These will not only give us a feel for the field, but as we will see later on, they will also become integral building blocks to describe more complex time series.

White noise

A basic but very important type of time series is known as **discrete white noise**, or simply **white noise**. In a white noise time series, the random variables that are generated all have a mean of 0, finite and identical variance σ_w^2, and the random variables at different time steps are uncorrelated with each other. Although some texts do not enforce this requirement, most texts also specify that the variables are also **independent and identically distributed (iid)** random variables.

The iid property essentially requires that each random variable come from the exact same distribution, such as a normal distribution with a particular mean and standard deviation. The property also requires that two variables from different time steps are not only uncorrelated with each other, but are also independent, which is a stronger requirement.

> It is a common misconception in statistics that if two variables are uncorrelated they must also necessarily be independent. While the converse is true, so that two independent variables are automatically uncorrelated, two uncorrelated random variables are not necessarily independent. For example, a random variable X with a normal distribution centered at 0 and a random variable Y, computed as X^2, are uncorrelated but clearly not independent of each other.

In this book, we'll include the iid requirement in the definition of the white noise time series. Finally, we'll note that a white noise time series drawn from a normal distribution is known as **Gaussian white noise**. We can easily generate some Gaussian white noise by sampling from a normal distribution with zero mean using the `rnorm()` function:

```
> set.seed(9571)
> white_noise <- rnorm(100, mean = 0, sd = 3.0)
```

The following plot shows our generated Gaussian white noise series:

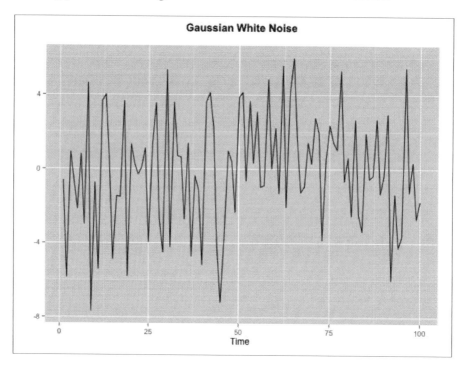

Fitting a white noise time series

Suppose we have collected some time series data and want to know if our time series is actually a white noise time series. One way to do this is to plot a **correlogram**. This is a graph that estimates the ACF function for pairs of time steps that are k steps apart. For different values of k, known as the **lag**, we should see zero correlation except for the case where $k = 0$. In this way, we are essentially testing for the uncorrelated property, which is one of the defining characteristics of a white noise series. We can easily do this in R via the `acf()` function:

```
> acf(white_noise)
```

Here is the ACF plot for the white noise series we generated earlier:

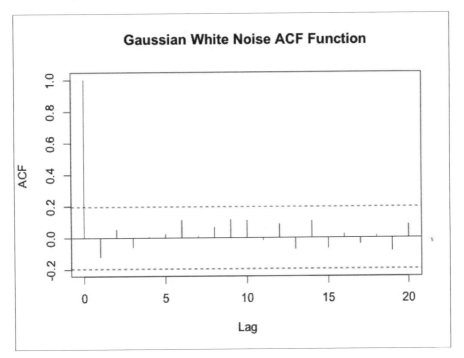

The dotted lines show a 95 percent confidence interval within which the value of the ACF function at a particular lag is not considered statistically significant (greater than zero). These values in practice will not be exactly zero due to sampling bias and in fact, we can reasonably expect to see 5 percent of them to be erroneously significant for a correlogram of an actual white noise series.

The correlogram we plotted does indeed match our expectations, whereby only the value at a lag of 0 is statistically significant. To fit our observed time series to a white noise series model, all we need is the variance as this is the only parameter of a white noise series. We can estimate this directly via the `var()` function, which gives a value very close to what we used to generate the sequence:

```
> var(white_noise)
[1] 9.862699
```

Random walk

Another very common type of time series is known as a **random walk**. This model has been used to describe the motion of pollen particles when placed on the surface of water, known as **Brownian Motion**, as well as for the price of stocks in the stock market. A time series that is a random walk is a time series in which the differences between successive time points are white noise. We can describe this process using a **recurrence relation**, that is to say, a relation in which a term in the sequence is defined as a function of terms that occur earlier in the sequence. When using a recurrence relation, we must also specify the initial condition(s) that must hold for the first term(s) in the sequence:

$$Y_t = Y_{t-1} + e_t$$
$$Y_1 = e_1$$

The first equation explains that a general term in the sequence at time t is related to the term in the sequence one time step earlier via the addition of the term e_t, which is a term from a white noise sequence. The second equation shows the starting condition of the random walk and says that the first term is also the first term of a white noise sequence. Essentially, we can think of a random walk as a sequence that adjusts its current value by a positive or negative amount according to a parallel white noise sequence.

A variant of the random walk is the random walk with drift. This differs from the regular random walk in that we also add a constant term a to every point in the series, and this is known as the **drift**. Due to this fact, the random walk with drift has a time varying mean of $t \times a$ (but the variance is the same as before).

From the definition of a random walk, it should be clear that at time step t, the term in a random walk arises from the sum of t iid variables with 0 mean and identical variance σ_w^2. These are, of course, the terms of a white noise series. Due to this fact, and because of the linearity of expectation and variance, we infer that the mean function of a random walk is 0 for all time points. By contrast, the variance is given by $t \times \sigma_w^2$. Consequently, in this time series, the variance continually increases over time. To simulate a random walk in R, we essentially need a cumulative sum of a white noise random series. We can do this with R's `cumsum()` function:

```
> set.seed(874234242)
> random_walk <- cumsum(rnorm(100, mean = 0, sd = 3.0))
```

Here's the plot of our random walk:

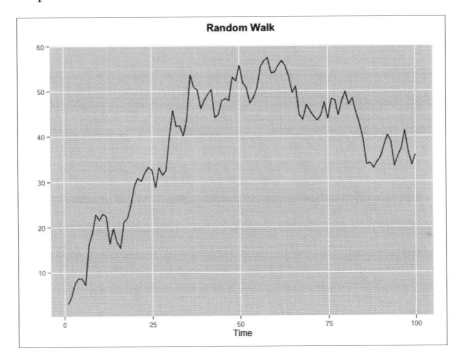

Fitting a random walk

A good way to see if a time series follows a random walk is to compute the successive differences between terms. The time series that is comprised of these differences should be a white noise time series. Consequently, were we to plot a correlogram of the latter, we should see the same kind of pattern characteristic of white noise, namely a spike at lag 0 and no other significant spikes elsewhere.

To compute successive term differences in R, we use the `diff()` function:

```
> acf(diff(random_walk))
```

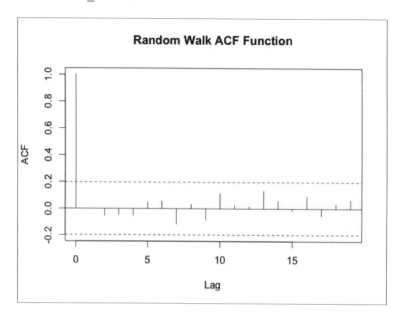

As expected, this plot looks very similar to the ACF plot of the white noise series we generated earlier in this chapter. Now that we have two examples of time series under our belt, we are ready to tackle an important new concept, stationarity.

Stationarity

We have often seen that in predictive modeling, we need to make certain important but limiting assumptions in order to build practical models. With time series models, one of the most common assumptions to make that render the modeling task significantly simpler is the **stationarity assumption**.

Stationarity essentially describes that the probabilistic behavior of a time series does not change with the passage of time. There are two versions of the stationarity property that are commonly used. A stochastic process is said to be **strictly stationary** when the joint probability distribution of a sequence of points starting at time t, Y_t, Y_{t+1}, ..., Y_{t+n}, is the same as the joint probability distribution of another sequence of points starting at a different time T, Y_T, Y_T+1, ..., Y_{T+n}.

To be strictly stationary, this property must hold for any choice of time t and T, and for any sequence length n. In particular, because we can choose $n = 1$, this means that the probability distributions of every individual point in the sequence, also known as the **univariate probabilities**, must be the same. It follows, therefore, that in a strictly stationary time series, the mean function is constant over time, as is the variance.

We also use a weaker form of stationarity, which very often tends to be sufficient for our needs. A stochastic process is **weakly stationary** when the mean function is constant over time and the autocovariance function depends only on the time lag between two points in the sequence. In symbols, this latter property can be written as:

$$\gamma_{t,t+k} = \gamma_{0,k}$$

Additionally, a weakly stationary stochastic process must have finite variance for all time points, something that is not necessary in the definition of a strictly stationary process. When we know that the variance is finite for all time points, a process that is strictly stationary is always also weakly stationary. As is custom, we will use the term *stationary stochastic process* or *stationary time series* to imply weak stationarity, and state strict stationarity explicitly where we require it. Armed with this new concept, we can simplify our formulae for the mean function, autocovariance, and autocorrelation for a stationary time series process respectively as:

$$\mu_t = \mu$$
$$\gamma_k = Cov(Y_t, Y_{t+k}) = E\left[(Y_t - \mu)(Y_{t+k} - \mu)\right]$$
$$\rho_k = \frac{\gamma_k}{\gamma_0}$$

Note that the autocovariance with a lag of 0, γ_0, is just the variance. Let's revisit the two examples of time series that we have seen so far from the perspective of stationarity. White noise is a stationary process as it has a constant mean, in this case of 0, and also a constant variance. Note also that the x axis of the ACF plot displays the time lag k rather than the position in the sequence.

In fact, to estimate the ACF plot, R's `acf()` function uses all pairs of values separated by a particular lag value irrespective of their position in the sequence, thus assuming stationarity. The random walk, on the other hand, does have a constant mean (not so in the case of the random walk with drift however) but it has a time varying variance and so it is non-stationary.

Stationary time series models

In this section, we will describe a few stationary time series models. As we will see, these can be used to model a number of real-world processes.

Moving average models

A **moving average (MA)** process is a stochastic process in which the random variable at time step *t* is a linear combination of the most recent (in time) terms of a white noise process. Concretely, we can write this in an equation as follows:

$$Y_t = e_t + \theta_1 e_{t-1} + \theta_2 e_{t-2} + \cdots + \theta_q e_{t-q}$$

In the previous equation, and henceforth, we will assume that the *e* terms are white noise random variables with mean 0 and variance σ_w^2. We can describe a moving average process in an equivalent way by making use of the **backshift operator**, *B*. The backshift operator is an operator that when applied to a random variable in a stochastic process at time *t*, produces the random variable at the previous time step, *t-1*. For example:

$$e_{t-1} = Be_t$$
$$e_{t-2} = Be_{t-1} = B^2 e_t$$

We can obtain random variables further back in time by successive applications of the backshift operator. B^2, for example, indicates the application of the backshift operator twice so that we go back two time steps. With that in mind, we can express an MA process using the backshift operator as follows:

$$Y_t = \left(1 + \theta_1 B + \theta_2 B^2 + \cdots + \theta_q B^q \right) \cdot e_t$$

The expression in parentheses is a polynomial of order q in terms of the backshift operator B. This polynomial is referred to as the **characteristic polynomial** of an MA process.

$$\theta(x) = 1 + \theta_1 x + \theta_2 x^2 + \cdots + \theta_q x^q$$

An MA process is always stationary regardless of the choice of coefficients θ or the order q of the process. We are, however, interested in the roots of the equation $\theta(x) = 0$. If the roots of this equation exceed 1 in absolute value, we say that the MA process is **invertible**. Invertibility is a highly desirable property of MA processes. Invertible MA processes have unique ACF plots, whereas MA processes that are not can share the same ACF plot.

For example, for an *MA(1)* process with a single θ coefficient, we get the same ACF plot when the coefficient is *1/θ*. The reader can verify this in a short while when we present the equation for the autocorrelation function. We will now explore some of the statistical properties of the MA process. Remembering that every *e* term is a white noise random variable, we can see that the mean of an MA process is constantly 0 and the variance is constantly given by the following expression, where we define θ_0 to be 1:

$$Var(Y_t) = \sigma_w^2 + \theta_1^2 \cdot \sigma_w^2 + \theta_2^2 \cdot \sigma_w^2 + \cdots + \theta_q^2 \cdot \sigma_w^2 = \sigma_w^2 \cdot \sum_{i=0}^{q} \theta_i^2$$

The autocorrelation function is given by the following:

$$\rho_k = \begin{cases} 1 & k = 0 \\ \dfrac{\sum_{i=0}^{q-k} \theta_i \theta_{i+k}}{\sum_{i=0}^{q} \theta_i^2} & 1 \le k \le q \\ 0 & k > q \end{cases}$$

Deriving the autocorrelation function is a little more tedious, so we leave it as an exercise for the interested reader. From the equation, the important observation to make is that the ACF of an MA process has nonzero values for lags below q, the order of that process, and 0 afterwards. This fact is not only useful in identifying an MA process through its ACF function, but also in estimating the order of the MA process, as we can take the largest lag that has a statistically significant nonzero value. We will simulate some MA processes to get an idea of this.

 For MA processes, and indeed all the time series models discussed in this chapter, there are a number of very useful references with examples in R. An excellent text from the Use R! series of *Springer* is *Introductory Time Series* by *Cowpertwait* and *Metcalfe*. We also recommend *Time Series Analysis With Applications in R, Cryer and Chan, Springer*.

In R, we can simulate MA processes (among others) using the `arima.sim()` function. This is actually a general function that we will use often in this chapter. To generate an MA process, we will use the n parameter to specify the length of the series and the `model` parameter to specify the parameters of the series we want to simulate. This, in turn, is a list in which we will set the vector of θ coefficients in the ma attribute and the standard deviation of the white noise terms in the sd attribute. The following is how we can generate 1,000 samples from the MA process $e_t + 0.84e_{t-1} + 0.62e_{t-2}$, where the white noise terms have a standard deviation of 1.2:

```
> set.seed(2357977)
> ma_ts1 <- arima.sim(model = list(ma = c(0.84, 0.62), sd = 1.2),
                      n = 1000)
> head(ma_ts1, n = 8)
[1] -2.403431159 -2.751889402 -2.174711499 -1.354482419
[5] -0.814139443  0.009842499 -0.632004838 -0.035627181
```

The `arima.sim()` function returns the result of the simulation in a special time series object that R calls ts. This object is useful for keeping track of some basic information about a time series and supports specialized plots that are useful in time series analysis. According to what we learned in this section, the ACF plot of this simulated time series should display two significant peaks at lags 1 and 2.

We will now plot this to confirm our expectations. In addition, we will also plot the ACF function of another simulated *MA(2)* process with coefficients 0.84 and -0.62 to show how we can also obtain negative values in the ACF coefficients:

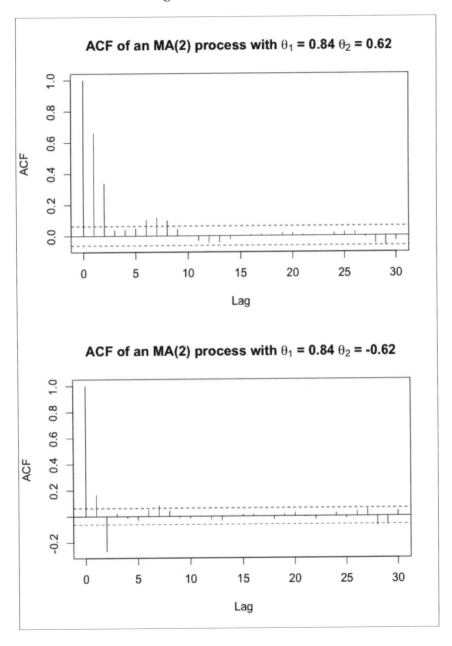

Autoregressive models

Autoregressive models (AR) come about from the notion that we would like a simple model to explain the current value of a time series in terms of a limited window of the most recent values from the past. The equation for an AR model of order p is:

$$Y_t = \varphi_1 \cdot Y_{t-1} + \varphi_2 \cdot Y_{t-2} + \cdots + \varphi_p \cdot Y_{t-p} + e_t$$

Collecting all the Y terms on the left and applying the backshift operator again yields:

$$\left(1 - \varphi_1 B - \varphi_2 B^2 - \cdots - \varphi_p B^p\right) \cdot Y_t = e_t$$

Unlike the MA process, the AR process is not always stationary. The condition for stationarity relies on the characteristic equation for the AR process, which is given by:

$$\varphi(x) = 1 - \varphi_1 x - \varphi_2 x^2 - \cdots - \varphi_p x^p$$

If the roots of this equation all have magnitude greater than 1, the process is stationary. The following two relations describe a necessary (but not sufficient) requirement for this to happen:

$$\varphi_1 + \varphi_2 + \cdots + \varphi_p < 1$$
$$\left|\varphi_p\right| < 1$$

This fact often helps us spot a non-stationary AR process through a quick examination of the coefficients. Note that a random walk is just an *AR(1)* with the first coefficient, φ_1, equal to 1. The autocorrelation function has a more complex form than is the case with the MA process. In particular, it does not have a cut-off property as in the MA process where all lag values greater than q, the order of the MA process, are zero.

For example, the autocorrelation function for an *AR(1)* process is given by:

$$\rho_k = \alpha^k, k \geq 0$$

We will simulate an *AR(1)* process with the `arima.sim()` function again. This time, the coefficients of our process are defined in the `ar` attribute inside the `model` list.

```
> set.seed(634090)
> ma_ts3 <- arima.sim(model = list(ar = c(0.74), sd = 1.2),
                      n = 1000)
```

The following ACF plot shows the exponential decay in lag coefficients, which is what we expect for our simulated *AR(1)* process:

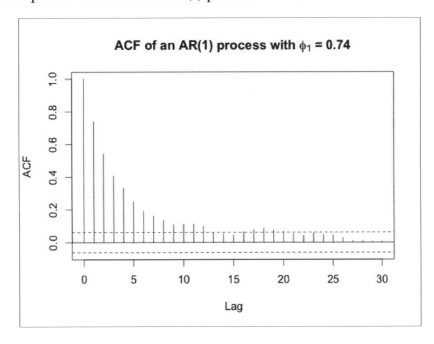

Note that with the moving average process, the ACF plot was useful in helping us identify the order of the process. With an autoregressive process, this is not the case. To deal with this, we use the **partial autocorrelation function** (**PACF**) plot instead. We define the partial autocorrelation at time lag, *k*, as the correlation that results when we remove the effect of any correlations that are present for lags smaller than *k*. By definition, the AR process of order *p* depends only on the values of the process up to *p* units of time in the past.

Consequently, the PACF plot will exhibit zero values for all the lags greater than p, creating a parallel situation with the ACF plot for an MA process where we can simply read off the order of an AR process as the largest time lag whose PACF lag term is statistically significant. In R, we can generate the PACF plot with the function `pacf()`. For our *AR(1)* process, this produces a plot with only one significant lag term as expected:

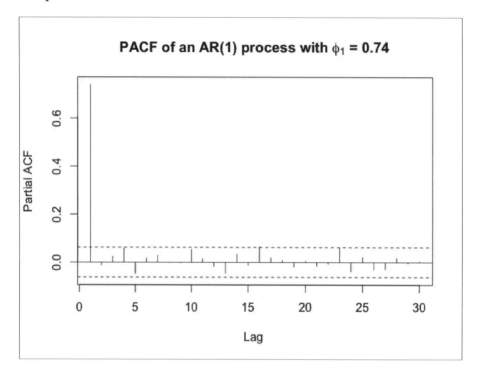

Autoregressive moving average models

We can combine the moving average and autoregressive models into a single model that has both elements of a moving average process and an autoregressive process. We call the generalized model a **moving average autoregressive (ARMA)** model. The general equation for an *ARMA(p, q)* process (that is, an ARMA process with a pth order autoregressive component and a qth order moving average component) is given by:

$$Y_t = \varphi_1 \cdot Y_{t-1} + \varphi_2 \cdot Y_{t-2} + \cdots + \varphi_p \cdot Y_{t-p} + e_t + \theta_1 \cdot e_{t-1} + \theta_2 \cdot e_{t-2} + \cdots + \theta_q \cdot e_{t-q}$$

Note that a purely moving average process *MA(q)* can be written as the ARMA process *ARMA(0, q)* and that a purely autoregressive process *AR(p)* can be written as the ARMA process *ARMA(p, 0)*. An ARMA process is stationary if the characteristic equation of the AR component $\varphi(x) = 0$ has roots whose magnitude is greater than unity. This is exactly the same condition as with a purely autoregressive model.

In a similar vein, the process is invertible if the characteristic equation of the MA component $\theta(x) = 0$ has roots whose magnitude is greater than unity. To uniquely determine an ARMA process, we further require that there be no common factors in the characteristic equations of the MA and AR components because they can cancel out, allowing us to obtain an equivalent but lower order ARMA process.

There are various techniques to fit ARMA models that usually consist of two parts. The job of the first part is to identify the order of the ARMA process by finding *p* and *q*. Once these have been chosen, the second part tries to estimate values for the coefficients of the AR and MA components, for example, by minimizing the sum of square errors between the observed sequence and the estimated sequence. In R, there are methods that perform this optimization for us, but later on in this chapter when we investigate real-world data sets, we will explore a method for choosing between trained models of a different order that relies on minimizing the AIC value.

Non-stationary time series models

In this section, we will look at some models that are non-stationary but nonetheless have certain properties that allow us to either derive a stationary model or model the non-stationary behavior.

Autoregressive integrated moving average models

The random walk process is an example of a time series model that is itself non-stationary, but the differences between consecutive points, Y_t and Y_{t+1}, which we can write as ΔY_t, is stationary. This **differenced sequence** was nothing but the white noise sequence, which we know to be stationary.

If we were to take the difference between consecutive output points of the differenced sequence, we would again obtain another sequence, which we call a **second order differenced sequence**.

Generalizing this notion of differencing, we can say that a **dth order difference** is obtained by repeatedly computing differences between consecutive terms d times, to obtain a new sequence with points, W_t, from an original sequence, Y_t. We can express this idea as:

$$W_t = \nabla^d Y_t$$

We can consequently define an autoregressive integrated moving average (ARIMA) process as a process in which the dth order difference of terms is a stationary ARMA process. An *ARIMA(p, d, q)* process requires a dth order differencing, has an MA component of order q, and an AR component of order p. Thus, a regular *ARMA(p, q)* process is equivalent to an *ARIMA(p, 0, q)* process. In order to fit an ARIMA model, we need to first determine an appropriate value of d, namely the number of times we need to perform differencing. Once we have found this, we can then proceed with fitting the differenced sequence using the same process as we would use with an ARMA process.

One way to find a suitable value for d is to repeatedly difference a time series and after each application of differencing to check whether the resulting time series is stationary. There are a number of tests for stationarity that can be used, and these are often known as **unit root tests**. A good example is the **Augmented Dickey-Fuller (ADF) test**. This test builds a regression model as follows:

$$\nabla Y_t = \varphi Y_t + \beta_1 \nabla Y_{t-1} + \beta_2 \nabla Y_{t-2} + \cdots + \beta_{k-1} \nabla Y_{t-k+1} + e_t$$

Here, k refers to the maximum number of time lags that will be included in the model. The null hypothesis of the ADF test is that the current time series is non-stationary and as a result, the regression model we just saw will predict a coefficient φ of approximately zero. If the time series is stationary, causing us to reject the null hypothesis, then the expected value of the coefficient is below zero.

We can find an implementation of this test in the R package `tseries` via the function `adf.test()`. This assumes a default value k equal to the largest integer that does not exceed the cube root of the length of the time series under test. The ADF test produces a *p*-value for us to examine. Values that are smaller than 0.05 (or a smaller cutoff such as 0.01 if we want a higher degree of confidence) are typically suggestive that the time series in question is stationary.

The following example shows the results of running the ADF test on our simulated random walk, which we know is non-stationary:

```
> library(tseries)
> adf.test(random_walk, alternative = "stationary")

    Augmented Dickey-Fuller Test

data:   random_walk
Dickey-Fuller = -1.5881, Lag order = 4, p-value = 0.7473
alternative hypothesis: stationary
```

As expected, our *p*-value is much higher than 0.05, indicating a lack of stationarity.

 Another unit root test is the **Philips-Perron test**, which in R we can run using the function PP.test(). The **Kwiatkowski-Phillips-Schmidt-Shin (KPSS)** test is yet another example of a unit root test. An implementation of this can also be found in the package tseries. In contrast with the previous two tests, the null hypothesis of this last test assumes stationarity, so the interpretation of the *p*-values is inverted.

Autoregressive conditional heteroscedasticity models

The key premise behind ARIMA models is that although the sequence itself was non-stationary, we could apply a particular transformation (in this case, by differencing the terms) in order to arrive at a stationary series. Thus, we essentially extended the range of possible types of time series we could model using the tools we have already learned this far, namely the autoregressive and moving average processes. Of course, many non-stationary processes cannot be described well with ARIMA models, so there are many other approaches to handling non-stationarity.

One such approach to building a model for a non-stationary time series is to make the assumption that the model is non-stationary because the variance of the model changes over time in a predictable way. It turns out that modeling the change of variance over time as an autoregressive process, thus using tools already familiar to us results in a model that has important applications in financial econometrics.

This model is known as the **autoregressive conditional heteroscedasticity (ARCH)** model. Heteroscedasticity is the opposite of homoscedasticity, which describes constant variance.

The equation for an ARCH model of order p is given by:

$$\varepsilon_t = w_t \cdot \sqrt{\alpha_0 + \sum_{i=1}^{p} \alpha_i \cdot \varepsilon_{t-i}^2}$$

In this process, we assume that our series terms, ε_t, have a zero mean and that the w_t terms are white noise. We can compute the variance of this series as follows:

$$Var(\varepsilon_t) = E\left[(\varepsilon_t - \overline{\varepsilon_t})^2 \right]$$

$$= E(\varepsilon_t^2)$$

$$= E(w_t^2) \cdot E\left(\alpha_0 + \sum_{i=1}^{p} \alpha_i \cdot \varepsilon_{t-i}^2\right)$$

$$= E\left(\alpha_0 + \sum_{i=1}^{p} \alpha_i \cdot \varepsilon_{t-i}^2\right)$$

$$= \alpha_0 + \sum_{i=1}^{p} E\left(\alpha_i \cdot \varepsilon_{t-i}^2\right)$$

$$= \alpha_0 + \sum_{i=1}^{p} \alpha_i \cdot E\left(\varepsilon_{t-i}^2\right)$$

$$= \alpha_0 + \sum_{i=1}^{p} \alpha_i \cdot Var\left(\varepsilon_{t-i}\right)$$

As we can see, the variance of the ARCH model at time t is a linearly weighted sum of the variances of the p most recent time periods in the past and so we have a recognizable AR process of order p. In this example, we've also made the assumption that the variance of the white noise process, w_t, is 1 just to highlight how the process is autoregressive; if the variance of the white noise process is not 1, then this simply introduces a constant multiplicative factor in the result, which does not change the autoregressive nature of the model.

Generalized autoregressive heteroscedasticity models

ARCH models are very popular in finance and for this reason they form the basis of many different extensions. We'll mention one extension here, the **generalized autoregressive heteroscedasticity (GARCH)** because its form is essentially an ARCH model with a moving average variance component added in. More specifically, the general form of a *GARCH(p, q)* process is:

$$\varepsilon_t = w_t \cdot \sqrt{h_t}$$

$$h_t = \alpha_0 + \sum_{i=1}^{p} \alpha_i \cdot \varepsilon_{t-i}^2 + \sum_{j=1}^{q} \beta_t \cdot h_{t-j}$$

Again, we can see that this is a clear extension of the *ARCH(p)* process, which is equivalent to a *GARCH(p, 0)* process.

Predicting intense earthquakes

Having reviewed several time series models, we are now ready for some practical examples. Our first data set is a time series of earthquakes having magnitude that exceeds 4.0 on the Richter scale in Greece over the period between the year 2000 and the year 2008. This data set was recorded by the Observatory of Athens and is hosted on the website of the University of Athens, Faculty of Geology, Department of Geophysics & Geothermics. The data is available online at http://www.geophysics.geol.uoa.gr/catalog/catgr_20002008.epi.

We will import these data directly by using the package RCurl. From this package, we will use the functions getURL(), which retrieves the contents of a particular address on the Internet, and textConnection(), which will interpret the result as raw text. Once we have the data, we provide meaningful names for the columns using information from the website:

```
> library("RCurl")
> seismic_raw <- read.table(textConnection(getURL(
  "http://www.geophysics.geol.uoa.gr/catalog/catgr_20002008.epi")),
  sep = "", header = F)
> names(seismic_raw) <- c("date", "mo", "day", "hr", "mn", "sec",
  "lat", "long", "depth", "mw")
> head(seismic_raw, n = 3)
```

```
     date mo day hr mn  sec      lat  long depth  mw
1 2000   1   1  1 19 28.3 41.950N 20.63     5 4.8
2 2000   1   1  4  2 28.4 35.540N 22.76    22 3.7
3 2000   1   2 10 44 10.9 35.850N 27.61     3 3.7
```

The first column is the date column and the second is the month column. The next four columns represent the day, hour, minute, and second that the earthquake was observed. The next two columns are the latitude and longitude of the epicenter of the earthquake. The last two columns contain the surface depth and earthquake intensity.

Our goal is to aggregate these data in order to get monthly counts of the significant earthquakes observed in this time period. To achieve this, we can use the `count()` function of the R package `plyr` to aggregate the data, and the standard `ts()` function to create a new time series. We will specify the starting and ending year and month of our time series, as well as set the `freq` parameter to `12` to indicate monthly readings. Finally, we will plot our data:

```
> library("plyr")
> seismic <- count(seismic_raw, c("date", "mo"))
> seismic_ts <- ts(seismic$freq, start = c(2000, 1),
                end = c(2008, 1), frequency = 12)
```

The following plot shows our time series:

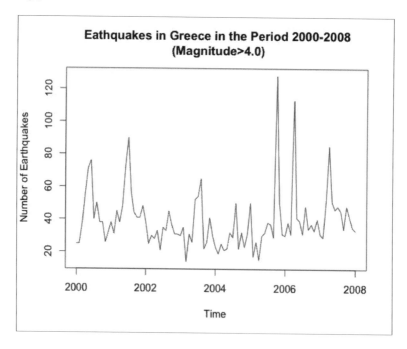

The data seems to fluctuate around 30 with occasional peaks, and although the largest two of these are more recent in time, there does not appear to be any overall upward trend.

We would like to analyze these data using an ARIMA model; however, at the same time, we are not sure what values we should use for the order. A simple way that we can compute this ourselves is to obtain the AIC for all the different models we would like to train and pick the model that has the smallest AIC. Concretely, we will first begin by creating ranges of possible values for the order parameters p, d, and q. Next, we shall use the expand.grid() function, which is a very useful function that will create a data frame with all the possible combination of these parameters:

```
> d <- 0 : 2
> p <- 0 : 6
> q <- 0 : 6
> seismic_models <- expand.grid(d = d, p = p, q = q)
> head(seismic_models, n = 4)
  d p q
1 0 0 0
2 1 0 0
3 2 0 0
4 0 1 0
```

Next, we define a function that fits an ARIMA model using a particular combination of order parameters and returns the AIC produced:

```
getTSModelAIC <- function(ts_data, p, d, q) {
  ts_model <- arima(ts_data, order = c(p, d, q))
  return(ts_model$aic)
}
```

When we talked about ARIMA processes in this chapter, we described them in terms of a zero mean. In R, many functions, such as the arima() function, center the results automatically for time series whose mean is nonzero by subtracting the mean of the time series from each point.

For certain combinations of order parameters, our function will produce an error if it fails to converge. When this happens, we'll want to report a value of infinity for the AIC value so that this model is not chosen when we try to pick the best model. The following function acts as a wrapper around our previous function:

```
getTSModelAICSafe <- function(ts_data, p, d, q) {
  result = tryCatch({
```

```
      getTSModelAIC(ts_data, p, d, q)
  }, error = function(e) {
    Inf
  })
}
```

All that remains is to apply this function on every parameter combination in our
`seismic_models` data frame, save the results, and pick the combination that gives
us the lowest AIC:

```
> seismic_models$aic <- mapply(function(x, y, z)
  getTSModelAICSafe(seismic_ts, x, y, z), seismic_models$p,
  seismic_models$d, seismic_models$q)
> subset(seismic_models,aic == min(aic))
   d p q     aic
26 1 1 1 832.171
```

The results indicate that the most appropriate model for our earthquakes time series
is the *ARIMA(1, 1, 1)* model. We can train this model again with these parameters:

```
> seismic_model <- arima(seismic_ts, order = c(1, 1, 1))
> summary(seismic_model)
Series: seismic_ts
ARIMA(1,1,1)

Coefficients:
         ar1      ma1
      0.2949  -1.0000
s.e.  0.0986   0.0536

sigma^2 estimated as 306.9:  log likelihood=-413.09
AIC=832.17   AICc=832.43   BIC=839.86

Training set error measures:
                      ME      RMSE      MAE      MPE      MAPE
    MASE         ACF1
Training set -0.2385232 17.42922 11.12018 -14.47481 29.84171
   0.8174096 -0.02179457
```

The `forecast` package has a very useful forecasting function, `forecast`, that can be applied to time series models. This, in turn, provides us with not only a convenient method to forecast values into the future, but also allows us to visualize the result using the `plot()` function.

> The `forecast` package also has an `auto.arima()` function that can be used to pick the order values of the ARIMA process, which is similar but slightly more sophisticated than the simple approach we present here.

Let's forecast the next ten points in the future:

```
> plot(forecast(seismic_model, 10))
```

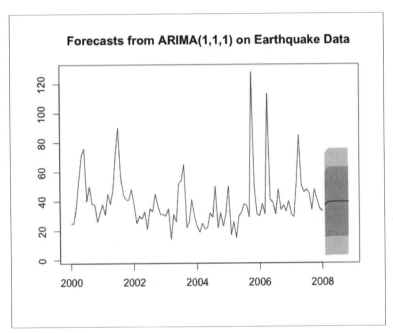

The plot shows that our model predicts a small rise in the number of intense earthquakes over the next few time periods and then predicts a steady average value. Note that the bands shown are confidence intervals around these forecasts. The spiky nature of the time series is reflected in the width of these bands. If we examine the autocorrelation function of our time series, we see that there is only one lag coefficient that is statistically significant:

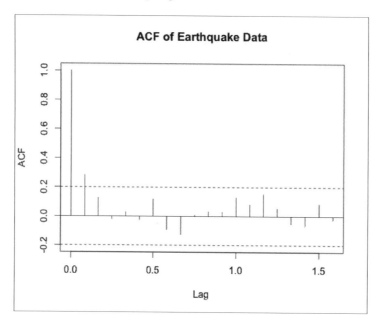

The profile of the ACF indicates that a simple *AR(1)* process might be an appropriate fit, and indeed this is what is predicted using the `auto.arima()` function of the `forecast` package. Repeating our forecast with an *AR(1)* model yields a result very similar to what we saw earlier. In fact, as indicated with the AIC values, this model is only slightly better than a white noise model (*AR(0)*), indicating that the time series that we have is very close to being white noise. This is not very surprising for our particular data set, which involves earthquakes produced at different epicenters around Greece. As a final note, we will add that if we want to inspect the coefficients of our fitted model, we can do so using the `coefficients()` function.

Predicting lynx trappings

Our second data set, known as the *lynx data set*, is a very famous data set and is provided with the core distribution of R. This was first presented in a 1942 paper by *C. Elton* and *M. Nicholson*, titled *The ten year cycle in numbers of Canadian lynx*, which appears in the *Journal of Animal Ecology*. The data consist of the number of Canadian lynx trapped in the MacKenzie river over the period 1821-1934. We can load the data as follows:

```
> data(lynx)
```

The following diagram shows a plot of the lynx data:

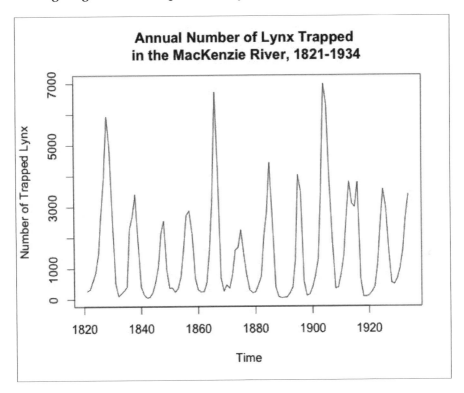

We will repeat the exact same series of analysis steps as we did with the earthquake data. First, we will create a grid of parameter combinations and use this to train multiple models. Then we will pick the best one on account of it having the smallest AIC value. Finally, we will use the chosen parameter combination to train a model and forecast the next few data points. The reader is encouraged to also experiment with `auto.arima()`.

```
> d <- 0:2
> p <- 0:6
> q <- 0:6
> lynx_models <- expand.grid(p = p, d = d, q = q)
> lynx_models$aic <- mapply(function(x, y, z)
  getTSModelAICSafe(lynx, x, y, z), lynx_models$p, lynx_models$d,
  lynx_models$q)
> subset(lynx_models,aic == min(aic))
      p d q       aic
124 4 2 5 1845.407
> lynx_model <- arima(lynx, order = c(4, 2, 5))
> plot(forecast(lynx_model, 10))
```

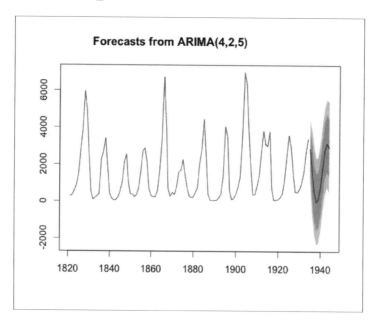

This time, we predicted a higher order ARIMA model and the forecasted value seems intuitively very reasonable given the observed time series. Even though the peaks of the time series are different, there is a much clearer seasonal pattern in the data.

Predicting foreign exchange rates

Our third and final data set will be constructed from a historical database of Euro Foreign Exchange Reference rates provided by the website of the European Central Bank. We can download a zipped archive containing the data from http://www. ecb.europa.eu/stats/eurofxref/eurofxref-hist.zip. When unzipped, this archive contains a file titled eurofxref-hist.csv, which we can directly import into R using the read.csv() function:

```
> eurofxref.hist <- read.csv("eurofxref-hist.csv",
                            stringsAsFactors = F)
> eurofxref.hist[1 : 6, 1 : 6]
        Date    USD    JPY    BGN CYP    CZK
1 2014-09-05 1.2948 136.27 1.9558 N/A 27.596
2 2014-09-04 1.3015 136.89 1.9558 N/A 27.662
3 2014-09-03 1.3151 138.11 1.9558 N/A 27.658
4 2014-09-02 1.3115 137.63 1.9558 N/A 27.784
5 2014-09-01 1.3133 136.97 1.9558 N/A 27.738
6 2014-08-29 1.3188 137.11 1.9558 N/A 27.725
```

As we can see, our data frame contains the conversion rates for several different currencies. As this file is continually updated by the Central Bank, downloading the file today will produce a data frame that begins at a more recent date than that shown. Note that the data are in reverse chronological order and that there are some gaps in the dates. These gaps occur on weekends or bank holidays when no trading took place.

We have chosen to focus on the time series of Euro to American Dollar exchange rates. As a first step, we will restrict the date range of our time series. This will allow all our analysis to be reproduced exactly irrespective of the date that the data is downloaded. Specifically, we will limit the rows of our data frame to the years 2005-2013 (both years inclusive) and produce a time series obtained by reversing the USD column (to sort the data chronologically):

```
> selector <- (eurofxref.hist$Date <= as.Date('2013-12-31')) &
             (eurofxref.hist$Date >= as.Date('2005-01-01'))
> eurofxref.hist <- eurofxref.hist[selector, ]
> euro_usd <- ts(rev(eurofxref.hist$USD))
```

Let's plot these data to see what it looks like:

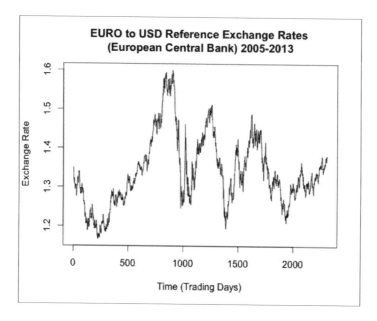

Here we will use the `fGarch` package, which provides us with the `garchFit()` function for training GARCH models. In finance, the *GARCH(1, 1)* process is quite commonly used, but as we know with a GARCH model, we are predicting the way the variance behaves over time. In order to model the behavior of the time series as a whole, we will also add an ARMA component.

We have repeated the steps to estimate the order of an ARIMA model, which we used with the previous two time series, and obtained that an *ARMA(4, 4)* model is appropriate for use with our economic time series. So we will investigate what a model with an *ARMA(4, 4)* and *GARCH(1, 1)* component predicts for our time series. With the `garchFit()` function, we need to specify the model parameters slightly differently via a formula:

```
> euro_usd_garch <- garchFit(~ arma(4,4) + garch(1, 1),
                     data  = euro_usd, trace = FALSE)
```

At the time of this writing, there is a documented issue with the fGarch package that prevents the `predict()` function from working when a model is trained with an ARMA component that is of a higher order than *ARMA(2, 2)*. For this reason, in the following plot, we will use this latter configuration.

With our model trained, we can now obtain a prediction:

```
> predict(euro_usd_garch, n.ahead = 20, plot = TRUE)
```

The following plot shows our forecast for this time series:

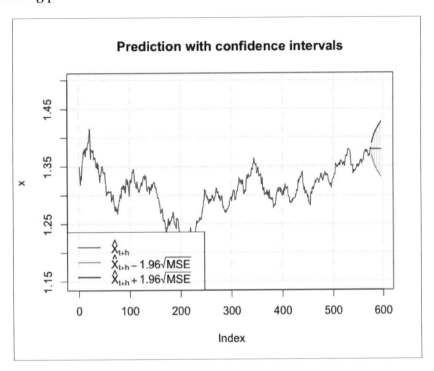

The prediction is that the series will decrease slightly in the next few time periods. Note how the GARCH component of our model causes our confidence interval to widen significantly over the next few time intervals.

Other time series models

In this chapter, we spent most of our time on studying models that describe a time series in terms of the patterns of correlations between different points in time. This approach led us to the ARIMA family of models, which we have seen are highly configurable and have successfully been employed in many real-world problems. There is a diverse array of methods that have been applied to the time series problem and in fact we have seen a few elsewhere in this book as well.

The neural networks that we studied in *Chapter 4, Neural Networks,* and the hidden Markov models that we saw in *Chapter 8, Probabilistic Graphical Models,* are two such examples. Sometimes, we can treat a time series as a regression problem, and so techniques from this area can be leveraged too.

One other important class of methods is **exponential smoothing**. There are two key premises behind methods that use this approach. The first of these is that a time series is usually decomposed into a number of different components. These include the **trend**, which describes a gradual shift in the mean of the time series, as well as the **seasonal** and **cyclical** components that contain patterns that repeat.

The second main idea is that if we remove trends and repeating patterns, we can predict the next time point as a weighted sum of the most recent time points where weights follow an exponential decay into the past. Thus, a forecast is computed as an exponentially weighted moving average. It has been shown that there are overlaps between the methods we have seen in this chapter and methods of exponential smoothing.

All the examples we have mentioned so far involve modeling how a time series behaves in time. Thus, the methods in question are known as **time-domain methods**. A radically different approach to modeling time series is to study their frequency properties using **frequency domain methods**, also known as **spectral methods**. The key intuition behind these methods is that we can decompose virtually any time series as a linear combination of sine and cosine waves of varying frequency, phase, and amplitude. This in turn stems from an initial intuition of decomposing a time series to find its periodic components, that is to say, the components that tend to repeat consistently over time.

Just as we used ACF and PACF plots to define the contribution of different time lags in the autocorrelation function of a time series, spectral methods make use of **spectral density plots** that show the contribution of different frequencies that make up a time series. The field of spectral analysis of time series has much in common with **digital signal processing**, drawing on important tools such as the **Fast Fourier Transform** and **wavelets**.

Aside from references given earlier in this chapter, an online textbook that discusses exponential smoothing as well as other techniques not mentioned here is *Forecasting: principles and practice, Rob J. Hyndman and George Athanasopoulos.* The URL is https://www.otexts. org/book/fpp. To learn more about digital signal processing, the definitive text introducing the field is *Digital Signal Processing, John G. Proakis and Dimitris K. Manolakis, Prentice Hall.*

Summary

The focus of this chapter was on understanding the fundamental tools that are useful in studying time series. Time series analysis is a very large field, but in this brief synopsis, we explored the basic concepts that are essential to further study. We started off by looking at some properties of time series such as the autocorrelation function and saw how this, along with the partial autocorrelation function, can provide important clues about the underlying process involved.

Next, we introduced stationarity, which is a very useful property of some time series that in a nutshell says that the statistical behavior of the underlying process does not change over time. We introduced white noise as a stochastic process that forms the basis of many other processes. In particular, it appears in the random walk process, the moving average (MA) process, as well as the autoregressive process (AR). These, in turn, we saw can be combined to yield even more complex time series.

In order to handle the non-stationary case, we introduced the ARIMA process, which tries to render a time series stationary through differencing. We also touched upon ARCH processes, which explicitly model how the variance of a non-stationary time series varies. ARCH models can be combined with ARMA models. Through a number of real-world data sets, we saw our models in action and explored a procedure to select suitable parameters for them. In particular, we noted that we often focus first on finding the order of a time series before learning the parameters of a time series model of that order. Finally, we wrapped up our discussion with a brief glimpse of some other important approaches to modeling time series.

In the next chapter, we'll look at topic models as a type of predictive model that has become very popular with the abundance of text available online. We will see that we can use topic models as a special case where our output is a mixture of different classes. At the same time, we will see how topic models can be used as a form of dimensionality reduction on a large feature set.

10
Topic Modeling

Topic modeling is a relatively recent and exciting area that originated from the fields of natural language processing and information retrieval but has seen applications in a number of other domains as well. Many problems in classification, such as sentiment analysis, involve assigning a single class to a particular observation. In topic modeling, the key idea is that we can assign a mixture of different classes to an observation. As the field is inspired from information retrieval, we often think of our observations as documents and our output classes as topics. In many applications, this is actually the case and so we will focus on the domain of text documents and their topics, this being a very natural way to learn about this important model. In particular, we'll focus on a technique known as Latent Dirichlet Allocation (LDA), which is the most prominently used method for topic modeling.

An overview of topic modeling

In *Chapter 8*, *Probabilistic Graphical Models*, we saw how we can use a bag of words as the features of a Naïve Bayes model in order to perform sentiment analysis. There, the specific predictive task involved determining whether a particular movie review was expressing a positive sentiment or a negative sentiment. We explicitly assumed that the movie review was exclusively expressing only one possible sentiment. Each of the words used as features (such as *bad, good, fun,* and so on) had a different likelihood of appearing in a review under each sentiment.

To compute the model's decision, we basically compute the likelihood of all the words in a particular review under one class, and compare this to the likelihood of all the words having been generated by the other class. We adjusted these likelihoods using the prior probability of each class so that when we know that one class is more popular in the training data, we expect to find it more frequently represented on unseen data in the future. There was no opportunity for a movie review to be partially positive so that some of the words came from the positive class and partially negative so that the rest of the words occurred due to the negative class.

The core premise behind **topic models** is that in our problem, we have a set of features and a set of hidden or latent variables that generate these features. Crucially, each observation in our data contains features that have been generated from a mixture of a subset of these hidden variables. For example, an essay, website, or news article might have a central topic or theme such as politics, but might also include one or more elements of other themes as well, such as human rights, history, or economics.

In the image domain, we might be interested in identifying a particular object in a scene from a set of visual features such as shadows and surfaces. These, in turn, might be the product of a mixture of different objects. Our task in topic modeling is to observe the words inside a document or the pixels and visual features of an image and from these determine the underlying mix of topics and objects respectively.

Topic modeling on text data can be used in a number of different ways. One possible application is to group together similar documents, either based on their most predominant topic or based on their topical mix. Thus, it can be viewed as a form of clustering. By studying the topic composition, most frequent words, as well as the relative sizes of the clusters we obtain, we are able to summarize information about a particular collection of documents.

We can use the most frequent words and topics of a cluster to describe a cluster directly and in turn this might be useful for automatically generating tags, for example to improve the search capabilities of an information retrieval service for our documents. Yet another example might be to automatically recommend Twitter hashtags once we build a topic model for a database of tweets.

When we describe documents such as websites using a bag of words approach, each document is essentially a vector indexed by the words in our dictionary. The elements of the vector are either counts of the various words or binary variables capturing whether a word was present in the document. Either way, this representation is a good method to encode text into a numerical format, but the result is a sparse vector in a high dimensional space as the word dictionary is typically large. Under a topic model, each document is represented by a mixture of topics. As this number tends to be much smaller than the dictionary size, topic modeling can also function as a form of dimensionality reduction.

Finally, topic modeling can also be viewed as a predictive task for classification. If we have a collection of documents labeled with a predominant theme label, we can perform topic modeling on this collection. If the predominant topic clustering we obtain from this method coincides with our labeled categories, we can use the model to predict a topical mixture for an unknown document and classify it according to the most predominant topic. We'll see an example of this later on in this chapter. We will now introduce the most well-known technique to perform topic modeling, Latent Dirichlet Allocation.

Latent Dirichlet Allocation

Latent Dirichlet Allocation (LDA) is the prototypical method to perform topic modeling. Rather unfortunately, the acronym LDA is also used for another method in machine learning, **Linear Discriminant Analysis**. This latter method is completely different to Latent Dirichlet Allocation and is commonly used as a way to perform dimensionality reduction and classification. Needless to say, we will use LDA to refer to Latent Dirichlet Allocation throughout this book.

Although LDA involves a substantial amount of mathematics, it is worth exploring some of its technical details in order to understand how the model works and the assumptions that it uses. First and foremost, we should learn about the **Dirichlet distribution**, which lends its name to LDA.

An excellent reference for a fuller treatment of Topic Models with LDA is the chapter *Topic Models* in the book *Text Mining: Classification, Clustering, and Applications*, edited by *A. Srivastava* and *M. Sahami* and published by *Chapman & Hall*, 2009. It can be found online at http://www.cs.princeton.edu/~blei/papers/BleiLafferty2009.pdf.

The Dirichlet distribution

Suppose we have a classification problem with K classes and the probability of each class is fixed. Given a vector of length K containing counts of the occurrence of each class, we can estimate the probabilities of each class by just dividing each entry in the vector by the sum of all the counts.

Now suppose we would like to predict the number of times each class will occur over a series of N trials. If we have two classes, we can model this with a binomial distribution, as we would normally do in a coin flip experiment. For K classes, the binomial distribution generalizes to the **multinomial distribution**, where the probability of each class, p_i, is fixed and the sum of all instances of p_i equals one. Now, suppose that we wanted to model the random selection of a particular multinomial distribution with K categories. The Dirichlet distribution achieves just that. Here is its form:

$$P\left(\overline{x} \mid \overline{\alpha}\right) = \frac{\Gamma\left(\sum_{k=1}^{K} \alpha_k\right)}{\prod_{k=1}^{K} \Gamma\left(\alpha_k\right)} \cdot \prod_{k=1}^{K} x_k^{\alpha_{k-1}}$$

This equation seems complex, but if we break it down to its constituent parts and label the symbols used, we will then be able to have a better understanding. To begin with, the $\bar{x}$ term is a vector with K components, x_k, representing a particular multinomial distribution. The vector $\bar{\alpha}$ is also a K component vector containing the K parameters, a_k, of the Dirichlet distribution. Thus, we are computing the probability of selecting a particular multinomial distribution given a particular parameter combination. Notice that we provide the Dirichlet distribution with a parameter vector whose length is the same as the number of classes of the multinomial distribution that it will return.

The fraction before the large product on the right-hand side of the equation is a normalizing constant, which depends only on the values of the Dirichlet parameters and is expressed in terms of the **gamma function**. For completeness, the gamma function, a generalization of the factorial function, is given by the following:

$$\Gamma(t) = \int_0^\infty x^{t-1} e^{-x} dx$$

Lastly, in the final product, we see that every parameter, a_k, is paired with the corresponding component of the multinomial distribution, x_k, in forming the terms of the product. The important point to remember about this distribution is that by modifying the a_k parameters, we are modifying the probabilities of the different multinomial distributions that we can draw.

We are especially interested in the total sum of the a_k parameters as well as the relative proportions among them. A large total for the a_k parameters tends to produce a smoother distribution involving a mix of many topics and this distribution is more likely to follow the pattern of alpha parameters in their relative proportions.

A special case of the Dirichlet distribution is the **Symmetrical Dirichlet distribution**, in which all the a_k parameters have an identical value. When the a_k parameters are identical and large in value, we are likely to sample a multinomial distribution that is close to being uniform. Thus, the symmetrical Dirichlet distribution is used when we have no information about a preference over a particular topic distribution and we consider all topics to be equally likely.

Similarly, suppose we had a skewed vector of a_k parameters with large absolute values. For example, we might have a vector in which one of the a_k parameters was much higher than the others, indicating a preference for selecting one of the topics. If we used this as an input to the Dirchlet distribution, we would likely sample a multinomial distribution in which the aforementioned topic was very probable.

By contrast, if the a_k parameters add up to a small number, this usually results in a peaky distribution. This is one in which only one or two of the topics are likely and the rest are unlikely. Consequently, if we want to model the process of drawing a multinomial with only a few topics selected, we would use low values for the a_k parameters, whereas if we want a good mix, we would use larger values. The following two plots will help visualize this behavior. The first plot is for a symmetric Dirichlet distribution:

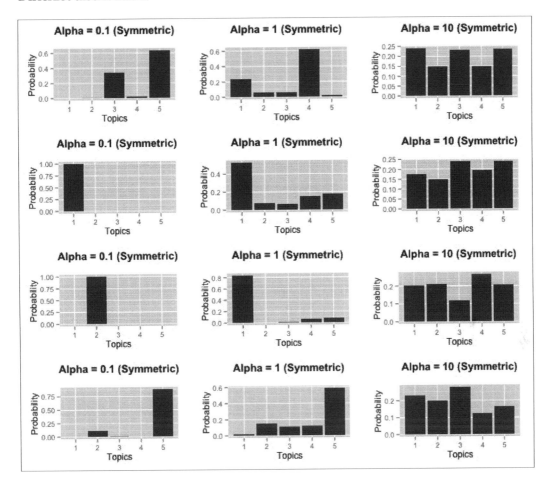

In this plot, each column contains four random samples of a multinomial distribution generated using a symmetric Dirichlet distribution for five topics. In the first column, all the a_k parameters are set to 0.1. Note that the distributions are very peaky and because all the a_k parameters are equally likely, there is no preference for which topic will tend to be chosen as the highest peak.

In the middle column, the a_k parameters are set to 1 and as the sum of the parameters is now larger, we are seeing a greater mix of topics, even if the distribution is still skewed. When we set the a_k parameters to the value of 10 in the third column, we see that the samples are now much closer to a uniform distribution.

In many scenarios, we use the Dirichlet distribution as a **prior distribution**; that is, a distribution that describes our prior beliefs about the multinomial distribution that we are trying to sample. When the sum of the a_k parameters is high, we tend to think of our prior as having very strong beliefs. In the next plot, we will skew the distribution of our a_k parameters to favor the first topic:

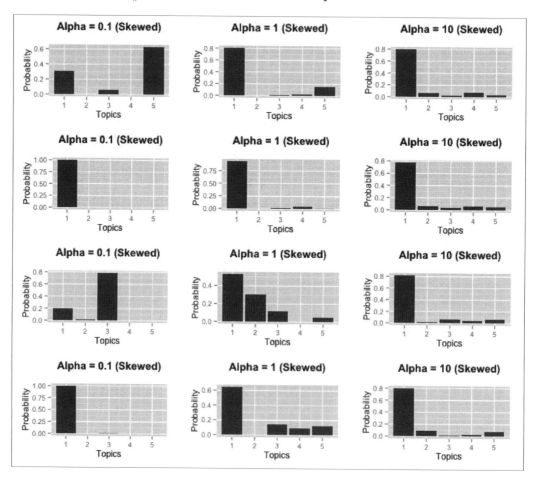

In the first column, the average value of the a_k parameters is 0.1, but we adjusted their distribution so that a_1, which corresponds to the first topic, now has a value four times as high as the others. We see that this has increased the probability of the first topic featuring prominently in the sampled multinomial distribution, but it is not guaranteed to be the distribution's mode.

In the middle column, where the average of the a_k parameters is now 1 but with the same skew, topic 1 is the mode of the distribution in all the samples. Additionally, there is still a high variance in how the other topics will be selected. In the third column, we have a smoother distribution that simultaneously mixes all five topics but enforces the preference for the first topic.

Now that we have an idea of how this distribution works, we will see in the next section how it is used in building topic models with LDA.

The generative process

We delved into the Dirichlet distribution with significant detail because it is at the heart of how topic modeling with LDA operates. Armed with this understanding, we'll now describe the **generative process** behind LDA.

The generative process is aptly named as it describes how the LDA model assumes that documents, topics, and words are generated in our data. This process is essentially an illustration of the model's assumptions. The optimization procedures that are used in order to fit an LDA model to data, essentially estimate the parameters of the generative process. We'll now see how this process works:

1. For each of our K topics, draw a multinomial distribution, φ_k, over the words in our vocabulary using a Dirichlet distribution parameterized by a vector a. This vector has length V, the size of our vocabulary. Even though we sample from the same Dirichlet distribution each time, we've seen that the sampled multinomial distributions will likely differ from each other.

2. For every document, d, that we want to generate:

    ○ Determine the mix of topics for this document by drawing a multinomial distribution, θ_k, from a Dirichlet distribution, this time parameterized by a vector β of length K, the number of topics. Each document will thus have a different mix of topics.

    ○ For every word, w, in the document that we want to generate:

        ○ Use the multinomial topic distribution for this document, θ_k, to draw a topic with which this word will be associated.

        ○ Use that particular topic's distribution, φ_k, to pick the actual word.

Note that we use two differently parameterized Dirichlet distributions in our generative process, one for drawing a multinomial distribution of topics and another for drawing a multinomial distribution of words. Although the model is simple, it does capture certain intuitions about documents and topics. In particular, it captures the notion that documents about different topics will, in general, contain different words in them and in different proportions. Additionally, a particular word can be associated with more than one topic, but for some topics it will appear with higher frequency than others. Documents may have a central topic, but they may also discuss other topics as well and therefore we can think of a document as dealing with a mixture of topics. A topic that is more important in a document will be so because a greater percentage of the words in the document deal with that topic.

Dirichlet distributions can be smooth or skewed, and the mixture of components can be controlled via the a_k parameters. Consequently, by tuning the Dirichlet distributions appropriately, this process can produce documents with a single theme as well as documents covering many topics.

At the same time, it is important to bear in mind the limitations of the model through some of the simplifying assumptions that it makes. The model completely ignores the word order inside a document, and the generative process is memoryless, in that when it generates the nth word of a document, it does not take into account the existing $n\text{-}1$ words that were previously drawn for that document.

Furthermore, LDA does not attempt to model any relationships between the topics that are drawn for a document so that we do not try to organize topics that are more likely to co-occur, such as weather and travel or biology and chemistry. This is a significant limitation of the LDA model, for which there are proposed solutions. For example, one variant of LDA is known as the **Correlated Topic Model (CTM)**, which follows the same generative process as LDA but uses a different distribution that allows one to also model the correlations between the topics. In our experimental section, we will also see an implementation of the CTM model.

The correlated topic model was presented in *A Correlated Topic Model of Science* by *D. M. Blei* and *J. D. Lafferty*, published by the *Annals of Applied Statistics* in 2007.

Fitting an LDA model

Fitting an LDA model to a corpus of documents essentially involves computationally estimating the multinomial topic and word distributions, φ_k and θ_d, that would most likely be able to generate the data assuming the LDA generative process. These variables are hidden or latent, which explains why the method is known as Latent Dirichlet Allocation.

A number of optimization procedures have been proposed to solve this problem, but the mathematical details are beyond the scope of this book. We will mention two of these that we will encounter in the next section. The first method is known as **Variational Expectation Maximization (VEM)** and is a variant of the well-known **Expectation Maximization (EM)** algorithm. The second is known as Gibbs sampling, which is a method based on **Markov Chain Monte Carlo (MCMC)**.

For a tutorial on the EM algorithm and VEM, we recommend *The Variational Approximation for Bayesian Inference* by *Dimitris G. Tzikas* and others in the November 2008 issue of the *IEEE Signal Processing Magazine*. For Gibbs sampling, there is a 1992 article in *The American Statistician* by *George Casella*, titled *Explaining the Gibbs Sampler*. Both are readable, but quite technical. A more thorough tutorial on Gibbs sampling is *Gibbs Sampling for the Uninitiated* by *Philip Resnik* and *Eric Hardisty*. This last reference is less mathematically demanding and can found online at
`http://www.cs.umd.edu/~hardisty/papers/gsfu.pdf`

Modeling the topics of online news stories

To see how topic models perform on real data, we will look at two data sets containing articles originating from BBC News during the period of 2004-2005. The first data set, which we will refer to as the *BBC data set*, contains 2,225 articles that have been grouped into five topics. These are *business, entertainment, politics, sports,* and *technology*.

The second data set, which we will call the *BBCSports data set*, contains 737 articles only on sports. These are also grouped into five categories according to the type of sport being described. The five sports in question are *athletics, cricket, football, rugby,* and *tennis*. Our objective will be to see if we can build topic models for each of these two data sets that will group together articles from the same major topic.

Both BBC data sets were presented in a paper by *D. Greene* and *P. Cunningham*, titled *Producing Accurate Interpretable Clusters from High-Dimensional Data* and published in the proceedings of the 9th European Conference on *Principles and Practice of Knowledge Discovery in Databases (PKDD'05)* in October 2005.

The two data sets can be found at `http://mlg.ucd.ie/datasets/bbc.html`. When downloaded, each data set is a folder containing a few different files. We will use the variables `bbc_folder` and `bbcsports_folder` to store the paths of these folders on our computer.

Each folder contains three important files. The file with the extension `.mtx` is essentially a file containing a term document matrix in sparse matrix form. Concretely, the rows of the matrix are terms that can be found in the articles and the columns are the articles themselves. An entry $M[i,j]$ in this matrix contains the number of times the term corresponding to row i was found in document corresponding to column j. A term document matrix is thus a transposed document term matrix, which we encountered in *Chapter 8, Probabilistic Graphical Models*. The specific format used to store the matrix in the file is a format known as the **Matrix Market format**, where each line corresponds to a nonempty cell in the matrix.

Typically, when working with texts such as news articles, we would need to perform some preprocessing steps, such as stop-word removal, just as we performed using the `tm` package in our example on sentiment analysis in *Chapter 8, Probabilistic Graphical Models*. Fortunately for us, the articles in these data sets have already been processed so that they have been stemmed; stop words have been removed, as have any terms that appear fewer than three times.

In order to interpret the term document matrix, the files with the extension `.terms` contain the actual terms, one per line, which are the row names of the term document matrix. Similarly, the document names that are the column names of the term document matrix are stored in the files with the extension `.docs`.

We first create variables for the paths to the three files that we need for each data set:

```
> bbc_folder <- "~/Downloads/bbc/"
> bbcsports_folder <- "~/Downloads/bbcsport/"

> bbc_source <- paste(bbc_folder, "bbc.mtx", sep = "")
> bbc_source_terms <- paste(bbc_folder, "bbc.terms", sep = "")
> bbc_source_docs <- paste(bbc_folder, "bbc.docs", sep = "")
```

```
> bbcsports_source <- paste(bbcsports_folder, "bbcsport.mtx",
                            sep = "")
> bbcsports_source_terms <- paste(bbcsports_folder,
                            "bbcsport.terms", sep = "")
> bbcsports_source_docs <- paste(bbcsports_folder,
                            "bbcsport.docs", sep = "")
```

In order to load data into R from a file in Market Matrix format, we can use the
readMM() function from the Matrix R package. This function loads the data and
stores it into a sparse matrix object. We can convert this into a term document matrix
that the tm package can interpret using the as.TermDocumentMatrix() function
in the tm package. Aside from the matrix object that is the first argument to that
function, we also need to specify the weighting parameter. This parameter describes
what the numbers in the original matrix correspond to. In our case, we have raw
term frequencies, so we specify the value weightTf:

```
> library("tm")
> library("Matrix")
> bbc_matrix <- readMM(bbc_source)
> bbc_tdm <- as.TermDocumentMatrix(bbc_matrix, weightTf)

> bbcsports_matrix <- readMM(bbcsports_source)
> bbcsports_tdm <- as.TermDocumentMatrix(bbcsports_matrix,
                            weightTf)
```

Next, we load the terms and document identifiers from the two remaining files and
use these to create appropriate row and column names respectively for the term
document matrices. We can use the standard scan() function to read files with a
single entry per line and load the entries into vectors. Once we have a term vector
and a document identifier vector, we will use these to update the row and column
names for the term document matrix. Finally, we'll transpose this matrix into a
document term matrix as this is the format we will need for subsequent steps:

```
> bbc_rows <- scan(bbc_source_terms, what = "character")
Read 9635 items
> bbc_cols <- scan(bbc_source_docs, what = "character")
Read 2225 items
> bbc_tdm$dimnames$Terms <- bbc_rows
> bbc_tdm$dimnames$Docs <- bbc_cols
> (bbc_dtm <- t(bbc_tdm))
<<DocumentTermMatrix (documents: 2225, terms: 9635)>>
Non-/sparse entries: 286774/21151101
Sparsity           : 99%
Maximal term length: 24
Weighting          : term frequency (tf)
```

```
> bbcsports_rows <- scan(bbcsports_source_terms, what =
                         "character")
Read 4613 items
> bbcsports_cols <- scan(bbcsports_source_docs, what =
                         "character")
Read 737 items
> bbcsports_tdm$dimnames$Terms <- bbcsports_rows
> bbcsports_tdm$dimnames$Docs <- bbcsports_cols
> (bbcsports_dtm <- t(bbcsports_tdm))
<<DocumentTermMatrix (documents: 737, terms: 4613)>>
Non-/sparse entries: 85576/3314205
Sparsity           : 97%
Maximal term length: 17
Weighting          : term frequency (tf)
```

We now have the document term matrices for our two data sets ready. We can see that there are roughly twice as many terms for the BBC data set as there are for the BBCSports data set and the latter also has about a third of the number of documents, so it is a much smaller data set. Before we build our topic models, we must also create the vectors containing the original topic classification of the articles. If we examine the document IDs, we can see that the format of each document identifier is <topic>.<counter>.

```
> bbc_cols[1:5]
[1] "business.001" "business.002" "business.003" "business.004"
[5] "business.005"

> bbcsports_cols[1:5]
[1] "athletics.001" "athletics.002" "athletics.003"
[4] "athletics.004" "athletics.005"
```

To create a vector with the correct topic assignments, we simply need to strip out the last four characters of each entry. If we then convert the result into a factor, we can see how many documents we have per topic:

```
> bbc_gold_topics <- sapply(bbc_cols,
                            function(x) substr(x, 1, nchar(x) - 4))
> bbc_gold_factor <- factor(bbc_gold_topics)
> summary(bbc_gold_factor)
     business entertainment       politics         sport
          510           386            417           511
         tech
          401
```

```
> bbcsports_gold_topics <- sapply(bbcsports_cols,
                         function(x) substr(x, 1, nchar(x) - 4))
> bbcsports_gold_factor <- factor(bbcsports_gold_topics)
> summary(bbcsports_gold_factor)
athletics   cricket  football    rugby    tennis
      101       124       265      147       100
```

This shows that the BBC data set is fairly even in the distribution of its topics. In the BBCSports data, however, we see that there are roughly twice as many articles on football than the other four sports.

For each of our two data sets, we will now build some topic models using the package topicmodels. This is a very useful package as it allows us to use data structures created with the tm package to perform topic modeling. For each data set, we will build the following four different topic models:

- LDA_VEM: This is an LDA model trained with the Variational Expectation Maximization (VEM) method. This method automatically estimates the *a* Dirichlet parameter vector.

- LDA_VEM_α: This is an LDA model trained with VEM but the difference here is that that the α Dirichlet parameter vector is not estimated.

- LDA_GIB: This is an LDA model trained with Gibbs sampling.

- CTM_VEM: This is an implementation of the **Correlated Topic Model (CTM)** model trained with VEM. Currently, the topicmodels package does not support training this method with Gibbs sampling.

To train an LDA model, the topicmodels package provides us with the LDA() function. We will use four key parameters for this function. The first of these specifies the document term matrix for which we want to build an LDA model. The second of these, k, specifies the target number of topics we want to have in our model. The third parameter, method, allows us to select which training algorithm to use. This is set to VEM by default, so we only need to specify this for our LDA_GIB model that uses Gibbs sampling.

Finally, there is a control parameter, which takes in a list of parameters that affect the fitting process. As there is an inherent random component involved in the training of topic models, we can specify a seed parameter in this list in order to make the results reproducible. Additionally, this is where we can specify whether we want to estimate the *a* Dirichlet parameter. This is also where we can include parameters for the Gibbs sampling procedure, such as the number of omitted Gibbs iterations at the start of the training procedure (burnin), the number of omitted in-between iterations (thin), and the total number of Gibbs iterations (iter). To train a CTM model, the topicmodels package provides us with the CTM() function, which has a similar syntax with the LDA() function.

Using this knowledge, we'll define a function that creates a list of four trained models given a particular document term matrix, the number of topics required, and the seed. For this function, we have used some standard values for the aforementioned training parameters with which the reader is encouraged to experiment, ideally after investigating the references provided for the two optimization methods:

```
compute_model_list <- function (k, topic_seed, myDtm) {
  LDA_VEM <- LDA(myDtm, k = k, control = list(seed = topic_seed))
  LDA_VEM_a <- LDA(myDtm, k = k, control = list(estimate.alpha =
                   FALSE, seed = topic_seed))
  LDA_GIB <- LDA(myDtm, k = k, method = "Gibbs", control =
                 list(seed = topic_seed, burnin = 1000, thin =
                 100, iter = 1000))
  CTM_VEM <- CTM(myDtm, k = k, control = list(seed = topic_seed,
                 var = list(tol = 10^-4), em = list(
                 tol = 10^-3)))
  return(list(LDA_VEM = LDA_VEM, LDA_VEM_a = LDA_VEM_a,
         LDA_GIB = LDA_GIB, CTM_VEM = CTM_VEM))
}
```

We'll now use this function to train a list of models for the two data sets:

```
> library("topicmodels")
> k <- 5
> topic_seed <- 5798252
> bbc_models <- compute_model_list(k, topic_seed, bbc_dtm)
> bbcsports_models <- compute_model_list(k, topic_seed,
                                         bbcsports_dtm)
```

To get a sense of how the topic models have performed, let's first see whether the five topics learned by each model correspond to the five topics to which the articles were originally assigned. Given one of these trained models, we can use the `topics()` function to get a vector of the most likely topic chosen for each document.

This function actually takes a second parameter *k*, by default set to 1, which returns the top *k* topics predicted by the model. We only want one topic per model in this particular instance. Having found the most likely topic, we can then tabulate the predicted topics against the vector of labeled topics. These are the results for the LDA_VEM model for the BBC data set:

```
> model_topics <- topics(bbc_models$LDA_VEM)
> table(model_topics, bbc_gold_factor)
```

```
              bbc_gold_factor
model_topics business entertainment politics sport tech
           1        11            174        2     0  176
           2         4            192        1     0  202
           3       483              3       10     0    7
           4         9             17      403     4   15
           5         3              0        1   507    1
```

Looking at this table, we can see that topic 5 corresponds almost exclusively to the *sports* category. Similarly, topics 4 and 3 seem to match to the *politics* and *business* categories respectively. Unfortunately, models 1 and 2 both contain a mixture of *entertainment* and *technology* articles and as a result this model hasn't really succeeded in distinguishing between the categories that we want.

It should be clear that in an ideal situation, each model topic should match to one gold topic (we often use the adjective *gold* to refer to the correct or labeled value of a particular variable. This is derived from the expression *gold standard* which refers to a widely accepted standard). We can repeat this process on the LDA_GIB model, where the story is different:

```
> model_topics <- topics(bbc_models$LDA_GIB)
> table(model_topics, bbc_gold_factor)
              bbc_gold_factor
model_topics business entertainment politics sport tech
           1       471              2       12     1    5
           2         0              0        3   506    3
           3         9              4        1     0  371
           4        27             16      399     3    9
           5         3            364        2     1   13
```

Intuitively, we feel that this topic model is a better match to our original topics than the first, as evidenced by the fact that each model topic selects articles from primarily one gold topic.

A rough way to estimate the quality of the match between a topic model and our target vector of topics is to say that the largest value in every row corresponds to the gold topic assigned to the model topic represented by that row. Then, the total accuracy is the ratio of these maximum row values over the total number of documents. In the preceding example, for the LDA_GIB model, this number would be (471+506+371+399+364)/2225 = 2111/2225= 94.9 percent. The following function computes this value given a model and a vector of gold topics:

```
compute_topic_model_accuracy <- function(model, gold_factor) {
  model_topics <- topics(model)
  model_table <- table(model_topics, gold_factor)
  model_matches <- apply(model_table, 1, max)
  model_accuracy <- sum(model_matches) / sum(model_table)
  return(model_accuracy)
}
```

Using this notion of accuracy, let's see which model performs better in our two data sets:

```
> sapply(bbc_models, function(x)
        compute_topic_model_accuracy(x, bbc_gold_factor))
  LDA_VEM LDA_VEM_a   LDA_GIB   CTM_VEM
0.7959551 0.7923596 0.9487640 0.6148315
> sapply(bbcsports_models, function(x)
        compute_topic_model_accuracy(x, bbcsports_gold_factor))
  LDA_VEM LDA_VEM_a   LDA_GIB   CTM_VEM
0.7924016 0.7788331 0.7856174 0.7503392
```

For the BBC data set, we see that the LDA_GIB model significantly outperforms the others and the CTM_VEM model is significantly worse than the LDA models. For the BBCSports data set, all the models perform roughly the same, but the LDA_VEM model is slightly better.

Another way to assess the quality of a model fit is computing the log likelihood of the data given the model, remembering that the larger this value, the better the fit. We can do this with the logLik() function in the topicmodels package, which suggests that the best model is the LDA model trained with Gibbs sampling in both cases:

```
> sapply(bbc_models, logLik)
  LDA_VEM LDA_VEM_a   LDA_GIB   CTM_VEM
 -3201542  -3274005  -3017399  -3245828
> sapply(bbcsports_models, logLik)
  LDA_VEM LDA_VEM_a   LDA_GIB   CTM_VEM
-864357.7 -886561.9 -813889.7 -868561.9
```

Model stability

It turns out that the random component of the optimization procedures involved in fitting these models often has a significant impact on the model that is trained. Put differently, we may find that if we use different random number seeds, the results may sometimes change appreciably.

Ideally, we would like our model to be **stable**, which is to say that we would like the effect of the initial conditions of the optimization procedure that are determined by a random number seed to be minimal. It is a good idea to investigate the effect of different seeds on our four models by training them on multiple seeds:

```
> seeded_bbc_models <- lapply(5798252 : 5798256,
            function(x) compute_model_list(k, x, bbc_dtm))
> seeded_bbcsports_models <- lapply(5798252 : 5798256,
            function(x) compute_model_list(k, x,
                bbcsports_dtm))
```

Here we used a sequence of five consecutive seeds and trained our models on both data sets five times. Having done this, we can investigate the accuracy of our models for the various seeds. If the accuracy of a method does not vary by a large degree across the seeds, we can infer that the method is quite stable and produces similar topic models (although, in this case, we are only considering the most prominent topic per document).

```
> seeded_bbc_models_acc <- sapply(seeded_bbc_models,
    function(x) sapply(x, function(y)
    compute_topic_model_accuracy(y, bbc_gold_factor)))
> seeded_bbc_models_acc
                [,1]      [,2]      [,3]      [,4]      [,5]
LDA_VEM   0.7959551 0.7959551 0.7065169 0.7065169 0.7757303
LDA_VEM_a 0.7923596 0.7923596 0.6916854 0.6916854 0.7505618
LDA_GIB   0.9487640 0.9474157 0.9519101 0.9501124 0.9460674
CTM_VEM   0.6148315 0.5883146 0.9366292 0.8026966 0.7074157


> seeded_bbcsports_models_acc <- sapply(seeded_bbcsports_models,
    function(x) sapply(x, function(y)
    compute_topic_model_accuracy(y, bbcsports_gold_factor)))
> seeded_bbcsports_models_acc
                [,1]      [,2]      [,3]      [,4]      [,5]
LDA_VEM   0.7924016 0.7924016 0.8616011 0.8616011 0.9050204
LDA_VEM_a 0.7788331 0.7788331 0.8426052 0.8426052 0.8914518
LDA_GIB   0.7856174 0.7978290 0.8073270 0.7978290 0.7761194
CTM_VEM   0.7503392 0.6309362 0.7435550 0.8995929 0.6526459
```

On both data sets, we can clearly see that Gibbs sampling results in a more stable model and in the case of the BBC data set, it is also the clear winner in terms of accuracy. Gibbs sampling generally tends to produce more accurate models but even though it was not readily apparent on these data sets, it can become significantly slower than VEM methods once the data set becomes large.

The two LDA models trained with variational methods exhibit scores that vary within a roughly 10 percent range on both data sets. On both data sets, we see that LDA_VEM is consistently better than LDA_VEM_a by a small amount. This method also produces, on average, better accuracy among all models in the BBCSports data set. The CTM model is the least stable of all the models, exhibiting a high degree of variance on both data sets. Interestingly, though, the highest performance of the CTM model across the five iterations performs marginally worse than the best accuracy possible using the other methods.

If we see that our model is not very stable across a few seeded iterations, we can specify the `nstart` parameter during training, which specifies the number of random restarts that are used during the optimization procedure. To see how this works in practice, we have created a modified `compute_model_list()` function that we named `compute_model_list_r()`, which takes in an extra parameter, `nstart`.

The other difference is that the `seed` parameter now needs a vector of seeds with as many entries as the number of random restarts. To deal with this, we will simply create a suitably sized range of seeds starting from the one provided. Here is our new function:

```
compute_model_list_r <- function (k, topic_seed, myDtm, nstart) {
    seed_range <- topic_seed : (topic_seed + nstart - 1)
    LDA_VEM <- LDA(myDtm, k = k, control = list(seed = seed_range,
                    nstart = nstart))
    LDA_VEM_a <- LDA(myDtm, k = k, control = list(estimate.alpha =
                    FALSE, seed = seed_range, nstart = nstart))
    LDA_GIB <- LDA(myDtm, k = k, method = "Gibbs", control =
                    list(seed = seed_range, burnin = 1000, thin =
                    100, iter = 1000, nstart = nstart))
    CTM_VEM <- CTM(myDtm, k = k, control = list(seed = seed_range,
                    var = list(tol = 10^-4), em = list(tol = 10^-3),
                    nstart = nstart))
    return(list(LDA_VEM = LDA_VEM, LDA_VEM_a = LDA_VEM_a,
                LDA_GIB = LDA_GIB, CTM_VEM = CTM_VEM))
}
```

We will use this function to create a new model list. Note that using random restarts means we are increasing the amount of time needed to train, so these next few commands will take some time to complete.

```
> nstart <- 5
> topic_seed <- 5798252
> nstarted_bbc_models_r <-
        compute_model_list_r(k, topic_seed, bbc_dtm, nstart)
> nstarted_bbcsports_models_r <-
        compute_model_list_r(k, topic_seed, bbcsports_dtm,
        nstart)
> sapply(nstarted_bbc_models_r, function(x)
  compute_topic_model_accuracy(x, bbc_gold_factor))
  LDA_VEM LDA_VEM_a    LDA_GIB    CTM_VEM
0.7959551 0.7923596 0.9487640 0.9366292
> sapply(nstarted_bbcsports_models_r, function(x)
  compute_topic_model_accuracy(x, bbcsports_gold_factor))
  LDA_VEM LDA_VEM_a    LDA_GIB    CTM_VEM
0.9050204 0.8426052 0.7991859 0.8995929
```

Note that even after using only five random restarts, the accuracy of the models has improved. More importantly, we now see that using random restarts has overcome the fluctuations that the CTM model experiences and as a result it is now performing almost as well as the best model in each data set.

Finding the number of topics

In this predictive task, the number of different topics was known beforehand. This turned out to be very important because it is provided as an input to the functions that trained our models. The number of topics might not be known when we are using topic modeling as a form of exploratory analysis where our goal is simply to cluster documents together based on the similarity of their topics.

This is a challenging question and bears some similarity to the general problem of selecting the number of clusters when we perform clustering. One proposed solution to this problem is to perform cross-validation over a range of different numbers of topics. This approach will not scale well at all when the data set is large, especially since training a single topic model is already quite computationally intensive when we factor issues such as random restarts.

A paper that discusses a number of different approaches for estimating the number of topics in topic models is *Reconceptualizing the classification of PNAS articles* by *Edoardo M. Airoldi* and others. This appears in the *Proceedings of the National Academy of Sciences*, volume 107, 2010.

Topic distributions

We saw in the description of the generative process that we use a Dirichlet distribution to sample a multinomial distribution of topics. In the LDA_VEM model, the a_k parameter vector is estimated. Note that in all cases, a symmetric distribution is used in this implementation so that we are only estimating the value of a, which is the value that all the a_k parameters take on. For the LDA models, we can investigate which value of this parameter is used with and without estimation:

```
> bbc_models[[1]]@alpha
[1] 0.04893411
> bbc_models[[2]]@alpha
[1] 10
> bbcsports_models[[1]]@alpha
[1] 0.04037119
> bbcsports_models[[2]]@alpha
[1] 10
```

As we can see, when we estimate the value of *a*, we obtain a much lower value of *a* than we use by default, indicating that for both data sets, the topic distribution is thought to be peaky. We can use the `posterior()` function in order to view the distribution of topics for each model. For example, for the `LDA_VEM` model on the BBC data set, we find the following distributions of topics for the first few articles:

```
> options(digits = 4)
> head(posterior(bbc_models[[1]])$topics)
                 1          2      3         4         5
business.001 0.2700360 0.0477374 0.6818 0.0002222 0.0002222
business.002 0.0002545 0.0002545 0.9990 0.0002545 0.0002545
business.003 0.0003257 0.0003257 0.9987 0.0003257 0.0003257
business.004 0.0002153 0.0002153 0.9991 0.0002153 0.0002153
business.005 0.0337131 0.0004104 0.9651 0.0004104 0.0004104
business.006 0.0423153 0.0004740 0.9563 0.0004740 0.0004740
```

The following plot is a histogram of the posterior probability of the most likely topic predicted by our four models. The `LDA_VEM` model assumes a very peaky distribution, whereas the other models have a wider spread. The `CTM_VEM` model also has a peak at very high probabilities, but unlike `LDA_VEM`, the probability mass is spread over a wide range of values. We can see that the minimum probability for the most likely topic is 0.2 because we have five topics:

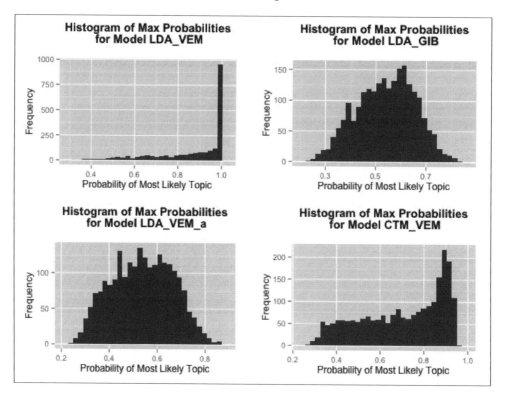

Another approach to estimating the smoothness of the topic distributions is to compute the *model entropy*. We will define this as the average entropy of all the topic distributions across the different documents. Smooth distributions will exhibit higher entropy than peaky distributions. To compute the entropy of our model, we will define two functions. The function `compute_entropy()` computes the entropy of a particular topic distribution of a document, and the `compute_model_mean_entropy()` function computes the average entropy across all the different documents in the model:

```
compute_entropy <- function(probs) {
    return(- sum(probs * log(probs)))
}


compute_model_mean_entropy <- function(model) {
    topics <- posterior(model)$topics
    return(mean(apply(topics, 1, compute_entropy)))
}
```

Using these functions, we can compute the average model entropies for the models trained on our two data sets:

```
> sapply(bbc_models, compute_model_mean_entropy)
    LDA_VEM LDA_VEM_a    LDA_GIB    CTM_VEM
  0.3119491 1.2664310 1.2720891 0.8373708
> sapply(bbcsports_models, compute_model_mean_entropy)
    LDA_VEM LDA_VEM_a    LDA_GIB    CTM_VEM
  0.3058856 1.3084006 1.3421798 0.7545975
```

These results are consistent with what the preceding plots show, which is that the `LDA_VEM` model, which is the peakiest, has a much lower entropy than the other models.

Word distributions

Just as with the previous section where we looked at the distribution of topics across different documents, we are often also interested in understanding the most important terms that are frequent in documents that are assigned to the same topic. We can see the *k* most frequent terms of the topics of a model using the function `terms()`. This takes in a model and a number specifying the number of most frequent terms that we want retrieved. Let's see the ten most important words per topic in the `LDA_GIB` model of the BBC data set:

```
> GIB_bbc_model <- bbc_models[[3]]
> terms(GIB_bbc_model, 10)
```

	Topic 1	Topic 2	Topic 3	Topic 4	Topic 5
[1,]	"year"	"plai"	"peopl"	"govern"	"film"
[2,]	"compani"	"game"	"game"	"labour"	"year"
[3,]	"market"	"win"	"servic"	"parti"	"best"
[4,]	"sale"	"against"	"technolog"	"elect"	"show"
[5,]	"firm"	"england"	"mobil"	"minist"	"includ"
[6,]	"expect"	"first"	"on"	"plan"	"on"
[7,]	"share"	"back"	"phone"	"sai"	"award"
[8,]	"month"	"player"	"get"	"told"	"music"
[9,]	"bank"	"world"	"work"	"peopl"	"top"
[10,]	"price"	"time"	"wai"	"public"	"star"

As we can see, given this list of word stems, one could easily guess which of the five topic labels we should assign to each topic. A very handy way to visualize frequent terms in a collection of documents is through a **word cloud**. The R package wordcloud is useful for creating these. The function wordcloud() allows us to specify a vector of terms followed by a vector of their frequencies, and this information is then used for plotting.

Unfortunately, we will have to do some manipulation on the document term matrices in order to get the word frequencies by topic so that we can feed them into this function. To that end, we've created our own function plot_wordcloud() as follows:

```
plot_wordcloud <- function(model, myDtm, index, numTerms) {

    model_terms <- terms(model,numTerms)
    model_topics <- topics(model)

    terms_i <- model_terms[,index]
    topic_i <- model_topics == index
    dtm_i <- myDtm[topic_i, terms_i]
    frequencies_i <- colSums(as.matrix(dtm_i))
    wordcloud(terms_i, frequencies_i, min.freq = 0)
}
```

Our function takes in a model, a document term matrix, an index of a topic, and the number of most frequent terms that we want to display in the word cloud. We begin by first computing the most frequent terms for the model by topic as we did earlier. We also compute the most probable topic assignments. Next, we subset the document term matrix so that we obtain only the cells involving the terms we are interested in and the documents corresponding to the topic with the index that we passed in as a parameter.

From this reduced document term matrix, we sum over the columns to compute the frequencies of the most frequent terms and finally we can plot the word cloud. We've used this function to plot the word clouds for the topics in the BBC data set using the LDA_GIB model and 25 words per topic. This is shown here:

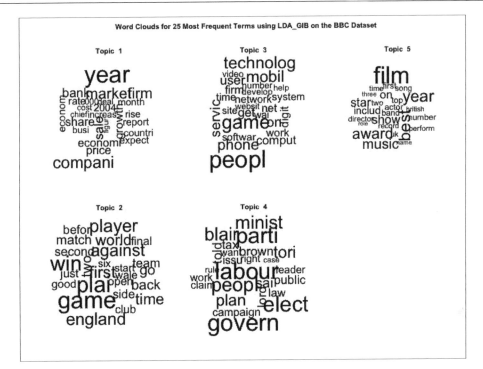

LDA extensions

Topic models are an active area of research and as a result, several extensions for the LDA model have been proposed. We will briefly mention two of these. The first is the **supervised LDA** model, an implementation of which can be found in the lda R package. This is a more direct way to model a response variable with the standard LDA method and would be a good next step to investigate for the application discussed in this chapter.

A second interesting extension is the **author-topic model**. This is designed to add an extra step in the generative process to account for authorship information and is a good model to use when building models that summarize or predict the writing habits and topics of authors.

The standard reference for supervised LDA is the paper *Supervised Topic Models* by *David M. Blei* and *Jon D. McAuliffe*. This was published in 2007 in the journal *Neural Information Processing Systems*. For the author-topic model, consult the paper titled *The Author-Topic Model for Authors and Documents* by *Michal Rosen-Zvi* and others. This appears in the proceedings of the 20th *conference on Uncertainty In Artificial Intelligence*.

Summary

This chapter was devoted to learning about topic models and after sentiment analysis on movie reviews, this was our second foray into working with real-life text data. This time, our predictive task was classifying the topics of news articles on the Web. The primary technique for topic modeling on which we focused was Latent Dirichlet Allocation (LDA). This derives its name from the fact that it assumes that the topic and word distributions that can be found inside a document arise from hidden multinomial distributions that are sampled from Dirichlet priors. We saw that the generative process of sampling words and topics from these multinomial distributions mirrors many of the natural intuitions that we have about this domain; however, it notably fails to account for correlations between the various topics that can co-occur inside a document.

In our experiments with LDA, we saw that there is more than one way to fit an LDA model, and in particular we saw that a method known as Gibbs sampling tends to be more accurate, even if it often is more computationally expensive. In terms of performance, we saw that when the topics in question are quite distinct from each other, such as the topics in the BBC data set, we could get very high accuracy in our topic prediction.

At the same time, however, when we classified documents with topics that are more similar to each other, such as the different sports documents in the BBCSports data set, we saw that this posed more of a challenge and our results were not quite as high. In our case, another factor that probably played a role is that both the number of documents and the available features were much fewer in number with the BBCSports data set. Currently, there is an increasing number of variations on LDA that are being researched and developed in order to deal with limitations in both performance and training speed.

Topic models can be viewed as a form of clustering, and this was our first glimpse in this area. In the next and final chapter on recommendation systems, we will delve more deeply into the field of clustering in order to understand the way in which websites such as Amazon are able to make product recommendations by predicting which products a shopper is most likely to be interested in based on their previous shopping history and the shopping habits of similar shoppers.

11

Recommendation Systems

In our final chapter, we'll tackle one of the most ubiquitous problems prevalent in the e-commerce world, namely that of making effective product recommendations to customers. Recommendation systems, also referred to as recommender systems, often rely on the notion of similarity between objects, in an approach known as collaborative filtering. Its basic premise is that customers can be considered similar to each other if they share most of the products that they have purchased; equally, items can be considered similar to each other if they share a large number of customers who purchased them.

There are a number of different ways to quantify this notion of similarity, and we will present some of the commonly used alternatives. Whether we want to recommend movies, books, hotels, or restaurants, building a recommender system often involves dealing with very large data sets. Consequently, we'll introduce a few ideas and options for working with Big Data using R to wrap up our exploration of building predictive models in R.

Rating matrix

A **recommendation system** usually involves having a set of users $U = \{u_1, u_2, ..., u_m\}$ that have varying preferences on a set of items $I = \{i_1, i_2, ..., i_n\}$. The number of users $|U| = m$ is different from the number of items $|I| = n$ in the general case. In addition, users can often express their preference by rating items on some scale. As an example, we can think of the users as being restaurant patrons in a city, and the items being the restaurants that they visit. Under this setup, the preferences of the users could be expressed as ratings on a five star scale. Of course, our generalization does not require that the items be physical items or that the users be actual people — this is simply an abstraction for the recommender system problem that is commonly used.

As an illustration, think of a dating website in which users rate other users; here, the *items* that are being rated are the profiles of the actual users themselves. Let's return to our example of a restaurant recommender system and build some example data. A natural data structure that is popularly used for recommendation systems is the **rating matrix**. This is an $m \times n$ matrix where the rows represent the users and the columns represent the items. Each entry, $e_{i,j}$, of the matrix represents the rating made by the user i for item j. What follows is a simple example:

```
> oliver   <- c(1,1,2,5,7,8,9,7)
> thibault <- c(5,9,4,1,1,7,5,9)
> maria    <- c(1,4,2,5,8,6,2,8)
> pedro    <- c(2,6,7,2,6,1,8,9)
> ines     <- c(1,3,2,4,8,9,7,7)
> gertrude <- c(1,6,5,7,3,2,5,5)
> ratingMatrix <- rbind(oliver, thibault, maria, pedro, ines,
                    gertrude)
> colnames(ratingMatrix) <- c("Berny's", "La Traviata", "El Pollo
    Loco", "Joey's Pizza", "The Old West", "Jake and Jill", "Full
    Moon", "Acropolis")
> ratingMatrix
```

	Berny's	La Traviata	El Pollo Loco	Joey's Pizza
oliver	1	1	2	5
thibault	5	9	4	1
maria	1	4	2	5
pedro	2	6	7	2
ines	1	3	2	4
gertrude	1	6	5	7

	The Old West	Jake and Jill	Full Moon	Acropolis
oliver	7	8	9	7
thibault	1	7	5	9
maria	8	6	2	8
pedro	6	1	8	9
ines	8	9	7	7
gertrude	3	2	5	5

Here, we have used a 10-point scale as a rating system, where 10 is the highest rating and 1 is the lowest. An alternative rating scale is a binary rating scale where 1 indicates a positive rating and 0 indicates a negative rating. This second approach would yield a binary rating matrix. How might we be able to use this rating matrix in order to inform a simple recommender system for other users?

Concretely, suppose that a new user, Silvan, has rated a few restaurants and we would like to make a recommendation for a suitable restaurant to which he has not been. Alternatively, we might want to propose a list of top three restaurants or even predict whether Silvan will like a specific restaurant he is currently considering.

One way to think about this problem is to find users that have similar views as Silvan on the restaurants that he has already rated. Then, we could use their ratings on restaurants that Silvan has not yet rated in order to predict Silvan's rating for those restaurants. This seems promising, but we should first think about how we might quantify this notion of similarity between two users based on their item ratings.

Measuring user similarity

Even with a very large database of users, chances are that for a real-world recommender system, it will be rare—if not massively unlikely—to find two people that would rate all the items in our item set with the exact same score. That being said, we can still say that some users are more similar than others based on how they rate different items. For example, in our restaurant rating matrix, we can see that Ines and Oliver rated the first four restaurants poorly and the last four restaurants highly and so their tastes can be considered far more similar compared to a pair like Thibault and Pedro, who sometimes agree and sometimes have completely opposite views on a particular restaurant.

By representing a user as their particular row in the rating matrix, we can think of a user as being a vector in an n dimensional space, n being the number of items. Thus we can use different distance measures appropriate for vectors in order to measure the similarity of two different users. Note that the notion of distance is inversely proportional to the notion of similarity and we can thus use measures of distance as measures of similarity by interpreting a large distance between two vectors as analogous to a low similarity score.

The most familiar distance metric for two vectors a and b is the **Euclidean distance**:

$$d_{euclidean}(a,b) = \sqrt{\sum_{i=1}^{i=n}(a_i - b_i)^2}$$

We can use R's built-in `dist()` function to compute all the pair-wise distances in our rating matrix as follows:

```
> dist(ratingMatrix, method = 'euclidean')
```

```
               oliver     thibault      maria       pedro        ines
thibault 12.529964
maria     8.000000 11.000000
pedro    10.723805  9.899495 10.246951
ines      3.316625 11.224972  6.082763 10.583005
gertrude 10.488088 10.344080  8.717798  8.062258 10.440307
```

The result is a lower triangular matrix because the Euclidean distance is a symmetric function. Thus, the entry for (`maria`, `pedro`) is exactly the same as for (`pedro`, `maria`) and so we only need to display one of these. Here, we can explicitly see that Ines and Oliver are the two most similar users as the distance between them is smallest. Note that we can also talk about the distances between items in terms of the similarity of the ratings they received from different users. All we have to do to compute this is to transpose the rating matrix:

```
> dist(t(ratingMatrix), method = 'euclidean')
                 Berny's La Traviata El Pollo Loco Joey's Pizza
La Traviata      8.366600
El Pollo Loco    6.708204    5.744563
Joey's Pizza     9.643651    9.949874      7.745967
The Old West    13.038405   12.247449     10.535654     7.810250
Jake and Jill   12.000000   11.575837     12.449900     9.848858
Full Moon       12.369317   10.246951      8.717798     9.486833
Acropolis       14.212670    8.831761     10.723805    11.789826
                 The Old West Jake and Jill Full Moon
La Traviata
El Pollo Loco
Joey's Pizza
The Old West
Jake and Jill    8.246211
Full Moon        8.062258      9.110434
Acropolis        8.831761      9.273618   7.549834
```

As we can see, the two most dissimilar restaurants (that is to say, those with the largest difference between them) are the *Acropolis* and *Berny's*. Looking back at the rating matrix, we should easily convince ourselves why this is the case. The former restaurant has received largely positive reviews across our user base whereas the reviews have been poor for the latter.

A commonly used alternative to the Euclidean distance (or L_2 norm, as it is also known) is the **cosine distance**. This metric measures the cosine of the smallest angle between two vectors. If the vectors are parallel to each other, meaning that their angle is 0, then the cosine distance is 0 as well. If the two vectors are at a right angle to each other, then they have the largest distance according to this metric. The cosine distance is given by:

$$d_{cosine}(a,b) = \cos(\theta) = \frac{a \cdot b}{\|a\|\|b\|}$$

Here, the numerator is the dot product between the two vectors and the denominator is the product of the magnitudes (typically computed via the L$_2$ norm) of the two vectors. The cosine distance isn't available as a method in the `dist()` function of R's base distribution, but we can install the `proxy` package, which enhances this function with a number of new distance metrics in order to compute the cosine distances for our rating matrix:

```
> library("proxy")
> dist(ratingMatrix, method = 'cosine')
            oliver      thibault      maria        pedro         ines
thibault  0.28387670
maria     0.12450495 0.23879093
pedro     0.20947046 0.17687385 0.20854178
ines      0.02010805 0.22821528 0.06911870 0.20437426
gertrude  0.22600742 0.21481973 0.19156876 0.12227138 0.22459114
```

Suppose instead that our users rated restaurants on a binary scale. We can convert our rating matrix into a binary rating matrix by considering all ratings above 5 to be positive and assigning them a new score of 1. The remaining ratings are all converted to a score of 0. For two binary vectors, the **Jaccard similarity** is given by the cardinality of the logical intersection divided by the cardinality of the logical union. The Jaccard distance is then computed as
1 minus this:

$$d_{jaccard}(a,b) = 1 - \frac{|a \cap b|}{|a \cup b|}$$

In a nutshell, what this is computing is one minus the ratio of the number of positions in which the two vectors both have a positive rating over the total number of positions in which either of the two vectors have a positive rating. Two binary vectors that agree in all their positive positions will be identical and thus have a distance of 0. Using the `proxy` package, we can show the Jaccard distance for our restaurant patrons as follows:

```
> binaryRatingMatrix <- ratingMatrix > 5
> dist(binaryRatingMatrix, method = 'jaccard')
            oliver      thibault      maria        pedro         ines
thibault  0.6000000
maria     0.2500000 0.5000000
pedro     0.5000000 0.6666667 0.6666667
ines      0.0000000 0.6000000 0.2500000 0.5000000
gertrude  1.0000000 0.7500000 1.0000000 0.8333333 1.0000000
```

The study of measurement and distance metrics is broad and there are many suitable metrics that have been applied to the recommender system setting. The definitive reference for distance metrics is the *Encyclopedia of Distances, Michel Marie Deza and Elena Deza, Springer*.

Collaborative filtering

Having covered distances, we are ready to delve into the topic of **collaborative filtering**, which will help us define a strategy for making recommendations. Collaborative filtering describes an algorithm, or more precisely a family of algorithms, that aims to create recommendations for a test user given only information about the ratings of other users via the rating matrix, as well as any ratings that the test user has already made.

There are two very common variants of collaborative filtering, **memory-based collaborative filtering** and **model-based collaborative filtering**. With memory-based collaborative filtering, the entire history of all the ratings made by all the users is remembered and must be processed in order to make a recommendation. The prototypical memory-based collaborative filtering method is **user-based collaborative filtering**. Although this approach uses all the ratings available, the downside is that it can be computationally expensive as the entire database is used in order to make rating predictions for our test user.

The alternative approach to this is embodied in model-based collaborative filtering. Here, we first create a model of the rating preferences of our users, such as a set of clusters of users who like similar items, and then use the model to generate recommendations. We will study **item-based collaborative filtering**, which is the most well-known model-based collaborative filtering method.

User-based collaborative filtering

User-based collaborative filtering is commonly described as a memory-based or lazy learning approach. Unlike most of the models we have built in this book, which assume that we will fit the data to a particular model and then use this model to make predictions, lazy learning simply uses the training data itself to make predictions directly. We saw an example of lazy learning with k-nearest neighbors in *Chapter 1, Gearing Up for Predictive Modeling*. In fact, the premise of the user-based collaborative filtering approach builds directly on the k-nearest neighbors approach.

Concretely, in user-based collaborative filtering, when we want to make recommendations for a new user, we will first pick a set of similar users using a particular distance metric. Then, we try to infer the ratings that our target user would assign to items that he or she has not yet rated as an average of the ratings made by these similar users on those items. We usually refer to this set of similar users as the user's **neighborhood**. Thus, the idea is that a user will prefer items that their neighborhood prefers.

Typically, there are two ways to define the user's neighborhood. We can compute a fixed neighborhood by finding the k-nearest neighbors. These are the k users in our database that have the smallest distance between them and our target user.

Alternatively, we can specify a similarity threshold and pick all the users in our database whose distance from our target user does not exceed this threshold. This second approach has the advantage that we will be making recommendations using users that are as close to our target user as we want, and therefore our confidence in our recommendation can be high. On the other hand, there might be very few users that satisfy our requirement, meaning that we will be relying on the recommendations of these few users. Worse, there might be no users in our database who are sufficiently similar to our target user and we might not be able to actually make a recommendation at all. If we don't mind our method sometimes failing to make a recommendation, for example because we have a backup plan to handle these cases, the second approach might be a good choice.

Another important consideration to make in a real-world setting is the problem of sparse ratings. In our simple restaurant example, every user had rated every restaurant. This rarely happens in a real situation, if ever, simply because the number of items is usually too big for a user to rate them all. If we think of e-commerce websites such as amazon.com, for example, it is easy to imagine that the most products that any user has rated is still only a small fraction of the overall number of products on sale.

To compute distance metrics between users in order to determine similarity, we usually incorporate only the items that both users have rated. Consequently, in practice, we often make comparisons between users in a smaller number of dimensions.

Once we have decided on a distance metric and how to form a neighborhood of users that are similar to our test user, we then use this neighborhood to compute the missing ratings for the test user. The easiest way to do this is to simply compute the average rating for each item in the user neighborhood and report this value. Thus for test user t and an item j for which the test user has not yet made a rating, we can predict the test user's rating for that item, $\hat{r}_{tj}$, as follows:

$$\hat{r}_{tj} = \frac{1}{|N(t)|} \sum_{u \in N(t)} r_{uj}$$

This equation expresses the simple idea that the predicted rating of our test user t for item j is just the average of the ratings made by the test user's neighborhood on this item. Suppose we had a new user for our restaurant scenario and this user had already rated a few of the restaurants. Then imagine that from these ratings, we discovered that our new user's neighborhood was comprised of Oliver and Thibault. If we wanted to make a prediction for what rating the test user would make on the restaurant *El Pollo Loco*, this would be done by averaging the ratings of Oliver and Thibault for this restaurant, which in this case would be the average of 2 and 4, yielding a rating of 3.

If our objective was to obtain a top-N list of recommendations for our user, we would repeat this process for all the items in the database, sort them by descending rating so that the highest rated items appeared first, and then pick out the top N items from this list. In practice, we would only need to check the items that at least one of the users in the new user's neighborhood has rated in order to simplify this computation.

We can make some improvements to this very simple approach. A first possible improvement comes from the observation that some users will tend to consistently rate items more strictly or more leniently than other users, and we would like to smooth out this variation. In practice, we often use Z-score normalization, which takes into account the variance of the ratings. We can also center each rating made by a user by subtracting that user's average rating across all the items. In the rating matrix, this means subtracting the mean of each row from the elements of the row. Let's apply this last transformation to our restaurant rating matrix and see the results:

```
> centered_rm <- t(apply(ratingMatrix, 1, function(x) x - mean(x)))
> centered_rm
          Berny's La Traviata El Pollo Loco Joey's Pizza
oliver     -4.00       -4.00          -3.00          0.0
thibault   -0.12        3.88          -1.12         -4.1
maria      -3.50       -0.50          -2.50          0.5
pedro      -3.12        0.88           1.88         -3.1
ines       -4.12       -2.12          -3.12         -1.1
gertrude   -3.25        1.75           0.75          2.8
```

	The Old West	Jake and Jill	Full Moon	Acropolis
oliver	2.00	3.0	4.00	2.00
thibault	-4.12	1.9	-0.12	3.88
maria	3.50	1.5	-2.50	3.50
pedro	0.88	-4.1	2.88	3.88
ines	2.88	3.9	1.88	1.88
gertrude	-1.25	-2.2	0.75	0.75

Even though both Ines and Gertrude originally rated Berny's with the same rating of 1, the centering operation has Ines rating this restaurant with a lower score than Gertrude. This is because Ines tends to make higher ratings on average than Gertrude and so the rating of 1 for Ines could be interpreted as a stronger negative rating than Gertrude's.

Another area of improvement concerns the way in which we incorporate the ratings of our new user's neighborhood to create the final ratings. By treating the ratings of all the neighboring users as equal, we are ignoring the fact that our distance metric may show that certain users in the neighborhood of the new user are more similar to the new user than others.

As we have already seen from the example of Jaccard similarity and Jaccard distance, we can often define a similarity metric from a distance metric by inverting it in some way, such as subtracting from one or taking the reciprocal. Consequently, for the distance metric of our choice, we can define its corresponding similarity metric and denote it with $sim(u,t)$. A user similarity metric takes high values for similar users, which are users for whom a distance metric takes low values.

With this clarification established, we can incorporate the similarity between users u and t in our previous equation by taking a weighted average of the ratings made by the neighboring users of the new user as follows:

$$\hat{r}_{tj} = \frac{1}{\sum_{u \in N(t)} sim(u,t)} \sum_{u \in N(t)} sim(u,t) \cdot r_{uj}$$

Other reasons why we might want to incorporate weights in the ratings made by other users include trust. For example, we might trust a user that has been using our restaurant recommendation service for a long time more than a more recent user. Equally, we might also want to consider the total number of items that a user has rated in common with the new user. For example, if a user has only rated two items in common with the new user, then even if the corresponding ratings made are identical, the evidence that these two users are indeed very similar is little.

All in all, the single largest difficulty with user-based collaborative filtering is that making recommendations for a test user requires access to the whole database of users in order to determine the user neighborhood. This is done by performing a similarity computation between the test user and every other user, an expensive process computationally. Next, we'll look at item-based collaborative filtering, which attempts to ameliorate this situation.

Item-based collaborative filtering

Item-based collaborative filtering is a model-based approach to collaborative filtering. The central idea underlying this method is that instead of looking at other users similar to the test user, we will directly recommend items that are similar to the items that have received a high rating by the test user. As we are directly comparing items instead of first comparing users in order to recommend items, we can build up a model to describe the similarity of items and then use the model rather than the entire database to make recommendations.

The process of building an item-based similarity model involves computing a similarity matrix for all pairs of items in our database. If we have N items, then we will end up with a similarity matrix with N^2 elements in total. To reduce the size of our model, we can store a list of the similarity values of the top k most similar items for every item in the database.

As k will be far smaller than N, we will have a very substantial reduction in the size of the data that we need to keep for our model. For every item in our database, this list of the k most similar items is analogous to the neighborhood of users for the user-based collaborative filtering approach. The same discussion regarding normalizing with respect to the bias and variance of user ratings in user-based collaborative filtering can be applied here. That is, we can compute item-to-item similarities after we normalize our rating matrix.

This approach is not without its shortcomings. In the memory-based recommender, a new user rating can automatically be incorporated into the recommendation process because that approach uses the entire database (rating matrix). Model-based collaborative filtering requires us to periodically retrain the model to incorporate information from these new ratings. In addition, the fact that the modeling process discards some information from the original rating matrix by retaining only a short list of the most similar items for each item in our database, means that it can sometimes make non-optimal recommendations.

Despite these drawbacks, the space and time performance of item-based collaborative filtering means that it has been very successfully applied in a large number of real-world settings. Model retraining can be done offline and automatically scheduled, and the non-optimality of recommendations can often be tolerated.

We can devise an analogous equation to what we saw for user-based collaborative filtering that explains how to predict a new rating using the item-based collaborative filtering model. Suppose we want to estimate the rating that our test user, t, would give to an item i, $\hat{r}_{ti}$. Suppose also that we already chose a similarity function, $sim(i,j)$, between a pair of items i and j, and from this we constructed our model. Using the model, we can retrieve the stored item neighborhood for the item in which we are interested, $S(i)$. To compute the predicted rating that our test user will make on this item, we calculate the weighted sum of the ratings our user has made on items that are similar to it:

$$\hat{r}_{ti} = \frac{1}{\sum_{j \in S(i)} sim(i,j)} \sum_{j \in S(i)} sim(i,j) \cdot r_{tj}$$

While this approach won't work if the user hasn't rated any items similar to the item in question, it does not require finding users that have similar preferences to the test user.

Singular value decomposition

In a real-world recommender system, the rating matrix will eventually become very large as more users are added to the system and the list of items being offered grows. As a result, we may want to apply a dimensionality reduction technique to this matrix. Ideally, we would like to retain as much information as possible from the original matrix while doing this. One such method that has applications across a wide range of disciplines uses **singular value decomposition**, or **SVD** as it is commonly abbreviated to.

SVD is a matrix factorization technique that has a number of useful applications, one of which is dimensionality reduction. It is related to the PCA method of dimensionality reduction that we saw in *Chapter 1, Gearing Up for Predictive Modeling*, and many people confuse the two. SVD actually describes just a mathematical method of factorizing matrices. In fact, some implementations of PCA use SVD to compute the principal components.

Let's begin by looking at how this process works. SVD is a matrix factorization process, so we start with an original matrix representing our data and express this as a product of matrices. In a dimensionality reduction scenario, our input data matrix would be the matrix where the rows are data points and the columns are the features; thus, in R, this would just be a data frame. In our recommender systems scenario, the matrix we use is our rating matrix. Suppose that we call our rating matrix D and we have m users (rows) rating n items (columns). The SVD factorization of this matrix is given by:

$$D_{m \times n} = U_{m \times n} \cdot \Sigma_{m \times n} \cdot V_{n \times n}^{T}$$

In the previous equation, U and V are square matrices and the matrix Σ is a matrix with the same dimensionality as our input matrix D. In addition, it is a diagonal matrix, meaning that all the elements of the matrix are zero except those on the leading diagonal. These elements are conventionally ordered from largest to smallest and are known as the **singular values** of the matrix D, giving rise to the name singular value decomposition.

Readers familiar with linear algebra will know that the eigenvalues of a matrix are often also described as containing information about the important dimensions of that matrix. It turns out that the eigenvalues of a matrix are related to the singular values through the following relationship—the singular values of a matrix D are the same as the square roots of the eigenvalues of the matrix product $D \times D^{T}$.

We can easily perform SVD on a matrix in R via the svd() function, which is available with R's base package. Let's see this with our existing ratingMatrix from before:

```
> options(digits = 2)
> (rm_svd <- svd(ratingMatrix))
$d
[1] 35.6 10.6  7.5  5.7  4.7  1.3

$u
        [,1]   [,2]    [,3]    [,4]    [,5]    [,6]
[1,] -0.44  0.48 -0.043 -0.401  0.315  0.564
[2,] -0.41 -0.56  0.703 -0.061  0.114  0.099
[3,] -0.38  0.24  0.062  0.689 -0.494  0.273
[4,] -0.43 -0.40 -0.521 -0.387 -0.483 -0.033
[5,] -0.44  0.42  0.170 -0.108 -0.003 -0.764
[6,] -0.33 -0.26 -0.447  0.447  0.641 -0.114
```

```
$v
          [,1]    [,2]   [,3]     [,4]    [,5]     [,6]
[1,]  -0.13  -0.255   0.30  -0.0790   0.013   0.301
[2,]  -0.33  -0.591   0.16   0.3234   0.065  -0.486
[3,]  -0.25  -0.382  -0.36  -0.0625  -0.017  -0.200
[4,]  -0.27   0.199  -0.36   0.5796   0.578   0.284
[5,]  -0.38   0.460  -0.30   0.1412  -0.556  -0.325
[6,]  -0.39   0.401   0.68   0.0073   0.239  -0.226
[7,]  -0.42   0.044  -0.26  -0.7270   0.369  -0.047
[8,]  -0.52  -0.161   0.11   0.0279  -0.398   0.628
```

The singular values are returned as a vector d, from which we can easily construct the diagonal matrix using the diag() function. To verify that this factorization really is the correct one that we expected, we can reconstruct our original rating matrix by simply multiplying the matrix factors that we have obtained:

```
> reconstructed_rm <- rm_svd$u %*% diag(rm_svd$d) %*% t(rm_svd$v)
> reconstructed_rm
       [,1] [,2] [,3] [,4] [,5] [,6] [,7] [,8]
[1,]    1    1    2    5    7    8    9    7
[2,]    5    9    4    1    1    7    5    9
[3,]    1    4    2    5    8    6    2    8
[4,]    2    6    7    2    6    1    8    9
[5,]    1    3    2    4    8    9    7    7
[6,]    1    6    5    7    3    2    5    5
```

One thing to note here is that if we were to attempt a direct equality check with our original matrix, we will most likely fail. This is due to rounding errors that are introduced when we store the factorized matrices. We can check that our two matrices are very nearly equal using the all.equal() function:

```
> all.equal(ratingMatrix, reconstructed_rm, tolerance = 0.000001,
          check.attributes = F)
[1] TRUE
```

The reader is encouraged to decrease the size of the tolerance and note that after several decimal points, the equality check fails. Though the two matrices are not exactly equal, the difference is so small that this will not impact us in any significant way. Now, once we have this factorization, let's investigate our singular values. The first singular value of 35.6 is many times larger than the smallest singular value of 1.3.

We can perform dimensionality reduction by keeping the top singular values and throwing the rest away. To do this, we'd like to know how many singular values we should keep and how many we should discard. One approach to this problem is to compute the square of the singular values, which can be thought of as the vector of **matrix energy**, and then pick the top singular values that preserve at least 90 percent of the overall energy of the original matrix. This is easy to do with R as we can use the cumsum() function for creating a cumulative sum and the singular values are already ordered from largest to smallest:

```
> energy <- rm_svd$d ^ 2
> cumsum(energy) / sum(energy)
[1]  0.85 0.92 0.96 0.98 1.00 1.00
```

Keeping the first two singular values will retain 92 percent of the energy of our original matrix. Using just two values, we can reconstruct our rating matrix and observe the differences:

```
> d92 <- c(rm_svd$d[1:2], rep(0, length(rm_svd$d) - 2))
> reconstructed92_rm <- rm_svd$u %*% diag(d92) %*% t(rm_svd$v)
> reconstructed92_rm
       [,1] [,2] [,3] [,4] [,5] [,6] [,7] [,8]
[1,]  0.68  2.0  1.9  5.1  8.3  8.0  6.7  7.2
[2,]  3.37  8.3  5.9  2.7  2.9  3.3  5.9  8.6
[3,]  1.10  3.0  2.4  4.1  6.4  6.3  5.9  6.7
[4,]  3.02  7.5  5.4  3.2  3.9  4.2  6.2  8.6
[5,]  0.87  2.5  2.2  5.1  8.1  7.9  6.8  7.5
[6,]  2.20  5.5  4.0  2.6  3.3  3.5  4.9  6.6
```

As we can see there are a few differences in the absolute values, but most of the patterns of different users have been retained to a large extent. Discarding singular values effectively introduces zeros in the leading diagonal of matrix D in the factorization so that this matrix ends up with entire rows and columns that only contain zeros. Consequently, we can truncate not only this matrix, but rows from the matrices U and V. Thus we reduce the size of the data that we have to store.

R and Big Data

Before we dive deep into building a few recommender systems using real-world data sets, we'll take a short detour and spend some time thinking about **Big Data**. Many real-world recommender systems arise out of the analysis of massive data sets. Examples include the product recommendation engine of amazon.com and the movie recommendation engine of Netflix.

Most, if not all, of the data sets that we have looked at in this book have been relatively small in size and have been chosen quite intentionally in order for the reader to be able to follow along with the examples and not have to worry about having access to powerful computing resources. These days, the field of predictive analytics, as well as the related fields of machine learning, data science, and data analysis in general, is heavily concerned with the importance of handling Big Data.

> The term Big Data has become a buzzword that has entered everyday conversation and as an inevitable result, we often encounter uses that reveal conflicting or muddled interpretations. For example, Big Data is not only concerned with the volume of a data set, but also covers issues such as how fast we need to process data in real time as well as the diversity of the data that we need to process. Consequently, volume, velocity, and variety are often referred to as the three *Vs* of Big Data. To learn more about this exciting field, an excellent reference is *The Big Data Revolution* by *Jason Kolb* and *Jeremy Kolb*.

The base R distribution is designed to operate with data that fits into computer memory. Often, the data we want to analyze is so large that processing it all in the memory of a single computer isn't possible. In some cases, we can take advantage of on-demand computing resources, such as Amazon's EC2, and have access to machines with over 100 GB of memory. To do this efficiently, however, we often need to be aware that processing very large data sets, even in memory, can still be very time consuming in R and we may continue to need a way to improve performance. Consequently, the approaches for handling Big Data in R can be roughly grouped into three broad areas.

The first approach to handling Big Data is to carry out sampling. That is, we will not use all of the data available to us to build our model, but will create a representative sample of these data. Sampling is generally the least recommended approach as it is natural to expect degradation in model performance when we use fewer training data. This approach can potentially work quite well if the size of the sample we are able to use is still very large in absolute size (for example, a billion rows) as well as in relative size with respect to the original data set. Great care must be taken in order to avoid introducing any form of bias in the sample.

A second approach to working with Big Data is to take advantage of distributed processing. The key idea here is to split our data across different machines working together in a cluster. Individually, the machines need not be very powerful because they will only process chunks of the data.

The *Programming with Big Data in R* project has a number of R packages for high-performance computing that interface with parallel processing libraries. More details on this project can be found through the project's website, http://r-pbd.org/, and by first starting out with the pbdDEMO package, which is designed for newcomers to this project.

Another alternative is to interface R to work directly with a distributed processing platform such as Apache Hadoop. An excellent reference for doing this is *Big Data Analytics with R and Hadoop* published by Packt Publishing. Finally, an exciting new alternative to working with Hadoop is the Apache Spark project. SparkR is a package that allows running jobs on a Spark cluster directly from the R shell. This package is currently available at http://amplab-extras.github.io/SparkR-pkg/.

The third possible avenue for working with Big Data is to work with (potentially on-demand) resources that have very high memory and optimize performance on a single machine. One possibility for this is to interface with a language such as C++ and leverage access to advanced data structures that can optimize the processing of data for a particular problem. This way, some of the processing can be done outside of R.

In R, the package Rcpp provides us with an interface to work with C++. Another excellent package for working with large data sets, and the one we will use in this chapter when we load some real-world data sets, is the package data.table, specifically designed to work with machines that have a lot of memory.

Loading data sets on the order of 100 GB on a 64-bit machine is a common use case when working with the data.table package. This package has been designed with the goal of substantially reducing the computation time of common operations that are performed on data frames. More specifically, it introduces the notion of a *data table* as a replacement data structure for R's ubiquitous data frame. This is not only a more efficient data structure on which to perform operations, but has a number of shortcuts and commands that make programming with data sets faster as well.

A critical advantage of this package is that the data table data structure is accepted by other packages anywhere a data frame is. Packages that are unaware of the data table syntax can use data frame syntax for working with data tables. An excellent online resource to learn more about the data.table package is an online course by *Matt Dowle*, the main creator of the package, and can be found at https://www.datacamp.com/courses/data-analysis-the-data-table-way. Without further ado, we will start building some recommender systems where we will load the data in data tables using the data.table package.

Predicting recommendations for movies and jokes

In this chapter, we will focus on building recommender systems using two different data sets. To do this, we shall use the `recommenderlab` package. This provides us with not only the algorithms to perform the recommendations, but also with the data structures to store the sparse rating matrices efficiently. The first data set we will use contains anonymous user reviews for jokes from the *Jester Online Joke recommender system*.

The joke ratings fall on a continuous scale (-10 to +10). A number of data sets collected from the Jester system can be found at `http://eigentaste.berkeley.edu/dataset/`. We will use the data set labeled on the website as *Dataset 2+*. This data set contains ratings made by 50,692 users on 150 jokes. As is typical with a real-world application, the rating matrix is very sparse in that each user rated only a fraction of all the jokes; the minimum number of ratings made by a user is 8. We will refer to this data set as the jester data set.

The second data set can be found at `http://grouplens.org/datasets/movielens/`. This website contains data on user ratings for movies that were made on the *MovieLens* website at `http://movielens.org`. Again, there is more than one data set on the website; we will use the one labeled *MovieLens 1M*. This contains ratings on a five-point scale (1-5) made by 6,040 users on 3,706 movies. The minimum number of movie ratings per user is 20. We will refer to this data set as the movie data set.

These two data sets are actually very well-known open source data sets, to the point that the `recommenderlab` package itself includes smaller versions of them as part of the package itself. Readers who would like to skip the process of loading and preprocessing the data, or who would like to run the examples that follow on smaller data sets due to computational constraints are encouraged to try them out using `data(Jester5k)` or `data(MovieLense)`.

Loading and preprocessing the data

Our first goal in building our recommender systems is to load the data in R, preprocess it, and convert it into a rating matrix. More precisely, in each case, we will be creating a `realRatingMatrix` object, which is the specific data structure that the `recommenderlab` package uses to store numerical ratings. We will start with the jester data set. If we download and unzip the archive from the website, we'll see that the file `jesterfinal151cols.csv` contains the ratings. More specifically, each row in this file corresponds to the ratings made by a particular user, and each column corresponds to a particular joke.

The columns are comma-separated and there is no header row. In fact, the format is almost exactly already a rating matrix were it not for the fact that the first column is a special column and contains the total number of ratings made by a particular user. We will load these data into a data table using the function `fread()`, which is a fast implementation of `read.table()` and efficiently loads a data file into a data table. We'll then drop the first column efficiently using the `data.table` syntax:

```
> library(data.table)
> jester <- fread("jesterfinal151cols.csv", sep = ",", header = F)
> jester[, V1 := NULL]
```

The last line used the assignment operator `:=` to set the first column, `V1`, to NULL, which is how we drop a column on a data table. We now have one final preprocessing step left to do on our data table, `jester`, before we are ready to convert it to a `realRatingMatrix` object. Specifically, we will convert this into a matrix and replace all occurrences of the rating of 99 with NA, as 99 was the special rating used to represent missing values:

```
> jester_m <- as.matrix(jester)
> jester_m <- ifelse(jester_m == 99, NA, jester_m)
> library(recommenderlab)
> jester_rrm <- as(jester_m, "realRatingMatrix")
```

Depending on the computational resources of the computer available to us (most notably, the available memory), we may want to try to process a single data set in its entirety instead of loading both data sets at once. Here, we have chosen to work with the two data sets in parallel in order to showcase the main steps in the analysis and highlight any differences or particularities of an individual data set with respect to a particular step.

Let's move on to the MovieLens data. Downloading the MovieLens 1M archive and unzipping reveals three main data files. The `users.dat` file contains background information about the users, such as age and gender. The `movies.dat` data file, in turn, contains information about the movies being rated, namely the title and a list of genres (for example, *comedy*) to which the movie belongs.

We are mainly interested in the `ratings.dat` file, which contains the ratings themselves. Unlike the raw jester data, here each line corresponds to a single rating made by a user. The line format contains the User ID, Movie ID, rating, and timestamp, all separated by two colon characters, `::`. Unfortunately, `fread()` requires a separator with a single character, so we will specify a single colon. The double-colon separator in the raw data results in us creating extra columns with NA values that we will have to remove, as well as the final column that contains the timestamp:

```
> movies <- fread("ratings.dat", sep = ":", header = F)
> movies[, c("V2", "V4", "V6", "V7") := NULL]
> head(movies)
    V1   V3 V5
1:   1 1193  5
2:   1  661  3
3:   1  914  3
4:   1 3408  4
5:   1 2355  5
6:   1 1197  3
```

As we can see, we are now left with three columns, where the first is the UserID, the second is the MovieID, and the last is the rating. We will now aggregate all the ratings made by a user in order to form an object that can be interpreted as or converted to a rating matrix. We should aggregate the data in a way that minimizes memory usage. We will do this by building a sparse matrix using the `sparseMatrix()` command from the `Matrix` package.

This package is loaded automatically when we use the `recommenderlab` package, as it is one of its dependencies. To build a sparse matrix using this function, we can simply specify a vector of row coordinates, a vector of matching column coordinates, and a vector with the nonzero values that fill up the sparse matrix. Remember, as our matrix is sparse, all we need are the locations and values for entries that are nonzero.

Right now, it is slightly inconvenient that we cannot directly interpret the User IDs and Movie IDs as coordinates directly. This is because if we have a user with a User ID value of 1 and a user with a User ID value of 3, R will automatically create a user with a User ID value 2 and create an empty row, even though that user does not actually exist in the training data. The situation is similar for columns. Consequently, we must first make factors out of our UserID and MovieID columns before proceeding to create our rating matrix as described earlier. Here is the code to build our rating matrix for the MovieLens data:

```
> userid_factor <- as.factor(movies[, V1])
> movieid_factor <- as.factor(movies[, V3])
> movies_sm <- sparseMatrix(i = as.numeric(userid_factor), j =
  as.numeric(movieid_factor), x = as.numeric(movies[,V5]))
> movies_rrm <- new("realRatingMatrix", data = movies_sm)
> colnames(movies_rrm) <- levels(movieid_factor)
> rownames(movies_rrm) <- levels(userid_factor)
> dim(movies_rrm)
[1] 6040 3706
```

It is a good exercise to check that the dimensions of the result correspond to our expectations on the number of users and movies respectively.

Exploring the data

Before building and evaluating recommender systems using the two data sets we have loaded, it is a good idea to get a feel for the data. For one thing, we can make use of the getRatings() function to retrieve the ratings from a rating matrix. This is useful in order to construct a histogram of item ratings. Additionally, we can also normalize the ratings with respect to each user as we discussed earlier. The following code snippet shows how we can compute ratings and normalized ratings for the jester data. We can then do the same for the MovieLens data and produce histograms for the ratings:

```
> jester_ratings <- getRatings(jester_rrm)
> jester_normalized_ratings <- getRatings(normalize(jester_rrm,
                                   method = "Z-score"))
```

The following plot shows the different histograms:

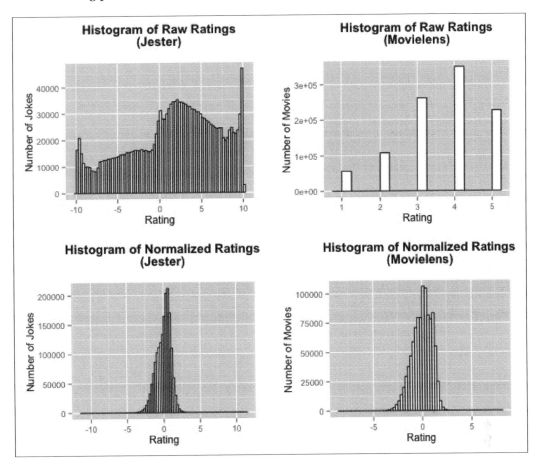

In the jester data, we can see that ratings above zero are more prominent than ratings below zero, and the most common rating is 10, the maximum rating. The normalized ratings create a more symmetric distribution centered on zero. For the MovieLens data with the 5-point rating scale, 4 is the most prominent rating and higher ratings are far more common than low ratings.

We can also look for the distribution of the number of items rated per user and the average rating per item by looking at the row counts and the column means of the rating matrix respectively. Again, the following code snippet shows how to compute these for the jester data and we follow up with histograms showing the results for both data sets:

```
> jester_items_rated_per_user <- rowCounts(jester_rrm)
> jester_average_item_rating_per_item <- colMeans(jester_rrm)
```

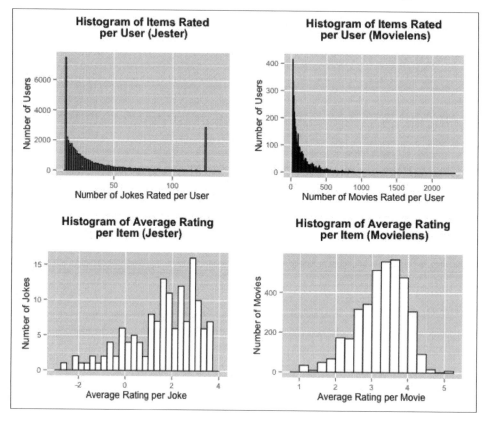

Both data sets show a curve in the average ratings per user that looks like a power curve. Most of the users have rated very few items, but a small number of very committed users have actually rated a very large number of items. In the Jester case, some have rated the maximum number of jokes in the data set. This is an exception and only occurs because the number of items (jokes) in this data set is relatively small. The distribution of the average joke rating is between -3 and 4, but for movies we see the whole range of the spectrum indicating that some users have rated all the movies they considered as completely awful or totally great. We can find the average of these distributions in order to determine the average number of items rated per user and the average rating of each item.

Note that we need to remove NA values from consideration in the Jester data set, as some columns may not have ratings in them:

```
> (jester_avg_items_rated_per_user <- mean(rowCounts(jester_rrm)))
[1] 34.10493
> (jester_avg_item_rating <- mean(colMeans(jester_rrm), na.rm = T))
[1] 1.633048
> (movies_avg_items_rated_per_user <- mean(rowCounts(movies_rrm)))
[1] 165.5975
> (movies_avg_item_rating <- mean(colMeans(movies_rrm)))
[1] 3.238892
```

Evaluating binary top-N recommendations

We now have some sense of what our data looks like for both data sets so we can start building some models. We will begin by looking at the problem of making top-N recommendations for a binary recommender system, which is simpler to do than when we have more granular data for ratings. Recall that a top-N recommendation is nothing but a list of *N* recommendations that are most likely to interest a user. To do this, we will use the jester data set and create a binary version of our rating matrix. We'll call any rating that is 5 or above a positive rating. As this may result in some users having no positive ratings, we'll also prune the rating matrix and keep only users with at least ten positive ratings under this scheme:

```
> jester_bn <- binarize(jester_rrm, minRating = 5)
> jester_bn <- jester_bn[rowCounts(jester_bn) > 1]
> dim(jester_bn)
[1] 13789    150
```

One of the advantages of the recommenderlab package is that it makes it very easy for us to compare results from several algorithms. The process of training and evaluating multiple algorithms for top-N recommendations begins by creating a list containing the definitions of the algorithms that we want to use. Each element in the list is given a name of our choice but must itself be a list containing a set of parameters for configuring a known algorithm. Concretely, the name parameter of this inner parameter list must be one that the recommenderlab package recognizes. It is possible to create and register one's own algorithm with this package, but our focus will be on existing implementations that more than suffice for our intents and purposes:

```
> algorithms <- list(
    "Random" = list(name = "RANDOM", param = NULL),
    "Popular" = list(name = "POPULAR", param = NULL),
```

```
"UserBasedCF_COS" = list(name = "UBCF",
                 param = list(method = "Cosine", nn = 50)),
"UserBasedCF_JAC" = list(name = "UBCF",
                 param = list(method = "Jaccard", nn = 50))
)
```

The RANDOM algorithm is a baseline algorithm that makes recommendations randomly. The POPULAR algorithm is another baseline algorithm that can sometimes be tough to beat. This proposes items in descending order of global popularity, so that for a top-1 recommendation, it will recommend the item with the highest average rating in the data set. We have chosen to try out two variants of user-based collaborative filtering for this example. The first one uses the cosine distance and specifies 50 as the number of nearest neighbors to use. The second one is identical but uses the Jaccard distance instead.

Next, we define an evaluation scheme via the function `evaluationScheme()`. This function records how we will split our data into training and test sets, the number of ratings we will take as given from our test users via the `given` parameter, and how many runs we want to execute. We will do a straight 80-20 split for our training and test set, consider 10 ratings from our test users as known ratings, and evaluate over a single run:

```
> jester_split_scheme <- evaluationScheme(jester_bn, method =
                     "split", train = 0.8, given = 10, k = 1)
```

Note that the `given` parameter must be at least as large as the smallest number of items rated by a user in our data set. We previously filtered the data set to ensure we have 10 items per user at least, so we are covered in our case. Finally, we will evaluate our list of algorithms in turn with our evaluation scheme using the `evaluate()` function. Aside from an evaluation scheme and a list of algorithms, we will also specify the range of *N* values to use when making top-N recommendations via the n parameter. We will do this for values 1 through 20:

```
> jester_split_eval <- evaluate(jester_split_scheme, algorithms,
                     n = 1 : 20)
RANDOM run
  1  [0.015sec/1.87sec]
POPULAR run
  1  [0.006sec/12.631sec]
UBCF run
  1  [0.001sec/36.862sec]
UBCF run
  1  [0.002sec/36.342sec]
```

We now have a list of four objects that represent the evaluation results of each algorithm on our data. We can get important measures such as precision by looking at the confusion matrices. Note that as we have run this experiment for top-N recommendations where N is in the range 1-20, we expect to have 20 such confusion matrices for each algorithm. The function getConfusionMatrix(), when applied to one of these objects, can be used to retrieve the folded confusion matrices in tabular format so that each row represents the confusion matrix for a particular value of N:

```
> options(digits = 4)
> getConfusionMatrix(jester_split_eval[[4]])
[[1]]
```

	TP	FP	FN	TN	precision	recall	TPR	FPR
1	0.5181	0.4819	18.47	120.5	0.5181	0.06272	0.06272	0.003867
2	1.0261	0.9739	17.96	120.0	0.5131	0.12042	0.12042	0.007790
3	1.4953	1.5047	17.49	119.5	0.4984	0.16470	0.16470	0.012011
4	1.9307	2.0693	17.06	118.9	0.4827	0.20616	0.20616	0.016547
5	2.3575	2.6425	16.63	118.4	0.4715	0.24215	0.24215	0.021118
6	2.7687	3.2313	16.22	117.8	0.4614	0.27509	0.27509	0.025791
7	3.1530	3.8470	15.83	117.2	0.4504	0.30508	0.30508	0.030709
8	3.5221	4.4779	15.46	116.5	0.4403	0.33216	0.33216	0.035735
9	3.8999	5.1001	15.09	115.9	0.4333	0.36069	0.36069	0.040723
10	4.2542	5.7458	14.73	115.3	0.4254	0.38723	0.38723	0.045890
11	4.6037	6.3963	14.38	114.6	0.4185	0.40927	0.40927	0.051036
12	4.9409	7.0591	14.04	114.0	0.4117	0.43368	0.43368	0.056345
13	5.2534	7.7466	13.73	113.3	0.4041	0.45345	0.45345	0.061856
14	5.5638	8.4362	13.42	112.6	0.3974	0.47248	0.47248	0.067360
15	5.8499	9.1501	13.14	111.9	0.3900	0.48907	0.48907	0.073066
16	6.1298	9.8702	12.86	111.1	0.3831	0.50604	0.50604	0.078836
17	6.4090	10.5910	12.58	110.4	0.3770	0.52151	0.52151	0.084592
18	6.6835	11.3165	12.30	109.7	0.3713	0.53664	0.53664	0.090384
19	6.9565	12.0435	12.03	109.0	0.3661	0.55187	0.55187	0.096198
20	7.2165	12.7835	11.77	108.2	0.3608	0.56594	0.56594	0.102095

To visualize these data and compare our algorithms, we can try plotting the results directly using the plot() function. For our evaluation results, the default is a plot of the true positive rate (TPR) versus the false positive rate (FPR). This is nothing other than the ROC curve, as we know from *Chapter 4, Neural Networks*.

```
> plot(jester_split_eval, annotate = 2, legend = "topright")
> title(main = "TPR vs FPR For Binary Jester Data")
```

Here is the ROC curve for the binary Jester data:

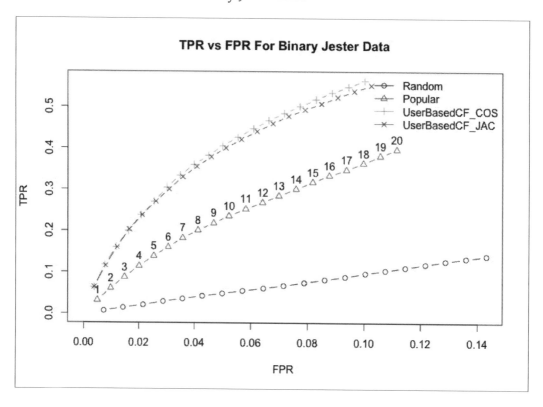

The graph shows that the user-based collaborative filtering algorithms perform better than the two baseline algorithms, but there is very little to separate these two, with the cosine distance marginally outperforming the Jaccard distance on these data. We can complement this view of our results by also plotting a precision recall curve:

```
> plot(jester_split_eval, "prec/rec", annotate = 2,
       legend = "bottomright")
> title(main = "Precision versus Recall Binary Jester Data")
```

Here is the precision recall curve for the binary Jester data:

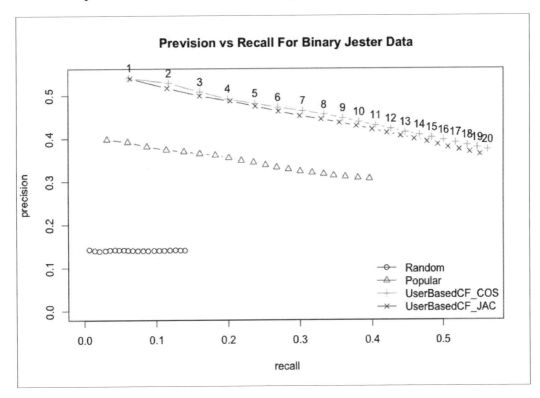

The precision recall curve paints a similar picture, with the user-based collaborative filtering algorithm that uses the cosine distance coming out as the winner. Note that the trade off between precision and recall surfaces in a top-N recommender system via the number of recommendations that the system makes. The way our evaluation scheme works is that we treat users in the test data as new users in the system that just contributed a certain number of ratings. We hold out as many ratings as the given parameter allows. Then, we apply our model in order to see if the ratings we suggest will agree with the ratings that remain. We order our suggestions in descending order of confidence so that in a top-1 recommendation system, we will suggest the item we believe has the best chance of interesting the user. Increasing N therefore is like casting a wider net. We will be less precise in our suggestions but are more likely to find something the user will like.

An excellent and freely available resource for recommendation systems is *Chapter 9* from the online textbook *Mining of Massive Datasets* by *Jure Leskovec, Anand Rajaraman,* and *Jeffrey David Ullman*. This book is also an excellent additional reference for working with Big Data. The website is `http://www.mmds.org/`.

Evaluating non-binary top-N recommendations

In this section, we will use the movies data set to see how we perform in the non-binary scenario. First, we will define our algorithms as before:

```
> normalized_algorithms <- list(
    "Random" = list(name = "RANDOM", param = list(normalize =
                "Z-score")),
    "Popular" = list(name = "POPULAR", param = list(normalize =
                "Z-score")),
    "UserBasedCF" = list(name = "UBCF", param = list(normalize =
                "Z-score", method = "Cosine", nn = 50)),
    "ItemBasedCF" = list(name = "IBCF", param = list(normalize =
                "Z-score")),
    "SVD" = list(name = "SVD", param = list(categories = 30,
                normalize = "Z-score", treat_na = "median"))
)
```

This time, our algorithms will work with normalized ratings by specifying the `normalize` parameter. We will only be using the cosine distance for user-based collaborative filtering as the Jaccard distance only applies in the binary setting. Furthermore, we will also try out item-based collaborative filtering as well as SVD-based recommendations. Instead of directly splitting our data, we demonstrate how we can perform ten-fold cross-validation by modifying our evaluation scheme. We will continue to investigate making top-N recommendations in the range of 1 to 20. Evaluating a moderately sized data set with five algorithms using ten-fold cross-validation means that we can expect this process to take quite a long time to finish depending on the computing power we have at our disposal:

```
> movies_cross_scheme <- evaluationScheme(movies_rrm, method =
        "cross-validation", k = 10, given = 10, goodRating = 4)
> movies_cross_eval <- evaluate(movies_cross_scheme,
        normalized_algorithms, n = 1 : 20)
```

To conserve space, we have truncated the output that shows us the amount of time spent running each iteration for the different algorithms. Note that the most expensive algorithm during training is the item-based collaborative filtering algorithm, as this is building a model and not just performing lazy learning. Once the process terminates, we can plot the results in the same way as we did for our binarized Jester data set in order to compare the performance of our algorithms:

```
> plot(movies_cross_eval, annotate = 4, legend = "topright")
> title(main = "TPR versus FPR For Movielens Data")
```

Here is the ROC curve for the MovieLens data:

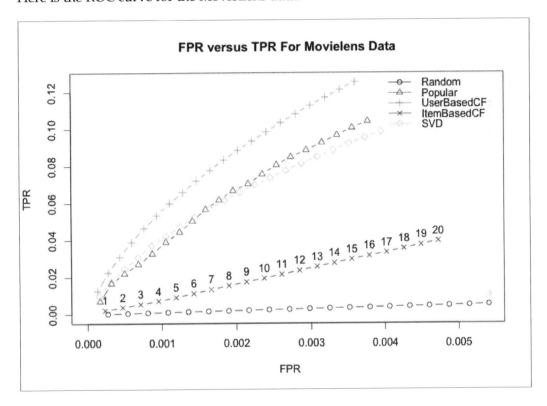

As we can see, user-based collaborative filtering is the clear winner here. SVD performs in a similar manner to the POPULAR baseline, though the latter starts to become better when N is high. Finally, we see item-based collaborative filtering performing far worse than these, outperforming only the random baseline. What is clear from these experiments is that tuning recommendation systems can often be a very time-consuming, resource-intensive endeavor.

All the algorithms that we specified can be tuned in various ways and we have seen a number of parameters, from the size of the neighborhood to the similarity metric, that will influence the results. In addition, we've seen that even for the top-N scenario alone there are several ways that we can evaluate our recommendation system, so if we want to try out a number of these for comparison, we will again need to spend more time during model training.

The reader is encouraged to repeat these experiments using different parameters and evaluation schemes in order to get a feel for the process of designing and training recommendation systems. In addition, by visiting the websites of our two data sets, the reader can find additional links to similar data sets commonly used for learning about recommendation systems, such as the book-crossing data set.

For completeness, we will plot the precision recall curve for the MovieLens data:

```
> plot(movies_split_eval, "prec/rec", annotate = 3,
        legend = "bottomright")
> title(main = "Precision versus Recall For Movielens Data")
```

Here is the precision recall curve for the MovieLens data:

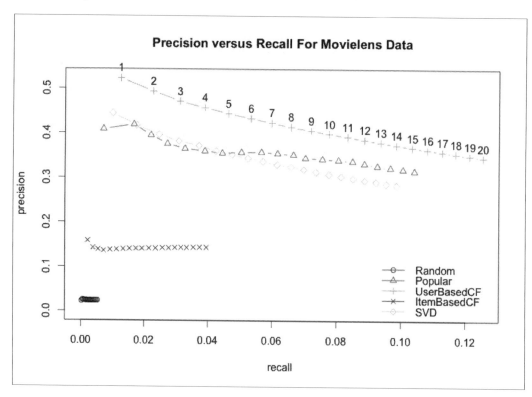

Evaluating individual predictions

Another way to evaluate a recommendation system is to ask it to predict the specific values of a portion of the known ratings made by a set of test users, using the remainder of their ratings as given. In this way, we can measure accuracy by taking average distance measures over the predicted ratings. These include the mean squared error (MSE) and the Root Mean Square Error (RMSE), which we have seen before, and the **mean average error (MAE)**, which is just the average of the absolute errors. We will do this for the regular (unbinarized) Jester data set. We begin as before by defining an evaluation scheme:

```
> jester_split_scheme <- evaluationScheme(jester_rrm, method =
  "split", train = 0.8, given = 5, goodRating = 5)
```

Next, we will define individual user- and item-based collaborative filtering recommenders using the `Recommender()` and `getData()` functions. The logic behind these is that the `getData()` function will extract the ratings set aside for training by the evaluation scheme and the `Recommender()` function will use these data to train a model:

```
> jester_ubcf_srec <- Recommender(getData(jester_split_scheme,
                            "train"), "UBCF")
> jester_ibcf_srec <- Recommender(getData(jester_split_scheme,
                            "train"), "IBCF")
```

We can then use these models to predict those ratings that were classified as known (there are as many of these as the `given` parameter specifies) in our test data:

```
> jester_ubcf_known <- predict(jester_ubcf_srec,
  getData(jester_split_scheme, "known"), type="ratings")
> jester_ibcf_known <- predict(jester_ibcf_srec,
  getData(jester_split_scheme, "known"), type="ratings")
```

Finally, we can use the known ratings to compute prediction accuracy on the ratings kept for testing:

```
> (jester_ubcf_acc <- calcPredictionAccuracy(jester_ubcf_known,
  getData(jester_split_scheme, "unknown")))
    RMSE      MSE      MAE
 4.70765 22.16197  3.54130
> (jester_ibcf_acc <- calcPredictionAccuracy(jester_ibcf_known,
  getData(jester_split_scheme, "unknown")))
    RMSE      MSE      MAE
 5.012211 25.122256  3.518815
```

We can see that the performance of the two algorithms is fairly close. User-based collaborative filtering performs better when we penalize larger errors (via the RMSE and MSE) through squaring. From the perspective of the mean average error, item-based collaborative filtering is very marginally better.

Consequently, in this case, we might make our decision on which type of recommendation system to use on the basis of the error behavior that more closely matches our business needs. In this section, we used the default parameter values for the two algorithms, but by using the `parameter` parameter in the `Recommender()` function, we can play around with different configurations as we did before. This is left as an exercise for the reader.

Other approaches to recommendation systems

In this chapter, we concentrated our efforts on building recommendation systems by following the collaborative filtering paradigm. This is a very popular approach for its many advantages. By essentially mimicking word-of-mouth recommendations, it requires virtually no knowledge about the items being recommended nor any background about the users in question.

Moreover, collaborative filtering systems incorporate new ratings as they arise, either through a memory approach, or via regular retraining of a model-based approach. Thus, they naturally become better for their users over time as they learn more information and adapt to changing preferences. On the other hand, they are not without their disadvantages, not least of which is the fact that they will not take into account any information about the items and their content even when it is available.

Content-based recommendation systems try to suggest items to users that are similar to those that users like on the basis of content. The key premise behind this idea is that if it is known that a user happens to like novels by *George R. R. Martin*, a fantasy and science fiction author, it makes sense that a recommendation service for books might suggest a similar author, such as *Robert Jordan*, for example.

Collaborative filtering systems, by their nature, require some sort of feedback system in order for the recommender to record a particular rating. In particular, they are ideal for leveraging **explicit feedback**, whereby the user logs an actual rating or score. **Implicit feedback** is indirect feedback, such as believing that a user likes a particular movie solely on the basis of the fact that they chose to rent that movie. Content-based recommendation systems are better suited to implicit feedback as they will use information about the content of the items to improve their knowledge about the user's preferences.

In addition, content-based recommendation systems often make use of a user profile in which the user may record what he or she likes via the form of a list of keywords, for example. Moreover, preference keywords can be learned from queries made by the user in the item database, if search is supported.

Certain types of content are more amenable to the content-based approach. The classic scenario for a content-based recommender is when the content is in the form of text. Examples include book and news article recommendation systems. With text-based content, we can use techniques from the field of information retrieval in order to build up an understanding of how different items are similar to each other. For example, we have seen ways to analyze text using bag of words features when we looked at sentiment analysis in *Chapter 8, Probabilistic Graphical Models*, and topic modeling in *Chapter 10, Topic Modeling*.

Of course, content such as images and video is much less amenable to this method than text. For general products, the content-based approach requires textual descriptions of all the items in the database, which is one of its drawbacks. Furthermore, with content-based recommendations, we are often likely to consistently suggest items that are too similar, that is to say that our recommendations might not be sufficiently varied. For instance, we might consistently recommend books by the same author or news articles with the same topic precisely because their content is so similar.

By contrast, the collaborative filtering paradigm uses empirically found relationships between users and items on the basis of preferences alone. Consequently, it can be far less predictable (though in some contexts, this is not necessarily good).

One of the classic difficulties that are faced by collaborative filtering and content-based recommendation systems alike is the **cold start problem**. If we are basing the recommendations we supply using ratings made by users or on the content that they somehow indicated they like, how do we deal with new users and new items for which we have no ratings at all? One way to handle this is to use heuristics or rules of thumb, for example, by suggesting items that most users will like just as the POPULAR algorithm does.

Knowledge-based recommendation systems avoid this issue entirely by basing their recommendations on rules and other sources of information about users and items. These systems usually behave quite predictably, have reliable quality, and can enforce a particular business practice, such as a sales-driven policy, with regards to making recommendations. Such recommenders often ask users specific questions in an interactive attempt to learn their preferences and use rules or constraints to identify items that should be recommended.

Often, this results in a system that, although predictable, can explain its output. This means that it can justify its recommendations to a user, which is a property that most examples of recommenders that follow the other paradigms lack. One important drawback of the knowledge-based paradigm besides the initial effort necessary to design it, is that it is static and cannot adapt to changes or trends in user behavior.

Finally, it is well worth mentioning that we can design hybrid recommendation systems that incorporate more than one approach. An example of this is a recommender that uses collaborative filtering for most users but has a knowledge-based component for making recommendations to users that are new to the system. Another possibility for a hybrid recommendation system is to build a number of recommenders and integrate them into an ensemble using a voting scheme for the final recommendation.

 A good all-round book that covers a wide variety of different recommender system paradigms and examples is *Recommender Systems: An Introduction* by *Dietmar Jannach* and others. This is published by *Cambridge University Press*.

Summary

In this chapter, we explored the process of building and evaluating recommender systems in R using the `recommenderlab` package. We focused primarily on the paradigm of collaborative filtering, which in a nutshell formalizes the idea of recommending items to users through word of mouth. As a general rule, we found that user-based collaborative filtering performs quite quickly but requires all the data to make predictions. Item-based collaborative filtering can be slow to train a model but makes predictions very quickly once the model is trained. It is useful in practice because it does not require us to store all the data. In some scenarios, the tradeoff in accuracy between these two can be high but in others the difference is acceptable.

The process of training recommendation systems is quite resource intensive and a number of important parameters come into play in the design, such as the metrics used to quantify similarity and distance between items and users. As the data sets we often encounter in this area are typically quite large, we also touched upon some key ideas of Big Data and took some first steps in working with the `data.table` package as one way of loading and manipulating large data sets in memory.

Finally, we touched upon alternatives to the collaborative filtering paradigm. Content-based recommendation systems are designed to leverage similarity between items on the basis of their content. As such, they are ideally suited to the domain of text. Knowledge-based recommendation systems are designed to make recommendations to users on the basis of a set of rules or constraints that have been designed by experts. These can be combined with the other approaches in order to address the cold start problem for new users or items.

Index

I

ID3 201
Independence of Irrelevant
  Alternatives (IIA) 115
independent and identically distributed
  (iid) 222, 283
information statistic 201
inhibitors 126
inner products 170, 171
intense earthquakes
  predicting 301-306
intercept 48
interquartile range 64
invertible 291
item-based collaborative filtering 348, 349

K

Kappa statistic
  defining 42
kernel functions 173
kernels
  about 172
  using 173
k-fold cross-validation 179
k-nearest neighbors 8, 9

L

laplacian smoothing 264
LDA
  about 315
  defining 317
  Dirichlet distribution 317-321
  generative process 321, 322
  LDA model, fitting 323
LDA extensions 337
LDA model
  fitting 323
  training 327
least absolute shrinkage 84, 85
letter patterns
  predicting, in English words 274-278
Likert scale 120
linear kernel 172
linear regression
  about 47, 48, 125

assumptions 48-51
classifying with 91-93
linear regression models
  assessing 61-63
  comparing 75
  outliers 78, 79
  performance metrics 71-74
  residual analysis 64-67
  tests, used for 68-71
link function 95
local kernel 173
logistic neuron 138, 139
logistic regression
  about 91, 94
  assumptions 97
  coefficients, interpreting 96, 97
  generalized linear models (GLMs) 95, 96
  maximum likelihood estimation 97-99
logistic regression models
  assessing 102, 103
  model deviance 104-108
  test set performance 108
logit function 96
lynx trappings
  predicting 307, 308

M

MAGIC Gamma Telescope data set
  attributes 233
  URL 233
Markov Chain Monte Carlo (MCMC) 323
Matrix Market format 324
matrix, recommendation systems
  rating 339, 340
  user similarity, measuring 341-343
maximal margin classification 163-168
maximal margin hyperplane 166
maximum likelihood estimation 97-99
mean 53
mean average error (MAE) 369
mean function 95, 282
Mean Square Error (MSE) 40, 56, 369
median 64
Missing At Random (MAR) 25
Missing Completely At
  Random (MCAR) 25

S

selection operator (lasso) 85
semi-supervised model 11
sensitivity 111
sentiment analysis
  URL 265
simple linear regression model
  about 48-52
  advantages 51
  regression coefficients, estimating 52-56
Singular Value Decomposition
    (SVD) 27, 349-352
slack variables 169
softmax function 114
spectral methods 312
splines 13
stationarity 288, 289
stationary time series model
  about 290
  ARMA model 296, 297
  autoregressive models (AR) 294-296
  moving average models 290-292
Statlog (Heart) data set
  working with 99-101
step function 128
stepwise regression 83
stochastic gradient boosting 238
stochastic gradient descent
  about 132
  defining 129-131
  gradient descent 132, 133
  local minima 132, 133
  logistic neuron 138, 139
  perceptron algorithm 133-138
stochastic model
  about 3
  example 3
stochastic process 281
stump 231
Sum of Squared Error (SSE) 40, 72, 148
supervised model 11, 12
support vector classification
  about 168-170
  inner products 170, 171
support vector machines 172, 173

synaptic neurotransmitters 126
synthetic 2D data
  class membership, predicting on 203-206

T

test set 33
tests, for linear regression 68-71
time-domain methods 312
time series
  defining 281, 282
  examples 283
  random walk 286, 287
  summary functions 282, 283
  white noise 283, 284
time series models
  defining 311, 312
topic modeling 315, 316
topics, of online news stories
  LDA extensions 337
  modeling 323-329
  model stability 330-333
  number of topics, finding 333
  topic distribution 333-335
  word distributions 335, 336
Total Sum of Squares (TSS)
  about 73
  formula 73
training set 33
tree models
  defining 187-190
tree pruning 196, 197
true negatives 44
true positives 44
Type I error 44
Type II error 44

U

UCI Machine Learning Repository
  URL 56
unit interval 21
unit root tests 298
unsupervised model 11, 12
user-based collaborative filtering 344-347

V

Variational Expectation Maximization (VEM) 323, 327
Viterbi algorithm 267

W

wavelet transform 207
white noise time series
  about 283, 284
  fitting 285, 286
wine quality
  URL 120
word cloud 336
word distributions 335, 336

Z

Z-score normalization 20

Thank you for buying
Mastering Predictive Analytics with R

About Packt Publishing

Packt, pronounced 'packed', published its first book, *Mastering phpMyAdmin for Effective MySQL Management*, in April 2004, and subsequently continued to specialize in publishing highly focused books on specific technologies and solutions.

Our books and publications share the experiences of your fellow IT professionals in adapting and customizing today's systems, applications, and frameworks. Our solution-based books give you the knowledge and power to customize the software and technologies you're using to get the job done. Packt books are more specific and less general than the IT books you have seen in the past. Our unique business model allows us to bring you more focused information, giving you more of what you need to know, and less of what you don't.

Packt is a modern yet unique publishing company that focuses on producing quality, cutting-edge books for communities of developers, administrators, and newbies alike. For more information, please visit our website at www.packtpub.com.

About Packt Open Source

In 2010, Packt launched two new brands, Packt Open Source and Packt Enterprise, in order to continue its focus on specialization. This book is part of the Packt Open Source brand, home to books published on software built around open source licenses, and offering information to anybody from advanced developers to budding web designers. The Open Source brand also runs Packt's Open Source Royalty Scheme, by which Packt gives a royalty to each open source project about whose software a book is sold.

Writing for Packt

We welcome all inquiries from people who are interested in authoring. Book proposals should be sent to author@packtpub.com. If your book idea is still at an early stage and you would like to discuss it first before writing a formal book proposal, then please contact us; one of our commissioning editors will get in touch with you.

We're not just looking for published authors; if you have strong technical skills but no writing experience, our experienced editors can help you develop a writing career, or simply get some additional reward for your expertise.

Data Manipulation with R

ISBN: 978-1-78328-109-1   Paperback: 102 pages

Perform group-wise data manipulation and deal with large datasets using R efficiently and effectively

1. Perform factor manipulation and string processing.

2. Learn group-wise data manipulation using plyr.

3. Handle large datasets, interact with database software, and manipulate data using sqldf.

Big Data Analytics with R and Hadoop

ISBN: 978-1-78216-328-2   Paperback: 238 pages

Set up an integrated infrastructure of R and Hadoop to turn your data analytics into Big Data analytics

1. Write Hadoop MapReduce within R.

2. Learn data analytics with R and the Hadoop platform.

3. Handle HDFS data within R.

4. Understand Hadoop streaming with R.

5. Encode and enrich datasets into R.

Please check **www.PacktPub.com** for information on our titles

R Object-oriented Programming

ISBN: 978-1-78398-668-2   Paperback: 190 pages

A practical guide to help you learn and understand the programming techniques necessary to exploit the full power of R

1. Learn and understand the programming techniques necessary to solve specific problems and speed up development processes for statistical models and applications.

2. Explore the fundamentals of building objects and how they program individual aspects of larger data designs.

3. Step-by-step guide to understand how OOP can be applied to application and data models within R.

Learning Data Mining with R

ISBN: 978-1-78398-210-3   Paperback: 314 pages

Develop key skills and techniques with R to create and customize data mining algorithms

1. Develop a sound strategy for solving predictive modeling problems using the most popular data mining algorithms.

2. Gain understanding of the major methods of predictive modeling.

3. Packed with practical advice and tips to help you get to grips with data mining.

Please check **www.PacktPub.com** for information on our titles

Printed in Poland
by Amazon Fulfillment
Poland Sp. z o.o., Wrocław